Public Expenditure

Public Expenditure

Its Defence and Reform

DAVID HEALD

Martin Robertson · Oxford

626318

First published in 1983 by
Martin Robertson & Company Ltd.
108 Cowley Road, Oxford OX4 1JF.
Reprinted 1984

British Library Cataloguing in Publication Data

Heald, David, 1947–
 Public expenditure.
 1. Finance, Public – Great Britain
 I. Title
 336.41   HJ1001

 ISBN 0–85520–418–4
 ISBN 0–85520–419–2 Pbk

Typeset by Freeman Graphic, Tonbridge
Printed and bound in Great Britain by
Billing and Sons Ltd., Worcester

For Hygeia

CONTENTS

Contents

LIST OF TABLES AND FIGURES

TABLES

FIGURES

List of Tables and Figures   xi

List of Tables and Figures

PREFACE

During much of the twentieth century public expenditure has grown inexorably in the UK and in other OECD countries, at least until the 1970s. There have been long periods of surprisingly little controversy, in which political debate centred more upon its rate of growth ('how much can the nation afford?') rather than upon its intrinsic merits. Public expenditure was a 'good thing' – more of it was better. There has been a sharp reaction against this earlier relaxed approach, in both academic and political circles. Many commentators are now prepared to assert aggressively that public expenditure is a 'bad thing'. The nature of the debate has therefore changed fundamentally, especially as this latter group has proved enormously influential with policymakers and the media. If the old orthodoxy sometimes crudely characterized the public/private dichotomy as good/bad, the converse is now frequently heard: public expenditure is a 'bad thing' – less of it is better.

I believe that the erstwhile promoters of high public expenditure have conceded too much, largely by default, to this counter-revolution in economic and political thought. After long periods without serious challenge, they were thoroughly unprepared to cope with either the sophistication or vigour of the attack. This book takes a critical look at the attack on big government, at least as far as this relates to public expenditure. It separates out the different but interwoven strands and assesses how seriously they ought to be taken as arguments against high public expenditure.

There have always been advocates of high public expenditure, such as Anthony Crosland (1956, 1974), who did not see the issues in the black and white terms characteristic of much looser writing. But he wrote at a time of confidence, when it could be assumed that higher public expenditure could be paid for out of an automatic annual increment in Gross Domestic Product (GDP). We live in much harder times to sustain such a view. As well as the dramatic change in the political climate towards public expenditure, the prospects for economic growth seem unprecedentedly poor. Nevertheless, this book can be seen within the broad tradition represented by Crosland, but the context and the problems which must be resolved have changed. It makes a

serious effort to confront the issues, both macroeconomic and microeconomic, which inevitably arise when public expenditure accounts for a
large proportion of output and the external environment is ominous.

Disagreements about public expenditure – in the academic literature as
outside – owe much to conflicting views about what the state should do. By
isolating these differences in value premises, it often proves possible to clarify
the issues of the debate. Even if nothing more, it becomes possible for those
who hold different views to agree to disagree, knowing exactly what
separates them. Throughout the book, I have attempted to be fair to positions
with which I disagree either on grounds of economic analysis or because I do
not subscribe to the value premises. Nevertheless, my own position underlies
the structure and form of the book. I would loosely describe that position as
being 'left-Keynesian'. In other words, I subscribe to the old consensus which
is under searching attack from the monetarist/free-market perspective.

The book is intended as a not uncritical defence of the role of public
expenditure within an industrialized economy. It defends public expenditure
in general, not every individual item of public expenditure in any country at
any time. The scope for better decisions is undeniable. The fact that it came to
be written could be seen as an indirect tribute to the influence of writers
adopting the view that public expenditure should be reduced as a method of
enhancing both efficiency and freedom. Their case deserves a careful answer
but I do not find it compelling.

The author of any book on such a wide-ranging topic owes enormous
debts, both to previous authors and to colleagues who have directly or
indirectly influenced the development of ideas and the formation of judgements. It is certainly the case with this book. Writing, then successive rounds
of editing and rewriting, has been a slow process, often painful but sometimes
exhilarating. Work started on the typescript in March 1980, though even that
built upon ideas for an ill-fated and never published collection of essays
which I started to edit as long ago as December 1976. The extended period
over which I have worked on this typescript owed something to my other
commitments but more to the breadth of my canvas, requiring me to leave the
shelter of my specialism in public finance and to branch out into diverse
literature, elsewhere in economics and far beyond. Not only did I have to
form views on subjects which I had never explicitly considered before but also
I found some of my well-established positions shifting, some subtly but others
more substantively.

I would like to thank the following authors, institutions and publishers for
permission to use material, usually for plotting Figures: George Bain and
Robert Price, together with Basil Blackwell Publisher Ltd and the editors of
the *British Journal of Industrial Relations* (for Figures 9.2 and 9.3); Sir Leo
Pliatzky and Basil Blackwell Publisher Ltd (for Figure 2.1); Terry Ward and
Robert Neild, together with the Institute for Fiscal Studies and Heinemann
Educational Books Ltd (for Figure 3.6); Mary Gregory, Andrew Thomson

and the editors of the *British Journal of Industrial Relations* (for Table 9.2); Andrew Dean and George Allen & Unwin Ltd (for Figure 9.7); OECD (for Tables 2.3, 9.1, 12.1 and 12.2); the Bank of England (for Figures 3.2, 3.4 and 3.5); the Central Statistical Office and HMSO for many of the other Figures, too numerous to mention individually; and Routledge & Kegan Paul Ltd for material in Chapter 5 which, in an earlier form, appeared as my contribution (Heald, 1980a) to a book edited by Noel Timms.

Academic colleagues, both in Glasgow and elsewhere, gave generously of their time, covering the typescript with indications of error, expressions of dissent and ticks of agreement. I thank them for their encouragement and guidance. David Steel (Exeter University), Jacki Charlton (Glasgow College of Technology), David Donnison, Christopher Hood and Michael Ingham (all Glasgow University), Peter Jackson (Leicester University), Colin Crouch and George Jones (both London School of Economics), Noel Timms (Newcastle University), Michael Keating and Richard Rose (both Strathclyde University), Albert Weale (York University), and two anonymous publisher's referees, read an earlier version of the entire typescript. Bob Elliott (Aberdeen University), Brian Smith (Bath University), Robert Goodin (Essex University), Phil Beaumont, Tom Campbell, Robin Downie, John Foster, Tom Schuller, Andrew Thomson and Gavin Wood (all Glasgow University), Andrew Likierman (London Business School), Peter Jones (Newcastle University), David Miller (Nuffield College, Oxford), and Richard Mowbray (Paisley College of Technology) read selected chapters. Their comments saved me from many errors, stimulated new insights and directions, and resulted in major improvements in exposition. My rejection of some of that advice, though never without careful consideration, makes me solely responsible for the remaining errors and for the judgements expressed. My greatest debt, however, is to Susan Wallace, not just for her invaluable research, editorial and bibliographical assistance. Perhaps even more crucial was her quiet confidence, at the times I despaired, that the book would be finished. Without all this help, the book *if* it had been completed would have been much inferior.

I hope that readers will judge that all this effort has been worthwhile and that the book will contribute towards a better understanding of the immensely important issues it considers. But, even more importantly, I trust that it is worthy of its dedication.

David Heald
Glasgow, January 1983

PART ONE

The Context

Part One provides a brief exposition of the context within which both the philosophical and policy issues must be considered. It surveys the political and economic environment which facilitated massive growth in the economic and social role of the state, reflected in dramatically increased levels of public expenditure. It establishes a link between the ascendancy of Keynesian ideas on macroeconomic policy with an enhanced role for the state in terms of direct service provision, an extended system of income transfers and other forms of intervention in the functioning of the market economy. Together these can be viewed as a broad consensus in favour of the Keynesian social democratic state.

However, this ascendancy was brief. It was undermined by the monetarist challenge to the Keynesian orthodoxy and by the revival of support for the free market as a more reliable instrument for achieving economic and social welfare than the state. This transformation of the intellectual climate in the 1970s was matched by a decisive electoral shift towards the political right in industrialized democracies. These political developments returned to office parties which, though earlier accepting the triumph of the Keynesian social democratic state, found renewed appeal in the revival of older doctrines.

Although this book operates on a wide canvas, it must be recognized that public expenditure is only one aspect of the activities of the modern state. It is not a measure of the power of the state. Furthermore, there are other forms of public policy which can act as substitutes for public expenditure. There are considerable ambiguities at the margin about what constitutes public expenditure, partly stemming from the fact that the public sector itself is a rather amorphous concept. Consequently, extreme care must be taken when interpreting the evidence about the level of public expenditure, particularly with reference to comparisons between different countries. The public expenditure/GDP ratio, often used as the basis of comparison both for one country over a period of time and between countries at the same time, is subject to severe limitations as an indicator.

The success of the monetarist challenge to the Keynesian macroeconomic orthodoxy has contributed towards the much more adverse climate for public

1

expenditure. Only part of this effect stems from the role which public sector borrowing plays in monetary growth. Arguably more important, monetarists' belief in the stability of the private sector and in the efficacy of market mechanisms encourages them to adopt a microeconomic stance which is critical of the discretionary activities of the state.

CHAPTER 1

The Tarnished Consensus

I CONSENSUS TRIUMPHANT

The radicals of a generation often suffer one of two fates. If unsuccessful, their pamphlets gather dust in libraries of record, of interest only to historians of thought. But if successful in shattering received ideas and practice, they subsequently become the conservatives of the next generation. This is archetypally the case with the advocates of the Keynesian social democratic state, a term used to embrace commitment to full employment, a willingness to use industrial intervention, and support for the public services character-istic of the welfare state.

It is not suggested that they were a well-defined or necessarily coherent group. Indeed, bitter political and academic controversies raged between them. As 'social democracy' has had specific though historically varying connotations, sometimes in a party sense, many adherents to the consensus would have rejected the label 'social democrat'. What they shared, however, was a conviction that beneficial state action was possible in the economic and social sphere. This distanced them sharply from both contemporary and later advocates of the minimal state. They lived in a confusing and frightening world: aware of the menace of fascism and communism; facing the threat of another war which would surpass the horror and destruction of the last; and more conscious than ever before of the ravages inflicted by unemployment and poverty in an industrialized society. They believed there must be a better way.

Such a context is vital to an understanding of why Keynesian ideas received such a ready and extensive welcome. They could be viewed alternatively as providing for the destruction or redemption of capitalism: indeed, they have been applauded and criticized for both. Which, if either, of these views is correct, depends critically on semantic questions (how does one recognize capitalism?) and on behavioural propositions about the consequences of certain policies. The term 'capitalism' is so loosely used, whether as a term of approval or of abuse, that its meaning becomes blurred. For example, there are the distinct questions of whether production is organized through

3

markets and whether there is private, public or cooperative ownership of the means of production. Moreover, there is the complex relationship between the state and the means of production, even where the latter are privately owned.

A strong case can be argued that Keynesian ideas facilitated the survival of a predominantly privately owned, market-oriented economy, albeit with a much enlarged non-market sector. Despite lengthy controversies over the balance of ownership, this is what the UK has remained. The work of John Maynard Keynes (for example, 1936) reduced the macroeconomic significance of ownership *per se*: the state did not require to own factories to be able to stimulate investment. Indirect methods of influence, via tax and expenditure instruments, became available as alternatives to ownership. Therein lay at least some of the appeal of Keynesianism to capitalists and establishment opinion.

Once the shock of accepting a positive economic role for the state had been absorbed, the possibilities became obvious. Judicious macroeconomic regulation on Keynesian principles could smooth out the cycles of boom and depression, thus demonstrating that Marxists were wrong when they argued that these were manifestations of the inherent self-destructiveness of capitalism. Instead of capitalism being abolished, it could be improved. The architects of the Keynesian revolution were not political or social revolutionaries: rather, as far-sighted members of the old social order, they saw how much else widespread misery and unemployment put at risk.

Keynes provided a respectable body of economic theory in which to frame an insight long familiar to those who lived close to empty bellies and idle hands: it is a scandalous waste of resources not to use men's labour amidst such evident scarcity. But this insight was traditionally based more on moral outrage than upon any coherent view of how this could be remedied. Keynes provided answers, even if rearmament proved in the event more important. However, the lesson once learnt was unlikely to be soon forgotten.

The appeal of Keynes's ideas to socialists rested not only in the prospect of banishing the spectre of mass unemployment but in the much more relaxed attitude this new stabilization role for the public sector generated towards its size. Indeed, the higher the ratio of public expenditure to GDP, the greater the leverage enjoyed by fiscal policy. This established a technical argument in favour of a large public sector. What had been remarkable in the years between the First and Second World Wars was that Labour, alleged by some of its opponents to be a revolutionary party, produced as leaders men of ultra-orthodox economic views. The acceptance of Keynesian ideas in academic and policy circles provided a cogent basis for the later development of Labour policies on the long road to 1945, an election which marked an overwhelming triumph for the ideology of the Keynesian social democratic state.

The conflicts of everyday politics should not disguise the extent to which the economic doctrines of the Conservative Party had changed dramatically.

Although 1945 did record a peaceful political and social revolution, there was much continuity as well. Many of the plans taken up by the Labour Government were inherited from the wartime coalition: witness the 1944 White Paper on full employment (Minister for Reconstruction, 1944) and the 1944 Education Act, neither of whose architects (William Beveridge and 'Rab' Butler respectively) were socialists. So Labour's victory marked not only an ephemeral electoral success but also reflected a fundamental realignment of both intellectual and political opinion. If the state could call upon its citizens to make the supreme sacrifice in war, it could turn its energies in peacetime to ensuring a decent life for them all.

Several younger and rising Conservative politicians were fully conscious of and shared in this changed mood. Perhaps the most significant was Harold Macmillan, whose later public image as a rather complacent Prime Minister has diverted attention away from his early radicalism. As the MP for Stockton-on-Tees, Macmillan represented an area devastated by the depression. This experience profoundly influenced the development of his views which became very receptive to Keynesian proposals and to ideas about economic planning (Macmillan, 1938). Although on the losing side in 1945, men like Macmillan ensured that the Conservative Party did not revert to its pre-1939 policies. Indeed, with a style possible only for a party which traditionally has not taken ideology too seriously, the Conservative Party accepted the verdict of 1945 and set out to prove that it could run the Keynesian social democratic state much better than Labour.

Thus followed a long period in which the climate for public expenditure growth could not have been more favourable. On any measure, it grew rapidly, as did public employment. The growth of the social programmes of the welfare state was assisted by the parallel run-down in military expenditure and employment. There could be more spending on social services without any increase in taxation. Both the services themselves and the jobs they created in the public and private sectors were valued by a generation which could remember having neither services nor jobs. Political competition between the major parties often revolved around the scale and efficiency of the public expenditure programmes they would deliver: Conservative ministers boasted about the number of new council houses built and National Health Service beds provided. For 30 years after 1945, few people, and even fewer active politicians, questioned the very existence of such programmes. The question was always: 'how much?' or 'when?', but not 'whether?'.

Politicians during this period knew what they were doing: sharply increasing the share of national resources taken by the state and allocated on non-market criteria. Claims that this history of public expenditure growth was solely a result of the self-interested machinations of either public bureaucracies or politicians are unconvincing. This is not to deny that such self-interest might have been a factor but simply to stress that the external environment was itself so favourable.

II CONSENSUS TARNISHED

Nothing could be clearer from the perspective of the early 1980s than that many of the assumptions and objectives of this consensus have been fundamentally challenged by recent developments. The world economy, after a sustained period of growth and prosperity, is now in the throes of a recession unparalleled since the 1930s. Mass unemployment has returned, with 25 million people unemployed in OECD countries in 1982, after a long period during which full employment had become regarded as a norm, almost as a right.

Furthermore, the heirs of Keynes are strangely silent, their self-confidence apparently shattered. Older traditions in macroeconomics have regained the upper hand. The strident abuse of Keynes, even by distinguished academic economists, is indicative of the general mood: he is now held to belong to his own category of the 'defunct economist' whose errors have seductively misled policymakers (Keynes, 1936, p. 383). This remarkable transformation clearly requires explanation, especially as developments in the wider political arena again mirror the intellectual realignment. There was a sharp move to the political right in most of the industrialized democracies during the 1970s. The relationship between this shift and the challenge within the academic world to the Keynesian social democratic orthodoxy is difficult to disentangle. Rather than look for direct links, it is perhaps more fruitful to explore indirect ones, especially in common sources of frustration with the existing order. A complete account will have to await the writing of the political, economic and intellectual history of the post-1945 period. It is sufficient here to present a sketch of the major factors.

Regardless of whether it could justifiably claim credit or not, the Keynesian social democratic state received powerful reinforcement from the post-1945 prosperity, with steady economic growth accompanied by full employment. Furthermore, unemployment was much lower than even the most enthusiastic advocates of Keynesian policies had initially believed possible, far exceeding the expectations of Keynes and Beveridge. For generations which had survived both depression and world war, the impression of success was irresistible. In time, however, serious problems began to emerge. Across the world, hitherto steady inflation gathered momentum and threatened to escalate out of control, with the UK proving particularly vulnerable. Although the post-war prosperity contrasted so sharply with the pre-war difficulties, the UK economy in fact performed badly on almost all indicators, except that of unemployment, when compared with its closest competitors. Indeed, there was a slowly dawning recognition of relative economic failure.

The 1964–70 Labour Government, under Harold Wilson, raised expectations of a direct onslaught on the underlying problems through its emphasis upon indicative economic planning. In reality, the result was a further period of intensifying relative failure and a growing public cynicism about economic and political life. Policy mistakes (such as the refusal to devalue in 1964) further aggravated deep-seated problems. More fundamentally, the cultural obstacles to UK economic growth proved much deeper and more impenetrable than was then understood. The loss of empire and of economic and political status on the world stage, despite victory in war, had proved traumatic, producing costly aberrations in policy as well as wider problems of maladjustment.

It was thus inevitable that those who had earlier claimed credit for perceived success would later be tarnished with blame for perceived failure. Expectations of even greater prosperity had been continually raised, only to be dashed from the mid-1960s onwards. The social lubricant of economic growth, on which Crosland (1956) had placed so much hope, dried up. More public expenditure meant higher taxation for it could no longer be financed out of growth. The liability to income taxation slipped dramatically down the income distribution: the traditional middle-class hostility to income tax spread to the working class.

Furthermore, the institutions of cash redistribution which were the hallmark of the Beveridge system began to lose popular assent. With the exception of old-age pensioners, the recipients of cash assistance, whether of the contribution-based unemployment pay or of social security benefits, suffered from attempts by parts of both the media and the political right to stigmatize them as 'scroungers'. This reflected a widespread belief that a large but undefined proportion of claimants were either unentitled to benefit (for example receiving unemployment pay while working) or were exploiting the system (for example receiving unemployment pay because workshy or not working because benefits were greater than earnings from work).

The recipients of state benefits were not the sole targets. Too much government, too powerful trade unions and (sometimes) too many immigrants provided complementary 'explanations' for economic decline. Sir Keith Joseph (1979) provided his own list of 'poisons' undermining economic performance:

> ... it isn't as if our problem is simply that there's been too much government. I reckon there are six, six poisons which wreck a country's prosperity and full employment: excessive government spending, high direct taxation, egalitarianism, excessive nationalisation, a politicised trade union movement associated with Luddism, and an anti-enterprise culture. Six of them. Now most of our rivals have one of these poisons, some of them have two, we're the only country in the world that has all six. And sometimes I think that the miracle is that with all these six poisons in our system we still do as relatively well as we do.

The election in May 1979 of the Conservative Government of Margaret Thatcher marked an outstanding victory for such views. Their substance might be disputed but not their popularity. This Government embarked upon the first serious attempt to dismantle the various legacies of the 1945 Labour Government, to a much greater extent than its manifesto had indicated.

As part of the rolling back of the state in favour of the market, some of the underlying premises of the Keynesian social democratic state were challenged. There began unprecedented questioning of public provision in areas such as housing and health which have been central pillars of the welfare state. Public intervention in industry was reduced with the nationalized industries being the subject of extensive privatization schemes. The emphasis which the 1979 Conservative Government placed upon restoring the operation of the free market stands in vivid contrast to the policies of its post-war Conservative predecessors. Its public pronouncements linked such policies to its commitment to a monetarist macroeconomic strategy. It gained support for such intellectual positions through its success in tapping the prevalent mood of right-wing populism, manifested in antagonism to taxation and the welfare state and in calls for tougher policies on law and order and on immigration.

This radicalization of the Conservative Party in the mid-1970s was profoundly influenced by the writings of Milton Friedman. Working at the University of Chicago, Friedman has established a formidable reputation as a monetary economist, challenging not only the Keynesian analysis of the events of the 1920s and 1930s but also breathing new life into the quantity theory of money. Initially regarded by the Keynesian establishment as brilliant but eccentric, Friedman persevered with his research analysing the relationship between inflation and money supply growth. Slowly at first, but later with astonishing rapidity, Friedman became the dominant figure in an emergent monetarist school, recruiting many of the most able younger macroeconomists as his disciples. As a skilful communicator and popularizer, he spread the message that the problems of inflation were the fault of governments failing to enforce proper monetary stringency, either through their desire to buy votes or through the fallacies of their Keynesian advisers. Automatic rules about the rate of monetary growth, as part of less government discretion generally, were his easily understood proposals.

Moreover, Friedman used his academic standing as a platform for advancing his views on wider economic and social issues (Friedman, 1962; Friedman and Friedman, 1980). The passion of his advocacy of free-market capitalism as the spring of both efficiency and freedom was only surpassed by that of his condemnation of the manifold activities of modern governments. *Capitalism and Freedom,* published in 1962, became an extremely influential book, providing inspiration for much of the later critique of 'big government'. His powerful advocacy of the minimal state demonstrated that the brief period of near-universal assent to the Keynesian social democratic state had ended.

Friedman's influence upon Conservative policy was channelled through two research institutes: the Institute of Economic Affairs which since its foundation in 1957 has published a steady stream of literature in support of monetarism and free-market economics; and the Centre for Policy Studies, founded in 1974 by Sir Keith Joseph in order to propound such positions within official Conservative circles and to develop policies, somewhat independently of the mainstream party machinery. The leading Conservatives who secured such a sharp realignment of policy were typically career politicians who had moved to the right rather than intellectuals with a longstanding commitment to either free-market or monetarist economics. The experience of the 1970–74 Conservative Government under Edward Heath had deeply scarred the memories of some of its members. Its initial enthusiasm for free-market policies had been quickly abandoned in favour of a strongly interventionist industrial policy, an overhasty reflation leading to extremely rapid money supply growth, and a rigid incomes policy which had culminated in an electoral defeat amidst a coal strike. These events left both a policy and personality vacuum, into which advocates of Friedmanite policies stepped.

The question immediately arises about what had sapped the vigour of the old orthodoxy. Alarmed by the failure either to achieve growth or to control inflation, its diverse adherents were publicly pilloried and beset by doubt. The view that the problems of the UK economy were more deep-seated than had been realized and that remedies were therefore complex and long term, inevitably sounded lame, especially in contrast to the mounting support for the clear-cut remedies of monetary discipline and less government. There were also aspects of the orthodoxy itself which made it vulnerable. Becoming the prevailing orthodoxy had stultified its development and a rather comfortable complacency had made it possible for awkward questions never to be asked. Such an absence of constructive criticism from within its own ranks had left it ill-prepared to respond to a hostile but sophisticated critique. Many examples will be cited in this book but, for the present, two will suffice. First, Keynesian policy proposals were popularized using a one-sector model which entirely neglected the role of money. Sophisticates knew better but allowed this practice to continue. Second, much of the analysis supporting the programmes of the welfare state was careless. Too often it was assumed without analysis or research that non-market methods of allocation of goods and services guaranteed allocation according to need and that such programmes were automatically progressive in their net impact.

Such deficiencies left the foundations of policy curiously exposed to probing by those critics with a good grasp of economic analysis and little sympathy for programme objectives. The Keynesian social democratic state therefore suffered at the hands of critics who turned against it the weapons of commitment and analysis, backed up by wider political support, through which it had itself triumphed. But to concede the contemporary pre-eminence of free-market and monetarist economics is not to acknowledge their validity.

CHAPTER 2

The Meaning of Public Expenditure

I INTRODUCTION

The most dramatic twentieth-century change in the economies of the industrialized world has been the increase in the proportion of GDP appropriated by the state. One popular measure, the public expenditure/GDP ratio, is a useful indicator, though its interpretation requires care. Athough there are differences in public expenditure growth rates between OECD member countries, the most striking fact is the broad uniformity of experience. This is in sharp contrast to the differences in economic 'success' (as measured by growth rates of GDP) and in political history (as characterized by wartime experiences, type of governmental institutions and ideological stance of governments). The pervasiveness of this 'growth of government', when intuitively a wide diversity of experience might have been expected, has attracted the attention of economists and political scientists.

Public expenditure constitutes the dispensation by the state on non-market criteria of economic resources which it has acquired from firms and households. This definition is deceptively simple, owing to the fact that the state is such a difficult concept to analyse. Which organizations form part of the state is both theory-dependent and subject to serious classification problems.[1] Furthermore, a number of key terms are used extremely loosely, sometimes reflecting analytical distinctions but more often either the persuasive use of language or an interchange of terms simply for variation. Both academic literature and public debate refer to the extended role of the state, the growth of government and the expansion of the public sector. Similarly, the terms 'state expenditure', 'government expenditure', and 'public expenditure' are all used. Given the broad canvas of this book, covering highly diverse literature, it is difficult to impose consistent usage on such terms. Following convention, this book uses the term 'public expenditure' rather than 'state expenditure' or 'government expenditure'. In general, 'state' is used as a more abstract term than 'government': for example, in the 'market versus the state'

10

debate, and in the various characterizations of societies as fitting alternative models, such as 'the minimal state' or 'the Keynesian social democratic state'. Unless qualified by its context, the term 'government' relates to central government and excludes local authorities and other public agencies. 'State' is therefore a broader concept than 'government', not just in coverage but also in the sense that it denotes more about the enduring features of a particular society.

There are not just conceptual and semantic problems: those of definition and measurement are acute. Before analysis can proceed, decisions must be taken as to which institutions have all or part of their outlays classified as public expenditure. Central and local government pose no difficulty on this score: all their expenditure is included within 'general government' expenditure which is the concept on which most international statistics are based. However, this is narrower than the rather imprecise concept of the public sector which also includes a wide range of other organizations, notably public enterprises and a host of *ad hoc* bodies established by the state to undertake certain kinds of activities and expenditure. The decisions which are taken as to whether and, if so, how such bodies are consolidated into public sector accounts have major implications for the public expenditure totals which are declared.

The apparent size of public expenditure also depends upon the accounting treatment of fees and charges for services. Public expenditure can be expressed on a gross or net basis. Where charges are very small relative to total expenditure, the effect is minimal (for example the National Health Service). However, where charges play a substantial role (for example public housing), there is a major difference between gross expenditure and net expenditure. Unfortunately, there is in the UK no standardized treatment of such income: sometimes they are treated as offsets to expenditure and immediately netted whereas in other cases they are treated as exchequer income and separately identified. The more that netting is the usual practice, the smaller will be the public expenditure totals revealed by the accounting system for any given level of public services.

Exhaustive public expenditure should be carefully distinguished from transfer payments. The key difference is that in the former case the state takes decisions about the pattern of final output, as with defence expenditure. In the latter case, the state redistributes purchasing power from the hands of one group of individuals (taxpayers) to those of another group (beneficiaries). There are greater or smaller overlaps between these groups depending upon the transfer payment under consideration. In the case of exhaustive public expenditure, the role of the market in output decisions is supplanted by governmental procedures, acting through political decision-makers and public bureaucracies. Decisions have to be taken about both scale (that is expenditure totals) and composition (for example the relative priorities attached to defence and education). Although output levels and allocations are established on non-market criteria, the market is generally maintained on the input side, with the state bidding for factors in competition with firms and households. However, certain markets for public sector inputs may be characterized by the state's monopsony power and the monopoly power of unionized public employees. In the case of transfer payments, the composition of final output depends upon the consumption decisions of individual recipients, consumer sovereignty thereby being respected. Nevertheless, decisions about the scale of such compulsory redistributions of purchasing power must be taken through political processes.

A further distinction is between public financing and public production. The fact that the costs of providing a service are met by the state is logically separate from the state itself producing the service. There are frequently alternative organizational models available through which public policy objectives can be pursued. For example, education could be publicly financed through the provision of either cash or vouchers to parents which could then be used to purchase educational services from private sector suppliers. Or, the state could make direct payments to these suppliers in order to enable children to attend school for reduced or zero fees. These mechanisms represent alternatives to the existing UK practice, dominated by both public ownership of educational institutions and public financing. Similarly, public production does not necessarily imply the primacy of tax finance: electricity in the UK is mainly publicly produced but costs are entirely covered by charges. Which of these alternative forms of public provision is chosen in any particular case is frequently the subject of intense political controversy.

II THE ARITHMETIC AND POLITICS OF PUBLIC EXPENDITURE/GDP RATIOS

Public expenditure, however defined in the accounting system, is only one dimension of the scale of the state's activities. The size of the public budget is not a measure of the power of the state which possesses many instruments which have either no or negligible impact upon public expenditure totals. Any comprehensive assessment must focus upon the full spectrum of such instruments and the external environment within which they are used. Furthermore, the relationships between the economic power of the state and other dimensions of power (for example the ability to maintain external security and domestic order) are clearly complex. For example, an authoritarian state could have a very low level of public expenditure relative to GDP, as did General Franco's Spain. The Scandinavian democracies provide examples of the converse – societies characterized by both extensive political liberties and high public expenditure/GDP ratios.

Unfortunately, it is necessary to labour what might appear an obvious point because some influential politicians and academics have sought to

Table 2.1: The arithmetic of public expenditure/GDP ratios

		Case 1		Case 2
		£		£
Public expenditure on goods and services			30	110
Public expenditure on transfers			80*	0*
Private expenditure: privately financed	30		70	
publicly financed	40		0	
	—	70	—	70
GDP		100		180
Public expenditure		110		110
GDP		100		180
Public expenditure/GDP ratio (× 100)		110%		61%

Note: *Excluded from GDP to avoid double counting of the transfers and of final expenditure.

attach an entirely inappropriate significance to public expenditure/GDP ratios. For example, Roy Jenkins (1976), then a member of a Labour Cabinet, warned that:

I do not think that you can push public expenditure significantly above 60 per cent and maintain the values of a plural society with adequate freedom of choice. We are here close to one of the frontiers of social democracy.

Similarly, Milton Friedman (1976) wrote an article in the same year entitled: 'The line we dare not cross: the fragility of freedom at "60%".' Much will be said in Chapter 4 about the complex relationship between public expenditure and freedom: here, the emphasis is upon clearing up confusions stemming from definitional questions, and establishing the significance of the ratio.

Although useful as a crude indicator of the relative size of public expenditure (and hence as a quick guide for both intertemporal and inter-country comparisons), the ratio is potentially misleading. The numerator includes transfer payments which are excluded from the denominator. Consequently, the ratio is not limited to 100 per cent: values above this are possible, if unlikely. Table 2.1 illustrates this point. It provides data for a hypothetical economy with two types of expenditure, public and private. Private expenditure is financed in two distinct ways: individuals earn rewards from market exchange (privately financed private consumption); and receive transfers from the state (publicly financed private consumption).

In the first column of Table 2.1, private expenditure financed from both these sources is £70. Public expenditure on transfers is £80. Although it seems odd that transfers could exceed private expenditure, this is possible if they are heavily taxed in the hands of the recipients (at 50 per cent in this example). The gross amount of such transfers is shown in Table 2.1 but recipients can obviously only spend the net amount. In this example, the state also spends £30 providing non-marketed public services such as education and health care. Public expenditure is £110 (£80 + £30) whilst GDP is £100 (£70 + £30). The public expenditure/GDP ratio is 110 per cent. Although real-world cases above 100 per cent are unlikely, such examples vividly illustrate the need for caution. The second column of Table 2.1 shows a further example: public expenditure on goods and services is now £110, there are no transfers and privately financed private expenditure is £70. Public expenditure is now £110 (£0 + £110) whilst GDP is £180, giving a much lower ratio of 61 per cent. In this case, however, the state abrogates consumer sovereignty as to patterns of output much more than in the first case.

Moreover, there are no hard and fast rules about what constitutes public expenditure, with the accounting treatment of particular items differing between countries and through time in the same country. The public sector can be usefully divided, for both statistical and analytical purposes, into three components: central government, local government and public corporations – though, in practice, line-drawing is frequently more difficult than this suggests. Overseas practice generally focuses upon the expenditure of 'general government' (i.e. central and local government) and excludes the activities of public enterprises. In several countries, these are usually incorporated under companies legislation and not established as public corporations. They are rarely consolidated into the public sector and hence do not affect public expenditure totals. In contrast, the UK has traditionally used a comprehensive definition of public expenditure, relating to the 'public sector' rather than to 'general government'. However, the obvious danger for any one country in using a broader definition is that unadjusted data will be presented as comparable. This happened quite commonly in the mid-1970s, creating the false impression that public expenditure in the UK was exceptionally high.

The potential for confusion and for manipulation of the figures is enormous, with the main limit on the latter being the recent growth of international data on standardized definitions (for example, OECD, 1982a, c). Nothing could bring home these dangers more forcefully than a retrospective look at Roy Jenkins's alarm about the imminent crossing of 'one of the frontiers of social democracy'. His warning, contained in a speech delivered in January 1976 at Llangefni, was prompted by a Treasury statement in the (then still to be published) 1976 White Paper (Treasury, 1976a) that the public expenditure/GDP ratio had reached 60 per cent in 1975/76. Taken together with the international comparisons considered later in this chapter, the evidence of Figure 2.1 and Table 2.2 makes his claim seem more and more incongruous. Indeed, it is much easier to excuse Milton Friedman for his lapse in failing to understand the mysteries of UK public expenditure conventions than it is a former Chancellor of the Exchequer, especially one who enjoyed a high reputation for his technical command.

Figure 2.1 plots five alternative measures of the UK public expenditure/ GDP ratio for the 1960s and 1970s. There is no reason to stop at five, other than the practical one that the graph would otherwise quickly become unreadable. The five which have been plotted were chosen from among the available alternatives either because of their historical or contemporary significance or because there is a consistent series on that basis covering the entire period. For ease of reference, a shorthand name is attached to each series:

(1) The *Jenkins* definition (bold line) is an attempt by the author to reconstruct the figures on which Jenkins based his Llangefni speech. Although the 60 per cent ratio was prominently cited in the 1976 White Paper (Cmnd 6393; Treasury, 1976a), the Treasury has been unable to trace the numbers on which the calculation was based (as opposed to explaining the methodology).[2] This definition relates to a broadly-defined public sector.

(2) The *Pliatzky* definition (dot-dashed line) is named after Sir Leo Pliatzky, formerly a Second Permanent Secretary at the Treasury, who devised and implemented the 1977 redefinition of public expenditure which narrowed the focus from the public sector to general government (Treasury 1976b, 1977; Pliatzky, 1982a).

(3) The *Cmnd 8494* definition (solid line), used in the 1982 public expenditure White Paper (Treasury, 1982a), is the direct descendant of the Pliatzky definition, the main difference being the former's inclusion of the net market and overseas borrowing of the nationalized industries. However, the definition has continued to change since 1977 in ways which are explained in the technical notes at the back of the annual public expenditure White Paper, a process which complicates the task of tracking the path of public expenditure on a consistent definition.

(4) The *Brittan* definition (dashed line) is named after Leon Brittan, the Chief Secretary to the Treasury, who provided a specially calculated series in a written parliamentary answer (Brittan, 1982c), describing it as the 'pre-1977 definition', though in fact it diverges from the Jenkins/ Cmnd 6393 numbers in a spectacular way.

(5) The *OECD* definition (dotted line) is the basis used for its international comparisons (for example, OECD, 1982c).

Whereas the five measures show a common pattern of fluctuations, there are pronounced differences in their levels, with the Jenkins series being an aberrant case. The series based upon the OECD definition provides a useful control, emphasizing the extent to which the pre-1977 UK definitions (Jenkins/Cmnd 6393 and Brittan) recorded consistently higher ratios than on this internationally standardized definition. However, the post-1977 UK definitions (Pliatzky and Cmnd 8494) consistently produce lower scores than

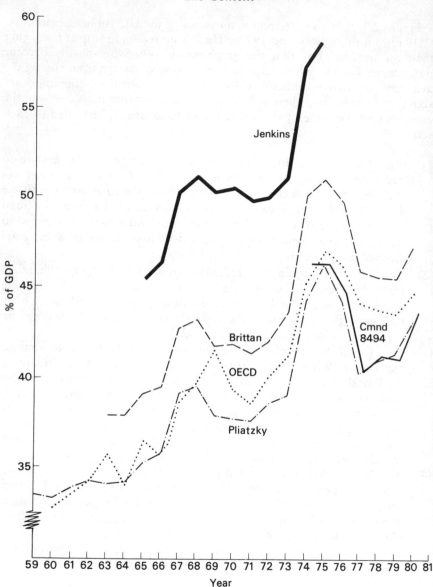

Figure 2.1 Alternative measures of the UK public expenditure/GDP ratio,
1959–81

Sources: For the 'Brittan' series: Brittan (1982c); for 'Cmnd 8494': Brittan (1982c) and Treasury (1982a, Vol. I, p. 7); for the 'Jenkins' series: Central Statistical Office (1976a); for the 'OECD' series: Table R8 of OECD (1982c); and for the 'Pliatzky' series: Pliatzky (1982a, p. 212).

Notes: The 'Cmnd 8494' entry which is for financial years rather than for calendar years has been displaced to the right by three months.

Table 2.2: The sensitivity of the public expenditure/GDP ratio to precise definitions

	Calendar year	1975	1976	1977		1978		1979		1980	
	Financial year	1974/75	1975/76	1976/77	1977/78		1978/79		1979/80		1980/81
Cmnd 6393 definition											
(1) Measure public expenditure and GDP in cash rather than volume terms										55.0*	
Jenkins definition											
(2) Exclude imputed value of rent from government owner-occupied non-trading property										?	
(3) Express GDP at market prices rather than at factor cost										(7.7)	
Brittan definition		50.8	49.6	45.8	45.8	45.5		45.4		47.3	
(4) Exclude nationalized industries' and certain other public corporations' capital expenditure but include their capital grants and net borrowing										(1.6)	
(5) Exclude debt interest to be met out of trading revenue										(3.4)	
(6) Include non-trading capital consumption										0.8	
Cmnd 8494 definition		46.2	46.2	44.5	40.3	41.2		41.0		43.1	43.6

Source: Brittan (1982c), Central Statistical Office (1982a,b).
Note: *The Jenkins ratio for 1980 is understated by the (no longer calculated) figure for imputed rent.

on the OECD definition, though the differences are much smaller. The divergence between the Jenkins and Brittan series reveals the scope for massaging the public expenditure/GDP ratio, according to whether high or low ratios are required. Although few of the entries in Table 2.2 can be completed from published data, the structure provides revealing insights. It is arranged to show how a reconciliation might be effected between the Cmnd 6393 and the Cmnd 8494 definitions, taking the Jenkins and Brittan definitions as intermediate steps.

Discussion of the 1977 redefinition has centred upon the revised treatment of nationalized industries (line 4) and of debt interest (line 5).[3] Table 2.2 shows just how misplaced that focus has been in terms of understanding the complete transformation of officially cited public expenditure/GDP ratios. The differences between the ratios calculated on the (pre-1977) Brittan definition and on the (post-1977) Cmnd 8494 definition are relatively small. For example, Brittan records 47.3 per cent for 1980 against Cmnd 8494's 43.1 per cent. It is the differences between the Jenkins/Cmnd 6393 and the Brittan scores which are significant, especially as they are calculated on the basis of the same definition of public expenditure. To move from Cmnd 6393 to Jenkins both public expenditure and GDP must be measured in cash, rather than in volume terms (line 1).[4] Then, to reach the Brittan definition, imputed rent must be excluded (line 2) and GDP at market prices substituted for GDP at factor cost (line 3).[5]

Table 2.2 reveals the extent to which the 1976 scare was a product of the Treasury's attempt to sell a story in support of public expenditure cuts. Within a year, the ominous figure of 60 per cent (Treasury, 1976a) was replaced by 46½ per cent (Treasury, 1977), an astonishing drop of 13½ percentage points, coupled with a new-found enthusiasm to explain that the ratio would be even lower if the overseas practice of excluding social security funds from public expenditure were adopted (Treasury, 1976b). The circumstances surrounding this redefinition highlight the political as well as technical content of such classificatory practice. The 1976 public expenditure White Paper (Treasury, 1976a) attached great prominence to the ratio reaching 60 per cent without making any of the necessary qualifications as to its interpretation. However, this statistic caught the attention of the media and of financial markets, leading to much misinformed comment. Somewhat hoist on its own petard, the Labour Government then narrowed the definition of public expenditure, bringing UK practice nearer to that of other OECD countries. Moreover, official calculations of the ratio have subsequently related public expenditure to GDP at market prices, not to the smaller GDP at factor cost.

III   POLICY SUBSTITUTES FOR PUBLIC EXPENDITURE

Public expenditure is used as a means of achieving policy objectives, whether protection of territory against foreign aggression or ensuring that old people can maintain some minimum standard of material well-being. Just as the objectives being pursued are diverse, public expenditure is only one means among several. It is therefore essential to examine the relationship between these alternative means before any firm conclusions can be drawn about public policy in different countries or about the respective merits of the various instruments. The resources of revenue, personnel and laws are processed through governmental organizations into programmes with specified policy outputs (Rose, 1981). It is immediately obvious that accounting totals will capture only the two of these resources which are converted into money (revenue and personnel) to the neglect of the third (laws). Resources can thus be directed to the achievement of public policy objectives without them ever being 'counted'. There are three main alternatives to public expenditure, all of which are 'law-intensive'. Because the extent to which these are used can vary sharply, the recorded amount of public expenditure is an incomplete, and potentially misleading, index.

Confiscation

Within its boundaries, the state claims and attempts to enforce a monopoly of legitimate violence. Therefore, it could always simply confiscate the resources which it requires, whether men for war or supplies such as foodstuffs and armaments. Amongst the many objections to such confiscation is the highly practical one that its repeated use provides very clear incentives not to possess the precise resources required by the state! Confiscation without compensation is rare. One significant example, involving only partial compensation, is military conscription. Conscripts are usually paid below the level of civilian wages, let alone sufficient to persuade them to supply their labour voluntarily in military occupations. Although laws could be passed authorizing confiscation, the state usually bids for resources in the market-place.

There are occasions, however, when the state requires specific resources (for example the nationalization of the assets of a particular firm; and the acquisition of particular land and property for road building or slum clearance) and uses powers of compulsory purchase. Public expenditure figures will be biased downwards if compensation is set at a level lower than market value. For example, but for conscription, the public expenditure cost of the Vietnam war to the US Federal Government would have been much higher. In contrast, given that there is no conscription in the UK, public expenditure figures do reflect this aspect of the cost of the Ulster troubles. An important part of the case for taxation is that its use enables the cost of public expenditure to be allocated between individuals on criteria (for example according to their ability to pay, or to the benefits they receive) rather than imposed upon those who directly supply the inputs.

Coerced private expenditures

In order to comply with regulatory legislation, firms and households undertake private expenditures which might reasonably be viewed as coerced. Environmental protection legislation compels firms to invest in equipment in order to reduce water or air emissions down to a statutorily prescribed level. Very little public expenditure is involved but the private costs to firms may be substantial, both in direct expenditure on pollution abatement equipment and in terms of opportunity costs as some (privately) efficient technologies may now be prohibited.

Coerced private expenditures include that part of the cost of regulation borne by firms and households. Examples can be found from many spheres, such as health and safety, and consumer protection. Whether such policies are justified raises issues beyond the concern of this chapter. Both careful scrutiny of costs and benefits and an assessment of alternative instruments to standards (for example taxes, and leaving it to bargaining between the affected parties) are necessary before this can be resolved. What is relevant here is that such coerced private expenditures are, at least in part, substitutes for public expenditure. Some or all of the costs of pollution abatement could be met instead through public expenditure on subsidies to firms to instal equipment, or relocation grants, or more public investment in sewage treatment facilities. Imposing the cost upon third parties' is therefore a method of achieving public policy objectives without incurring public expenditure.

The notion of coerced private expenditures could be extended much further. State intervention in the market through such instruments as price controls, tariffs and import restrictions are other examples of public policy objectives being pursued without the costs appearing as public expenditure. The extent and complexity of the implicit costs and benefits arising from the various forms of state intervention are formidable obstacles confronting the construction and interpretation of comparative international data (Tait and Heller, 1982).

Tax expenditures

There are numerous occasions when governments face a policy choice between public expenditure and tax expenditures (that is allowances against tax). Examples include child benefit versus child tax allowances, investment grants versus capital allowances, and housing subsidies versus mortgage tax relief. Tax expenditures have rarely been acknowledged to be relevant to public expenditure decisions, let alone explicitly planned. What start as small concessions often grow to become major deductions from exchequer revenue. Willis and Hardwick (1978) calculated that the yield of UK income tax would have been 40 per cent higher in 1973/74 if there had been no tax expenditures in that year. They advocated a tax expenditures budget. A small step was made in the 1979 public expenditure White Paper (Treasury, 1979a) which introduced the practice of giving the estimated costs of a large number of tax allowances and listed those on which no valuation could then be put.

Tax expenditures require attention for a number of reasons. First, they constitute a further hazard in the way of valid inferences from cross-sectional data (if the extent of reliance upon them varies between countries) and from time series data (if their relative importance in a country changes).

Second, the use of tax expenditures would make it possible for governments to exaggerate or conceal the true extent of changes in the size of public expenditure. An important example is provided by the 1979 Conservative Government's statutory sick-pay scheme which altered the existing arrangements for the first eight weeks of sickness. Under the new scheme, administration has been passed from the Department of Health and Social Security to employers, who recover the cost of statutory sick pay by deducting it from their remittances of national insurance contributions. This change is, therefore, a combination of coerced private expenditures and the substitution of tax expenditures for public expenditure on benefits. With employers now carrying the administrative costs, there is a public expenditure saving on this item of £30 million. There are savings of national insurance benefit of £365 million, offset by reduced payments from employers which fall by £565 million. However, accompanying changes will produce more income, from sickness pay becoming taxable (£130 million) and from higher national insurance contributions (£125 million) (Department of Health and Social Security 1982a, b). It is typical of the myopia surrounding the question of tax expenditures that the 1982 public expenditure White Paper referred to the scheme solely in terms of the gross public expenditure savings of £355 million with no mention of such offsets (Treasury, 1982a, Vol. II, p. 50).[6]

Third, it has been argued that the benefits from tax expenditures are distributed much more unequally than those from public expenditure. Field, Meacher and Pond (1977) have described them as the 'hidden welfare state'.

Fourth, there is often widespread reluctance to accept that exemption from taxation is equivalent to the receipt of public expenditure.[7] An important example relates to the favourable tax treatment of owner-occupation: the value of imputed rent is not taxed yet tax relief is granted on mortgage interest payments; and the proceeds of the sale of an individual's main residence are exempt from capital gains tax. In contrast, public housing subsidies are classified as public expenditure and are often criticized for being subsidies on grounds which logically should be, but frequently are not, extended to the implicit subsidies favouring owner-occupation.

Fifth, partly because they are not accounted for, planned or controlled and partly because of their appeal to parties of the political right with commitments to cut public expenditure, tax expenditures seem likely to grow in significance. This is by no means solely a British phenomenon. For example Doern (1981, p. 144) criticized the Canadian Royal Commission on Financial Management and Accountability (Lambert, 1979) for its inadequate discussion of the role of tax expenditures which he predicted: '... wil increasingly become the instrument through which various interests in Canadian society seek favours from government.' The reason why tax expenditures are neglected is that public accounting systems have been devised to ensure that 'public money' is used for the purposes intended. The focus has therefore been upon cash dispensed rather than revenue sacrificed. Indeed, tax expenditures are usually regarded as 'private money', not 'public money'.

Confiscation, coerced private expenditures, tax expenditures and public expenditure are different methods of achieving public policy objectives. Disputes about the choice of instrument often mask disputes about those objectives, as well as reflecting disagreement about the impact of particular organizational forms. Both values and analysis are therefore involved.

IV   THE EXPENDITURE RECORD

This is a book about ideas, rather than about the detailed historical record. Furthermore, the discussion of policy substitutes in the previous section has highlighted the problems inherent in the interpretation of public expenditure statistics. This task is difficult enough in the context of data for a single country, in which case 'local knowledge' will often indicate those areas requiring extreme care. In the context of international comparisons, the pitfalls are even more formidable. Despite such warnings, however, this chapter would be seriously incomplete without a brief discussion of the expenditure record. Without it, the 'problems' of public expenditure, real and imagined, could not be set in their proper context.

The UK experience

The seminal work on the growth of public expenditure in the UK was undertaken by Peacock and Wiseman (1961). They recorded spectacular growth over the period of their study: from 8.9 per cent of GNP in 1890 to 36.6 per cent in 1955. However, these were both peacetime years, with much higher figures being recorded in wartime, for example, 51.7 per cent in 1918 and 73.9 per cent in 1943. In their explanation both of the extent and timing of growth, they emphasized that wars and major social disturbances seemed to exert an upwards displacement effect. Although the ratio fell back sharply on the return to peacetime, it remained far above the level of the earlier period of peace. This time profile made them emphasize the role of changed perceptions about tolerable types and levels of taxation, fundamentally altered by such events. It also reinforced their scepticism, initially philosophical, about Wagner's Law, the proposition that an expanding role for the state in the economy is an inevitable feature of economic development (Wagner, 1883).

Perhaps the major reason why Peacock and Wiseman's study became so well known was their achievement in constructing an expenditure series over such a long period. Official statistics are often available on a consistent basis for a surprisingly short period. Even then, consistency is problematical, owing to problems of both classification and the movement of particular activities either between the public and private sectors or between the components of the public sector. For practical reasons, resort must be made to the national income accounts which employ a rather different definition of public expenditure from that used in the annual public expenditure White Papers.[8] When these sources are available as alternatives, the White Paper possesses the important advantage that the expenditure figures for the historical years are adjusted on to the public expenditure definition and classifications used for the planning years. Because the White Papers only provide figures for the previous five years, the analysis of trends must be conducted on the basis of the national income accounts figures, even though they have not been reworked on to a common classification. Such difficulties notwithstanding, Figures 2.2 to 2.5 chronicle the main features of public expenditure growth and compositional change. They all relate to general government rather than to a more broadly defined public sector. Although the graphical exposition inevitably suppresses much detail, its visual impact assists the identification of broad trends and is therefore consonant with the contextual objectives of this chapter.

Figure 2.2 records the growth of public expenditure over the post-war period, highlighting its division between volume and price elements. Two series are plotted at current prices: general government expenditure (solid line) and general government expenditure on goods and services (dashed line). Although their time paths did sometimes diverge, both increased twenty-five-fold over the period 1946–81. The dot-dashed line plots general government expenditure on goods and services at 1975 prices, the year on which all the constant price tables in the national income accounts are now based (Central Statistical Office, 1982a, b). This series, which is calculated by applying relevant price indexes to the components of public expenditure, is only available back to 1962. Over the years 1962–81, general government expenditure on goods and services increased by 910 per cent at current prices but by only 33 per cent at constant prices. There is no equivalent constant price series for general government expenditure, partly because of the conceptual difficulties attached to the choice of deflator for other categories of expenditure. Leaving aside for later discussion the implications of any divergence between the deflator for public sector costs used above and the GDP deflator, it can be safely concluded that it has been increases in prices,

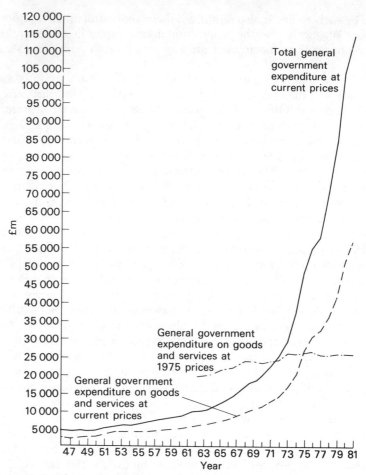

Figure 2.2 The growth of general government expenditure, 1946–81
Source: Central Statistical Office (1982b, pp. 14, 51 and 151).
Notes: The series for general government expenditure on goods and services at 1975 prices can only be taken back to 1962 through a lack of constant price figures for earlier years covering general government domestic fixed capital formation. The Central Statistical Office do not publish any estimates of total general government expenditure (i.e. including, *inter alia*, transfers) at 1975 prices.

not in volume, which have been the dominant factor in higher public expenditure on goods and services.

Much of the popularity and resilience of the public expenditure/GDP ratio stems from its appeal as a method of overcoming the problems of interpretation introduced by inflation. For the period 1946–81, Figure 2.3 expresses general government expenditure and general government expenditure on goods and services (both in current prices) as a percentage of GDP at market

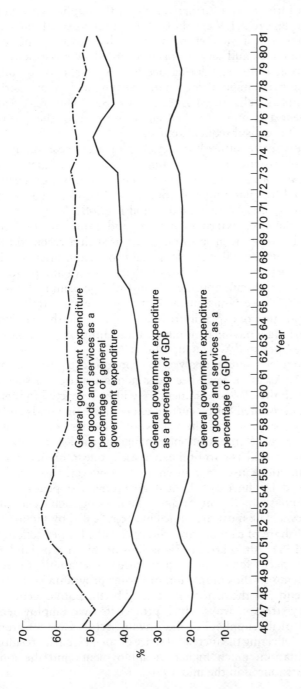

Figure 2.3 General government expenditure/GDP ratios, 1946–81
Source: Central Statistical Office (1982b)

prices. The first ratio is yet a further variant of the public expenditure/GDP ratios plotted in Figure 2.1 Viewed over such a long period, the changes in these ratios look much smaller than might have been expected. Most significantly, the goods and services ratio recorded almost exactly the same value in 1981 as in 1946. The dot-dashed line expresses goods and services expenditure as a percentage of the total, revealing a slow but fairly steady decline from its peak value of 64.5 per cent in 1953. The crisis years of the mid-1970s appear as a hump on the long-term trends of the two ratios, to which there has been a subsequent return.

Figure 2.4 shows expenditure by function, plotting the cumulative percentage of the total represented by the functions indicated. The analysis must use the functional categories of the national income accounts, not the functional programmes used for planning and control, and is restricted by the availability of consistent data to the limited period 1966–81. The functions of the minimal state (defence, external relations and protective services) have remained a fairly constant proportion. Even in such a recent time period, there has been a substantial increase in the proportion attributable to the 'core' welfare state (education, libraries and arts; health and personal social services; social security; and housing): from 48.07 per cent in 1966 to 54.68 per cent in 1981. The establishment of the welfare state transformed the functional composition of expenditure, with defence and the servicing of the national debt no longer having their nineteenth-century importance (44.9 per cent in 1890; Peacock and Wiseman, 1961, p. 186.)

Figure 2.5 provides a similar analysis by economic category, for the longer period 1946–81. As there have been distinctive features to such compositional changes in the 1970s, commentary will be restricted to this decade. The proportion accounted for by current expenditure on goods and services has been slowly rising, as has the wages and salaries component of that category. But the latter compositional change in total public expenditure should not be overstated as part of the increase is due to higher employment taxes (such as national insurance surcharge). However, this trend is much more pronounced in the case of local government expenditure (Heald, 1982c), thus emphasizing the importance of analysing such trends at a more disaggregated level. The most dramatic change revealed by Figure 2.5 is the sharply reduced share of capital expenditure: from 11.1 per cent in 1971 to 4.0 per cent in 1981. Alternative explanations of this abrupt fall have been advanced: lower needs for capital expenditure, for example, on education and housing, owing to the completion of earlier programmes and changed demographic trends; or the distortions caused by the public sector responding to budgetary stress in ways which protect its own employment at the expense of that of its suppliers in the private sector. Current grants have grown strongly, reflecting the increased share of social security resulting from an ageing population, much higher unemployment, and the indexation arrangements introduced in the mid-1970s.

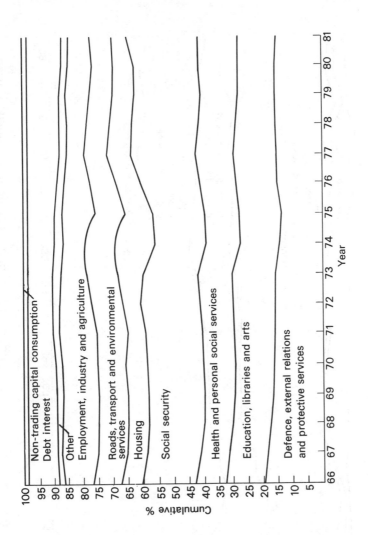

Figure 2.4 The composition of general government expenditure: analysis by function, 1966–81

Source: Central Statistical Office (1982a) and earlier volumes of the Blue Book.
Notes: This figure has been plotted using Table 9.4 of successive Blue Books. When the definition of public expenditure was narrowed to general government in 1977, the years back to 1966 were revamped in this Table ('Analysis of total [general government] expenditure'), published for the first time in the 1977 Blue Book (Central Statistical Office, 1977). This replaced the earlier Table ('Analysis of public expenditure') which covered the combined expenditure of general government and public corporations.
Figures for earlier years on the new basis have never been published.

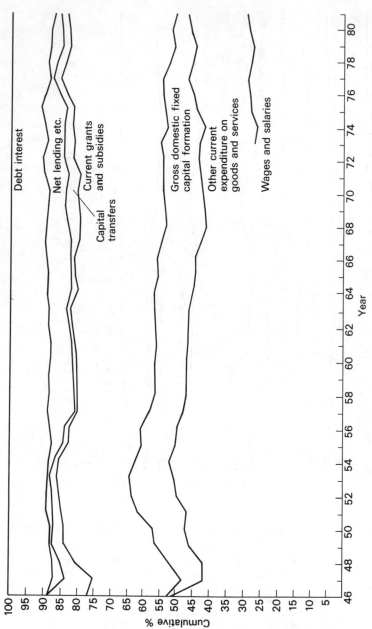

Figure 2.5 The composition of general government expenditure: analysis by economic category, 1946–81

Source: Central Statistical Office (1982b)

International comparisons

The view that public expenditure in the UK was abnormally large gained widespread currency in the mid-1970s, partly as a result of comparisons being drawn between the UK's public expenditure/GDP ratio on the then broad definition and ratios for other countries calculated on much narrower bases. Such a misunderstanding influenced the climate of opinion, lending support to the view that excessive public expenditure was a prominent factor in poor economic performance. The one-sentence first paragraph of the 1979 Conservative Government's first public expenditure White Paper (Treasury, 1979c) read: 'Public expenditure is at the heart of Britain's present economic difficulties.' When such a bald statement appears in the key planning document, it becomes even more important to examine UK developments with the aid of an international perspective.

The most reliable basis for international comparisons is the OECD's annual statistical volume summarizing the national accounts of member countries on the UN standardized system (for example, OECD, 1982a). Table 2.3 shows public expenditure/GDP ratios for the period 1960–80 for those member countries for which standardized data are available (OECD, 1982c). Member countries are divided into three groups: 'EEC-Europe' which typically displays high ratios; 'other Europe' which is more diverse, with high ratios in the high-income Scandinavian countries but low ratios in low-income southern Europe; and 'non-Europe' which, though high-income, displays only low or medium ratios. There are, of course, exceptions to these broad generalizations: for example, Greece has a low ratio, just having been 'promoted' into EEC-Europe and still having much in common with the rest of southern Europe; Finland is well below the rest of Scandinavia; and Japan remains a middle-income country, unlike other 'non-Europe' members of OECD.

Over the period, the UK has gone down the league of international ratios. Given its poor economic performance which has made it one of the poorest EEC countries, such a development is unsurprising. An OECD study (1978) calculated the elasticity of total public expenditure with respect to GDP over the period 1960–76, with the values being greater than 1 for all member countries. In other words, a 1 per cent increase in GDP is associated with a greater than 1 per cent increase in total public expenditure. In fact, the value for both the UK and the average for OECD was 1.21 per cent. The final column of Table 2.3 gives the increase in percentage points over the period 1960–80 for those countries for which the required annual entries are available. The UK's increase of 12.0 percentage points is not much different from that of France (+11.6) or West Germany (+14.9) but far below Belgium (+21.4), the Netherlands (+28.8) and Sweden (+34.6). However, such comparisons must be interpreted with care, recognizing that different rates of growth of GDP will, for any given expenditure elasticity of greater than 1,

		1960	1961	1962	1963	1964	1965	1966	1967	19·
A.	**EEC-EUROPE**									
	1. Belgium	30.3	29.8	30.5	31.5	30.8	32.3	33.5	34.5	36
	2. Denmark	24.8	27.1	28.1	28.6	28.4	29.9	31.7	34.3	36
	3. France	34.6	35.7	37.0	37.8	38.0	38.4	38.5	39.0	40
	4. Greece	17.4	17.4	18.4	18.7	19.8	20.6	21.5	23.6	23
	5. Ireland	28.0	29.7	29.5	30.5	31.8	33.1	33.6	34.8	35
	6. Italy	30.1	29.4	30.5	31.1	31.8	34.3	34.3	33.7	34.
	7. Luxembourg	30.5	30.3	32.2	32.1	32.3	33.3	35.0	37.5	37.
	8. Netherlands	33.7	35.4	35.6	37.6	37.8	38.7	40.7	42.5	43.
	9. United Kingdom	**32.6**	**33.4**	**34.2**	**35.6**	**33.9**	**36.4**	**35.6**	**38.5**	**39.**
	10. West Germany	32.0	33.4	35.2	35.9	35.7	36.3	36.5	38.2	37.
B.	**OTHER EUROPE**									
	11. Austria	32.1	32.3	33.6	34.7	38.2	37.9	38.3	40.5	40.
	12. Finland	26.7	26.0	27.4	29.2	30.5	31.3	32.5	33.4	33.
	13. Iceland	28.2	24.0	23.9	26.0	27.6	28.4	28.4	32.2	33.
	14. Norway	29.9	29.7	31.5	33.1	33.1	34.2	34.8	36.4	37.
	15. Portugal	17.0	19.3	18.8	20.3	20.4	20.1	20.3	20.9	20.
	16. Spain	13.7	13.0	12.8	13.0	18.7	19.6	19.5	21.1	21.
	17. Sweden	31.1	31.0	32.4	34.6	34.8	36.0	38.1	40.0	42.
	18. Switzerland									
	19. Turkey	—	—	18.0	19.1	20.5	20.6	20.6	21.0	21.
	20. Yugoslavia									
C.	**NON-EUROPE**									
	21. Australia	22.1	23.7	23.5	23.3	23.7	25.6	25.6	26.3	25.
	22. Canada	28.9	30.0	30.0	29.5	28.9	29.1	30.1	32.1	33.·
	23. Japan	20.7	20.6	23.1	23.2	23.2	22.7	23.3	22.7	22.·
	24. New Zealand									
	25. United States	27.8	29.2	29.0	29.0	28.4	28.0	29.2	31.2	31.·
D.	**TOTAL OECD**	28.5	29.5	29.9	30.2	29.9	30.1	30.8	32.2	32.·

Source: Table R8 of OECD (1982c).

Notes: n/a = not available.

The data in this table are measured according to the standard definitions of the OECD–UN system of accounts. The definition of public expenditure used is 'total outlays of government'

'1	*1972*	*1973*	*1974*	*1975*	*1976*	*1977*	*1978*	*1979*	*1980*	*Increase in percentage points 1960–1980*
0	38.8	39.1	39.4	44.5	45.1	46.6	47.9	49.5	51.7	+ 21.4
0	42.6	42.1	45.9	48.2	47.8	48.9	50.6	54.0	56.0	+ 31.2
3	38.3	38.5	39.7	43.5	44.0	44.2	45.2	45.4	46.2	+ 11.6
8	22.0	21.1	25.0	26.7	27.4	29.0	29.9	29.7	30.3	+ 12.9
5	38.8	39.0	43.0	47.5	46.8	45.5	46.4	48.9	—	n/a
6	38.6	37.8	37.9	43.2	42.2	42.5	46.1	45.5	45.6	+ 15.5
3	37.0	35.7	36.1	48.9	49.7	52.7	51.8	52.1	60.2	+ 29.7
5	48.1	48.7	50.8	55.9	55.9	56.0	57.5	59.5	62.5	+ 28.8
4	**40.0**	**41.1**	**45.2**	**46.9**	**46.1**	**44.1**	**43.7**	**43.5**	**44.6**	**+ 12.0**
9	39.7	40.5	43.4	47.1	46.4	46.5	46.5	46.4	46.9	+ 14.9
7	39.8	41.3	41.9	46.1	46.9	46.8	49.7	48.8	48.5	+ 16.4
8	33.2	31.9	32.9	37.1	38.3	39.5	39.1	38.5	38.2	+ 11.5
6	33.6	35.5	36.6	38.7	33.9	34.0	—	—	—	n/a
0	44.6	44.6	44.6	46.6	48.5	50.2	52.3	51.4	49.4	+ 19.5
3	22.7	21.3	24.7	30.3	35.1	—	—	—	—	n/a
6	23.2	23.0	23.1	24.7	26.0	27.5	29.3	30.5	32.4	+ 18.7
5	46.4	44.9	48.1	49.0	51.9	57.9	59.6	65.1	65.7	+ 34.6
1	22.5	—	—	—	—	—	—	—	—	n/a
2	26.3	26.8	30.4	32.4	32.9	34.3	33.7	33.2	34.1	+ 12.0
6	37.2	36.0	37.4	40.8	39.6	40.6	41.0	39.3	40.7	+ 11.8
8	21.8	22.1	24.5	27.3	27.9	29.0	31.1	31.6	32.7	+ 12.0
2	31.9	31.2	32.9	35.4	34.4	33.5	33.1	32.8	33.2	+ 5.4
1	33.3	33.1	35.0	38.2	37.7	37.7	38.2	38.6	39.4	+ 10.9

Notes cont.)
hich is the sum of lines 23, 28, 29 and 30 less line 26 in Table 9 of OECD (1982a) Vol. II. The
try for 'Total OECD' is a weighted average for those countries for which information is
vailable.

lead to different increases in the ratio. The surge in the UK's ratio from 197:
to 1975 (+5.8 points) was paralleled elsewhere, focusing attention upon
external events such as the effects of OPEC price increases, rather than jus
specific weaknesses in the UK's system of public expenditure control. In
contrast, the subsequent holding of the ratio at the 1975 level was less typical
many countries experienced further large increases in the second half of the
1970s.

If increases in the public expenditure/GDP ratio count as evidence of sin
there are many sinners. Although higher incomes tend to lead to higher ratios
ideology and the consequent political choices about the respective roles of the
market and the state can modify this relationship. For example, the USA has
not shared the rapid expenditure growth characteristic of other high-income
OECD countries. Ratios are not just the outcome of technological relationships linking expenditure levels to income and demographic factors: values
and preferences, working through political processes, play a crucial role.

V   CONCLUSION

Whatever uncertainties may attach to any precise measure, public expenditure has increased massively during the twentieth century.[9] At the middle of
the century, the powerful combination of Keynesian ideas on macroeconomic
policy and the development of the welfare state provided both a stimulus and
a facilitator. Although such broad trends are clear, the detailed record must
be studied with great care, given the widespread misconceptions about the
size of public expenditure relative to GDP. Public expenditure is but one
instrument of public policy. If too much attention is attached to setting
precise targets for the public expenditure/GDP ratio, it is likely to encourage
the substitution of policies which do not count towards this ratio for those
which do. However undeveloped the existing statistics on coerced private
expenditures and tax expenditures may be, they are directly relevant to any
comprehensive measure of the extent to which the state modifies the use of
resources in an otherwise market economy.

CHAPTER 3

The Monetarist Challenge

I THE VULNERABILITY OF THE KEYNESIAN ORTHODOXY

Monetarists made heavy inroads in the 1970s into the Keynesian citadels, both academic and governmental. Macroeconomic policy in the UK switched decisively from Keynesian concerns with demand management and fine tuning towards monetarist concerns with the Public Sector Borrowing Requirement (PSBR) and money supply growth. This change of emphasis preceded, but was accelerated by, the election of a Conservative Government in 1979.

In no sense could a single chapter in this book elucidate all the subtleties of the debate between monetarists and Keynesians, let alone adjudicate between the rival camps. The purpose of this chapter is different. Whilst sidestepping many of the controversies related to the adoption by governments of monetarist prescriptions, it seeks to clarify the implications of monetarism for the role, scope and level of public expenditure. The extent of the monetarists' success in first challenging the Keynesian framework of macro-economic policy and then substituting their own, requires explanation.

There would seem to be three reasons why the Keynesian framework had become so vulnerable. First, as the dominant orthodoxy of the post-war period, it received blame for the emergence of stagflation and for failing to provide successful remedies. Second, macroeconomic policy as practised by 'Keynesian' governments was predicated upon a one-sector model, even though the two-sector IS-LM analysis was the orthodoxy of academic Keynesians.[1] It was the resulting passivity of monetary policy upon which Milton Friedman seized. His commanding personal influence, both as a researcher and as a communicator, established the intellectual prestige of monetarism and stimulated other work within its theoretical framework. Third, whereas memories of mass unemployment had faded, experience of inflation was immediate, resulting in a major upwards readjustment in the levels of unemployment which were perceived to be politically and socially tolerable. This faded memory made the idea that unemployment is 'voluntary' more acceptable. Contrast, for example, public attitudes towards unemployment and the unemployed during the 1950s and 1960s (which many would now characterize as a period of fairly sustained over-full

employment) with that of the 1970s and 1980s (in which large-scale
unemployment re-emerged). Fatalism about the level of unemployment and
growing hostility towards the unemployed would seem a not unreasonable
characterization of public attitudes in the later period. This changed climate
proved fertile ground for the acceptance and dissemination of monetarist
ideas on how to defeat inflation.

II   THE LINK BETWEEN MONETARISM AND THE FREE MARKET

A priori, there does not seem any necessary link between the view that control
of monetary growth should be the cornerstone of macroeconomic policy and
any particular view about the desirable level of public expenditure. The
respective merits of fiscal and monetary policy seem a long way removed from
both the question of the level of public expenditure and the wider one of the
role of the public sector. Yet there do exist in practice strong ideological
overtones to the monetarist position. It is necessary to scrutinize the internal
logic of the monetarist case to establish whether acceptance of it does in fact
lead to advocacy of a low level of public expenditure. Alternatively, is it that
monetarist policy conclusions are of particular appeal to those who favour
low public expenditure on quite separate grounds?

The presumed link

In public debate, it is frequently assumed that a monetarist stance on
macroeconomic policy will necessarily be accompanied by a free-market, and
hence anti-public expenditure, stance on microeconomic issues. Some writers
have emphasized that the logical connection is much weaker than is usually
assumed. For example, Vane and Thompson (1979, p. 195) concluded that:
'It is possible to be a monetarist without possessing right-wing political
leanings and similarly to be a right-wing politician without being a monetarist.' Very much depends upon what the terms 'right-wing' and 'left-wing'
are taken to mean in this context. If they refer to opposition to, or support for,
private ownership of the means of production, this statement might hold.
Indeed, some Marxists have incorporated monetarist mechanisms into their
theories of capitalist crisis. However, left-wing and right-wing are frequently
used in a rather different sense: meaning support for, or opposition to, state
intervention in the market economy. In turn, this intervention operates at two
different levels: macroeconomic intervention in the form of an active fiscal
policy, possibly backed up by prices and incomes policies; and extensive
microeconomic intervention resulting in a large proportion of output being
transferred out of the market.
    The Keynesian social democratic state has been interventionist in both
senses. Because of the way in which Keynesian macroeconomic policies

mproved the climate for public expenditure growth, abandonment of such
policies may also have environmental implications. This is perhaps one of the
reasons why the left-wing monetarist academic and the right-wing non-
monetarist politician are in practice rather difficult to find. The political
significance of monetarist ideas lies in their success in breaking up the loose
coalition which had sustained the accommodation in favour of the Keynesian
social democratic state: it eroded one pillar of its theoretical foundation. It
was not accidental that, when the Conservative Party embraced monetarist
views, there was a simultaneous transformation in its attitudes towards the
role of the public sector.

The characteristic features of monetarism

Monetarism and belief in the free market are powerfully combined in the
writings of Milton Friedman. Before making an assessment of the logical
rather than personal links, it is necessary to examine what constitutes
monetarism. Attempting to answer this question, Mayer (1978, p. 4) advanced twelve propositions which he considered were the 'basic building
blocks' of monetarism. Whilst demonstrating that they form a coherent
group, he noted:

> These twelve items are, of course, not all equally significant. The first
> four are the basic ones and can be used to define monetarism.
> Monetarists need not accept any of the other eight. But monetarists do
> tend to accept these other eight propositions too.

Although there have been other attempts to define the meaning of monetarism, Mayer's analysis is the best known and highlights the uneasy mix of
the technical and the ideological. In what follows there has been some
paraphrasing in order to make the material more readily accessible but,
where there is any danger of ambiguity, his own phraseology is also given.
   Mayer's four defining propositions were:

(1)   Changes in the money stock are the dominant determinant of changes
      in money income (quantity theory of money).
(2)   Changes in the quantity of money will induce portfolio substitution by
      individuals, across a wide range of assets, not just financial ones but
      also physical assets such as property and consumer durables (the
      monetarist transmission process).
(3)   Left to itself, the market economy has a self-correcting mechanism in
      the long run which limits macroeconomic instability (the inherent
      stability of the private sector).
(4)   Irrespective of the initial source of the change in the money supply, it
      will have given and predictable effects, even if knowledge about the

structure of this process and the lags involved is imperfect (the irrelevance of allocative detail and belief in the fluid capital market).

Mayer's eight supplementary propositions were:

(5)   Focus on the price level as a whole rather than on individual prices.
(6)   Reliance on small rather than large econometric models.
(7)   Use of the reserve base or similar measure as the indicator of monetary policy.
(8)   Use of the money stock as the proper target of monetary policy.
(9)   Acceptance of a monetary growth rule.
(10) There is no long-run trade-off between unemployment and inflation which would give policymakers a choice between alternative combinations. The 'natural rate of unemployment' is the rate at which expectations held about future changes in the price level are vindicated by events. Its level is determined by microeconomic factors, such as the nature of the labour market and tax/transfer policy, and by the frictional, structural and seasonal characteristics of the economy. If a government attempts to reduce unemployment below the natural rate, the result will be ever-accelerating inflation (the expectations-augmented Phillips curve).
(11) A relatively greater concern about inflation than about unemployment compared to other economists.
(12) Dislike of government intervention.

An evaluation of such building blocks will not be attempted in this book. What should be noted is that, whilst a number of them are primarily technical, others have much more ideological content, notably (3), (11) and (12). Taken together, they have clear implications for the proper economic role of the state.

The direct implication is to reject activist demand management policies: public expenditure thus loses its stabilization role. The indirect implications are much more far-reaching for public expenditure itself. Adherence to (3) and (12) encourages a preference for private rather than public sector activity. Explicit within monetarism is an image of smoothly working competitive markets. Rather less explicit is an unfavourable view of the political process, manifesting itself in propositions such as (9), designed to limit the discretion of elected politicians and of bureaucrats. It is often proposed that the central bank should be insulated from the political system, thus moving the control of the money supply outside the domain of political competition. Monetarists are therefore likely to draw upon schools of thought which manifest similar attitudes to discretionary state action (for example the political writings of Milton Friedman and Friedrich von Hayek; and the Virginian 'public choice' school). These bodies of writing reinforce the monetarist analysis by providing a theoretical foundation for the argument that the instability of modern economies stems not from the private sector but from the political system. It is such reinforcement which accounts for the vigour of the critique of the Keynesian social democratic state.

The way in which monetarist and free-market views are mutually reinforcing is an important key to understanding why monetarist views are often interpreted as 'right-wing', to be embraced or rejected on such grounds rather than on an appraisal of their merit. One of the immediate causes of monetarism's identification with a right-wing political stance in the UK has been that its most prominent exponents to British audiences have included Milton Friedman, Enoch Powell and Sir Keith Joseph. It is also clear that they appreciated the role which monetarism played within their wider economic and political philosophy. However, a fear that such an association would lead to the rejection of monetarist policy prescriptions on irrelevant grounds was articulated by Samuel Brittan (1976), himself both a monetarist and an advocate of the free market, in an 'open letter' to Milton Friedman, which he published as an article in *The Financial Times*. Brittan who, as an extremely influential economic journalist, did much to spread monetarist ideas in the UK, sharply rebuked Friedman for not distinguishing between: 'Friedmanite economics and the personal opinions of Milton Friedman', thus creating: 'a danger that your strong expression of what is purely speculative and personal may discredit the more securely established parts of your analysis'.

Propositions (1) to (12) can be seen to incorporate an uneasy mix of technical and ideological statements. If monetarists are correct in their technical propositions, the present shift of macroeconomic policy towards its new focus on monetary aggregates will be sustained. If that were all, the implications are fairly limited. Keynesian deflation (focusing on public expenditure cuts and tax increases) might not seem that different in kind from monetarist deflation (focusing on reducing the rate of growth of the money supply and using fiscal policy as an instrument to support this objective). Too much ideological significance can be read into the choice of fiscal or monetary instruments: there is an element of illusion in the characterization of the former as more interventionist than the latter.

Under this set of specified circumstances, it should be possible for economists and politicians of wide-ranging persuasions to adopt the new methods of macroeconomic control. Hence, the fears expressed that such methods would be rejected on irrelevant grounds are well placed. Nevertheless, it should by now be clear that the controversy extends much wider because of the strength of monetarists' belief in the efficacy of private markets, the inherent stability of the private sector, and the destabilizing effects of the public sector.

However, the discussion so far has attributed too much unity to monetarist thought (Burton, 1982). The Treasury and Civil Service Committee's inquiry into monetary policy (1981a) highlighted the growing divisions, both theoretical and on policy, between the 'gradualist' monetarists, such as, Milton Friedman and David Laidler, and the 'new classical' monetarists, such as Patrick Minford. A new generation of monetarist models has been constructed, heavily influenced by the 'rational expectations' revolution set in motion by Robert Lucas and Thomas Sargent. The theory of rational expectations describes the formation of expectations about future movements in the economy, stating that these are formed in accordance with economic agents' perceptions of how the economy works and are not subject to any systematic bias or error. Individuals use information with complete efficiency in pursuit of their own interests, knowing the true probabilities attached to possible outcomes, given all the publicly available information. In response to the charge that such assumptions are wildly unrealistic, the standard defence of positive economics is used: it is not the assumptions which matter but the predictive success of models containing them compared with that of the available alternatives (Minford and Peel, 1981).

On policy, the new classicals advocate the defeat of inflation through sharp reductions in monetary growth whereas the gradualists urge deceleration. Even less scope is conceded for activist fiscal or monetary policy: their inflationary consequences would be fully anticipated by economic agents, thus eliminating any output effects. Complete wage and price flexibility, downwards as well as upwards, is assumed. The hostility to the Keynesian social democratic state is even more pronounced, with tax/transfer policy blamed for causing extensive unemployment, all of which is 'voluntary': the restriction of benefits and an assault on union power are policy priorities (Minford and Peel, 1981). Tobin (1981, p. 30) described the new classicals as:

> ... a second wave of monetarism, a second counter-revolution that has absorbed and breathed new life into the first, a movement both more reactionary and more revolutionary than its predecessor.

III   CROWDING OUT

The idea of 'crowding out' was developed by the monetarist writers Karl Brunner and Allan Meltzer and quickly passed into popular usage in the 1970s. It was a term taken to mean that the private sector was being squeezed out by the growth of the public sector. Independently, Bacon and Eltis (1976) also stressed the pre-empting of resources from the private sector, though the mechanisms were different. 'Crowding out' is a term with an ominous ring, implying that the process is undesirable. Brunner and Meltzer (for example, 1978) were quite explicit about their view that much public output has a low or negative value. There are thus two issues: first, the relative value at the margin of public and private output; and, second, whether higher public output necessarily leads to an offsetting fall in private output.

It is the second of these issues which is the concern of this section. When the economy is consistently operating at the full employment level of output, any increase in the level of public expenditure at a particular point in time must be at the expense of private expenditures. One of the most fundamental Keynesian propositions is that, when the economy is operating below the full employment level of output, higher public expenditure will, through the multiplier process, generate higher output. It is sometimes possible to have both more private output and more public output. The exponents of the crowding out hypothesis have vigorously disputed this core proposition.

Criticisms of Keynesian multipliers

The crude version of the Keynesian multiplier rests upon the assumption that there are hitherto unutilized factors of production 'waiting' to be brought into productive use. This is clearly a special case, more plausible in the depths of depression than in the typical circumstances of the post-war period. Nevertheless, this qualification was frequently lost sight of in popular debates on macroeconomic policy.

There is, however, a fundamental weakness in the traditional exposition of Keynesian multiplier analysis: the disregard of the government's budget constraint. Analysis has often been couched in terms of the government increasing its spending by £100 million and, given a multiplier of, say, 2, GDP increasing by £200 million. The flaw in this example is its incompleteness. Even in an economy with unutilized resources, this increased government expenditure has to be financed by some combination of increases in taxation, government borrowing, or the money supply. Even within the more sophisticated IS-LM framework, the absence of any government budget constraint encouraged the treatment of fiscal and monetary policy as separate compartments and obscured their essential interdependence. For example, an expansionary fiscal policy has monetary consequences: the increased government deficit must be financed through the creation of either money or debt. If analysis focuses solely upon the impact of higher public expenditure and fails to examine the monetary repercussions on the rest of the economy, it will be seriously incomplete (Burrows, 1979).

Types of crowding out

As the term 'crowding out' is frequently used very loosely, it is necessary to specify the mechanisms through which it is believed to take place. Two distinct types of mechanism have been identified: physical crowding out and financial crowding out. Physical or direct crowding out occurs when the state pre-empts real resources such as manpower and materials. Bacon and Eltis (1976) argued that public employment growth had been directly at the expense of the (predominantly private) market sector. However, they failed to demonstrate that the market sector had wanted the manpower absorbed into the public sector. Much of the growth in public employment took the form of part-time females (Wilkinson and Jackson, 1981) during a period when the market sector was shedding employees, mainly full-time males. The combination of these trends suggests that more caution is required. Bacon and Eltis's crowding out might alternatively be viewed as the result of conscious choices either to absorb in the public non-market sector manpower unwanted in the market sector or to change the balance between the market and non-market sectors. The essence of their argument was that the balance had shifted too far towards the non-market sector: the mechanisms were themselves less important.

Monetarist writers stress financial or indirect crowding out (Stein, 1982). Care has to be taken with the term 'financial' because these effects are believed to operate not only through interest rates. If additional public expenditure is financed by higher public borrowing, interest rates must rise so that a money supply target can be met. Higher interest rates will have two effects: first interest-sensitive private expenditures, notably on investment, house-building and consumer durables, will be reduced; second, higher domestic interest rates will attract an inflow of capital, thus pushing up the exchange rate. This process will damage the market prospects of both exporting industries and those facing competition from imports, with consequential effects for investment, output and employment. If the higher public expenditure is financed by an increase in the money supply, thus breaching monetary targets, there will be an upwards revision of inflationary expectations as households attempt to maintain their real money balances.

Most Keynesians would accept that these effects are plausible but would deny that they are sufficiently strong to cancel out the stimulating effects of higher public expenditure. It is very difficult to resolve such arguments because both sides are unconvinced by each other's evidence. For example, the Treasury (1981a) argued that each £1 of higher public investment would be exactly offset by a £1 reduction in private expenditures. The evidence presented by runs on the Treasury's own macroeconomic model suggests that this would not be the case. The model indicated that, both in cases where existing money supply targets were held and in those where they were relaxed, crowding out was less than 100 per cent. In other words, there was a net increase in output. In some favourable circumstances, there was negative crowding out: more public expenditure led to more private expenditures as well. When these runs on the Treasury model were commissioned by the Treasury and Civil Service Committee (1981c), there was the curious spectacle of the Treasury announcing that it had no faith in the answers obtained from its own model.[2]

These severe disagreements about the impact of public expenditure on the private sector have major implications. If it is believed that the macro-economic effects of public expenditure are beneficial, a much more sympathetic climate is thus created for decisions on totals. Once the macroeconomic effects are believed to be damaging and short-run changes for stabilization purposes viewed as worthless if not perverse, an important pillar supporting the post-war role of public expenditure crumbles.

IV MONETARIST POLICIES AND THE PSBR

Although explicit targets for money supply growth had been adopted before May 1979, the new Conservative Government embraced monetarism as a virtue rather than as a necessity. This section will explore the link between its monetarist convictions and its policies towards public expenditure. The essence of its strategy was to refuse to accommodate a high rate of inflation by means of restricting the growth of the money supply. It believed that control over the money supply would produce a downwards revision of inflationary expectations in line with monetary growth targets. What was required was both the necessary technical means and public confidence in the Government's strength of purpose. On this view, exogenous shocks, such as from an increase in raw material prices, would not lead to higher inflation as there would be offsetting price falls. The strains imposed by the rate of money supply growth being held below the inflation rate would be taken by the price level rather than by the volume of economic activity. This conclusion stems from the emphasis upon expectations adjustments and on wage and price flexibility.

The accounting link between the nominal PSBR and £M3 growth

The PSBR constitutes the link between the Government's focus upon monetary growth and its policies towards the level of public expenditure. This link, which has been central to the Government's macroeconomic case for public expenditure cuts, deserves careful attention because it has been the subject of much dispute. Figure 3.1 shows the build up of the PSBR for the period 1963/64 to 1981/82, distinguishing between government transactions on current, capital and financial accounts. When interpreting this and subsequent graphs, it should be remembered that the customary sign convention leads to the PSBR (the shortfall of revenues over expenditure) being plotted as a positive figure and therefore above the horizontal axis. Consequently, the public sector current balance (that is current receipts minus current expenditure) will be drawn below the horizontal axis if it is positive (current surplus) but above if it is negative (current deficit). Two different measures of public sector saving are shown in Figure 3.1. The dot-dashed line plots the public sector current balance and the dotted line the narrower measure of the general government current balance. The latter, which excludes the savings (that is retained profits and depreciation charges) of public corporations, is parallel to the public expenditure definitions and

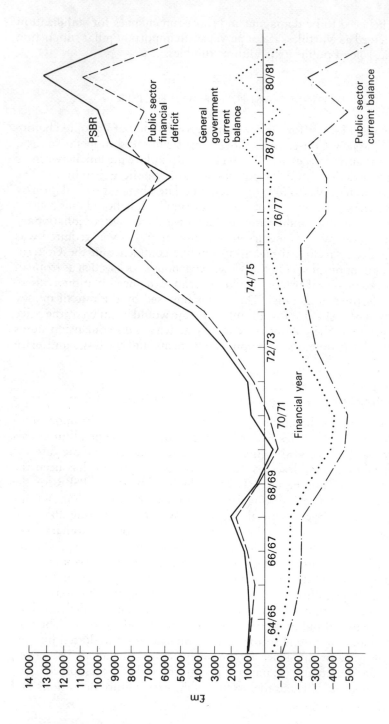

Figure 3.1 *The build up* of *the PSBR, 1963/64 to 1981/82*

Source: Alexander and Toland (1980) updated from Central Statistical Office (1983a) and from unpublished sources.

the time series reviewed in the previous chapter. Whereas policy and statistics now revolve around the narrower general government expenditure, it is the broadly defined PSBR which has been central to the macroeconomic policy debate. The extent of public sector saving should be stressed because of the popularity of homilies such as 'the public sector should learn to live within its means, just like private firms and households'. In practice, the public sector has usually more than covered its current expenditure from current receipts, with borrowing covering part of its capital and financial transactions in a way which would be judged entirely proper in the private sector. The reduced level of general government saving in the 1970s was a reflection of the budgetary strains induced by inflation and recession.

The dashed line plots the public sector financial deficit, calculated as the current balance plus the difference between capital expenditure and capital receipts. The vertical distance between this line and the dot-dashed line (public sector current balance) measures net capital expenditure. Having considered the current and capital accounts, the final step is to bring in the financial account. The PSBR is the sum of the financial deficit and net financial transactions, a miscellaneous category including net lending to the private sector. The PSBR is an all-inclusive measure for the public sector, including the borrowing of central government, local authorities, national-ized industries and other public corporations, but netting out intra-public sector transactions. The size of the PSBR therefore depends in part upon the subdivision of economic activity between the public and private sectors. Consequently, care is required in making inter-country comparisons if either accounting conventions or the public/private split differs.[3] It is clear from Figure 3.1 that the PSBR reached unprecedented levels in the 1970s, of an entirely different order from those of the 1960s, though the fact that the graph is drawn in current prices makes it unsuitable for detailed interpretation of events over a period characterized by high and variable rates of inflation. Nevertheless, the changing relative size of public sector saving and the PSBR indicates much greater reliance on external finance as the means of financing transactions on capital and financial accounts.

Before subjecting these trends to detailed analysis, the accounting link between the PSBR and the growth of the money supply can be specified. From amongst the various alternatives available, the definition of the money supply in terms of which UK monetary targets are now framed is sterling M3 (£M3). The PSBR can be financed either by borrowing or by money creation. The impact of any given PSBR upon £M3 depends upon the way in which it is financed. To the extent that the government can sell public sector debt to the UK non-bank private sector, the PSBR does not add to the growth of £M3, thus making such sales an important intermediate policy target. Figure 3.2 shows the accounting link between changes in £M3 and the PSBR. The growth in £M3 is measured on the upper part of the vertical axis. The PSBR only contributes towards £M3 growth to the extent that it is unfunded: the

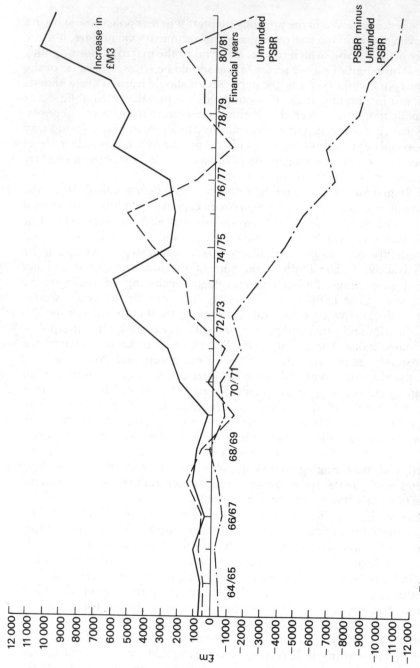

Figure 3.2 The PSBR's 'direct' contribution to the growth of £M3, 1963/64 to 1981/82

Source: Central Statistical Office (1983a) and from unpublished material supplied by the Bank of England.

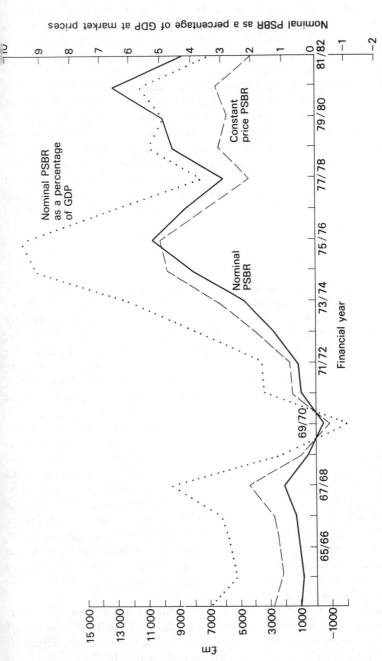

Figure 3.3 Nominal and constant-price PSBR, 1963/64 to 1981/82

Source: Alexander and Toland (1980) revised and updated from Central Statistical Office (1982b) and from unpublished sources.
Notes: Both the nominal PSBR (solid line) and the constant-price PSBR (dashed line) are plotted against the left-hand vertical axis. The PSBR/GDP ratio (dotted line) is plotted against the right-hand vertical axis.

funded part which is financed from the UK non-bank private sector is excluded from £M3 growth. The unfunded PSBR is the difference between the PSBR and the UK non-bank private sector's net acquisition of public sector debt (for example national savings and gilt-edged stock) and can take both positive and negative values. If the graph of the unfunded PSBR is above the horizontal axis, this indicates a positive contribution to £M3 growth: if below, a negative contribution. Finally, the difference between the PSBR (treated as positive if the government is borrowing) and the unfunded PSBR (treated as positive if not all the PSBR is covered by funding) is plotted on the lower part of the vertical axis. Therefore, the vertical distance (treated as positive) between the dashed line and the dot-dashed line indicates the size of the PSBR in each year. Although it is essential not to confuse statements of accounting identities with propositions about economic behaviour, Figure 3.2 shows that *ex post* the direct contribution of the PSBR to £M3 growth has been very limited.

Alternative measures of the PSBR

Although the nominal level of the PSBR rose to unprecedented heights in the 1970s, the significance of this development has been the subject of divergent assessments. Five alternative measures of the PSBR have been calculated: the nominal PSBR; the constant-price PSBR; the inflation-adjusted PSBR; the constant-employment PSBR; and the demand-weighted PSBR. There is often confusion between the second and third: the term 'real PSBR' is variously used to denote the constant-price PSBR (Alexander and Toland, 1980; Peacock and Shaw, 1981) and the inflation-adjusted PSBR (Treasury and Civil Service Committee, 1981b).

One reason for the intensity of disputes about the significance and policy implications of the levels reached by the PSBR in the 1970s and early 1980s is that some of these various adjustments can transform how events are interpreted. In Figure 3.3, covering the period 1963/64 to 1981/82, the solid line represents the nominal PSBR (in current prices) and the dashed line the constant-price PSBR at 1975 prices. The path of the *nominal PSBR* reveals a sharp contrast between the 1960s and 1970s. However, the *constant-price PSBR*, which eliminates the effects of inflation, moderates this contrast. Another way of removing the influence of inflation on the nominal PSBR is to express it as a percentage of GDP. Plotted as a dotted line, this closely mirrors the path of the constant-price PSBR, revealing a sharp fall in the late 1970s after peaking dramatically at 9.6 per cent in 1975/76.

Calculations of the *inflation-adjusted PSBR*, undertaken by economists at the Bank of England, provide an inflation-adjusted estimate, setting off against the nominal PSBR the gains to the public sector from the effects of inflation on its nominal debt (Taylor and Threadgold, 1979; Bank of England, 1982). Figure 3.4 plots the inflation-adjusted PSBR which for most

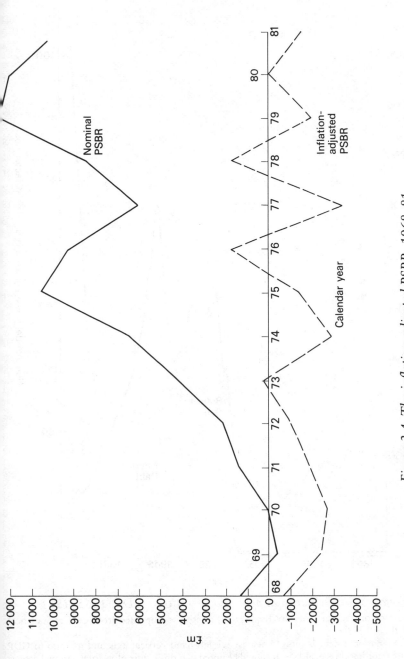

Figure 3.4 The inflation-adjusted PSBR, 1968–81

Source: Plotted from a table supplied by the Bank of England and based on the methodology of Taylor and Threadgold (1979) and Bank of England (1982).

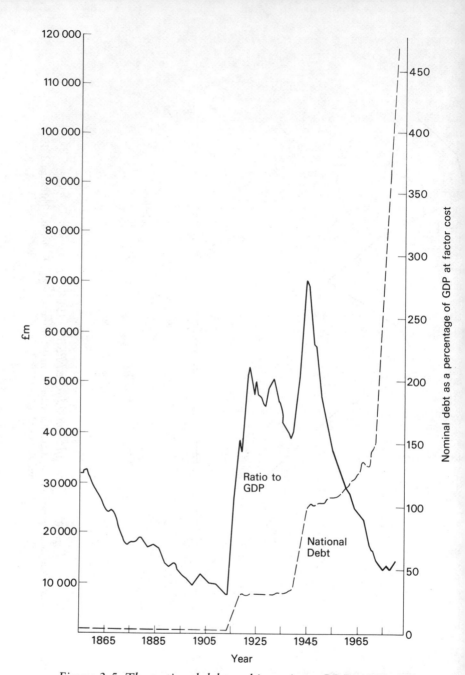

Figure 3.5 The national debt and its ratio to GDP, 1855–1981

Source: Based on the data used by Reid (1977) revised and updated from Central Statistical Office (1982b, 1983b).

Notes: The national debt is plotted against the left-hand vertical axis and its ratio to GDP against the right-hand vertical axis. It should be noted that this Figure plots total national debt as a percentage of GDP at factor cost. It therefore includes 'official holdings' and takes the narrower version of GDP. If the 1981 ratio were calculated as market holdings as a percentage of GDP at market prices, it would be 38 per cent rather than 54 per cent.

years is a negative figure, dramatically transforming the high nominal PSBR and making the public sector a net saver. The reason for the scale of this adjustment can be seen from Figure 3.5. It shows that, despite increases in the national debt, its ratio to GDP at factor cost has fallen dramatically since 1945 and that the high nominal PSBRs of the 1970s have steadied, not reversed this trend (Reid, 1977).

The nominal PSBR tends to increase in a recession as tax revenues fall alongside output and employment, and certain kinds of expenditure rise, notably social security benefits. The *constant-employment PSBR* is an attempt to remove such cyclical effects, by calculating what the PSBR would have been had the level of activity remained constant. A large number of assumptions are required in such calculations: for example, the composition of the additional demand. Furthermore, the estimates depend upon the econometric model used to generate them, meaning that alternative calculations are possible (Hartley and Bean, 1978). Ward and Neild (1978) calculated the constant-employment budget balance, adjusting the public sector's net acquisition of financial assets (the financial deficit of Figure 3.1) rather than the PSBR itself. They emphasized how the adjusted figures show the experience of the late 1970s in a dramatically different light: the public sector moves into 'surplus'. In Figure 3.6, the constant-employment budget balance is compared with its unadjusted counterpart. For 1949–77, the solid line plots Ward and Neild's calculations of these variables, denoted by a solid line and a dotted line respectively. However, the sensitivity of the levels of such adjusted measures, if not of their fluctuations, can be seen from the upwards displacement of the constant-employment budget balance shown by Ward's latest estimates (Ward, 1982). His revised estimates, covering 1971–81, are plotted by a dashed line, with the unadjusted counterpart being shown by a dot-dashed line.[4]

Various kinds of public expenditure and revenue may have different multiplier effects on output: for example, higher social security benefits will increase demand by more than equivalent reductions in higher income tax rates because of different marginal propensities to consume. The *demand-weighted PSBR* is calculated by weighting expenditure and revenue items by their respective multipliers. Such calculations which rely upon simple income-expenditure models are an extreme Keynesian construction and have been criticized as such by the Treasury (1982b).

Such an array of adjusted measures of what seemed at first sight a simple concept is a reflection of deeply divided views about the significance of the PSBR. A term unknown before the 1970s (Peacock and Shaw, 1981) has been thrust to the centre of the policy debate.[5]

The economic relationship between the PSBR and £M3 growth

The consequence of a high nominal PSBR is that governments will maintain

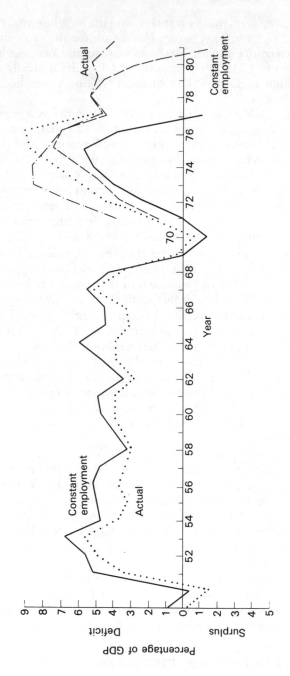

Figure 3.6 Constant employment budget balance: Ward and Neild's estimates, 1949–81

Source: Ward and Neild (1978) and Ward (1982).

Notes: Two series for both actual and constant employment budget balances are plotted, the first from Ward and Neild (1978) and the second from Ward (1982). See footnote 4 to this chapter for a discussion of the relationship between the two series.

interest rates at a higher level than they would otherwise be, in order to carry out the funding programme. The 1979 Conservative Government's declared objective of steadily reducing the PSBR as a percentage of GDP was designed to facilitate the achievement of its unconditional monetary targets with less pressure on the private sector through high nominal interest rates. In its medium-term financial strategy, the Government placed great emphasis upon the reduction in the PSBR because of the assumed link between the PSBR and £M3 but stressed that the planned reduction in the PSBR/GDP ratio was not intended to be interpreted as a target path, unlike the parallel monetary targets (Treasury, 1980a).

There are, however, fundamental disputes about the economic relationship between the PSBR and changes in £M3. Leaving aside Keynesian doubts about the significance of any such relationship, there is the question of which of the following is relevant to the growth of the money supply: (a) the nominal PSBR or only the unfunded part? (b) the nominal PSBR or the inflation-adjusted PSBR? The importance of the nominal PSBR has been repeatedly stressed by the Treasury (1980d) in its exposition of the 1979 Conservative Government's monetary policy. The balance of the expert evidence received by the Treasury and Civil Service Committee (1980b) was against such an emphasis. Although the Treasury view was supported by Minford (1981), doubts extended beyond the predictably hostile Keynesians such as Kaldor (1980, 1982) and Hahn (1980) to embrace gradualist monetarists such as Friedman (1980) and Laidler (1980). For example, Friedman argued that:

> The key role assigned to targets for the PSBR, on the other hand, seems to me unwise for several reasons. (1) These numbers are highly misleading because of the failure to adjust for the effect of inflation. (2) There is no necessary relation between the size of the PSBR and monetary growth. There is currently such a relation, though even then a loose one, only because of the undesirable techniques used to control the money supply. . . . (3) The size of the PSBR does affect the level of interest rates. However, given monetary growth, the major effect on interest rates is exerted by the real PSBR not the nominal PSBR. . . . (4) Emphasis on the PSBR diverts attention from the really important aspects of government fiscal policy: the fraction of the nation's output that is diverted to uses determined by government officials . . . (pp. 56–7).

In turn, Laidler wrote:

> I do not believe that the links in the British Economy between the balance of the budget and the public sector borrowing requirement on the one hand, and the rate of money creation on the other, are so

clearcut and rigid that the adoption of monetary targets has any strong implications for the conduct of fiscal policy (p. 53).

Friedman's reference to the 'real PSBR' should be interpreted as to the inflation-adjusted PSBR.

The Treasury's emphasis (1981e) upon the nominal PSBR stems in part from an assumed economic relationship and in part from the techniques which have been used to control the money supply. This policy can be characterized as using interest rates as an instrument for controlling the demand for money rather than by acting directly on the monetary base. The distaste with which academic monetarists regard such procedures has stimulated a debate on the techniques of monetary control (Treasury, 1980c; Treasury and Civil Service Committee, 1980a; Congdon, 1982). Within the context of existing techniques, the Treasury's medium-term financial strategy envisaged a sharp reduction in the PSBR/GDP ratio, intended to relieve the pressure that high nominal interest rates exert on the private sector. Control over the nominal PSBR is thus seen as an essential counterpart to the attainment of money supply targets.

If higher interest rates are required to fund a higher nominal PSBR, upwards pressure will be exerted on the exchange rate, thus increasing £M3 through the ensuing inflow of funds. Individuals may respond to an increase in their wealth as represented by higher government debt in order to re-establish their desired portfolio balance. Such mechanisms mean that the funded PSBR, as well as the unfunded PSBR, may contribute to the growth in the money supply: the first, indirectly, and the second, directly (Bank of England, 1981a, b). Alternatively, a higher funded PSBR might not lead to higher interest rates because the multiplier effects on income have increased the level of savings. The evidence presented to the Treasury and Civil Service Committee (1981a) illustrated both the wide variety of theoretical propositions and the difficulty in discriminating between them. David Hendry (1981a; b, p. 94), one of the specialist advisers, dismissed the Treasury's econometric work (1981e) on the relationship between the PSBR and £M3 growth, commenting: '. . . only someone already believing in the basis of the current policy could find such evidence "convincing".' More generally, none of the existing econometric work is capable of convincing the opponents of the theory tested.

Technical issues can frequently, but not always, be resolved through an appeal to the facts using econometric techniques. However, the margins for looking at the same facts in different ways are often extremely large. Conflicts over macroeconomic policy have an ideological as well as technical dimension. There is something of an irony in the strength of the conviction in positive economics displayed by Vane and Thompson (1979) and by Cobham (1978), in the light of the rebuke delivered by Brittan (1976) to its most distinguished advocate (Friedman, 1953). Given the limitations of existing empirical practice, attention inevitably turns back to the assumptions.

Differences in UK macroeconomic models reflect conflicting judgements about how the economy works (for an exposition, see Minford, 1980). For example, the (Keynesian) Cambridge Economic Policy Group model incorporates prices in goods and labour markets which are extremely sticky, particularly in a downwards direction. In contrast, Minford's (new classical) Liverpool model assumes that prices and wages respond flexibly to demand and supply conditions. Such different model specifications lead to profoundly different policy conclusions. It would seem to stretch credibility to deny that at least part of the explanation for these differences stems from the model-builders' sharply contrasting attitudes towards the role of the state in the market economy.

Different model specifications lead to divergent predictions and policy judgements. Whereas Keynesian models rarely show 100 per cent crowding out even in the presence of money supply targets, monetarist models sometimes do (Bank of England, 1981a). The extent of wage and price flexibility built into the model will be a key factor in determining in what proportions lower monetary growth cuts output rather than inflation. There is a spectrum of views, running from new classical monetarists (small output effects) through gradualist monetarists (limited output effects provided that there is gradual deceleration) and 'pragmatic' Keynesians (serious output effects) to 'anti-monetarist' Keynesians (dramatic output effects) (Treasury and Civil Service Committee, 1981a).

The PSBR and the level of public expenditure

Within the framework set by the 1979 Conservative Government's medium-term financial strategy, control of the money supply is regarded as sufficient for the control of inflation. Discretionary monetary policy is rejected in favour of the pursuit of a pre-specified monetary growth rule which is unconditional in the sense that it does not vary with either output growth or external shocks (such as further oil price increases). Other policy instruments, such as changes in taxes, public expenditure and interest rates, are to be used in order to facilitate the achievement of the monetary target. It is thus rather misleading to talk in terms of a rejection of an active fiscal policy. Taxation and public expenditure might be changed vigorously. What is fundamentally different, however, is that the purpose of such changes is to support the attainment of the unconditional monetary target and not as part of a Keynesian attempt to regulate directly the level of economic activity. Both public expenditure cuts and tax increases are designed to reduce the PSBR, thus lowering the level of interest rates consistent with the monetary target, and causing less 'crowding out' of private expenditures. This view contrasts sharply with the Keynesian emphasis upon the depressing effects of a lower PSBR on the level of output.

The implications of the adoption of such policies for the level of public expenditure should be examined carefully. First, the direct implications for the level of public expenditure of a desire to control the PSBR are relatively small. The PSBR is solely the difference between revenue and expenditure. Strict control of the PSBR limits the use of borrowing as a financing source: the same level of public expenditure can still be sustained through a greater reliance on taxation. However, various indirect effects might be postulated: for example, governments would be less willing to incur such high levels of expenditure if it all had to be tax-financed. Nevertheless, this is a behavioural proposition about how governments act rather than an economic proposition about an inherent link between the public expenditure/GDP ratio and the PSBR/GDP ratio.

Second, the feedbacks between different parts of the government's expenditure and taxing functions are highly complex and, on certain key issues, little understood. At first sight, the PSBR can be reduced by a policy of cutting the planned level of public expenditure, say, on education. Although such a policy would reduce outlays on that programme, there may be repercussions upon other programmes. Within a welfare state, displaced employees have automatic entitlements to a wide range of cash and kind benefits. In this context, displaced employees include not only redundant teachers. They also embrace newly trained teachers who never obtain teaching posts and other employees, possibly far removed from teaching, who are pushed into unemployment by the intensified competition for other jobs. Consequently, lower expenditure on education will be accompanied by higher expenditure on certain other programmes, notably social security. Furthermore, the Exchequer will lose income tax revenue and, if the spending of those now unemployed falls, indirect tax revenue as well.

No satisfactory estimates for these complex interactions are available for the UK. However, piecemeal evidence suggests that, particularly in the first year, these feedbacks can be very high: the 'first round' effects (that is excluding 'second round' effects such as lower VAT receipts) of the increase in unemployment of 1 million was estimated as £3400 million (Treasury, 1981b, c). The net improvement in the PSBR of a £1000 million reduction in public expenditure programmes such as education will be far smaller than this figure. It is even possible that in the first year the net effect might be negative. Such interactions cast serious doubts about any strategy conceived in terms of sharply reducing the public expenditure/GDP ratio during a major recession.

If the benefit to the PSBR from a given reduction in public expenditure on goods and services turns out to be small, let alone negative, successive reductions will be required in order to approach any such target. So far, the focus has been upon the interactions between different parts of the government's own finances and not upon any multiplier effects of expenditure cuts upon the rest of the economy. A determined pursuit of such policies might produce a downwards spiral of public expenditure and of GDP. Recessions are very bad news for finance ministries. Either the pursuit of such PSBR/GDP targets must be abandoned or the mechanisms of the welfare state which generate such troublesome feedbacks must be challenged. Many of these feedbacks were previously regarded as beneficial automatic stabilizers which provided a cushion to the level of economic activity during recession. Pursuit of a PSBR/GDP ratio is an attempt to defeat the operation of such automatic stabilizers.

V CONCLUSION

By examining certain monetarist propositions and then the implementation of an avowedly monetarist economic strategy, this chapter has shown that monetarism contains features which make it naturally attractive to those of a free-market philosophical persuasion. The link is undeniably an elusive one to handle. It should always be couched in terms of appeal, rather than of logical necessity. It is possible to subscribe to a monetarist position on macroeconomic policy and also advocate the vigorous use of tax and public expenditure policies to secure goals such as income redistribution and the provision of public services. Yet few prominent monetarists actually do this: the reason must lie in the image of the market and of the state running through monetarist thought.

The monetarist and free-market perspectives fit neatly together. When the invisible hand works smoothly, the monetarist diagnosis and prescription is reinforced, thereby generating powerful arguments against both discretionary demand management and an 'over-generous' tax/transfer system. Furthermore, the blame for high 'voluntary' unemployment during any adjustment process is attributed not to failings of the market economy but to the operation of collective institutions, be they trade unions (for example resistance to real wage cuts) or the state (for example high unemployment benefits, and subsidized public sector housing inhibiting labour mobility). The prescribed policy is therefore to free the market by curtailing the activities of the state and the operation of trade unions. Faith in the efficacy of the invisible hand affects not only the perceived scope for stabilization policy but the entire economic role of the state.

The direct implications of monetarism for public expenditure operate through the more restrictive outlook towards the PSBR because of its assumed links with the target monetary aggregates. This restricts the amount of public expenditure which can be financed by borrowing but leaves open the amount to be financed by taxation. However, the indirect implications, flowing from the belief that the invisible hand works well, are more significant, constituting the contribution which monetarism has made towards the emergence of a cogent anti-public expenditure school of thought.

PART TWO

Values

The breakdown of consensus about the economic and social role of the state
owes much to the renewed intensity of disputes about values. Some of these
debates are new but others are echoes of earlier debates about how the
extension of political democracy would influence the operation of a market
economy. This part of the book explores the meaning of freedom, efficiency
and equality, with a view to identifying the impact upon them of the growth
of public expenditure. Dramatically conflicting claims are often voiced: for
example, that public expenditure either destroys or secures freedom. Disputes about values will not necessarily be resolved by an analysis of the
underlying concepts. Nevertheless, it provides an opportunity to consider the
extent to which these different claims hinge upon subtle differences in
meaning or upon facts which might be subjected to verification. None of these
three values is without its own ambiguities: there are severe tensions between
alternative formulations of each of them. Furthermore, the three values can
conflict, making it necessary to trade one off against the others. In the periods
of easy consensus which facilitated the explosive growth of public expenditure, it was possible to ignore such dilemmas: that is no longer possible.

CHAPTER 4

Freedom

I INTRODUCTION

Libertarian arguments have played an increasing role in the case which has been made against public expenditure. They form part of wider arguments in favour of limiting the state, emphasizing the ways in which its activities diminish individual freedom. Although public expenditure is only one dimension of the activities of the modern state, its impact upon the nature and extent of freedom has assumed importance in both the academic and political debate. The threat posed by public expenditure to freedom is a direct consequence of a definition of freedom in terms of free exchange within a market system. The argument runs as follows. Markets allow individuals to make personal decisions about the factors they will supply and about the goods and services they will consume. The decentralization of economic decisions thus achieved through the market system promotes freedom of choice and protects individuals from the power of the state and of producer groups. Public provision, financed by taxation, prevents the consumer from exercising his freedom of choice and from indicating his preferences to the producer through the signalling role of the price mechanism.[1] The free market is thus the only system consistent with the exercise of personal freedom, choice and responsibility.

This argument requires careful examination, not least because it has shown resilience and appeal. The purpose of this chapter is to explore the philosophical issues involved.

II THE NATURE OF FREEDOM

Few people, irrespective of their views, would deny being in favour of freedom. Such evaluative overtones make it an even more difficult concept to handle. So deeply entrenched is the word, that values, other than freedom, are advocated in its name. In English, the nouns 'freedom' and 'liberty' are typically used interchangeably. They generate the adjectives 'free', and liberal', 'libertarian' and 'liberalist'. Such usage proves extremely trouble-some when efforts are made to ascribe precise meanings so that proper distinctions can be drawn. The adjective 'liberal', both when self-ascribed and ascribed by others, is applied to those who embrace mutually exclusive positions. Many of those who would in the everyday language of political debate now be described as conservatives regard themselves as liberals. In turn, they would deny the adjective 'liberal' to many who embrace this description in the political arena.

Such terminological confusion reflects a reversal of the meaning of liberalism between the nineteenth and the twentieth centuries. What had once unambiguously counterposed individual freedom against state coercion had come to indicate a willingness to use the state as a vehicle for promoting individual welfare. Neither side of this argument is willing to renounce its claim. It is therefore impossible to use terms consistently and the context must always be examined carefully. In this book, the term 'liberalist', sometimes used by economists who consider themselves liberals in the nineteenth-century sense, is not used, though the term 'market liberal' is applied to economists such as Milton Friedman. 'Libertarian' is only used to refer to those, such as Robert Nozick, who press their advocacy of the minimal state much further than most market liberals. The term 'radical right', as a broad description of the new-style critics of the Keynesian social democratic state, embraces both market liberals and libertarians.

An important contribution towards clarifying the issues involved was made in his inaugural lecture by Sir Isaiah Berlin. He distinguished two alternative conceptions of the concept of liberty: negative freedom and positive freedom (Berlin, 1958).[2] Given the influence exercised by this lecture, it is helpful to organize the following discussion around it.

Negative freedom

Berlin considered that the meaning of negative freedom must be sought in the answer to the question:

> What is the area within which the subject – a person or group of persons – is or should be left to do or be what he is able to do or be, without interference by other persons? (pp. 121–2)

This conception is concerned with the absence of interference from others, constraining the area of action of the individual. The choice of vocabulary is itself significant: the term 'interference' is far from being a neutral one, reflecting the persuasive use of language. Coercion is bad, although it may have to be applied in particular cases in order to prevent greater evils. Non-interference, as the opposite of coercion, is valued for itself. The wider the area of non-interference possessed by the individual, the wider is his freedom.

Liberty in this sense means freedom *from*: the absence of interference beyond a shifting and recognizable, though disputed, frontier drawn between the area of private life and that of public authority. Berlin observed that this conception of liberty was used by the classical English political philosophers even though they disagreed as to where these lines should be drawn compiling different catalogues of individual liberties to be defended. Nevertheless, they used common arguments for 'keeping authority at bay'. Whereas limitations must necessarily be placed by law upon the area of an individual's actions, there should exist a certain minimum area of personal freedom which should on no account be violated.

The analysis of negative freedom raises four issues which are relevant to the concerns of this book: the source of coercive constraints upon the individual; the relationship between negative freedom and voluntary exchange; the position of negative freedom as one of several values and the relationship between negative freedom and representative government.

The source of coercive constraints. The source of coercive constraints upon the actions of the individual is identified by Berlin in the following way: 'without interference *by other persons*' (p. 122; italics added). The italicized words are crucial, for much misunderstanding and disagreement can be traced to them. They allow interpretation as: another individual, a collective body such as a trade union, a corporate body such as a firm, or the state itself. But it has been the activities of the state which have dominated the concerns of philosophers.

The radical right has extensively cited such warnings about the necessity for proper limits upon the state. The state is represented as the source of coercion and the market as the source of freedom. But such a simple dichotomy presumes too readily that the operation of the market, dependent as it is upon legally enforceable private property rights, does not itself generate unfreedoms as well as freedoms. Cohen (1979) argued that this is precisely what the institution of private property does, and denied the alleged identity between capitalism and freedom. He made use of an example, in which he wishes to use a yacht which is the private property of Morgan. However, Morgan would restrain him, if necessary with the support of the state's law-enforcement agencies, thus restricting the actions of Cohen. On a literal reading of Berlin's definition, this would qualify as an infringement of negative freedom.

The freedoms bestowed upon individuals by private property consist in the freedoms to buy and to sell the goods, services and factors owned by the individual. The key word is 'owned'. These freedoms to use or dispose, which are extensive and very real under capitalism, generate a matching set of unfreedoms, whereby non-owners are precluded from either using or disposing. All property rules necessarily extend both freedoms and unfreedoms. The notion that private property constitutes economic freedom can only be rescued by altering Berlin's definition to make the last phrase read: 'without *unjustified* interference by other persons'. If this amended definition is combined with a moral endorsement to private property, Morgan may now justifiably prevent Cohen from using his yacht. Cohen's freedom is held not to be diminished because Morgan's action is justified. The switch from an 'empirical' to a 'normative' definition of freedom is a crucial, though often unremarked, step (Jones, 1982). On an empirical definition, whether an individual is free or unfree is settled with reference to explicit empirical criteria. Differences in values will lead to the advocacy of different empirical definitions, not to disagreements about whether any given set of criteria is met, an assessment independent of any judgement about the desirability or justifiability of the condition itself. In contrast, values are present, explicitly or implicitly, in a normative definition of freedom. If freedom is defined normatively in a way which requires non-interference with the individual's right to property, any policy of redistribution must accordingly infringe upon his freedom. What has happened, however, is that the shift to this particular normative definition has transformed the debate, moving it away from the original concern with freedom itself towards a new focus upon the status and justification of these property rights (Jones, 1982). Almost any claim can be made in the name of freedom provided that a 'suitable' normative definition is adopted.

If the meaning of economic freedom is so narrowed to mean using, buying or selling the goods which one owns, capitalism does indeed provide it. But this is a narrow interpretation of economic freedom, much dependent upon a moral endorsement of private property, which allows it to be said that Morgan's restrictions are justified. If, however, economic freedom is defined more widely, then capitalism, which constitutes a complex system of freedoms and unfreedoms, provides one particular form of it. This recognition that a normative definition is involved is important, particularly as advocates of limiting the concept of liberty to its negative conception often criticize others for confusing freedom with other values. A valid defence of private property might be based upon the argument that its property rules restrict freedom less than communal property rules, or on arguments of efficiency, but not on a claimed identity between private property and economic freedom. Libertarians such as Robert Nozick, who advocate free-market capitalism and the minimal state, themselves use a normative definition.

Freedom and voluntary exchange. Berlin stressed that mere incapacity (for example, an inability to read because of blindness) does not necessarily constitute an infringement of liberty. Such impairments to an individual's fulfilment of his purposes, however damaging, should not be represented as an absence of freedom:

Coercion implies the deliberate interference of other human beings within the area in which I could otherwise act. You lack political liberty or freedom only if you are prevented from attaining a goal by human beings (p. 122).

However, Berlin attached qualifications to this statement. He made a distinction between liberty and the conditions which make it of value to the individual, recognizing that economic deprivation might be so severe as to diminish greatly the value of liberty. This qualification applies with particular force to the freedom to buy and sell in the market-place. Furthermore, he acknowledged that whether a particular action is prevented 'by human beings' can itself be the subject of controversy. Whether a lack of resources with which to undertake transactions in the market-place is viewed as an infringement of liberty will depend critically upon the theories which are upheld to explain this condition. If this stems from an individual's lack of ability, it does not. If, however:

> ... I believe that my inability to get a given thing is due to the fact that other human beings have made arrangements whereby I am, whereas others are not, prevented from having enough money with which to pay for it, that I think myself a victim of coercion or slavery (Berlin, p. 123).

Adherence to such a view depends upon acceptance of particular economic and social explanations of the sources of the individual's poverty. Such themes have long pervaded Marxist and other socialist writings about capitalism, neatly encapsulated in Tawney's observation (1913, p. 112): '... what thoughtful rich people call the problem of poverty, thoughtful poor people call with equal justice the problem of riches'. Socialists have maintained that the man-made 'arrangements' of capitalism can be viewed as 'interferences' with the freedom of those subject to it. Herein lies a fundamental source of conflict between socialists and the philosophical advocates of free-market capitalism. But this issue also differentiates market liberals from other liberals. Whereas Friedman views capitalism almost as the source of negative freedom, Berlin accepts that on certain social explanations it might be said to diminish it (Macpherson, 1973a, b).

Those writers who can see no compulsion involved in the operation of market capitalism stress that it is the essence of market exchange that participation in market transactions is voluntary. A counter to this view can be found in Berlin's denial that the existence of negative freedom is conclusively established by the existence of more than one alternative: 'The mere existence of alternatives is not ... enough to make my action free (although it may be voluntary) in the normal sense of the word' (p. 130). His particular example related to when, in a totalitarian state, he betrays his friend, under threat of imprisonment, torture, death or simply loss of job. Options, amongst which he might choose, remain open: few people would argue that he has acted freely. On a much less dramatic scale in that only livelihood is involved, those without property are in this position under free-market capitalism.

Freedom as one of several values. Berlin was scathing about attempts to clothe other values in the language of liberty:

> ... a sacrifice is not an increase in what is being sacrificed, namely freedom, however great the moral need or the compensation for it. Everything is what it is: liberty is liberty, not equality or fairness or justice or culture, or human happiness or a quiet conscience (p. 125).

His essay made a plea not to overextend the concept of liberty so as to render it empty of meaning. In no sense did he suggest that an absolute value should be placed on negative freedom. Indeed, he stressed that, on occasions, it must be traded-off against some other value. Such views were held by philosophers in the English classical tradition, a point of importance because of the way in which some free-market economists draw upon these writers in a way which implies otherwise.

Negative freedom and representative government. Negative freedom implies little about the form of government, solely about the spheres of human life upon which it should not encroach. Berlin wondered whether both scholars and minorities might not have had greater liberty in the Prussia of Frederick the Great or in the Austria of Joseph II than in many later democracies:

> ... liberty in this sense is not incompatible with some kinds of autocracy, or at any rate with the absence of self-government. Liberty in this sense is principally concerned with the area of control, not with its source.... Self-government may, on the whole, provide a better guarantee of the preservation of civil liberties than other regimes, and has been defended as such by libertarians. But there is no necessary connexion between individual liberty and democratic rule. The answer to the question 'Who governs me?' is logically distinct from the question 'How far does government interfere with me?' (pp. 129–30).

Free-market writers are much more concerned with the second question than with the first. Indeed a characteristic feature of the current wave of writing from the radical right is the bleak view of democratic politics contained in it, a position which is considered at various points in this book.

Positive freedom

Many philosophers have considered that liberty, conceived as the mere absence of external human constraints, is much too narrow. This view has stimulated the development of the conception of positive freedom, concerned with freedom *to* rather than freedom *from*. Partly because of the way in which adherence to this conception has been claimed by regimes which have ruthlessly violated the requirements of negative freedom, the reaction of liberals to such ideas is typically hostile. Berlin, who shared this antipathy, considered that the meaning of positive freedom must be sought in the answer to the question: 'What, or who, is the source of control or interference that can determine someone to do, or be, this rather than that?' (p. 122).

Running throughout the doctrine of positive freedom is the metaphor of self-mastery: the individual's wish to be his own master. Various interpretations have been given to the nature of the struggle within the individual. It can be conceived of as a struggle for supremacy between two parts of the individual's self, the contestants being:

(1)   The individual's 'reason', or 'higher nature', or 'real' or 'autonomous' self.
(2)   The individual's 'unbridled impulses', or 'irrational desires', or 'lower nature', or 'empirical' or 'heteronomous' self.

An individual's freedom consists not in the absence of external constraints but in the victory of his 'rational' self over his 'animal' self: the idea of self-discipline is central. The 'lower nature' has to be rigidly disciplined if the individual is ever to realize his full potential as a rational human being. Self-mastery involves self-control and self-direction: this is the doctrine of liberation by reason.

Whereas no constraint can of itself enhance negative freedom, some constraints may enhance positive freedom. Language is used in a persuasive way, distinguishing between constraints which inhibit the expression of the higher and lower natures. In nothing is this more clear than in the use of the words 'liberty' and 'licence'. Through the choice made between these words, both the absence of constraint, and an expression of approval or disapproval, is announced. Liberty, the unfettered exercise of the rational will, is quite different from licence, the indulgence of non-rational desires or passions. Cranston (1967) noted that such persuasive use of language is age-old: John Milton, who disliked political constraints but approved of moral constraints, wrote:

> Licence they mean when they cry liberty
> For who loves that must first be good and wise.
> (Sonnet XII)

Milton's royalist opponents could reasonably have accepted his distinction, but reversed the labels!

But such persuasive use of language is not what causes alarm about the conception of positive freedom. Provided that the source of control is self-discipline, no real difficulties are caused for the defenders of negative freedom, even though they may be very unhappy at the use of the word. These difficulties emerge when the transition is made from a theory of 'rational freedom' to one of 'enforceable rational freedom', with a switch from an individualistic to a social ethic and from self-discipline to an externally imposed discipline. Freedom is then 'enforced' upon the individual: the antithesis of freedom and authority disappears as freedom comes to mean submission to rational authority.

Instead of the division being between two parts of the individual's self, the distinction is sometimes drawn between the individual and some wider social entity, whether a tribe, race, church or state, of which the individual forms a part. The individual represents the 'lower nature' and the social entity the 'higher nature'. This organic metaphor is then used to justify the exercise of control by the social entity over the individual, as a method of achieving freedom for the latter as well as for the whole. External discipline has replaced self-discipline, and it is called freedom.

Nevertheless, the potential for abuse inherent in such metaphors does not mean that the issues raised by the conception of positive freedom can be safely neglected. Taylor (1979) has warned against the temptation to fall back on a narrow negative conception, from which position all extensions to the meaning of freedom can be vigorously rejected, for such a step involves abandoning so much terrain central to the liberal tradition in which the importance placed upon self-realization is the main reason why freedom is valued so highly. The extent to which philosophical debate becomes dominated by extreme caricatures of the two conceptions adds greatly to the appeal of such a position. There is, however, an important asymmetry. Whereas few of the advocates of positive freedom subscribe to the extreme version but have this pinned upon them by their opponents, many of the supporters of the negative conception do wish to restrict the meaning of freedom to the absence of external human contraints.

Taylor identified a number of reasons why a line neither can nor should be drawn around the extreme negative conception, as constituting a secure defence against excesses of totalitarian oppression being justified in the name of the extreme version of positive freedom. First, there is the aggregation problem: how are the different violations of negative freedom occurring in societies with contrasting social and economic institutions to be added up so that a comparison can be made? If no weighting is allowed, reflecting judgements about the significance of particular violations, all that can be done is to count either the number of constraints or the frequency at which they cause violations. On this basis, Albania can be argued to be a freer society than the UK. Albania has abolished religion whereas the UK has not However, there are less traffic lights in Tirana per head of population than in London.[3] On plausible assumptions about the proportion of the population of Tirana otherwise wishing to worship and that of London wishing to move around that city, Albania can thus be pronounced a freer society on the basis of a lower per capita rate of violations. But this is obviously a preposterous line of argument for the freedom of worship is almost universally recognized to be of profoundly more importance than such minor restrictions on personal mobility as imposed by traffic lights. Such judgements about significance are derived from a deeply-rooted cultural knowledge which readily labels some external constraints as trivial but others as fundamentally destructive of human potential. Accordingly, such traffic regulations are seen to be very different from restrictions on personal mobility designed to prevent travel to certain parts of a country. What is thereby introduced, however, is a recognition that any discussion of the extent of freedom in a particular society is unintelligible without such external validation of relative significance. The move from an empirical definition to a normative definition is thus inevitable, despite the way in which the ground is thereby shifted to the reasons why freedom is itself valued.

Second, the nature of the constraints which are regarded as obstacles to freedom is the source of much disagreement. On the extreme negative view, only external constraints attributable to human agency are allowed. However, Taylor noted the circumstances in which it is intelligible to speak of internal obstacles to freedom, such as when an individual cannot fulfil his deepest purposes because of fear, addiction or uncontrolled emotion. In contexts in which the individual may wish to repudiate some of his desires, the removal of existing external constraints upon his actions cannot necessarily be interpreted as an increase in his freedom. Moreover, there may be difficult, extreme cases in which the individual is so mistaken about his purposes that he cannot be allowed to be the final arbiter: Taylor cites the missions of Charles Manson and Andreas Baader. Such exceptional examples illustrate the more general point that, however much it might seem to open undesirable doors, some second-guessing of the individual cannot be avoided.

Third, and more immediately relevant to the impact of public expenditure on the extent of freedom, is the kind of external constraints which are considered to restrict freedom. Miller (1983) has sought to develop an 'expanded' negative conception which broadens the nature of the external constraint allowed. One of the factors leading to the adoption of the positive conception has been a reaction against narrowly-defined constraints. Insistence upon freedom *to* has often been a reaction against the hollow formality of many cases of freedom *from*, such as the beggar dining at the Ritz. Indeed, the terms 'negative freedom' and 'positive freedom' are frequently used in a way different from that of Berlin: simply to mean respectively 'the absence of

Table 4.1: MacCallum's triadic relationship

	Variable		Representing
the	FREEDOM		
of	SOMETHING	x	An agent or agents
from	SOMETHING	y	Preventing conditions such as constraints, restrictions, interferences and barriers
to	DO / NOT DO / BECOME / NOT BECOME	z	Actions or conditions of character or circumstances

legal impediments' and 'the presence of economic resources'. Miller contended that issues such as poverty can be handled with more insight by widening the negative conception of freedom, treating economic factors as constraints, rather than by introducing the positive conception. So much of substance clearly depends upon whether the relevant constraints are interpreted narrowly or broadly, in turn reflecting alternative social and economic theories about their origin and moral significance. Which constraints are judged to be due to 'arrangements made by other persons' is thus crucial.

MacCallum's triadic relationship

In an influential article, MacCallum (1967) argued that the traditional distinction between the negative and positive conceptions is not a useful one but a source of widespread confusion about the real differences separating writers. What is at stake, he claimed, are not two different conceptions of freedom but two different, both incomplete, representations of one complex relationship. Implicit in all statements about freedom is a triadic relationship having the structure shown in Table 4.1. There is always an agent (x), a preventing condition (y), and an action or state of character (z). For statements about freedom to be intelligible, they must contain all three variables which, even if not made explicit, can be filled in: x is free *from* y to *do* (etc.) z. Whenever philosophers speak of freedom *from* or freedom *to*, the other part of the triadic relationship is always implicit.[4] Each group of writers emphasizes one part, at the expense of the other, but the underlying disagreements can only be appreciated when the relationship is viewed as a whole. MacCallum was uneasy about attempts to split writers into two groups, one favouring negative freedom and the other positive freedom, stressing the diversity of possible positions, reflecting independent choices on x, y and z.

The discussion in Section IV of this chapter, exploring the impact of the welfare state on the freedom of the individual, will adopt MacCallum's triadic relationship as the basis for organizing the diverse material. It is particularly helpful in attempting to unravel the frequent confusion between two different issues: separating whether a particular action constitutes interference and reduces freedom from whether such interference is justified. A major reason for so much disagreement about the meaning of freedom can be located in the failure to specify carefully all three parts of the triadic relationship. Originating partly in logical error and partly in the intermingling of advocacy with analysis, there has been a confusion between these two different issues. If freedom is defined to include A but not B, it is often wrongly inferred that A has been shown to be more important than B. If freedom is defined in such a way that laws restrict it but a lack of economic resources does not, the second is not necessarily less important or less urgently requiring remedy. Definitions do not settle questions of relative importance. By insisting upon careful specification of the complete triadic relationship, MacCallum's framework thus provides a means of structuring analysis of the conflicting claims made about the impact of public expenditure on freedom.

III   FREE ECONOMY – STRONG STATE

The radical right claims that the growth of public expenditure has diminished freedom. The free market is advocated, with explicitly libertarian arguments being used to justify a reduction in the size and scope of the public sector. These libertarian arguments are believed to reinforce the efficiency arguments which will be examined in Chapter 5. Just as Milton Friedman's economic writings fired the monetarist counter-revolution against the Keynesian orthodoxy, so his political writings, notably *Capitalism and Freedom* (Friedman, 1962), stimulated the growth of a vigorous literature in defence of free-market capitalism and against the Keynesian social democratic state. Together with Hayek (1944, 1976), he is the inspiration behind much recent work in the UK, as in the USA.

Whereas it would be wrong to attempt to impose too much unity upon such writings, common themes clearly emerge. With certain exceptions, they can be characterized by the maxim of 'free economy – strong state', coined by the nineteenth-century German neo-liberal, Rustow (Friedrich, 1955; Gamble, 1979). Although the free-market case is usually presented as a general attack on the state, that is misleading. It is certain types of state activity which are strongly disliked whereas others receive strong sanction. There is the desire to change the relationship between the state, the market and the polity: whether the state would emerge from this transformation weaker or stronger is open to contention.

The destruction of liberty by the Keynesian social democratic state

Before examining the issues in a structured way, it is useful to gain the flavour of this literature by quoting at some length from one of its leading British exponents. Charles Rowley falls neatly into the Rustow mould, as the following quotations show. Many of the crucial issues, particularly those concerning the relationship of the free market and the strong state, can be focused much more closely through an examination of his work rather than that of more measured, but less explicit, writers.

In his contribution to an Institute of Economic Affairs conference, he stated:

> In one sense the title of this conference, *The Taming of Government,* is misleading. In my view, the growth of the public sector, given the political system, has weakened rather than strengthened government, both central and local (Rowley, 1979a, p. 114).

Rowley desired constitutional reforms which would strengthen government but severely curtail its activities. If constitutional reforms are not feasible, he saw three alternative futures for the UK: the first was Latin American-style hyperinflation and the second was continuing economic weakness and decline through the continuation of early 1979 policies:

> Yet a third is for democracy to be sacrificed in the name of economic efficiency and for Britain to be ruled by the gun. . . .
> Such a solution, however unpalatable, cannot be ruled out if labour market violence continues to escalate at all in Britain during the next few critically important years. It is better by far, however, to experiment with constitutional reform designed to re-introduce market constraints on the exercise of power (p. 117).

Elsewhere, he has argued that the conception of freedom relevant to liberalism is negative freedom:

> . . . freedom to choose is not a means to some higher political or economic end. It is an end in itself. The freedom . . . is negative and not positive, ensuring an individual of no particular opportunities, economic or otherwise, but leaving him free to choose among such alternatives as are available to him, without restrictions arising from the coercive influence of other individuals. Freedom is not construed from the liberal viewpoint as effective power over political and/or economic resources. Indeed, this latter view of freedom is a negative of liberalism (Rowley, 1978b, p. 239).

Furthermore the growth of the public sector has reduced freedom:

> The nation which gave birth to *The Wealth of Nations* and which for
> long was viewed as a model for political democracy is veering perilously
> close to the destruction of its market economy and to its replacement by
> bureaucratic dictatorship (Rowley, 1979b, p. 11).

> That they [Rowley's constitutional proposals] appear as stark and
> substantial as many will think they do, illustrates only how far Britain
> has slipped from liberty towards a totalitarian state. . . . In the absence
> of some such surgery, however, democracy as we know it in Britain is
> likely to disappear over the coming decade, just as liberty as we used to
> know it has disappeared during the 1970s (p. 21).

> . . . British citizens are fast losing such important liberties as freedom of
> choice of occupation and consumption which have long been viewed as
> the hallmarks of British civilisation (Rowley, 1979a, p. 112).

Rowley wished to repel threats to negative freedom and to reverse earlier
encroachments. He recognized that different negative freedoms may conflict,
making coercion inevitable. Therefore, negative freedoms must be ranked,
thus opening up the potential for conflict amongst those who subscribe to the
primacy of negative freedoms, but disagree on rankings:

> . . . liberals inevitably are required to assess the sources of the most
> significant threats to individual liberties, which are seen to stem from
> concentrations of political and economic power, whether in the hands
> of the State, of bureaucrats, of firms, of organized labour or indeed of
> private citizens. For liberals are aware of the potential for coercive
> abuse characteristic in significant discretionary power, believe that all
> power corrupts and recognize the difficulty of eliminating discretionary
> power when once it has been established. For this reason, liberals have a
> preference for a system that encourages voluntary exchange via com-
> petitive market processes. . . .
> For these reasons, liberals rank the freedom of markets, of competition
> and entry and the freedoms of choice in consumption and occupation
> significantly higher than the freedoms of contract and of collusion since
> these latter may be *abused* to destroy the basis of a liberal order – as is
> the present situation in the United Kingdom. Liberals will endorse
> *coercive interventions of an appropriate nature* to ensure the domi-
> nance of the former over the latter freedoms whenever they are in
> conflict (Rowley, 1979b, pp. 12–13; italics added).

That negative freedoms conflict is a well-established conclusion. But Rowley is arguing that negative freedoms can be *abused*, thus justifying 'coercive interventions of an appropriate nature'. 'Liberals', in Rowley's sense, are prepared to use the power of the state to suppress one set of negative freedoms in order to sustain another set: the choice criterion is their own assessment of relative value. Systematically, those which are to be suppressed are those relating to groups rather than to individuals, and particularly, those generating a centre of power not emanating from the institutions of private property and competitive markets. Few writers who support free-market capitalism and the minimal state are as explicit as Rowley about the extent of state power required to establish and sustain them. The economic role of the state, within this framework, is to protect property rights, to enforce contracts and to prevent anti-competitive behaviour. There may be little direct state economic activity but the state performs the role of defending existing property rights and of enforcing the virtues of competitive markets upon reluctant capitalists and combining workers. The source of legitimacy for this exercise of state power is rarely explicitly stated. It must rest upon a belief in the beneficence of the market system, even where this is not recognized by capitalists or workers.

One consistent feature of industrial capitalism has been the emergence of trade union organization despite early attempts by employers and the state to suppress this development. The right of free association, in the labour market context as in others, has become a major distinguishing feature between the pluralist Western democracies and totalitarian states, whether in Eastern Europe or elsewhere. Removing such rights (as opposed to marginal procedural changes) would require drastic surgery and extensive use of both the judicial and security arms of the state. There are those within the free-market school who would propose radical action. Rowley's proposed constitution would 'withdraw the rights of all public employees to unionize and to take industrial action in pursuit of wage bargains' and make the closed shop unconstitutional (Rowley, 1979b, p. 21). A formidable use of state power would be required to enforce such constitutional prohibitions.

The legitimacy of such state action would be challenged, partly because the underlying premise of the beneficence of markets, competition and private ownership is itself disputed. Sometimes the realization of the resulting paradox is present. Dearlove (1980) noted that at least some of the participants at an IEA conference (Littlechild *et al.*, 1979) appreciated that the 'taming of government' first involved making it 'more ferocious'. Very illiberal policies may be necessary to maintain the desired framework for the market and to combat the expected opposition to the state's withdrawal from its economic and welfare role. Despite their rhetoric about the overweening state, free-market writers often yearn for the simpler world of the 'strong state' (authoritatively carrying out a limited range of functions) to replace the Keynesian social democratic state (struggling to accommodate conflicting social and economic pressures).

A characteristic of the Keynesian social democratic state has been the growth of public expenditure. Rowley (1979b, p. 13) traced the growth of the public expenditure/GDP ratio in a section headed 'The threat from collective choice'. Implicitly at least, he used this ratio as an index of freedom: the lower the ratio, the more extensive is negative freedom. All technical problems with this ratio will be set aside in the following discussion, in order to focus exclusively upon the central issue. There are two very different questions: first, are decisions on the composition of output to be taken by individuals or by the state; and second, should the state compulsorily transfer resources from one set of individuals to another?

On the first question, market liberals prefer economic decisions to be taken by individuals rather than by the state. Apart from the efficiency gains accruing from the pattern of output more closely reflecting individual preferences, it is held to be intrinsically valuable that individuals take their own decisions. If the proposition that individuals should take decisions on the pattern of output were accepted, what would be the implications for public expenditure? The most striking impact would be on its composition. The state would not supply private goods (that is those which are not 'public goods' in the technical sense considered in Chapter 5). It would try to secure its redistributive aims through more extensive use of the tax/transfer system, thereby substituting 'publicly financed private consumption' for 'public expenditure on goods and services'. Individuals, not the state, would therefore decide the composition of output. During the 1970s, the decade in which Rowley considered that 'liberty as we used to know it' disappeared, it was mainly transfers, not exhaustive expenditure, which accounted for the increases in public expenditure.

On the second question, there are extensive implications for public expenditure if the legitimacy of the state redistributing resources between individuals is itself disputed. Attention has now switched from individuals' decisions in goods markets (on the composition of their consumption) to their decisions in factor markets (on which factor services they will supply). The operation of the tax/transfer system involves the state taking income, earned from the supply of factor services, from some individuals and then redistributing it to others. In opposition to such policies there is the assertion of the rights of those receiving factor incomes to keep that income, and not to have it confiscated by the state for redistribution on criteria entirely remote from the functioning of the market system.

This challenge is much more fundamental to the state's budgetary role, relating to both the scale and composition of public expenditure and to the legitimacy of the redistributive dimension of the public budget. It is articulated using efficiency arguments (for example the damage which redistributive policies inflict upon factor markets) to supplement the libertarian claim that the individual should retain the full fruits of his factor supply decisions. Modifications to the existing pattern of factor ownership will be the natural consequence of market processes, working through voluntary exchange. However, state action to alter coercively the prevailing pattern of factor ownership (that is property rights) is held to constitute an explicit threat to freedom.

The primacy of market freedoms

The radical right's conception of freedom is inextricably linked to the exercise of individual choice within markets and to the definition and protection of property rights. Freedom is therefore a market-related concept. Freedom exists whenever individuals may, unhindered by the state, exploit whatever market opportunities lie open to them. The desired separation of the economy from the polity is almost complete. The polity's role is to sustain the framework which both facilitates the operation of the market economy and also insulates the economy from direct intervention by the polity. Public expenditure thereby diminishes freedom because it substitutes judgements emanating from the state about the composition of output for unconstrained market outcomes and is a mechanism for coerced transfers of income between individuals.

Such a conception of freedom would appear to set extremely narrow limits to state activity. In terms of the range of state activity, this is unquestionably true. In terms of its intensity, the consequences are more ambiguous. The framework-setting role of the minimal state is its crucial function, encompassing:

(1) The definition and enforcement of property rights, the maintenance of competitive markets and the preservation of internal order.
(2) The organization of external defence.

The activities under (1) are required for the continued operation of competitive markets and are prerequisites of freedom because of the way in which freedom has been defined. The exercise of freedom within markets is impossible prior to the definition of property rights. Any dilution of property rights by the state therefore reduces its extent. Freedom is entirely unrelated to the distribution of property rights and is undermined by any attempt by the state to alter the distribution emerging from market processes. Such a position is directly in conflict with Cohen's (1979) view that the definition of property rights has a dual effect: it confers freedom upon the propertied and unfreedom upon the propertyless.

Nevertheless, the framework-setting functions of the state which receive strong sanction from free-market writers impose severe restrictions on individual behaviour. Certain of the resulting constraints can be particularly far-reaching: for example, the delineation of citizenship rights, the exercise of immigration control, the enforcement of military service, restrictions on behaviour defined as 'anti-state' activity, and subjection to the police and judiciary. Although some such restrictions on individual behaviour are an accepted feature of any industrialized society, they diminish negative freedoms, thus showing that these may conflict and that there may be tradeoffs against other values.

The activities under (2) are of a completely different kind, namely the preservation of the territorial integrity of the state. The notion of freedom has changed. What is at stake is the preservation of the collectivity, usually now defined in terms of the nation state. Freedom within markets is a very different concept from that of the maintenance of the territorial and political integrity of the nation state. Berlin (1958) refused to extend the name of freedom to one of its most common uses in the context of groups: the 'national freedom' of a people. He acknowledged the pervasive influence of this idea but described it as the search for status or proper recognition. He noted the cruel irony whereby the achievement of national liberation by previously subject peoples in Africa and Asia often led to a reduction of negative freedom. Whatever the reservations of philosophers, such usage is widespread, partly because of the favourable overtones of the word 'freedom'.

Advocates of free-market capitalism and the minimal state wish to restrict the meaning of freedom to its negative conception. A few are consistent in their view of the individual's obligations to the state and of the supremacy of negative freedom. The majority, however, particularly those involved in public life, combine libertarianism in the economic sphere with a strongly developed sense of patriotism. Unannounced moves between the two meanings are frequent. A delightful example is provided by Stein's (1980) statement to the US Senate's Committee on the Budget. Alongside a casual discussion of the possibilities of conscription, he proposed the establishment of a 'Subcommittee on Paying for Survival', as part of a plan to double real defence spending as a proportion of GNP so that Americans do not 'lose our freedom' because of a neglect of defence expenditure. In contrast, he supported the abolition of the 'great and wasteful society', manifested in nondefence programmes which are not worthwhile or are untested.

The external security role of the state is one of the most explicitly coercive tasks it ever undertakes, and seriously threatens the individual's market freedoms. Conscription, compulsory purchase, high taxation, forced saving and goods rationing are typical features of a wartime economy which abrogate market freedoms. The peacetime counterparts are less dramatic but nevertheless exist, notably taxation, embargoes on trade with potential enemies and sometimes conscription. The individual's market freedoms are curtailed in order to achieve a collective goal (victory in war; external security in peace). Furthermore, the loss of negative freedom is much wider than this diminution of market freedoms. The individual may be conscripted to fight and kill enemies defined as such by the state; be exposed to premature death; and be liable to imprisonment should he decline to fight or to execution for treason should he support the enemy.

Three conclusions can be drawn. First, market freedoms are thus revealed not to be the absolute values sometimes implicit in arguments against non-defence expenditures. Second, decisions on national security are taken by the institutions of the state. This observation would be trivial but for the selective nature of the free-market critique which has directed its fire against the economic and welfare activities of the state. But if the state is identified as inefficient, riddled with the self-interest of politicians and bureaucrats, and oppressive of freedom, it seems curious to place so much faith in the conduct of its national security role. Third, that role frequently involves the exercise of intense social and legal pressures to secure the individual's conformity with the wishes of the state. The obligation of the individual to the state and to his fellow citizens is asserted in its most dramatic form. He is forcibly prevented from applying any form of individualistic calculus to his participation in war. A high value on his own life, possibly coupled with few property rights to defend, might make acquiescence to the demands of the foreign power his most favoured option. He is compelled to accept the decision of the state: his only remedy is through collective action designed to reverse that decision.

The fundamental point should now be clear: political and economic philosophies which embody such a paradox about the relationship of the individual and the state should be probed carefully as to the meaning attached to the word 'freedom'.

Market freedoms and political freedom

An insistence upon a separation between the economy and the polity is intended to establish a clear distinction between economic freedom (taken to mean market freedoms) and political freedom. The insistence of pro-capitalist writers such as Friedman (1962), Hayek (1944) and Norman (1979) that capitalism is a pre-condition for political freedom has obscured this point. Whatever the posited links, the conceptual distinction remains important. In the last resort, the relationship is an empirical question. Undeniably, the industrialized capitalist democracies of the West have a much better record at preserving negative freedoms than the communist states of Eastern Europe. But the issue around which this book revolves is the impact within a democracy of public expenditure of varying proportions of GDP: are the Netherlands and Sweden, the only countries to breach the 60 per cent barrier on OECD definitions, notably less free than the USA?

For all their rhetoric, free-market writers concentrate on the economy and not on the polity: market freedoms and not political freedoms (of speech, religion, assembly or franchise) have been the focus of attention. The

Values

potential for tension between market freedoms and political freedoms should be clear. Political freedoms in modern democracies are distributed on strictly egalitarian presumptions. In contrast, the pattern of resource ownership is highly unequal. Consequently, although each individual possesses the same market freedoms, the incidence of material return from them is markedly unequal. Any group which has a limited stake in the existing distribution of property rights and of economic welfare may attempt to use its influence in the political system in order to improve its position. Such a strategy has been explicitly adopted by reformist political parties on the left.

The dangers which universal suffrage posed for the established order were well-recognized in nineteenth-century debates. Much of the recent advocacy of constitutional reform (Littlechild, 1978, 1979; Rowley 1978b, 1979a, b) to limit the activities of the state has been a semi-conscious echo of such fears about democracy. The emphasis has been upon limiting the power of politicians and bureaucrats: the purpose and practical consequences are to limit the ability of individuals *qua* voters to influence the economy. Constitutional limits on the activities of the state would perform a parallel role to the earlier restrictions on the franchise. Nevertheless, there has been some thinking aloud about the possibility of removing the franchise from bureaucrats and welfare beneficiaries.[5]

It would be wrong to overstress the direct link between free-market academics and the political right. Members of the first group are probably somewhat diverse in their self-perceived political affiliation, a fact reflected in their contrasting views about the desirable extent of redistribution. Yet it is clear that their attachment to markets and private enterprise, and antipathy towards state welfare and state enterprise, make such views attractive to the political right. The implementation of their public policy proposals would rely heavily on the political right enjoying power. This raises the paradox of the traditional authoritarianism of the political right (upholding values such as patriotism and social order, and wanting guns instead of butter) and the belief in freedom (defined as absence of constraints on the individual's choices) of the free-market academics.

There is a further twist to the irony in that the political left in Western industrialized countries often combines interventionism in the economic sphere with libertarianism in the civil and political spheres. Writing about Britain, Gamble (1979) has stressed the populism of the political right which has heavily emphasized issues such as immigration, law and order and social security abuse. The undoubted electoral appeal of such views has far-reaching consequences. The political right has used the parable of market efficiency and freedom but has combined it with inconsistent positions. For example, the pursuit of economic freedom is used as a justification for the relaxation of exchange controls at the very time at which methods of more rigorous immigration control are introduced. Away from the context of market relationships, other measures are taken which diminish the rights of

:he individual in relation to certain state agencies, for example, the police.

The other major tension between market freedoms and political freedoms :elates to their very different implications for non-state collective action. Freedom of association and of assembly are integral parts of political freedom. They may lead, however, to anti-competitive behaviour, alleged to .indermine both market efficiency and market freedoms.

IV   FREEDOM AND THE WELFARE STATE

The rise in the public expenditure/GDP ratio has been the necessary counterpart of the establishment of the welfare state. Such major changes in the nature of the economic and social system can be expected to have had implications for the nature and extent of freedom. Goodin (1982) has attempted to evaluate the impact, conducting his discussion in terms of MacCallum's triadic relationship. However, he first cited Berlin (1958) in support of the view that it is wrong to locate the case for the welfare state solely in the conception of positive freedom, in contrast to the case for the free market grounded in negative freedom. The case for the welfare state can also be made in terms of negative freedom. He then identified nine different claims about the impact of the welfare state on freedom and attempted to assess their validity and significance. The six claims purporting to show a reduction in freedom will be examined first, followed by the three contrary claims.

Claim 1: Infringement of property rights

The welfare state reduces the freedom
of   taxpayers
from legal obstacles
to   dispose of their property as they please.

Discussion of this claim has been unduly influenced by profound disagreements over a related issue. Lindblom (1977) criticized market liberals such as Friedman (1962) for their failure to recognize the coercion inherent in market economies, reflecting the fact that private property is itself a barrier to freedom. Rather than this neglect being incidental, Friedman's political writings revolve around the view that the market enhances freedom whilst the Keynesian social democratic state destroys it. However, the state and the market constitute different barriers to freedom, impinging upon different but overlapping groups of individuals. For example, the free rider problem means that the state must coerce individuals if there is to be an efficient level of supply of public goods or an optimal (however determined) scale of redistribution. Perhaps in reaction to Friedman, a number of authors have challenged the claim that the state diminishes freedom when its redistributive policies infringe property rights. For example, Goodin (1982, pp. 156–7) contended:

> The distribution of property rights – and their redistribution – is necessarily a constant sum game. Freedoms taken away from one person are given to another, or from a person in one capacity (e.g., landowner) are returned to him in another (e.g., rambler). No net loss of freedom for society as a whole, as distinct from individuals within it, is involved in redistributive taxation.

Jones (1982) advanced a similar argument but Loevinsohn (1977, p. 239) went much further, claiming that redistribution enhanced freedom if the following condition were met:

> . . . by redistributing property, a government can decrease the overall extent to which people's desires for material goods go unsatisfied, so that overall it will become less important to people to use or consume property from which they are legally barred.

The fundamental error in such arguments is the confusion between freedom and utility. The fact that property is taken to be constant-sum does not imply that freedom is constant-sum. Even if all the standard objections to Loevinsohn's claim that redistribution will allow more important desires to be satisfied are set aside, it remains a proposition about utility, only tangentially about freedom. Furthermore, there is a difference between clearly-defined rights to certain goods based on the institution of private property and the much more conditional rights to certain goods based on redistribution through the political process and which can always be terminated or reversed. The abrogation of property rights through a policy of redistribution must inevitably generate uncertainty as to how property rights will be affected in the future. This claim is not a conclusive argument against redistribution but its strength should be acknowledged.

Claim 2: Imposition of uniformity

The welfare state reduces the freedom
of   citizens
from legal regulations
to   display diverse tastes for certain public services.

There is some truth in this statement: how much depends crucially upon the form which public provision takes. For example, it is stronger when provision is centralized rather than decentralized: local decision-making can facilitate diversity between communities. Whatever the form, the taxes necessary to finance provision reduce the disposable income of individuals and therefore

heir capacity to exhibit diverse tastes through the market-place. The
question of private purchases arises when the services are not pure public
goods. However, such would be a reasonable characterization of most public
xpenditure, and certainly that on the welfare state. There is an important
difference between the following arrangements:

1) Where public provision is free at the point of consumption but
   individuals are nevertheless able to move out of the public sector and
   make purchases in the private sector.
2) Where private purchases are prohibited.

The welfare state usually adopts form (1): state education and health care are
free' in the UK but there are no prohibitions on the private sector, though its
development is clearly retarded by 'free' public provision. Abolishing private
education is more restrictive of market freedoms than simply providing state
education. In specific cases, there may be a direct clash between securing the
egalitarian objectives considered in Chapter 6 and maintaining such market
freedoms. Claim 2 has no relevance to most cash transfers.

Claim 3: Paternalism

The welfare state reduces the freedom
of   citizens generally, and welfare recipients especially,
from   legal obstacles
to   pursue their own preferences.

The welfare state does, by the way in which it changes the relative prices faced
by individuals, channel consumption in certain directions, for example,
towards education, health and housing. In that sense, it can therefore be
regarded and perhaps condemned as paternalist. However, a certain degree
of paternalism is implicit in the objective of 'limiting the domain of
nequality' which is central to the idea of the welfare state (see Chapter 6). But
t should be noted that many public expenditure programmes are less
paternalist than a whole range of other public policies: for example,
differential taxation of tobacco and alcohol; compulsory safety belts; and
health and safety at work legislation. An analysis of particular cases is
required in order to assess whether the benefits from these policies are worth
the costs including, *inter alia,* such restrictions on freedom.

Claim 4: Red tape

The welfare state reduces the freedom
of   welfare recipients
from   legal or bureaucratic obstacles
to   live their lives as they please.

Eligibility criteria abound in the welfare state, particularly in the case of cash benefits. For example, the unemployed must be available for work; there are earnings limits attached to the receipt of state pensions; and a woman with children may not cohabit without prejudicing her own entitlement to benefit. Undeniably, some conditions are in practice extremely insensitive and are sometimes applied in a thoughtless manner, thereby causing unnecessary distress to welfare recipients. However, Goodin posed the interesting question of whether some such constraints are not a necessary feature of the welfare state. When 'public money' has been voted for specific purposes eligibility rules are inevitable if there are to be any guarantees that these objectives are met. They serve as a rationing mechanism for the resources at the disposal of a given programme. Paradoxically, a claim that these conditions reduce freedom would be based on a positive concept. Using a negative concept, however, it would be emphasized that welfare recipients are not coerced to accept benefit but accept a package of cash and conditions, in an analogous way that conditions, mainly payment, must be met in market exchange.

Claim 5: The creation of dependency

The welfare state reduces the freedom
of   welfare recipients
from psychological and economic pressures
to   pursue alternative social and political arrangements.

This claim comes in alternative forms, rooted in very different political assumptions. The radical right have claimed that welfare recipients are broken in spirit: whereas markets encourage self-reliance, welfare states breed reliance. Anarchists claim that mutual aid institutions are atrophied through the substitution of state provision for older forms of community self-help. Would-be revolutionaries claim that the welfare state is a method of buying off revolution. There is remarkably little evidence, rather than rhetoric, to support the first. There is some truth in the second, though public policy can make use of such agencies in particular cases. The third has some historical truth: how it is assessed depends upon what gains and losses are expected from the revolution!

Claim 6: The irreversibility of the welfare state

The welfare state reduces the freedom
of   citizens
from bureaucratic and political obstacles
to   pursue alternative social and political arrangements.

The radical right has made extensive use of the public choice literature in order to argue that coalitions of bureaucrats and recipients conspire to prevent the reversal of welfare state measures. It is alleged that the democratic political process is so loaded in favour of excessive public expenditure that new constitutional rules are required. Major programmes are indeed difficult to reverse. However, it is clear that, under existing constitutional arrangements, politicians such as Margaret Thatcher and Ronald Reagan have harnessed an electoral backlash against the welfare state. Despite the obstacles, such administrations, if they stayed in office over a reasonable period, would by various privatization schemes have a major impact on the welfare state: for example, by reducing the participation rate in the public sector for health and education and thus weakening political support for such spending.

Claim 7: The reduction of poverty

The welfare state increases the freedom

of   welfare recipients

from social and economic obstacles

to   live their lives as they please.

The most frequent claim in terms of freedom which is made for the welfare state is that it frees many people from the debilitating poverty they would otherwise suffer. The case is usually argued in terms of positive freedom, stressing freedom *to*. Opponents of the welfare state quickly seize upon the unfavourable image of this conception, deriving from its use in defence of totalitarianism, and attempt to discredit through association both the justification of the welfare state in terms of freedom and its characteristic institutions and policies. The ambitious programme of redistribution canvassed by Field (1981) in the name of freedom was denounced by Green (1982, p. 243) as 'paternalistic collectivism', said to reflect the onset of 'state worship'. The appeal of MacCallum's framework is the way in which it focuses attention upon each part of the triadic relationship, showing how both *from* and *to* are implicit in all statements about freedom, even when not spelled out. Although the scope for impassioned rhetoric remains boundless, it becomes much more difficult to construct a convincing argument for exclusive support for *to* and absolute rejection of *from*. Furthermore, the conventional argument that the welfare state enhances freedom *to* through an increase in the options available to an individual can readily be reconstructed in terms of enhancing freedom *from,* provided that a lack of resources is included within the types of external constraint defined to reduce freedom (Miller, 1983). The real dividing line is thus identified to rest less in which of the two conceptions of freedom is adopted, more in the nature and source of the external constraints judged to be freedom-relevant. There is no reason

why the advocates of the welfare state should consent to normative defini
tions of freedom which include in this category all constraints inposed by the
state but none emanating from the market. Whilst refusing to allow
libertarians and market liberals to expropriate for themselves the language o
freedom, they must themselves avoid the error of confusing equality (or other
values) with freedom.

Claim 8: The capacity to act on moral principles

The welfare state increases the freedom
of   citizens
from   practical and psychological constraints
to   act upon seriously-held moral principles in public affairs.

Through the institutions of the welfare state, it is possible to remove the
allocation of a limited range of 'essential' items from the market and to ensure
that they are distributed equally, without regard to ability to pay. Some
deeply-held moral principles are sensitive to contamination, only being safe if
protected from the mundane considerations introduced by the market. Some
items, such as love and patriotism, are believed to be things which 'money
cannot buy', being debased when they are bought and sold. In the welfare
state, certain 'needs' are given absolute priority over ordinary wants, even
though there are well-established objections to any such partitioning of needs
from wants. Removed from the market, it is possible to have an allocation of
such items according to a moral principle (that is allocation according to
need), rather than according to ability to pay.

Claim 9: The capacity to act impartially

The welfare state increases the freedom
of   citizens
from   psychological obstacles
to   display moral impartiality.

The presence of uniformity limits the extent of partiality and favouritism. A
rule of uniformity obliges everyone to behave in a more ethical manner. It acts
as a substitute for a condition of pervasive uncertainty in which the individual
would be unaware of how a decision on the level of public services would
affect his own interests, because he would not know his own future position
in society and hence his reliance upon them. Historically, the psychological
sacrifices imposed by major wars have propelled extensions to the welfare
state, as the reality of common sacrifice has been translated into procedures
for social policy. Individuals are freed from the necessity of solely pursuing
self-interest. Furthermore, the mere fact that all must use the same facilities is

kely to generate pressure for higher quality services than if the more affluent
an opt out of the public sector.
  Goodin (1982, p. 149) had begun his article by observing:

The relationship between freedom and the welfare state surely is, at best
and at worst, a mixed one. In some ways, the welfare state promotes
certain kinds of freedom for certain people. In others, it restricts those
or other freedoms for those or other people.

After examining the nine claims, he concluded that the net effect of the
welfare state has been to increase freedom. But there is, in practice, no
common scale for balancing gains and losses which would allow such a
strong conclusion, either way. More fundamentally, however, it must be
remembered that the welfare state cannot be judged, nor has to be justified,
solely on its effects on freedom: its performance against all criteria is more
important than on a single one. What Goodin's analysis achieves is to
structure arguments in a careful way, directing attention towards evidence
for and against the various claims and encouraging reflection about how far
the answers depend upon the particular form welfare state provisions
actually takes. It extends the debate beyond impassioned rhetoric about the
destruction of liberty.

<h2 style="text-align:center">V CONCLUSION</h2>

Free-market writers have argued that the growth of public expenditure has
diminished freedom. The purpose of this chapter has been to elucidate the
conception of freedom underlying such arguments and to relate them to the
wider philosophical debate. Their conception of freedom has been shown to
be inextricably linked to the exercise of individual choice within markets and
to the definition and protection of property rights. They want the state to be
limited in scope. Nevertheless, such a state remains coercive because the
operation of a well-ordered market system requires that the state possesses
and can enforce a 'monopoly of legitimate violence'. The extent of explicit
coercion will depend in part upon the severity of conflicts, for example, over
distribution.
  Milton Friedman, as one of the most influential exponents of such views,
stresses the role of the state in protecting property, enforcing contracts,
controlling the money supply, maintaining internal law and order and
promoting external security. This limited portfolio of state activities will
appeal to those of a particular ideological persuasion and to particular social
groups. A wider portfolio (including, for example, the welfare state and a
commitment to full employment) will appeal to those of a different ideological persuasion and to different social groups. The crucial point is that
various kinds of state activity have differential impacts.

Negative freedoms are restricted, because they conflict with each other, o in order to achieve other objectives. It is a tenable ideological position that the sum of such coercion should be minimized, though there is no available measurement scale. Yet the fact that freedom has been restricted to protec other freedoms and to secure one set of other objectives (for example interna and external security), leaves it open for others to argue that differen negative freedoms should be assigned priority and that some negative freedoms should be further restricted to secure other objectives (for example economic and social equality). Furthermore, the individual's relationship with the state cannot be characterized solely in terms of the presence or absence of restraints on market behaviour because state power is used eithe to uphold or modify the existing structure of property rights. It is a multi faceted relationship, ranging far beyond this aspect alone. The label 'liber tarian' can be conceded too readily to those solely committed to 'libertarian ism with respect to buying and selling' (Cohen, 1979, p. 10). Whereas some economists who adopt a strong free-market stance carry their libertarianism over to other issues, this does not extend either to all their colleagues or to the vast majority of right-wing politicians who advocate the free market in the political arena. Indeed, the latter in practice often hold rather authoritariar views on a range of social issues, impinging closely on matters of negative freedom. Moreover, they frequently advance strongly nationalist concep- tions of the individual's duty towards the state. When governments of the right claim the sanction of libertarianism for an attack on trade unions anc the welfare state, the ambivalence of their attitude to the state should always be remembered.

CHAPTER 5

Efficiency

I INTRODUCTION

The fact of scarcity makes the efficient use of available resources so crucial. It is apparent that the methods by which resources are allocated between competing uses may be relevant to the efficiency with which they are used. Public expenditure involves the state limiting the area of operation of the market and substituting non-market methods of allocation. There are, therefore, issues of economic efficiency relevant to the division of economic activity between the sphere of the market and that of the state.

The purpose of this chapter is to explore such issues of economic efficiency in a way which parallels the previous chapter's discussion of freedom. Because of the nature of the topic, it is the most technically difficult chapter in the book, particularly for the non-economist. Every attempt has been made, by means of careful exposition, to minimize such difficulties. But the reader who does find the material difficult is urged to persevere, as an understanding of such technical issues is a prerequisite for the analysis of the appropriate spheres of the market and the state.

II CONCEPTIONS OF EFFICIENCY

Efficiency can be regarded as the economist's value: it is not the sole value but one which can only be neglected at a heavy cost in terms of both economic welfare and the ability to achieve social objectives. Questions of efficiency have an important bearing upon:

(1) The division of economic activity between the market and non-market sectors.
(2) The division of the market sector between its public and private components.
(3) The operation of the public non-market sector, both with regard to the allocation of resources between competing uses and the amount of inputs which are required in order to achieve any given objective.

85

The economist's conception of efficiency is wider than the popular meaning of the term. Furthermore, it rests upon value judgements which should be clearly specified. There are two dimensions to economic efficiency which it is useful to regard as separate, though interrelated: allocative efficiency and X-efficiency.

Allocative efficiency

The entire apparatus of Paretian welfare economics is dedicated to the task of providing criteria for judging alternative allocations of resources, whether these resources are goods or factors of production. The search for allocative efficiency is its systematic theme, in which the concept of Pareto optimality plays the central role. An allocation of resources is described as Pareto optimal if no one can be made better off without making at least one person worse off. It is, therefore, concerned with securing the maximum amount of gains from trade (using 'trade' in its widest sense, meaning voluntary exchange).

Paretian welfare economics develops propositions about the desirability of alternative allocations of resources. As such they are necessarily based on value judgements. It is important to make these explicit because there has developed an unfortunate tendency, particularly in 'textbook' literature, to claim either (a) that the Pareto criterion rests on objective grounds; or (b) that the underlying value judgements are generally acceptable, uncontroversial or innocuous. By making explicit the underlying value judgements, which are much stronger than may appear at first sight, it becomes easier to appraise the significance of the Pareto criterion. The four key value judgements are:

(1) The concern is with the welfare of all individuals in the society rather than with that of some entity called 'society' or 'state' or with that of some special group or class.
(2) Any non-economic factors affecting an individual's welfare can be ignored: it is assumed that the allocation of economic resources can be separated from social, psychological and political factors provided that they do not impinge directly upon the processes of market exchange.
(3) An individual should be considered the best judge of his own welfare: in other words, there is complete consumer and producer sovereignty.
(4) If any change in the allocation of resources increases the welfare of at least one person without reducing that of any other, then the change should be considered to have increased social welfare.

Such assumptions are the tools of trade of the Paretian welfare economist. They are inherently individualistic as opposed to collectivist: (1) and (4). They reject paternalism: (3). They impose a clear separation between the economy and the polity: (2). Such features of Paretianism accounted for its traditional association with competitive capitalism. However, it subsequently developed in directions which made ambivalent its implications for the role of the state.

Pareto optimality can be conceptualized as three sub-problems; of exchange efficiency, of technical efficiency and of overall Pareto efficiency. A brief and inevitably technical explanation is now provided.[1] *Exchange efficiency* is concerned with ensuring that any given bundle of consumption goods is allocated between individuals in such a way so as to render impossible any further reallocations of goods which would make one person better off without making another person worse off. This can be achieved by allowing individuals to adjust their consumption packages in response to relative prices.

Exchange efficiency requires that the marginal rate of substitution between any two goods should be equal for all consumers. The marginal rate of substitution measures a consumer's willingness to give up one good in exchange for another. When this is equal for all consumers, no further reallocations are possible which satisfy the condition that no one should be made worse off. When fixed quantities of two goods must be divided between two consumers, there are many alternative allocations which satisfy the necessary condition for exchange efficiency that marginal rates of substitution should be equal. In the Edgeworth box,[2] these points are indicated by a tangency between an indifference curve of one person with an indifference curve of the other. The contract curve is the locus of such tangencies. All points on the contract curve are efficient: all points off it are inefficient. Each point on the contract curve represents a different distribution of utility between the two persons. The criterion of exchange efficiency thus identifies the contract curve but provides no mechanism for ranking the points on it.

An almost identical analysis, this time using an Edgeworth production box rather than the consumption box, establishes the necessary conditions for *technical efficiency*, meaning the optimal combination of factors of production. The marginal rates of substitution between any two factors must be equal for all goods which are produced. When this condition is satisfied, it is not possible to reallocate factors so that more of one good is produced but no less of any other good. The contract curve again distinguishes efficient from inefficient allocations. Each point on it represents a different output mix.

The analysis so far has focused upon the allocation of fixed quantities of consumption goods between individuals (exchange efficiency) and of factors of production between goods (technical efficiency). The next step is to consider the optimal composition of output: *overall Pareto efficiency*. The slope of the transformation curve measures the rate (described as the marginal rate of transformation) at which one good must be sacrificed in order to obtain more of another good (that is its marginal cost). The necessary conditions for technical efficiency are met at all points on, rather than inside, the transformation curve. Overall Pareto efficiency is achieved when the marginal rate of transformation (the slope of the transformation curve) is equal to the common marginal rate of substitution (the slope of the indifference curves which are equal at all points on the contract curve).

At such a point of overall Pareto efficiency, no further reallocation of good or factors can make one person better off without simultaneously makin another person worse off. There is, however, no single allocation of resource which alone is Pareto optimal. Instead, there is an infinite number of suc points, each corresponding to different distributions of welfare. Which o these is reached depends critically upon the initial distribution of facto endowments which provides the starting point for market exchange. How ever, the Pareto criterion itself provides no mechanism for choosing betwee these outcomes.[3]

For a market economy to achieve overall Pareto optimality the followin; conditions must hold: there is perfect knowledge; all individuals aim t maximize their utility; there are no externalities; there is perfect competitio between all buyers and sellers; and all producers are profit maximizers. Thi is a formidable list. Indeed, breaches of such assumptions provide the startin; point for the development of the theory of market failure.

The concept of Pareto optimality is the criterion of allocative efficienc against which alternative allocations of resources can be judged. It provide key insights about the efficiency properties of perfect markets. It emphasize that allocative efficiency requires prices to be everywhere equal to margina cost. It confers an important, though not unqualified, blessing upon th operation of real-life market economies. The historical link between the free market economy and overall Pareto optimality has stemmed from th frequent identification of the latter with universal perfect competition. I fact, other mechanisms could result in an allocation of resources which is ar overall Pareto optimum. It was the important insight of Lange (1938) anc Lerner (1944) that a decentralized socialist economy could also secure th fundamental requirement that prices everywhere should equal marginal cost But the stringency of the assumptions on which both results depend must be stressed.

X-*efficiency*

When the necessary conditions for allocative efficiency were formulated above, the assumption of profit maximization guaranteed that firms would produce any given output at the minimum attainable cost. Taken together with the other assumptions, this ensured that the economy would operate on, and not inside, the transformation curve. However, this assumption has been challenged by Leibenstein who accused economists of misdirecting their energies and of misunderstanding where the opportunities for improving economic welfare really lay. He argued that the welfare cost of the direct resource misallocation from distortions such as monopoly is very small compared with the costs imposed by more inputs than are absolutely necessary being used to produce any given level of output. He introduced the term 'X-inefficiency' to describe such losses. Rather than provide a formal definition in his original article, Leibenstein (1966) preferred the expositional device of citing examples, often involving the failure to adopt, or to maintain the use of, best-practice techniques. Later, he defined the degree of X-inefficiency as: '... the difference between maximal effectiveness of utilization [of inputs] and actual utilization' (Leibenstein, 1975, p. 582). The achievement of allocative efficiency requires that all X-inefficiency has been eliminated. Whereas economists have frequently made the presumption of X-efficiency and then concentrated their attention upon allocative issues, Leibenstein argued that X-inefficiency is pervasive throughout the economy and that economists simply assumed away the real problem of efficiency, the one recognized as such by non-economists.

Leibenstein's explanation of the sources of X-inefficiency has evolved over time, with his later work (1973, 1975, 1976) containing behavioural propositions and mechanisms entirely missing from the original 1966 article. Rather than assume that the firm is a unit with a single brain which takes decisions, he focused upon how the individuals employed in the firm (firm members) take decisions about their supply of effort within constraints imposed by the firm's internal organizational structure and its external market environment. As labour contracts can never be fully specified and detailed policing is expensive and sometimes counterproductive, the firm member has considerable discretion as to how his job is interpreted and how much effort he will supply. However, his maximization of utility is constrained by the pressures exerted by other firm members with whom accommodations must be sought.

Leibenstein thus wished to redirect microeconomics away from the analysis of markets back to the internal processes of the firm. Nevertheless, he stressed that the external market environment impinges upon such processes: competition is seen as a source of external pressure which constrains the degree of X-inefficiency but does not eliminate it (Leibenstein, 1973). There is obviously a similarity between Leibenstein's work and the behavioural theories of the firm (Cyert and March, 1963; Williamson, 1975). Optimizing by the firm, rather than by its members, is rejected as an assumption, thus removing the pillar upon which the achievement of X-efficiency was based. The problem of efficiency is reinterpreted in a very different light. Such theoretical developments, originating in the analysis of the private firm, will be shown to have major relevance to the economics of the public sector.

III   THE EFFICIENCY CASE AGAINST PUBLIC EXPENDITURE

Efficiency arguments against public expenditure constitute an important part of the case against public provision as articulated in the UK by the Institute of Economic Affairs (IEA). This research institute has acted as a channel through which various strands of free-market writing have been communicated to British audiences. Despite its ideological stance, it has established fo itself a position of substantial influence within the economics profession and recruited as its authors economists of high professional standing. The majo strands of thought which recur in its publications are: the monetarist schoo revitalized by Milton Friedman of the University of Chicago; the 'law and economics' school at the University of Chicago such as Harold Demsetz William Landes and Richard Posner, who have analysed the economi implications of property rights and of legal systems; the public choice schoo represented by James Buchanan, Gordon Tullock and Richard Wagner of the Virginia Polytechnic Institute; and the Austrian tradition represented by Friedrich von Hayek.

Pamphlets from the IEA have covered almost every area of public provision beyond the narrow limits of the minimal state: for example housing, health, social services, education, libraries, transport, roads, parking, fire, water, refuse and seaside facilities. Day summarized the IEA's theme as:

> . . . the philosophy that where the benefit of a particular service is clearly identifiable as going to the particular individual, then there is a good case for that individual paying the price and choosing whether or not he takes the benefit of that service . . . (quoted in Harris and Seldon, 1976, p. 23).

Although the IEA consistently emphasizes that it has no collective view, there are clearly defined policy positions which characterize most (if not all) IEA pamphlets. The common themes are much more striking than any diversity of opinion among authors. Many IEA publications are polished and persuasive, with their appeal to economists owing much to the way in which they apply standard microeconomic tools in order to derive policy conclusions. They are far more tightly argued than much of the social policy literature which is one of their major targets. The fundamental weakness of the IEA literature is not to be found in any lack of internal coherence or cogency but in its presentation of the underlying assumptions as unchallengeable (Heald, 1980a).

The IEA's main policy conclusions can be summarized as follows:

(1) Services should not be provided free of user charge. To the extent that, say, health and education are provided by the public sector, users should pay fees.
(2) Wherever possible, public provision should be replaced by private provision.
(3) Choice can be restored to public services by the use of vouchers (for example for education).
(4) Whatever income redistribution is desired should be implemented through cash transfers and not benefits in kind.

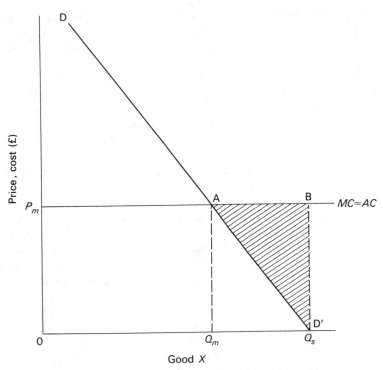

Figure 5.1 How 'free' provision causes waste

Conclusion (4) will not be discussed here in any detail as it is subsequently examined in Chapter 6. Conclusions (1), (2) and (3) are concerned with the alleged inefficiency of public provision. They are examined in turn but an evaluation is postponed until later.

'Services should not be provided free'

Figure 5.1 illustrates the allocative efficiency rationale of this conclusion. On the horizontal axis is plotted the quantity of good X (which might be education) and on the vertical axis is plotted its price and cost: DD' is the individual's demand curve for good X. For simplicity, it is assumed that the cost per unit of output is constant: hence marginal cost (MC) equals average cost (AC).

The optimal level of output is $0Q_m$ units which satisfies the condition that price should equal marginal cost. This level of output would emerge from a perfectly competitive market in which all consumers of X pay the market price $0P_m$. This outcome can now be contrasted with what will happen if the government provides good X to consumers 'free of charge' at the point of consumption and meets the costs of production out of taxation. Consumers will now wish to consume $0Q_s$ units of good X, indicated by the point at which the demand curve DD′ intersects the horizontal axis. $0Q_s$ is the desired level of output under 'free' state provision in the absence of non-price rationing.

Consumers derive utility from each of the extra units between $0Q_m$ and $0Q_s$. But they value each of these extra units (Q_mQ_s) at less than its marginal cost. Extra benefits from the expansion of output are measured by the area Q_mAQ_s and the extra costs by Q_mABQ_s. There is a net loss (shaded area ABQ_s) resulting from the substitution of 'free' state provision for market pricing. Public provision of good X is therefore 'wasteful' in the sense that it will lead to an expansion of output beyond the level for which consumers would have been willing to pay.

Two other sources of allocative inefficiency may arise. First, there will be distortions introduced by the taxes which are required to finance the 'free' provision. Second, it is possible that, because of other claims on public revenue and of resistance to further taxation, output will not be expanded to $0Q_s$. The government will decide upon the level of output (possibly on quite arbitrary grounds) and then use non-price rationing to allocate the good between consumers. Unlike the price mechanism, such rationing procedures do not ensure that the goods are allocated to those who value them most (in the sense of willingness to pay), thus breaching the necessary conditions for allocative efficiency. Furthermore, not only are resources absorbed in the rationing process but also there is the possibility of the abuse of bureaucratic power, made possible by the existence of discretion.

'Substitute private for public provision'

This conclusion rests upon the claim that public production is inherently less X-efficient than private production because there is no residual claimant who can appropriate to himself the benefits from higher X-efficiency. Figure 5.2 reproduces the demand curve DD′ of Figure 5.1 There are, however, now two different cost curves, each representing both MC and AC. A subscript 's' denotes public production and a subscript 'm' denotes private production. The cost curves for public production are drawn at the same level as the corresponding curves in Figure 5.1 As private production is assumed to embody a higher level of X-efficiency, the cost curves for it are drawn below those for public production.

The desired level of public production at zero prices remains at $0Q_s$. However the perfectly competitive output level has changed: price now equals marginal cost at output $0Q_m'$ where DD′ intersects MC_m. Public production at $0Q_s$ is still allocatively inefficient. Even though $0Q_m'$ is greater than $0Q_m$, it remains below $0Q_s$. The loss from allocative inefficiency is given by the diagonally shaded area (EFQ_s). There is now a further loss due to the X-inefficiency of public production. This is shown by the vertically

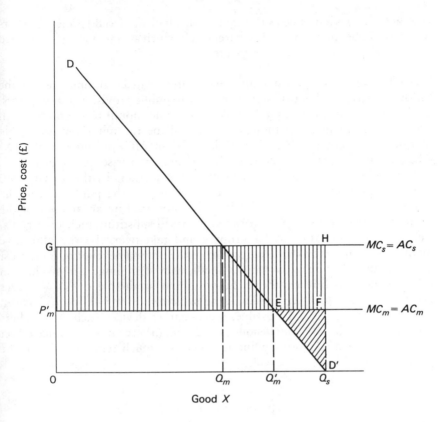

Figure 5.2 X-inefficiency and public provision

shaded area (P'_mGHF) which lies between MC_s and MC_m measured up to the level of output under public production ($0Q_s$).

'Use vouchers to discipline public production'

Where a service is not transferred to the private sector, choice of supplier can be restored to the consumer by the introduction of vouchers. These would be redeemable for the purchase of the specific service from alternative suppliers. In this way, incentives for X-efficiency are introduced, thus simulating market disciplines in the public sector. Education vouchers have been advocated by, *inter alia,* Peacock and Wiseman (1970) and Maynard (1975). The pattern in which parents redeemed such vouchers is presented as a mechanism for measuring the efficiency of particular schools, with a flow of pupils away from the 'unsuccessful' ones. Although many varieties of voucher schemes have been suggested, most advocates would prefer vouchers which could be supplemented by parents out of private income and redeemed with either public or private suppliers.

The efficiency case against public expenditure can be summarized in the following way. Market pricing is preferable to public provision at zero prices. Unlike competitive firms, public services have no inbuilt mechanism which promotes X-efficiency. Although neither will be the minimum attainable marginal cost curve, MC_m will be lower than MC_s reflecting higher X-efficiency in the private sector. Under private enterprise, X-inefficiency is contained by the policing of management and workers by the owners who can appropriate to themselves any cost savings. In the public sector, the interests of the consumer are likely to be subverted by an alliance of the producers (management and workers) who will substitute their own goals, free from the sanction of bankruptcy and take-over. To the allocative inefficiency, caused by the departure from the optimal level of output, must be added the additional loss from X-inefficiency stemming from production costs being even further above the minimum attainable ones. Wherever possible, private production should be substituted for public production. Where this option is not possible, quasi-market devices such as vouchers should be introduced. Conclusions (1), (2) and (3) are an interconnected set of policy recommendations pointing towards a much reduced role for the public sector.

IV   MARKET FAILURE

Figures 5.1 and 5.2 are simple but powerful constructions which conveniently summarize much criticism of the public sector as inefficient and wasteful. But are they compelling? The case presented by Figure 5.1 against public expenditure as allocatively inefficient entirely neglects the issue of market failure. Paretian welfare economics has ambivalent implications for the 'market versus the state' debate. Although it has been used systematically in IEA pamphlets as an argument for the market, it has also constituted the justification advanced for much state intervention. In recognition of this ambivalence, writers such as Rowley and Peacock (1975) have explicitly distanced themselves from the Paretian tradition.

Through its emphasis upon externalities, public goods and monopoly, Paretian welfare economics severely undermined the general case for the free market as an efficient allocator of resources. Much of the advocacy of the market in preference to the state implicitly pictures the private sector in terms of perfectly competitive markets in which the output of every good is expanded up to the point at which price equals marginal cost. The aura attached to perfect competition is transferred to any kind of competition.

This stands in contrast to the opposite fallacy of assuming an omniscient state. Instead of comparing the perfect market with the imperfect state or vice versa, the imperfect market must be compared with the imperfect state.

The acknowledgement that there may be various types of market failure complicates the analysis and makes the conclusions much less clear-cut. There is an extensive literature on market failure but only two topics, externalities and public goods, will be systematically considered. The question of increasing returns to scale, with the ensuing propensity for monopolies to be created, will not be examined. Neither will the topic of uncertainty which is a potent source of market failure. Subsequently, there will be a section on consumer surplus because of its relevance to the question of whether, in particular contexts, prices have efficiency-generating properties.[4]

Externalities

There are two types of interdependence within any market system. First, there is that essential interdependence communicated by the market process itself. The choices of one household on consumption packages and factor supplies influence the choices faced by other households through their effects on relative prices. It is this signalling of resource scarcities which is the central function of prices. Second, the key idea about externalities is that of untraded interdependence: the effects upon utility and production functions are direct and not through the market mechanism. Environmental pollution is an example of negative (that is undesirable) externalities: it provided Pigou's (1920) original example of the smoky factory chimney. It has often been argued that health, housing and education generate external benefits to third parties (that is positive externalities).

Instead of a rule to set price equal to marginal cost, the revised rule, which secures the socially optimal level of output, is to set marginal social benefit equal to marginal social cost. However, in practice, the measurement of social benefits and social costs presents severe methodological and empirical problems (Pearce, 1978). Figure 5.1 was drawn on the assumption that good X provides benefits to the consumer alone. If there are external benefits, new issues are raised which are considered in Figure 5.3. For example, good X might again be education and wider literacy may confer benefits upon others. The conclusion that state provision of good X is too large and wasteful no longer necessarily holds.

To the construction of Figure 5.1 has been added the demand curve EE' which measures the willingness to pay of both direct consumers and those receiving external benefits. The external benefit of any unit of good X is measured by the vertical distance between EE' and DD': for example, for the Q_mth unit, it is AJ. EE' is drawn on the arbitrary, but plausible, assumption that the external benefit of a unit of good X diminishes as output of good X increases.

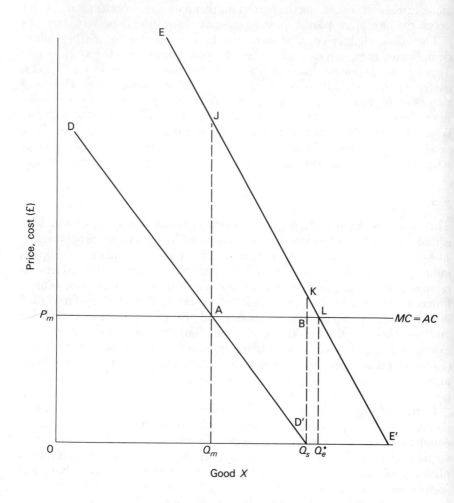

Figure 5.3 The optimal output of a publicly provided good yielding external benefits

The perfectly competitive market output is at $0Q_m$ at which marginal private benefit (Q_mA) equals price ($0P_m$). But marginal external benefit is equal to AJ and marginal social benefit is equal to Q_mJ. Therefore, $0Q_m$ cannot be the socially optimal output. Even if consumers expand their consumption to the point where marginal private benefit equals zero ($0Q_s$), marginal social benefit (Q_sK) still exceeds marginal cost ($0P_m$). The socially optimal output is where marginal social benefit equals marginal social cost. This is at $0Q_e^*$ where Q_e^*L equals $0P_m$.

It must be stressed that the result that there is no 'waste', even if state provision is expanded to the point where marginal private benefit equals zero, is entirely dependent upon how the curves have been drawn. If EE' intersected the MC curve to the left of Q_s, there would be 'waste' in the sense that the social value of marginal units is less than their social cost. However, the purpose of Figure 5.3 is to expose the over-simplicity of Figure 5.1. Very little is known about the shape of EE' but that is no excuse for simply assuming away the issue of external benefits.

The presence of externalities means that the pursuit of self-interest by individuals and firms will not necessarily lead to a socially optimal allocation of resources. This analysis easily leads on to the advocacy of state intervention to 'correct' the misallocation of resources, as it did historically. For example, Pigou recommended taxes and subsidies to alter the choices faced by individuals and firms so that they would take their decisions in the light of social rather than private costs and benefits.

In Figure 5.3, the socially optimal output could be reached if the purchasers of good X were paid a subsidy equal to the marginal external benefit. This subsidy would be equal to the vertical distance between EE' and DD'. The most obvious difficulty is the informational requirements: the size of the marginal external benefit must be known for all levels of output which will inevitably include some far removed from practical experience. The operation of such a subsidy system would involve administrative costs and would absorb public revenue. Furthermore, its design and implementation inevitably raise questions about the motives, altruistic or self-interested, of public decision-makers. Underlying many of the policy proposals derived from welfare economics is an image of the state as omniscient and selfless. If, however, objectives other than maximizing social welfare are pursued, the cost of such 'state failure' has to be set against the cost of market failure before any final policy conclusion can be reached. The problem of state failure is the subject of Section VI of this chapter.

The existence of externalities does not lead directly to proposals for either public ownership or public provision at zero prices. Their inclusion in the analysis does, however, sanction state intervention in the market, provided that the benefits from such action exceed its costs. The role which this idea has played in sanctioning state intervention provoked Rowley (1978a, p. 13) to claim: 'Society might be far better off if the problem of social cost had never been discovered.' In IEA pamphlets on the welfare state, it is usually asserted that the benefits of public spending are largely privately appropriated. By thus downgrading the importance of externalities, IEA authors seek to resist both the case for government action in the specific policy sphere and the general sanctioning of intervention. The link between externalities and 'free' public provision is thereby indirect: their introduction has damaged the proposition that the government should simply stand aside from the market economy.

Public goods

The concept of public goods is a development from the theory of externalities. There are severe terminological dangers which must be guarded against. 'Public good' and 'private good' are technical terms: they do not mean goods produced by the public and private sectors respectively. Samuelson (1954, 1955) defined a pure public good as a good which exhibits both:

(1) Non-rivalry in consumption: one person's consumption does not reduce the amount available for others.
(2) Non-excludability: it is impossible to exclude from benefit a person who refuses to contribute to the cost.

A large theoretical literature has developed the necessary conditions for Pareto optimality for an economy with both public goods and private goods. These are different from those for an economy with only private goods. The logic of this difference is simple. By the non-rivalry assumption, one individual's enjoyment of the pure public good does not in any way diminish any other individual's enjoyment. By the non-excludability assumption, one individual cannot be prevented from enjoying the units of the public good paid for by any other individual. The relevant criterion for allocative efficiency is that the joint marginal willingness to pay of all individuals should be equal to the marginal cost.[5]

Samuelson's major insight was that, though it is possible to develop the appropriate efficiency conditions for an economy with public goods, there is no mechanism through which a market economy can achieve this overall Pareto optimum because of non-rivalry and non-excludability. The pursuit of individual self-interest, which guides an economy with only private goods to satisfy the efficiency conditions, now prevents the achievement of the revised efficiency conditions. Individuals have the incentive to become free riders (that is benefit without paying) as they can reduce their own contribution towards the cost of the public good by under-declaring their preferences for it within any voluntary exchange framework. A decentralized market cannot achieve the optimal level of output, meaning that there must be some form of state intervention.

Pure public goods do not necessarily involve public production as well as public financing: they could be publicly financed but privately produced. Despite the literature's recognition of the fallacy of jumping from technical property to mode of provision, this logical error is frequently committed. It operates in two opposite directions. First, it presumes too readily that certain goods must be publicly produced because of their public good properties. Second, it leads to the proposition that the public sector should produce public goods and the private sector private goods. The delineation of the respective roles of the public and private sectors is thereby reduced to the task of classifying goods along the public/private spectrum. In practice, the public sector produces goods which range from the pure public (for example defence) to the pure private (for example motor cars). Any attempt either to predict or to prescribe the range of public sector activities from the technical property of 'publicness' will result in highly restrictive conclusions. The division of activities between the public and private sectors cannot be simply reduced to the technical properties of the goods in question.

Consumer surplus

Although prices play a crucial role in promoting allocative efficiency, there are well-established cases in economic theory when allocative efficiency can be improved by the alteration or suppression of prices. Consumer surplus is the difference between the consumer's willingness to pay for a good and the amount actually paid. Dupuit (1844), a French highway engineer, introduced the idea of consumer surplus and developed it as a highly sophisticated argument against tolls on bridges and roads. His insights and subsequent theoretical developments have provided some powerful results which are highly relevant to the role of charges for the use of public facilities.

Figures 5.4 and 5.5 illustrate the argument against tolls. In Figure 5.4, DD' is the demand curve for journeys over a bridge across a major river. Marginal and average operating costs are assumed to be zero and marginal and average toll collection costs are OT. The bridge is assumed to be privately owned by a profit maximizer. The bridge owner sets marginal revenue equal to marginal cost: these curves intersect at E which corresponds to $0Q_t$ crossings. The toll is $0P_t$ and profits are TP_tBE.

Although $0Q_t$ is the profit maximizing level of crossings, it is not the socially optimal level. At $0Q_t$, marginal benefit (Q_tB) exceeds marginal cost (Q_tE). This marginal cost consists exclusively of the cost of collecting the toll since marginal operating cost has been assumed to be zero. Total utility can be measured by the area under the demand curve DD' up to the actual number of crossings.[6] When tolls exist, consumer surplus is calculated as total utility minus tolls paid. In Figure 5.4, the total utility of $0Q_t$ crossings is $0ABQ_t$ and consumer surplus is P_tAB. If the toll is abolished, marginal cost is zero. The number of crossings is now $0Q_s$ and consumer surplus, which is identical to the total utility from crossings, is $0AQ_s$. The socially optimal level of output is now achieved: travellers value all crossings up to $0Q_s$ at which marginal benefit equals marginal cost, both of which are zero.

Figure 5.5 reproduces Figure 5.4 so that areas can be shaded without obscuring the essentials of the original diagram. The horizontally shaded area ($0P_tBQ_s$) is the gain in consumer surplus when the toll is abolished. The vertically shaded area ($0TEQ_t$) is the real resource saving from abolishing toll collection. The diagonally shaded area (TP_tBE) is the loss of the bridge

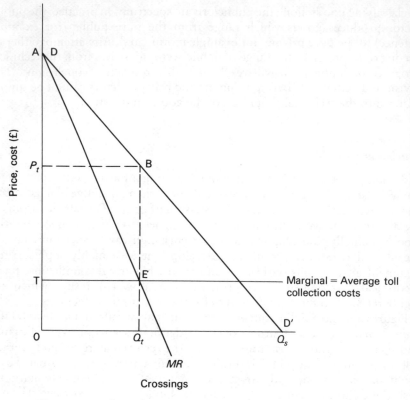

Figure 5.4 The consumer surplus case for toll-free bridges

owner's profits. Therefore, the net benefit from abolishing the toll is:

Q_tBQ_s $+ (0P_tBQ_t - TP_tBE)$ $+ 0TEQ_t$ $= Q_tBQ_s + 2(0TEQ_t)$

consumer   + additional   + real   = net gains from
surplus of   consumer surplus   resource   abolition of
generated   on existing   savings   tolls
traffic   traffic minus   through
              the loss of   ending of
              bridge owner's   toll
              profits   collection

Three caveats should be noted. First, the assumption has been made that it is valid to add up the shaded areas of Figure 5.5. This involves the assumption

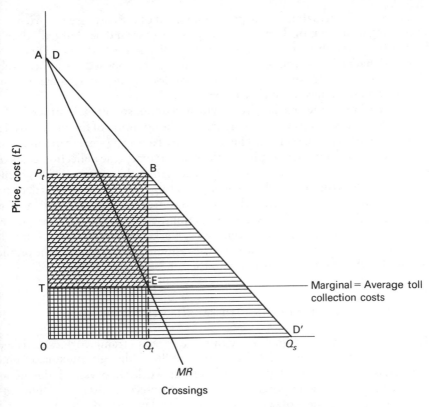

Figure 5.5 Gains and losses from abolition of a toll

that toll revenue, the bridge owner's profits and consumer surplus are all equally socially valuable. Second, the effects of the taxes, which will be required to finance toll-free bridge construction, have been neglected. The purpose of tolls on estuarial crossings in the UK has been to cover such historical costs, with negligible attention being paid to allocative efficiency. Moreover, tolls on such bridges have never succeeded in achieving even this narrow objective. Third, the possibility of congestion has been assumed away in the analysis of Figures 5.4 and 5.5. When the bridge is subject to congestion, there is an efficiency case for a toll which should be set equal to marginal social cost.

Dupuit's efficiency argument against tolls on bridges extends to other public facilities which exhibit zero or very low marginal operating cost once the decision to provide the facility has been taken. Examples would include public parks, open spaces, beaches and museums, provided that demand is not so high relative to capacity so as to cause congestion. Nevertheless, IEA publications have advocated pricing for all these public services. This paradox emphasizes that a powerful component of the IEA case for pricing is something nearer a moral imperative ('consumers should be charged') than a search for Paretian efficiency (see, for example, Seldon (1977)). There are severe dangers in assuming that any pricing, as opposed to allocatively efficient pricing, is desirable. The role of prices within a particular institutional framework has to be closely examined.

One feature of the market from which economists often abstract is the presence of transactions costs. In Figure 5.5, the abolition of the toll secured a real resource saving of $0TEQ_t$. The operation of a pricing system involves the use of resources and the abolition of the toll eliminates the collection costs of the bridge owner. But these are far from being the only costs: travellers incur time losses due to the toll, higher vehicle operating costs and the cost of detours to avoid the toll. These are additional resource savings once the toll is abolished. The price mechanism involves transactions, policing and enforcement costs which are frequently neglected in market versus the state debates. It is often assumed without evidence that the rationing mechanisms of the public sector absorb far more resources than their market counterparts.

V QUESTIONING THE PARETIAN FRAMEWORK

The analysis so far has remained within the Paretian framework established by the four value judgements listed on page 86. Although much economic analysis is indeed confined within such a framework, these value judgements should themselves be exposed to scrutiny. Non-economists are often surprised at the willingness of economists to suspend judgement about them and to operate within their confines. Much of this section is devoted to considering the implications of relaxing one or more of them. But, first, a different line of criticism of the Paretian tradition should be considered, one which provides strong reinforcement of the case for the market.

The significance of property rights

A new literature, much of it either originating from or heavily influenced by the University of Chicago, has criticized the Paretian tradition for failing to emphasize the critical role of property rights in securing efficient resource allocation. It is argued that too much attention has been paid to the derivation of efficiency conditions, conceived within a static view of the market economy and too little to the forces promoting or hindering efficiency. In contrast, a well-defined system of property rights is held to ensure that economic decisions will be taken by those whose self-interest is conducive to efficiency. Many of the cases of market failure have been reinterpreted in terms of a defective allocation of property rights. Instead of state intervention through systems of taxes, subsidies or public provision, a better definition of property rights is advocated. The best-known articulation of such a view is Coase's (1960) criticism of the Pigovian tax/subsidy solution to the problem of externalities: if property rights are sufficiently well-defined, bargaining between parties is judged preferable to state intervention.[7] The pursuit of self-interest within a system of property rights is identified as the strength of the market economy. It is contrasted with the attenuation of property rights inherent in the activities of the state. This view underlies much of the growing literature on state failure, considered in Section VI of this chapter.

Exogenous preferences

Although economists have been willing to apply their methods of analysis to political and social questions, they have paid limited attention to the crucial stage of preference formation. Consumer preferences are usually treated as exogenous (that is given from outside the economic model). As well as being exogenous, an individual's indifference curves are usually held to be independent of those of any other individual. Given these assumptions, it is then possible to prove the efficiency properties of a market economy.

The reasons for this lack of curiosity about the process of preference formation are complex. Relaxing the exogenity assumption reintroduces problems of subjectivity. It might also encourage contentious judgements about the circumstances in which the preferences of individuals could be overridden. This is, however, an anticipated consequence rather than something logically inherent in such an extension of the analysis. Taking consumer preferences as exogenous and as sovereign imposes constraints upon the directions in which the subsequent analysis may develop. It diverts attention away from the process of preference formation: individual preferences, as revealed through market exchange, are to be counted. The analysis of the influence of class, culture, location and time on the preference patterns of individuals is judged to be irrelevant.

The limits of consumer sovereignty

The concept of allocative efficiency was defined with reference to individual preferences. There is clearly a libertarian dimension to assumption (3) on page 86 which results in individual preferences, as articulated through the exercise of consumer and producer sovereignty, being fundamental to the concept of efficiency. The view that there is some source of external judgement about the social value of particular patterns of consumption is rejected. Consequently, attempts by governments to alter freely chosen consumption packages (for example to encourage the consumption of education and to discourage the consumption of tobacco) are likely to be condemned as paternalist. In the economics literature, 'paternalist' is more frequently used as a pejorative term than in a descriptive sense. This climate perhaps explains the popularity of externality arguments about both education and tobacco, hinging upon the benefits and/or costs to third parties arising from the individual's consumption decisions. This is safe territory because there are well-established reasons why market exchange cannot accommodate such effects. No challenge is thereby posed to the 'correctness' of the consumption decision itself.

However, much of the wider public debate about both education and tobacco is not about postulated external effects (for example the benefits of living in a literate society and the nuisance caused by smoking) but whether these individual decisions correctly take into account the full range of benefits and costs to the individual. In other words it challenges the assumption of individual rationality. Smokers smoke, drinkers drink, and motorists would drive without safety belts, goes the argument, even though the costs exceed the benefits on their own *ex post* evaluation. Various reasons have been suggested to explain this paradox: individuals are held to underestimate the risks attached to certain kinds of consumption activity; the extent of habituation for certain kinds of consumption may mean that present consumption decisions are heavily constrained by past ones; and individuals' decisions are held to be constrained by the social context of consumption in which certain types of consumption confer, or are claimed to confer, social status.

The possibility therefore arises that the government may have much better information than individuals on some of these risks, for example the statistical probabilities of death or injury. There may be circumstances under which the government does indeed know best the consequences of individual decisions. In some cases, but not in others, it would be possible to verify or disprove such claims as to fact. Nevertheless, very different attitudes could be adopted if the claims were verified. It could be argued that such evidence did nothing to challenge the ethical supremacy of the presumption in favour of consumer sovereignty. Alternatively, the government could be urged to disseminate this information to consumers or to alter consumer choices by the use of taxes, regulations or prohibitions. The policy advocated will depend upon both the degree of commitment to the principle of consumer sovereignty and the circumstances of the particular case.

There are three other reasons for the advocacy of the principle of consumer sovereignty to be qualified rather than absolute. First, very large resources are utilized in advertising campaigns designed, at least in part, to alter consumer preference patterns. It is at least incongruous to view such activity by the private sector as acceptable yet then deny to elected governments any role in shaping consumption patterns. Second, the apparent democracy of counting everybody's preferences as equally valid and important is partly spurious: resource allocation depends upon the distribution of purchasing power as well as upon the distribution of preferences. Third, consumer preferences are usually defined over goods and factors. However, other issues arise when consumers are not indifferent as to which social groups they are associated with during the process of consumption. Some consumers may be prejudiced against, for example, Jews or blacks or women or the working class. It is not difficult to construct an argument in favour of the formation of private clubs to provide services like education, health or golf which explicitly exclude the unwanted social group. It is therefore unsafe to regard consumer sovereignty as sacrosanct once the possibility has been introduced that utility does not solely depend upon the individual's own consumption package.

Preference correction and merit wants

The conventional presumption in favour of consumer sovereignty excludes the possibility that individuals might voluntarily accede to restrictions being placed by governments upon their consumption patterns. It is possible that individuals will be willing to vote for legislation (for example compulsory safety belts; anti-drink and drive measures such as breathalysers; anti-heroin laws; and compulsory school attendance) which effectively restricts their own and other consumers' freedom of choice. Certain kinds of consumption, which would be freely chosen by at least some consumers, are thereby made illegal.

Burrows (1977) has argued that such cases of preference correction should be recognized as such and not explained through a postulated chain of consumption externalities. He suggested two alternative explanations of this paradox of why consumers should agree to prohibit activities which they might otherwise undertake. First, individuals might have two sets of preferences concerning an activity: a higher ordering relating to the individual in an objective, detached frame of mind; and a lower ordering relating to the individual when faced by temptation. Second, the difference between the two levels of ordering may reflect the voter's recognition that as a consumer he is ill-informed about the consequences of certain kinds of consumption.

There are two separate dimensions to this issue of preference correction. First, certain kinds of consumption are either prohibited or made more expensive through taxation. Drugs such as heroin fall into the former category and alcohol into the latter. Second, through either the enforcement of minimum standards or public provision financed out of taxes, governments may impose a pattern of consumption which would not be freely chosen by consumers. Musgrave (1959) used the term 'merit wants' in cases where the presumption of consumer sovereignty is dropped: most economists use the term 'merit good'. However, he never developed the concept very far and it received a very unsympathetic reception from most economists, wedded to the view that the individual is always the best judge of his own welfare.

Free-market writers dismiss the merit good argument as invalid, based upon an authoritarian and organic view of the state, and embodying the paternalist view that 'the government knows best'. They contrast this with their own individualistic view that society's wishes can be no more than the sum of the wishes of the individuals who make up that society. The concept of merit goods is held to challenge the view that there is no mythical entity called 'society' and to deny that the individual is the best judge of his own welfare. However, Collard (1976) noted in his review of Rowley and Peacock (1975) that, despite their emphasis upon individual preferences, the authors were not prepared to allow individuals to vote for collective provision. For a certain range of goods, the welfare state involves such a substitution of political processes for individual decisions in the market-place. Public provision of goods which are not pure public goods in the technical sense has often been subjected to such a charge of paternalism. However, this is an issue which can best be analysed in Chapter 6 which examines the reasons why in-kind programmes play such a significant role in the welfare state.

The social context of consumption

By forcefully rejecting assumption (2) on page 86 that the economic dimension can be separated from the non-economic, Hirsch (1977) explored the reasons why individuals might support collective action which restricted their consumption choices. He rejected the view that the binding constraints on economic growth were shortages of natural resources. Doomwatch forecasts had been based upon a failure to comprehend the adaptability of a market economy to scarcities of particular natural resources and to the resulting changing relative prices.

Hirsch, however, identified severe constraints on future economic growth: these were the 'social limits to growth'. He contended that the traditional assumption that the economic and non-economic dimensions could be separated had led to a failure to appreciate the distinction between:

(1) 'Conventional' goods which are reproducible on any desired scale, given the availability of the appropriate factors and technologies.
(2) 'Positional' goods which are not so much valued for themselves but for the social status which the act of consumption confers on individuals. More factors and more efficient technologies can produce more of the good, such as an academic degree, but it cannot reproduce more of the social status which was formerly attached. Once more of the positional good is available, it fails to perform as effectively its role as a screening device and may cease to be a positional good.

Economic growth therefore entails internal contradictions. Individuals expect from it not just more goods but more of the social status hitherto associated with positional goods. Frustrated expectations are inevitable because economic growth can make available more conventional goods but

1ot more positional goods. He therefore viewed the process of economic growth as intensifying social conflict rather than alleviating it, in sharp contrast to Crosland's vision (1956) of greater economic equality and social cohesion.

In his judgement, the fundamental dilemma of the market economy is that too many of its actors have absorbed its ethos of the pursuit of self-interest resulting in a depleted moral legacy. There is no longer any internal mechanism or invisible hand capable of harmonizing their actions to the common good. The consequence has been an increasingly bitter struggle between individuals and groups over the distribution of income. This has resulted in much greater conflict in the realm of industrial relations which provides most groups with their sole direct mechanism for challenging the existing distribution. The heightened perception of self-interest has spread to occupational groups previously outside the arena of industrial conflict, many of them employed in the public sector. The steadily growing complexity and interdependence of economic life has accentuated the economy's vulnerability to both conventional and new forms of disruption. Paradoxically, the increased willingness to use power in the pursuit of sectional interest has been coupled with a growing intolerance of the social and economic inequality stemming from unequal life chances and from the outcome of previous struggles over distribution.

Hirsch predicted that there will be a trend towards 'reluctant collectivism' involving the regulation of incomes. Certain goods will be taken out of the market and allocated on non-market criteria. Unless the non-reproducibility of positional goods is fully recognized, it will prove impossible to maintain social harmony. Plans which appear rational at the level of the individual can be seen at the level of society to be incapable of fulfilment because of the intrinsic scarcity of positional goods. It is therefore meaningful to speak about society's views as being potentially different from the sum of the views of the constituent individuals in isolation. Recognizing that relative consumption is vitally important, individuals may be prepared to use collective institutions to restructure the set of consumption opportunities facing them as consumers. This is clearly something which they cannot do as individual consumers when they must take the available choices as given.

VI STATE FAILURE

The 'invisible hand' of the market has retained its appeal for economists ever since Adam Smith (1759, 1776) coined the metaphor. Fascination about its workings, even when not accompanied by unbridled enthusiasm for market outcomes, is the common characteristic which sets economists aside from their fellow human beings. Fascination rather than enthusiasm is indeed the correct description for economists have always been the source of the most

perceptive criticisms both of individual markets and of the market system
Much effort has been expended in refining the theory of market failure, at
both the microeconomic (for example externalities) and macroeconomic (for
example persistent unemployment) levels of analysis. But there are two
fundamental criticisms which can be levelled against mainstream economics
First, the Paretian tradition partitioned off the economic from the non-
economic parts of human activity, leading to a neglect of values other than
efficiency. Second, neoclassical economics did not have a theory of the state
an omission which became crucial when the move was made from the
analysis of market failure towards particular policy prescriptions, usually
involving some form of state action (Whynes and Bowles, 1981).

This absence of a theory of the state exerted a decisive influence over the
development of policy prescriptions. Market failure has long been the
starting point of expositions of the economic rationale of state action. After a
whole variety of market failures has been dissected, attention then turns to
the design of policy instruments to be used by the state in order to improve the
allocation of resources: for example, the use of taxes or subsidies in order to
deal with the problem of externalities. The potential difficulties associated
with this approach ought to have been obvious, yet were neglected in a
literature which became more and more entranced with the optimal design of
policy instruments, oblivious to the question of whether they would be
implemented in the manner intended. Such implementation would require
public officials to be altruistic (maximizers of social welfare and untainted by
self-interest); omniscient (about cost and demand conditions); skilled in the
use of the analytical techniques of Paretian welfare economics; and committed to its underlying value judgements.

Such requirements were left implicit, distracting attention from the fact
that the existence of market failure is only a necessary condition for state
intervention to improve resource allocation, not a sufficient condition. This
limited vision of economists was due in part to their desire to develop a corpus
of theory and analytical techniques which were 'ethically neutral'. This was
often believed to have been done by concentrating on the operation of
markets and on efficiency: the consideration of equity, let alone of political
processes, required extra and 'unscientific' value judgements. At a critical
historical period, this emphasis on the technician role made the economics
profession more sympathetic than it might otherwise have been to the spread
of state intervention which prefaced the Keynesian social democratic state.

The failure to analyse the operation of the state constituted a weak link in
the economic justification of the public sector, a ready target for the later
revival of support for the free market and the minimal state. Buchanan (1962)
made the well-founded criticism that Paretian welfare economics is an 'open
system' which examines markets and their failures but treats state action as
exogenous. In a properly defined 'closed system', state action is itself
endogenous, to be subjected to a parallel analysis to that of the market,

hereby exposing its causes and weaknesses. Before firm conclusions can be drawn about the appropriate economic role of the state, either in general or in particular contexts, the costs of market failure must be weighed against those of state failure resulting from 'remedial' intervention.

Over the past twenty years, however, there has developed a new body of economic literature, designed to probe this logical jump by analysing the interrelationships between economics and politics. Under the general label of public choice theory' can be found highly disparate writings, held together by a common desire to apply analytical economic techniques but distinguished by sharply divergent philosophical positions. This is brought out most starkly by comparing the version of public choice theory associated with the Virginia Polytechnic Institute, with the version associated with Kenneth Boulding. Whereas the former is strongly free market and hostile to the Keynesian social democratic state, almost the reverse is true of the latter. But it is the Virginian version which has become influential, providing telling criticisms of the public sector which supplement the critique based on monetarism and traditional free-market economics. Ever alert, the IEA has published both Virginian authors (James Buchanan, Gordon Tullock and Richard Wagner) and their British adaptors (John Burton, Stephen Littlechild and Charles Rowley). However, much of this literature fails to heed Buchanan's own warning that the advantages and failings of both the market and the state must be simultaneously weighed: a state characterized by budget-maximizing bureaucrats and vote-seeking politicians is contrasted with an idealized version of the market.

Although the discovery that the state and democratic political processes contain their own defects would surprise neither political scientists nor practitioners, it has contributed towards the shift in the centre of gravity of the economics profession, with a renewed distrust of the state enhancing the appeal of market solutions. But the ideological overtones of some strands of the public choice literature provide no reason for rejecting either the subject matter or the general approach. Indeed, on closer examination, the scope for divergent policy conclusions becomes apparent, as evidenced by the dispute, considered below, about whether or not the public budget is automatically too large in a democracy. Taking a broad view of what constitutes 'state failure', it is useful to distinguish four types. Each of them is briefly explained in a parallel manner to the earlier treatment of market failure.

The failure of collective choice mechanisms

The market and politics are alternative mechanisms for aggregating preferences, the former relying upon the information communicated by individual decisions in the market-place and the latter, in a democratic country, by the casting of votes. Whereas 'votes' in the market are unequally distributed, the presumption of strict equality now usually guides the distribution of votes in the political system. For any given distribution of 'votes' and preferences, the market will generate a unique result, working through its inbuilt aggregation system. In contrast, all collective choice mechanisms such as voting suffer from severe aggregation problems, in the sense that the outcome will be determined at least in part by the choice of one from the many available alternative aggregation rules. For example, the outcome is sensitive to both the voting system (for example first-past-the-post versus proportional representation) and the sequence in which alternative options are taken.

Ever since Arrow's (1951) seminal contribution on collective choice, formidable mathematical elegance has been devoted towards unravelling the problems he revealed. His impossibility theorem stated that it is impossible to aggregate individual preference orderings into a consistent social ordering which meets certain (apparently) minimal conditions: namely, that social orderings should respond positively to individual orderings; should not be imposed upon society by a single individual; should be able to rank all possible states; and that the social ordering of two alternative states is independent of the ordering of irrelevant alternatives.[8]

The end result of such efforts has been to emphasize the difficulties inherent in devising procedures through which public decisions may consistently and accurately reflect individual preferences. On an analytical level, it rules out the presumption of a 'social indifference map' with the neat and convenient properties of an individual's indifference map, thus removing a potentially powerful tool of analysis. Similarly, it means that a social welfare function, embodying distributional judgements, cannot be derived from individual preferences if Arrow's 'minimal' conditions have to be met. So, even if the public official is altruistic and wishes to maximize a social welfare function based on individual values, collective choice procedures will not provide either consistent or unambiguous results. On a philosophical level, such problems with collective choice mechanisms have provided those who stress the primacy of individual preferences with a further argument for maximizing the sphere of the market and minimizing that of the state.

The 'over-expanded' public sector

Quite apart from such difficulties with the concept of social welfare, there is no reason to presume that public officials, whether politicians or bureaucrats, would wish to maximize it. In place of the altruistic public official, implicit in the earlier policy prescriptions, are now to be found the vote-seeking politician and the budget-maximizing bureaucrat. The pioneering contribution to the economic theory of democracy was made by Downs (1957) who, viewing politicians as utility-maximizers contended that their utility functions contained other arguments such as ideology and chances of re-election as well as social welfare. In such models, the 'median-voter' played a pivotal role, with competing parties bidding for his support. Niskanen (1971, 1973) subsequently applied a similar economic methodology to the behaviour of bureaucrats, assigning budget size the role of dominant argument in their utility functions. Both these theoretical developments emphasized the existence of discretion within political rather than market systems of allocation. They identified two distinct sources of distortion: the first in the relationship between voter and politician and the second in that between politician and bureaucrat.

On the first, it is claimed that the benefits and costs of public expenditure are inaccurately perceived: there is a systematic and persistent fiscal illusion at work. Unfortunately, as with most arguments based upon such illusions, it is possible to argue the case either way, with the public sector being judged either 'too large' or 'too small', depending upon the precise form of that illusion. Buchanan and Tullock (1962) argued that the benefits of public expenditure are overestimated because much of it is designed to satisfy interest groups which are politically mobilized to promote particular items. There is no similar mobilization of taxpayers as a result of the tax burden being more evenly spread. In opposition, Downs himself (1960), whilst accepting that certain items may be over-expanded through that mechanism, contended that the overall result is that the budget is too small because the benefits of much public expenditure are diffuse and not appropriable by individuals whereas tax shares are keenly felt. Similarly, Galbraith's (1958) aphorism of 'private affluence and public squalor' claimed that public expenditure was undervalued.

Neither version is capable of being subjected to systematic empirical testing because of the problem of measuring benefits and costs. Although it is the former which now commands the stage, discrimination between them must rest heavily upon the exercise of judgement. But there are reasons for treating such theories with caution. Given economists' customary emphasis upon individual rationality, scepticism seems to be in order when appeal is made to systematic and persistent errors in perceiving benefits and costs. If clear-headed and rational *qua* consumer, it seems odd if the individual *qua* voter is consistently deceived. Furthermore, it is not clear in what direction the chance of re-election or the ideological preference variables would bias the relative shares. The chance of re-election variable might be expected to depend upon the prevailing public mood towards the public sector and the taxation system, very different in the 1980s from the 1960s.

The second source of distortion stems from the fact that the politician cannot directly carry out the business of government but relies for its execution upon the bureaucracy. This term, which is used both descriptively and pejoratively, refers to the permanent administrative machinery of the state. Niskanen's application of economic methodology to bureaucratic decision-making has been influential. The politician and bureaucrat have a relationship best viewed as one of bilateral monopoly: the politician is the sole supplier of funds to the bureau (department or agency) and the bureau is the sole provider of the output which the politician values. By definition, the output of the bureau is non-marketed, whether as a result of its technical public good properties or of a prior political decision.

The absence of a market valuation of output makes the politician's task of monitoring exceptionally difficult: how can he assess the level of security provided by the existing defence budget or the efficiency with which it is managed? Niskanen assumed that, unlike the bureaucrat, the politician does not know the cost function and must infer output levels from the bureau's level of activity, as measured by its physical inputs and its total budget. Given the discretion provided by this environment, Niskanen (1971, p. 38) considered what objectives might be pursued by the bureaucrat:

> Among the several variables that may enter the bureaucrat's utility function are the following: salary, perquisites of the office, public reputation, power, patronage, output of the bureau, ease of making changes, and ease of managing the bureau. All of these variables except the last two, I contend, are a positive monotonic function[9] of the total *budget* of the bureau during the bureaucrat's tenure in office.

In his formal model, however, he assumed that a bureau will seek to maximize its budget subject to the constraint that its budget covers the costs of production. This compression of the utility function into a simple budget-maximizing mould is clearly a crucial step, justified by Niskanen on the contention that all except the last two cited objectives are positively related to budget size.

A simplified version of Niskanen's model is represented in Figure 5.6. The perceived output of the bureau (Q) is measured along the horizontal axis and marginal benefit (MB) and marginal cost (MC) on the vertical axis. If the bureau were to seek to maximize social welfare, it would choose that level of output at which the marginal benefit of an extra unit of output equalled its marginal cost: this Pareto-efficient output level is indicated by $0Q_0$, given by the intersection of the marginal benefit and marginal cost curves. However, the bureaucrat is a budget-maximizer, constrained only by the politician's willingness to supply funds. The area of the triangle E, defined by the marginal benefit and marginal cost curves, measures the consumer surplus accruing from the production of $0Q_0$ units. But the politician, lacking information on these marginal curves, will be willing to supply funds provided that total benefit equals total cost. Consequently, the bureau is able to expand output further, up to $0Q_1$ at which output the area of triangle F, denoting the excess of costs over benefits for this additional output, is equal to the area of triangle E. The bureau is thus able to expropriate the consumer surplus on intramarginal units, using this to facilitate output expansion beyond the Pareto-efficient level. Although refinements can be added to Niskanen's basic model, this diagrammatic representation captures the essential ideas (for a fuller discussion, see Jackson (1982)).

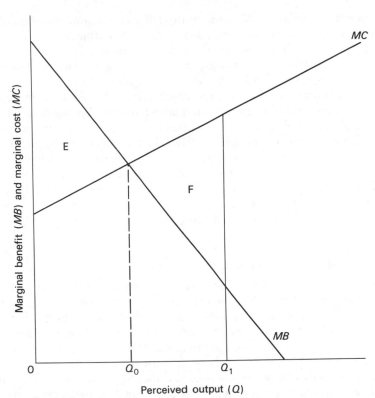

Figure 5.6 Niskanen's model of budget over-expansion

Generalizing Niskanen's result of excessive output from the individual bureau to the public non-market sector as a whole lends support to the hypothesis that the public budget will be too large. Given his assumptions, however, this result is hardly surprising. Instead of bureaucrats being viewed as entirely altruistic (maximize social welfare), they are now seen as entirely selfish (maximize budgets subject to a funding constraint). Furthermore, the external constraints are represented as being extremely weak, stemming from the absence of output measures, in contrast to the market disciplines exerted over the private sector.

As with theories of over-expansion through political rather than bureaucratic distortion, Niskanen's model is difficult to test in a rigorous way as this in turn requires output measures, so that marginal benefit can be set against marginal cost. Attention is thus directed back towards the logical structure of the model and its behavioural assumptions. It starts from a clearly unfavourable view of the public sector, relying upon an assumption about bureaucratic motivation which is as implausible as the assumption of pure altruism: no regard for the public interest is allowed to intrude. But it should be noted that any degree of self-interest will, in the context of severe monitoring difficulties, mean deviations from the optimal level and mix of output.

More fundamentally, however, the external constraints upon the public non-market sector are not just economic but ideological. How tightly these ideological constraints bind will vary both through time and from programme to programme. In a society characterized by markets, individual property ownership and economic inequality, non-market methods of allocation are always likely to offend powerful interests, especially when there is a redistributive element. Though much weakened during the ascendancy of the Keynesian social democratic state, the ideology of the market has revived, intensifying the constraints on funding the non-market sector. Although Niskanen's model provides valuable insights as to how particular bureaucracies may work if subjected to weak external constraints, it is more convincing as a model of distorted composition than of excess public sector output.

The rising real unit cost of public sector output

The growth of public expenditure has reflected not just more extensive provision of public services but also their rising real unit cost. This latter trend is widely acknowledged to have occurred, though precise quantification faces the familiar difficulty that there are no satisfactory output measures. For example, the procedure adopted in the national income accounts is to value public services simply on the basis of the cost of the factor inputs. Such a procedure not only disregards many of the alleged problems of state failure ('public services are worth less than their cost') but also assumes that there is zero productivity growth ('higher output comes only from more inputs'). Accounting conventions should never be confused with statements about economic reality.

There are two polar explanations of the tendency for the real unit cost of public sector output to increase through time (often described as the 'relative price effect'). Although it is possible to adopt an eclectic position, believing that both processes are at work, it is useful at this stage of the analysis to differentiate them sharply. Their implications for the future of public expenditure are so dramatically different: the first encourages an acceptance of steadily rising public expenditure/GDP ratios as an inevitable facet of an industrialized society but the second leads to proposals for the vigorous privatization of public sector activities. On the second view, but not on the first, the relative price effect is a dimension of state failure.

'*Baumol's disease*'. Baumol (1967) attributed the fiscal crisis of urban local authorities to the technological structure of the public services which they provide. Although conceding that reality would be more a spectrum rather than a simple dichotomy, he argued that a distinction should be drawn between two types of economic activity:

(1) Technologically *progressive* activities in which economies of scale, capital accumulation and innovation result in cumulative increases in output per man.

(2) Technologically *non-progressive* activities in which none of this is possible.

It should be noted that these terms, despite their ring, are not being used in an evaluative sense. The distinction between the two types of activity relates to their technology, not to differences in X-efficiency. As real living standards rise, the real unit costs of activities in the non-progressive sector will increase relative to those in the progressive sector. Both sectors have to compete for labour in the same market and the non-progressive sector will also face trade union pressure to maintain 'comparability' with the progressive sector. Baumol assigned manufacturing to the progressive sector, and most public services, and some private ones, to the non-progressive sector.

The urban fiscal crisis was attributed by Baumol (1967, pp. 423–4) to a paradox: the 'explosion in external costs' demanded state intervention to improve resource allocation and income distribution but the provision of public services would become ever more expensive because of this problem of 'unbalanced growth' (Baumol and Oates, 1979). This condition has become known as 'Baumol's disease', with the sufferers being identified as the 'personal services' in which: '. . . there is frequently an intimate connection between the quantity of labour used in supplying them and the quality of the end product' (Baumol and Oates, 1975, p. 242). Many of the polar examples of activities in the non-progressive sector which have been cited in the literature come from the performing arts. Despite the massive improvements in labour productivity in the manufacturing sector in the period since their first performances, there are still as many parts in an Ibsen play (Peacock, 1969) or a Schubert trio (Baumol and Oates, 1972). Reducing the amount of labour input may not be possible in certain activities without simultaneously reducing the quality of output. If the public sector were characterized by non-progressive activities to a much greater extent than the private sector, a steady increase in the relative cost of its activities would be predicted. Baumol (1967, p. 415) vigorously emphasized that this process could not be resisted. Inherent in the technological structure of non-progressive activities are:

> . . . forces working almost unavoidably for progressive and cumulative increases in the real costs incurred in supplying them. As a consequence, efforts to offset these cost increases, while they may succeed temporarily, in the long run are merely palliatives which can have no significant effect on the underlying trends.

If Baumol's model has any validity, there are profound implications for both the planning and control of public expenditure and for the conduct of public sector industrial relations (see Chapters 8 and 9).

'The absence of incentives for X-efficiency'. The second explanation attributes the relative price effect to X-inefficiency in the public sector: not only is it higher than in the private sector but this differential also grows through time. For example, Peacock (1980, p. 43) stated:

> I have strong doubts about the soundness of the argument that the barriers to productivity growth in public sector activities lie in technology of public service output. I believe these barriers to be institutional.

Similarly, Niskanen contended that public sector production is more X-inefficient than that of the private sector due to the absence of appropriate internal incentives. With the profit motive gone, there is no residual claimant who can appropriate the savings from higher X-efficiency. When Leibenstein developed that concept, he did so primarily with reference to the private sector. However, among the economic contexts in which X-inefficiency might be expected to emerge, he cited the following example:

> ... Low pressure on firms may exist because of considerable inability on the part of buyers of the services to understand the nature of the product. For example, this may be true of hospital services, or certain types of government-operated services (1975, p. 604).

Neither the private nor the public sectors have inbuilt mechanisms which guarantee efficiency in the Paretian sense: both are imperfect. However, Leibenstein (for example, 1973) has consistently and forcefully stressed the role of competition, both actual and potential, in containing X-inefficiency. The public non-market sector is much less exposed to competition than the private sector. For organizations within it, the possibility of institutional death is more remote. The question therefore arises as to whether other mechanisms, such as external scrutiny, budgetary stress or simply commitment to service objectives, are capable of taking the place of competition as constraints upon X-inefficiency. But his examples above are more directed towards the consumer's problems of comprehension and monitoring, less at whether production is public or private, monopolistic or competitive. It should be remembered that these are three separate questions, distinctions to which attention will return.

Figure 5.6 illustrated only part of Niskanen's critique of public sector waste: the allocative inefficiency stemming from excessive output. In the exposition above, MC was interpreted as the minimum attainable marginal cost curve. Niskanen would interpret it as the marginal cost curve under public production, assumed to lie above the marginal cost curve if production were private. More extensive X-inefficiency is thus piled upon allocative inefficiency. But just as budget maximization was asserted not proved, so with the inferiority of public production. The theoretical mechanisms, and any evidence in their support, is therefore a matter of vital importance.

Wolf (1979) identified four problems likely to be associated with the activities of non-market organizations, a category extending beyond the state to embrace organizations such as foundations, churches and voluntary bodies which receive all or part of their revenue other than from the proceeds of marketed output. Three of his four types of non-market failure could be viewed as sources of X-inefficiency. Wolf's choice of terminology deliberately paralleled that which is already familiar from the analysis of market failure:

1) *Internalities and private goals*: the monitoring of goals has been removed from the discipline of the market and now depends heavily upon the self-discipline of those running the organization. Goals other than maximizing the cost effectiveness of the organization may be chosen: for example, pioneering technical advance even where economically unviable.

2) *Redundant and rising costs*: where output is difficult to define and measure, the monitoring of costs may be defective with the result that there are both redundant costs and a tendency for real costs to increase over time.

3) *Derived externalities*: public policies have unpredicted side effects which frequently impose additional costs on both public and private organizations, with the result that new programmes may sometimes be introduced to rectify the damage done by existing ones.

His fourth case, *distributional inequity*, draws attention to the fact that the requirements of equity, in the spheres of both power and economic welfare, can be breached by non-market as well as by market mechanisms. But that is a topic which falls conveniently into Chapter 6.

If private is more X-efficient than public, a clear policy direction is defined. Most authors commenting upon this issue judge that this is indeed the case (Niskanen, 1971; the various contributors in Borcherding, 1977; Mueller, 1979; Wolf, 1979; Peacock, 1980). For example, Niskanen's policy proposals have included the privatization of entire functions or at least of production through the use of tendering and of contracting; the establishment of overlapping bureaux in order to create competition for funds; and the design of personal financial incentives for bureaucrats, such as allowing the retention of a proportion of cost savings. The common theme running through such proposals is the creation of greater competition, real or simulated.

The relative performance of public and private organizations is a subject characterized by strong assertion and little systematic evidence. Given the formidable methodological problems involved in devising appropriate tests and the obvious ideological import, it is perhaps unsurprising that there are disputes about relative efficiency. But there is a disturbing tendency, even in articles making constructive analytical contributions, to fall back on a kind of casual empiricism long since discredited as a form of economic evidence. It is possible to cite 'horror stories' about any organization but exceptionally difficult to assess either their accuracy or significance, never more so than when they relate to the state.

With such warnings, the question of the relative efficiency of public and private sector production will be set on one side, pending the discussion in Part Three of those characteristics of public sector activities which stand in the way of systematic answers. The judgement which is struck between the two explanations of the relative price effect (Baumol's disease versus growing X-inefficiency) is of critical importance, not least for practical decisions. For example, increases in the relative cost of education may be due either to its inherently non-progressive character or to the resistance of management and unions to new technologies. Arguments about the need to maintain small class sizes because of a postulated link with quality might simply be a sophisticated cover for resisting the introduction of techniques such as televised lectures and computerized learning which would threaten both budgets and jobs. Rising relative costs may therefore be a result of the nature of the activity, growing X-inefficiency or some combination of both.

The political business cycle

The pursuit of self-interest by politicians is alleged to destabilize the macroeconomy, generating political business cycles synchronized to the election cycle. The quest for electoral success encourages politicians to 'buy' votes by manipulating the economy so that in the immediate pre election period there is a combination of politically popular features, such as low unemployment and high growth, even though this is unsustainable as it has been purchased at the expense of higher inflation after the election. Given the assumed myopia of the electorate, which focuses only upon the government's recent record, this is a viable electoral strategy as the consequential unpalatable measures will have been forgotten by the time of the next election. Such models have been taken to provide reinforcement for the view that the instability of modern economies stems from the public sector, rather than from the private sector.[10]

VII CONCLUSION

The problem of state failure has been established as an analogue to that of market failure. Decisions about the respective roles of the market and the state will in part hinge upon judgements made about the relative importance of market failure and of state failure. However, efficiency is not the sole value and the choice between the market and the state as the allocative mechanism in a particular context may have different implications for the realization of other values, such as freedom and equality. But there is a tendency for judgements to cluster: those who rate the market highly in terms of efficiency tend to regard it as the vehicle of freedom, treating the claims of equality relatively lightly. If state failure is judged the greater threat, the arguments in favour of the minimal state are thereby strengthened. When reliance on the state is unavoidable, organizational models combining public financing with private production are likely to be preferred. Alternatively, a conclusion in favour of an extensive state could be argued in terms of the pre-eminence of market failure or of the overriding claims of equality, or both. Even from this perspective, action by the state should be preceded by an assessment of the consequences. Furthermore, the state must develop mechanisms of its own which will perform for the non-market public sector those functions which are performed by the market for the private sector.

Efficiency emerges as a much more complex concept than is initially apparent: the distinction between allocative efficiency and X-efficiency is crucial. The presumption that the market system is efficient in both senses depends upon a much stricter set of assumptions than is often acknowledged. There are strong, if often implicit, value judgements underlying such conceptions of efficiency. Within the Paretian tradition, emphasis has been placed upon the development of the theory of market failure which has stressed the concepts of externalities and public goods. The emergent theory of state failure stresses that the existence of market failure is not a sufficient condition for state intervention: the possibility that it might worsen, rather than improve, the allocation of resources has to be considered. In other words, the problem of state failure has to be set against the problem of market failure. It will be clear from the discussion in this wide-ranging chapter that there is no consensus about their relative importance. Here, the concern has been with the efficiency case for and against the economic activities of the state. However, the growth of such activities has also been justified with appeal to another value often believed to be in conflict with efficiency. It is to the claims of equality that attention is now turned.

CHAPTER 6

Equality

I INTRODUCTION

The idea of equality, often advocated in the name of social justice, has played a crucial role in stimulating the development of the welfare state, thereby sanctioning the consequent growth of public expenditure. Advocates of the welfare state have argued that the patterns of social and economic inequality generated by the interaction of unequal starting positions and the process of market exchange, unjustly limit the life chances of certain individuals and classes. Their remedy is to use the power of the state to mitigate these inequalities, relying upon a complex web of policies and institutions. Whatever the precise form they take, the state acquires an extensive, often pervasive role in economic and social life. The establishment of the welfare state thus raises a number of interconnected philosophical and policy issues: for example, the claims of equality to be a moral justification for altering the market-determined pattern of rewards; the wider implications of such an extended role for the state; and the extent to which the establishment of the welfare state has actually reduced inequality.

In face of the formidable difficulties confronting attempts to provide complete answers to such questions, this chapter adopts the limited objectives of assessing the contribution made by the idea of equality to public expenditure growth and of reviewing the extent to which the welfare state has in fact satisfied the egalitarian hopes pinned upon it. It would therefore be straying beyond the concerns of this chapter to become involved in a detailed discussion of either the libertarian theory of justice (Nozick, 1974) or of the liberal theory of justice (Rawls, 1972). However, these constructions should be interpreted as attempts by their respective authors to provide both procedural and substantive answers to profound philosophical questions concerning the relationships between individual, market and state. The voluminous debates generated by the publication of their two books are an indication of how the questions posed, if not always the frameworks and solutions, have struck chords, even amongst those such as economists who often treat such ultimate questions with disdain.

The process of market exchange produces a distribution of welfare which is contingent upon, *inter alia,* the initial definition of property rights. Market

120

processes lead to a distribution of welfare which is unlikely to satisfy any patterned principle of justice. Such a patterned principle of justice is one which enables judgements to be made about particular distributions. Libertarian philosophers such as Robert Nozick strongly deny the validity of any patterned principle. He argued that what matters is justice in acquisition: individuals have acquired their present holdings through the working of institutions and processes which conform to principles of justice. Any attempt by the state to implement patterned principles immediately comes into conflict with individual freedom. The only defensible principle of justice is held to be justice in acquisition, not justice in distribution. Moreover, Nozick held that a free-market economy, operating in the context of a well-defined system of property rights, will satisfy the necessary conditions for justice in acquisition.

Whereas rectification of earlier injustices, both of acquisition and transfer, are judged permissible, Nozick (1974, p. 169) indicted policies of redistribution for violating the rights of individuals, claiming that: 'Taxation of earnings from labor is on par with forced labor.' He grounded his defence of private property in natural right, not in utilitarian arguments relating to efficiency (Becker, 1977). He accorded the right to property priority over the right to life and self-preservation, claiming descent for his theory of property from Locke (1690). However, Locke's justification of property in the context of an exchange economy was based upon utility and consent, rather than upon a labour theory of property acquisition which established natural rights to that property (Drury, 1982). Locke cannot properly be cited in support of Nozick's view that redistributive policies are inherently illegitimate, a position forming part of the latter's rejection of anything beyond the minimal state.

Nevertheless, Nozick's book raises an issue worthy of much greater attention than it usually receives from those who favour systematic policies of redistribution. One of the difficulties of applying any principle of justice in distribution is that factors, goods, income and wealth do not exist independently but are already 'attached' to defined individuals in the sense that they have existing property rights over them. Consequently, attempts to redistribute them involve the infringement or attenuation of the property rights of these existing holders. For Nozick, this argument is decisive as he refused to allow any trade-off of individual property rights against a wider public interest. Although market liberals appeal to such libertarian arguments in their defence of the market-determined distribution of rewards against modification by the state, they are typically unwilling to press the logic as far as Nozick. Yet Milton Friedman's advocacy of a state-provided safety net in the form of negative income tax should, on this view, be judged just as illegitimate as a comprehensive welfare state (for discussions on this point, see Jones (1982) and Sugden (1982)). The force of Nozick's argument stems from its absolute prohibition. Once that is breached, his libertarian concerns are unlikely to prove decisive when the question becomes one of degree.

Policies of redistribution undertaken in the name of equality must confront three questions:

(1)   Are patterned principles of justice legitimate?
(2)   If so, what should these patterned principles be?
(3)   What types of state intervention in the economy are required to establish and then sustain such patterns?

Clearly, the pursuit of distribution according to need in the context of a market economy will require extensive and continuous intervention to restore the desired distribution or to limit deviations from it. Attention to such questions brings the realization that equality often seems a vague and contradictory idea, more conducive to applause or denunciation than helpful as a guide to practical policy. A major purpose of this chapter is to assess whether any precise meaning can be attached to it, a task undertaken in conjunction with a review of the claims made for equality as a value requiring that the state should in certain areas overrule the market. Although the terms 'equity' and 'social justice' are often used interchangeably, equality should be recognized to be a different concept. It constitutes just one answer to what social and economic arrangements and outcomes are to be considered equitable or just. An equal outcome is not necessarily a just outcome, even leaving aside the problem of defining equal in such contexts. Rights, desert and needs might each be considered as principles of social justice (Miller 1976). Although this chapter will concentrate upon the claims and signifi cance of equality, it is appropriate to begin the analysis by focusing upon the wider issue of the relationship between equity and efficiency.

II   THE RELATIONSHIP BETWEEN EQUITY AND EFFICIENCY

Public policies designed to reduce inequality will have implications for the efficiency of the market economy. These effects are complex, partly because of the way in which the concept of efficiency is itself formulated. A commitment to reduce inequality represents a specific equity objective. It will help the subsequent discussion of policy if the relationship between efficiency and equity is first explored in a formal manner. The equity principle is left unspecified, other than that it embodies judgements about distribution rather than merely about the processes through which distribution is settled.

It is possible for different allocations of resources all to be Pareto optimal what differentiates them is that they correspond to different distributions of welfare between individuals. Pareto optimality is an efficiency concept and provides no mechanism for judging between such distributions. An economy characterized by extreme inequality (for example rich landowners and poverty-stricken peasants) may be Pareto optimal. This is simply a technical condition: it is not possible by any reallocation of goods and factors to make one person better off without making at least one other person worse off. The Pareto criterion does not sanction making the poor better off, however large his potential gain, if this also means making one rich person worse off. It takes its reference point as the status quo. Therefore the implications of the Pareto principle for distribution depend upon the starting point which itself might be characterized by extreme or limited inequality.

This separation of questions of efficiency from those of equity has profound analytical implications. Economists have often succumbed to the temptation of assuming that distribution is ideal, pursuing the more tractable efficiency questions but never then returning to relax this assumption. Equity questions have often been neglected or treated in a casual, *ad hoc* manner. Economics has never possessed a concept of equity capable of ranking allocations of resources in a similar way to that in which the Pareto criterion can rank allocations of resources in terms of efficiency. When the neoclassical revolution in welfare economics banned interpersonal comparisons of utility, it made the concept of equity much more difficult to handle.

The use of the Pareto criterion of efficiency to sanction or to disallow certain reallocations of goods between individuals makes it clear that there are two separate distributional issues:

(1) The initial distribution of factor endowments which constitutes the starting point from which exchanges take place.
(2) The distribution of gains from exchange.

The Pareto criterion takes the first as given exogenously and treats the second as a matter of indifference. The fourth assumption on page 86 implies that the increase in social welfare is independent of the distribution of gains. The moves which are sanctioned are those which reallocate goods in such a way so as to make at least one person better off and no one else worse off. Whenever the necessary conditions for efficient allocation are breached, these opportunities will exist. Such an efficiency criterion is blind to the identity of the gainers. All it insists upon is that there are no losers, defined in absolute terms. This clearly involves the assumption that gains to the rich are as 'socially valuable' as gains to the poor. It also places the focus upon absolute levels of welfare and not on relative positions.

Adopting this value judgement is sometimes described as being 'neutral' about distribution. This claim is only valid if neutral is understood in the very narrow sense of presuming that distributional questions are of no significance or that there is no legitimate mechanism for making the necessary interpersonal comparisons. Economists are understandably uncomfortable about the source and ethical base of explicit income weights which are purported to make comparable the gains and losses of different income groups. Nevertheless, the strength of the value judgement involved in the assumption tha everyone's income is equally valuable (that is implicit weights of unity fo everyone) should itself be recognized.[1]

Valuable insights into the relationship between equity and efficiency can be derived by combining the Pareto criterion with a social welfare function. A social welfare function embodies a judgement about distribution: each of its successive contours identifies distributions yielding equal aggregate welfare The formal analysis is contained in the Appendix and the results summarized here.

The Pareto criterion is concerned with securing an efficient allocation of resources and very different allocations might all satisfy the necessary technical conditions. Each of these allocations will correspond to different distributions of welfare between individuals. If distribution is an issue, a social welfare function is required in order to supplement the Pareto criterion. Despite an extensive literature, there is no satisfactory solution as to the mechanisms for deriving such a social welfare function, should it be required to be derived from the preferences of individuals rather than externally imposed. The social welfare function used for expositional purposes in Figure 6.2 in the Appendix demonstrates that, if there is a judgement in favour of more equal rather than less equal distributions, some inefficient allocations might be ranked more highly than some efficient ones.

The typical focus of economic analysis upon efficiency to the neglect of equity has one defence. It is valid if it is possible to have lump-sum transfers of utility. This hypothetical tool justifies reaching the utility frontier (see Figure 6.2) at any point because it is subsequently possible to move along it. If lump-sum transfers are feasible, equity can therefore be separated from efficiency. Although this is an appealing story, the reality of taxes and transfers is much more bleak. All instruments of tax/transfer policy do break some of the efficiency conditions for Pareto optimality, particularly those concerned with the work/leisure choice. Unfortunately, efficiency and equity cannot be so easily disentangled.

III THE MEANING OF EQUALITY

Equality is a much more complex and elusive concept than either its advocates or detractors usually acknowledge. Exactly what is understood by the term is crucially relevant to its implications for the scale and composition of public expenditure. There are many alternative formulations of equality, some of which are mutually consistent and some not. Its influence over the development of the welfare state has been as an ideal, not as a numerically achievable objective.

Given the frequent presumption that equality and freedom must necessarily conflict in all circumstances, it is worth stressing that the idea of equality played an influential role in the development of liberalism, both as a political movement and as an intellectual tradition (Berlin, 1956; Wollheim, 1956). Berlin maintained that the 'irreducible minimum of the ideal of equality' is that: 'Every man to count for one and no one to count for more than one' (p. 301). Furthermore he claimed: 'The assumption is that equality needs no reasons, only inequality does so' (p. 305). This means that all human beings: '. . . should in every respect be treated in a uniform and identical manner, *unless there is sufficient reason not to do so*' (pp. 302–3; italics added). The critical step is obviously establishing what constitutes 'sufficient reason', distinguishing good from bad, relevant from irrelevant. For example, t might be judged that efficiency is, but birth is not, a sufficient reason for a particular inequality. This example is Berlin's but his judgement of 'sufficient reason' could be challenged by someone holding different values.

Berlin distinguished two conceptions of equality which, although these are not his terms, can be understood as procedural equality and substantive equality. Procedural equality involves the application of 'rules' (whether moral principles, laws or rules of a game) which impose a measure of equality n the sense that the rule should be applied to all affected parties. It is a readily understandable complaint that too many exceptions are being made without specific rules to back them: this is a plea for procedural equality. If the logic of substantive equality is pursued to the limit, it would mean the imposition of complete uniformity, necessarily enforced by 'a highly centralized and despotic authority' (p. 314). This fear, characteristic of liberals, made Berlin emphasize that: 'equality is one value among many' (p. 319).

This idea of equality is both complex and beset by internal contradictions, manifest in both academic reflection and political argument. It is thus necessary to analyse its structural characteristics in order to clarify its meaning. Accordingly, Rae (1981) devised a 'grammar of equality', distinguishing five dimensions: (a) the subject of equality; (b) the domain of equality; (c) the value of equality; (d) the problem of indivisibilities; and (e) the measurement of equality. Each of these dimensions will now be examined n turn and will subsequently help to structure the substantive discussion.

The subject of equality

Subjects of equality can be of two main types: (a) individual-regarding; or (b) block-regarding. Under (a), equality is required between individual subjects. However, there is a crucial distinction within (a) between (a, i) simple subjects (equality is required between all subjects in the subject class) and (a, ii) segmental subjects (having sub-divided the subjects of equality into two or more mutually exclusive sub-classes, equality is required within sub-classes but not between). Under (b), the subjects of equality are first divided into two or more mutually exclusive sub-classes and then equality is required between sub-classes but not within.

The following examples are helpful in illustrating these distinctions: (a, i) universal suffrage; (a, ii) the provision of public services in which entitlement is defined by age, family or employment status; and (b) 'equal but separate' facilities for different races or sexes or equal median incomes for males and females. Such examples highlight the importance of how broadly the class of equals is defined: inclusionary and exclusionary means broad and narrow classes of equals respectively. By adopting a sufficiently exclusionary definition, all manner of systematic inequalities can be represented as equalities, for example, equality between white Protestant males. Furthermore, the achievement of inclusionary equalities requires the centralization of the relevant power. The social classifications which can be used to define blocks or segments are innumerable: for example, race, sex, age, location, or native tongue. The achievement of block-regarding equality (for example equal median incomes for males and females) does not mean that individuals, whether male or female, have equal incomes. Equalities often conflict.

The domain of equality

The domain of equality refers to the classes of objects which are to be allocated equally. Analysis of the domain raises three issues: (a) whether the domain is broad or narrow; (b) whether the domain is 'straightforward' or not; and (c) if not 'straightforward', whether equalities are marginal or global.

On (a), the domain can be defined either broadly or narrowly. It can be limited to formal political and legal equality or extended into the economic and social sphere. The definition of the domain is crucial to debates about the role of public expenditure: it is an issue which will be raised in Section IV of this chapter.

On (b), the meaning of 'straightforward' in this context must be explained. The domain of allocation is the class of objects which a given agent X presently controls for the purposes of allocation. The domain of account is the class of objects over which another agent Y seeks equality. The domain is straightforward if X's domain of allocation covers Y's domain of account: X could make an equal allocation over the full domain of Y's account. If this condition does not hold or if some objects in the domain of account, but outside the domain of allocation, are unequally divided, straightforward equality is not attainable.

On (c), the fact that the domains are not straightforward leads to a distinction between marginal equalities and global equalities. In the first case, the objects in the domain of allocation are equally divided but there are not equal outcomes because of the lack of correspondence between the two domains. Global equalities result in equalization of the domain of account by one of two methods. Compensatory inequality is the unequal division of a domain of allocation so as to offset other inequalities which lie outside this omain but inside a domain of account: it involves 'inequality in the name of quality' such as positive discrimination. The redistribution of domains restablishes the straightforward condition by either diminishing the domain of ccount or by enlarging the domain of allocation. Whereas the former nvolves a contraction of the equality objective, the latter constitutes a method of achieving it. For example, all existing wealth holdings might first e confiscated so that total wealth could subsequently be equally distributed.

The value of equality

The pursuit of equality has to be squared with the fact of human diversity. There are two distinct approaches: (a) lot-regarding equality; and (b) person-egarding equality. For (a) to be satisfied, each individual must place the same aluation on his own lot as on any other individual's lot. In most cases this vill mean making lots identical: for example, everyone has one vote or the ame housing. Under (b), each individual must place the same valuation on his own lot as all other individuals place on theirs. Lot-regarding equality is n insensitive equality rule as it ignores all variations in needs and prefernces. In contrast, person-regarding equality recognizes that such variations re relevant to a meaningful equal treatment. But, unlike (a), (b) requires nterpersonal comparisons of utility, themselves banished for economists by Pareto (1906) and Robbins (1938).

The problem of indivisibilities

Whereas goods are usually capable of physical division, other things which re valued, such as status and position, are not. However, equality is often udged relevant to the question of access to them. In such cases, a principle of qual opportunity is frequently cited. This can take two forms: (a) prospect-egarding equal opportunity; and (b) means-regarding equal opportunity. Under (a), individuals have equal opportunities for X if each has the same probability of attaining X. Nothing about the particular individual affects the esult: a lottery is a good example. Under (b), individuals have equal opportunities for X if each has the same instruments for attaining X. The ocus is upon equal rules and equipment, thus securing not equal prospects of uccess but legitimately unequal prospects of success. The decathlon and IQ ests are good examples.

If the relevant talents are unequally distributed, every policy of means-egarding equal opportunity must thus violate equal prospects and vice versa. But the choice of criteria with which to regulate this competition is not itself neutral. IQ tests may be culturally specific and inequalities in other domains may bias the result: for example, ill-fed athletes do not win decathlons. However, an attempt to secure prospect-regarding equal opportunity, whether through handicapping or quota systems, will breach means-regard-

Values

ing equal opportunity. The conflict is particularly acute in the case of block regarding equalities: quotas by race or sex discriminate against individual outside the 'compensated' group.

The measurement of equality

In any realistic society there cannot be a simple dichotomy between equalit and inequality: it is a matter of degree. The difficulty then arises of judgin which of two allocations is the more equal. Rae (1981) examined four separate but related, criteria of relative equality.

(1)   *The maximin criterion*: any allocation which improves the position o the least advantaged subject is more equal ('maximin' standing fo 'maximizing the minimum').
(2)   *The ratio criterion*: any allocation which increases the ratio between th lesser entitlement and the greater is more equal.
(3)   *The least difference criterion*: any allocation which reduces the absolut difference between the greater entitlement and the lesser is more equal
(4)   *The minimax criterion*: any allocation which diminishes the entitlemen of the more advantaged subject is more equal ('minimax' standing fo 'minimize the maximum').

Unless the object to be divided remains constant, these four criteria do no give identical answers as to the relative equality of alternative allocations. T the conceptual difficulties associated with equality are added severe mea surement problems confronting any statistical exercises.

IV   LIMITING THE DOMAIN OF INEQUALITY

The most established aspects of equality in democratic societies are to b found in the existence of equality before the law and of equality of forma political rights such as universal suffrage. Despite their profound significance these entail negligible direct public expenditure costs, thus providing a cogen reminder that governments possess resources other than money. However formal equality in the legal and political spheres may be less significant thar appears at first sight, if economic inequalities are so great as to prevent thes rights being fully exercised. In the twentieth century, there has been ar extension of concern to inequalities in economic and social conditions. Thi development owed much initially to philanthropists such as Seebohn Rowntree who, moved by the desperate poverty around them, collectec information and organized voluntary relief. Later, the state extended its rol in the alleviation of poverty, not only in response to the demands of ar industrializing economy and of preparations for war, but also to the clamou for social reform from working-class parties emerging alongside the extendec franchise.

Appeal has often been made to the idea of equality as a justification for such policies. Williams (1962) has distinguished three recurrent arguments in favour of equality. First, there is the appeal to common humanity, emphasizing the 'equality of men as men'. Despite manifold differences, human beings possess a number of common characteristics: for example, speaking a language; using tools; living in societies; possessing the capacity to feel pain and affection and engage in reflective thought; and feeling a desire for self-respect. It is the significance of these common characteristics which makes intelligible the claim that certain political and social arrangements may neglect the moral claims which arise from their possession. Second, it is argued that, despite the extensive differentiation of intellectual and physical abilities, men have equal moral capacities to pursue their own purposes. It is thus essential to look behind the professional, social or technical roles attaching to individuals and which assign unequal status, in order to consider their views and purposes as men. The significance of this step is enhanced by the extent to which the prevailing social arrangements themselves condition man's consciousness of his role in society: for example, 'the happy slave'. Third, the idea of equality is frequently cited in certain circumstances in which it is readily agreed that individuals are unequal. Certain goods have to be distributed, or more generally the conditions of access to them arranged. The question of what constitutes 'sufficient reason' for unequal treatment again arises. It is often contended that inequalities of need (for example, ill health) or of merit (for example, intellectual ability) are sufficient reasons for unequal consumption of medical care and higher education, respectively, whereas inequalities of birth or income are not.

Tawney (1931) was the most persuasive advocate of the 'strategy of equality', involving extensive state action designed to limit economic and social inequalities. He explicitly rejected the view that all that was required was the equal distribution of income and wealth.

It is not the division of the nation's income into eleven million fragments, to be distributed, without further ado, like cake at a school treat, among its eleven million families. It is, on the contrary, the pooling of its surplus resources by means of taxation, and the use of the funds thus obtained to make accessible to all, irrespective of their income, occupation, or social position, the conditions of civilization which, in the absence of such measures, can be enjoyed only by the rich.

It is possible for a society, experience suggests, by thus making the fullest possible provision for common needs, to abolish, if it pleases, the most crushing of the disabilities, and the most odious of the privileges, which drive a chasm across it (Tawney, 1964, p. 122).

Equality as conceived by Tawney in no sense requires the imposition of uniformity:

'. . . equality of provision is not identity of provision. It is to be achieved, not by treating different needs in the same way, but by devoting equal care to ensuring that they are met in the different ways most appropriate to them, as is done by a doctor, who prescribes different regimens for different constitutions, or a teacher who develops different types of intelligence by different curricula. The more anxiously, indeed, a society endeavours to secure equality of consideration for all its members, the greater will be the differentiation of treatment which, when once their common human needs have been met, it accords to the special needs of different groups and individuals among them (Tawney, 1964, pp. 49–50).

Tawney was clearly aware of the relevance of many of the distinction emphasized by Rae's grammar of equality: his advocacy of person-regarding equality has rarely been matched.

The strategy of equality would have to be implemented within the context of a market economy, albeit one modified by state intervention. There are two distinct sources of the extensive economic and social inequalities generated by such an economy. First, the distribution of welfare within even a perfectly functioning market economy depends upon the initial distribution of factor endowments (property rights). Individuals start with different stocks of land and capital (inheritance). Second, the operation of the market economy establishes a set of prices for factor services which depend, *inter alia*, upon factor availabilities, known techniques of production, and preferences. The distribution of income both between individuals and 'classes' of factor owner emerges from this myriad of separate decisions.

It is sometimes wrongly suggested that this emergent income distribution reflects desert. Although effort and prudence are relevant, so are many other factors. The very high earnings of some professional footballers reflect a high scarcity premium on certain abilities which may have no value in another society. A landowner may receive massive windfall gains because events elsewhere in the world suddenly make it economic to develop oil deposits under his ground. A desire to defend the income distribution emerging from the market against modification by the state can be argued in two ways: first, on the libertarian grounds that redistribution offends the principle of justice in acquisition; and, second, that the efficient functioning of a market economy requires that the rewards of factor suppliers are not attenuated. In turn, those who advocate patterned principles of justice which involve a commitment to reducing inequality must both argue the validity of patterned principles and counter the alleged impact on efficiency.

The historical evolution of the welfare state, made possible by massive increases in public expenditure, has reflected a commitment to reduce the social and economic inequalities resulting from the operation of the market economy. The welfare state has had two arms: the development of the extensive system of cash transfers; and the parallel growth of social expenditure on 'in-kind' programmes such as education and health. It has been recognized that inequality is deeply embedded in the social structure of modern societies. Inequalities in income and wealth are themselves socially sanctioned and resistant to redistributive policy. The transfer part of the welfare state has focused primarily upon the contingencies of the life cycle (for example support for children and old people) and upon those events such as ill health and unemployment which impair the individual's capacity to make market exchanges.

The second arm of the welfare state reflected a fairly wide consensus that there was an (imprecisely defined) set of goods to which access should not be determined solely by ability to pay. Redistributive policy has therefore focused upon establishing some measure of equal access to these goods, whilst not attempting to remove the underlying differences in ability to pay. Such a policy has been variously described as 'the strategy of equality' (Tawney, 1931) and as 'specific egalitarianism' (Tobin, 1970). It incorporates a rigid insistence on removing certain inequalities whilst adopting a more relaxed attitude to those income inequalities surviving the operation of the tax/transfer system. Its advocates stress that certain goods are fundamental to the life chances of individuals born into an unequal and socially stratified society.

There is an important logical contrast between policies designed to ensure a minimum standard provision for all and those designed to ensure equal standards. In practice, specific policies tend to have mixed objectives. Minimum standards can reduce inequality but will never produce equality. State old age pensions are a good example of the former in that supplementary private provision through both occupational schemes and private savings are themselves encouraged by tax expenditures. Individuals can therefore reallocate their lifetime consumption through time. There are other cases, however, where the objective of equal provision is at least attempted. One of the philosophical rationales of the NHS was that of equal access for equal need. Such an objective can only be achieved if there is public control, not only over the NHS, but also over the private health sector. If individuals can either opt out, or selectively opt in and out, the equal provision objective is defeated. It does not directly defeat the minimum standards objective though it may do so indirectly by altering the political climate towards public expenditure on health.

The equal provision objective much more explicitly limits the individual's ability to make alternative private arrangements. It is on such issues that the conflict between the strategy of equality and market freedoms is most acute. Both Tawney (1931) and Crosland (1956) emphasized the extent to which the existence of the private sector in education can be a powerful mechanism for transmitting inequalities through generations, whether through better provision or through the establishment of social networks. Thoroughgoing attempts to pursue the strategy of equality may therefore in particular case involve prohibitions on private market purchases.

Tobin (1970) has acknowledged that attempts to distribute certain rights privileges and duties to all members of society, independent of their income and wealth, generate conflicts with market freedoms and with efficiency Certain transactions are universally prohibited in democratic societies: fo example, the buying and selling of votes. He also cited the prohibition afte the American Civil War of the practice of wealthy parents buying substitute for their conscripted sons. In such cases, attempts to ensure an egalitaria distribution run into direct conflict with the economist's standard assump tion that voluntary exchange is beneficial to both parties. On the much broader issue of the scope for removing certain goods from the market, Tobir (1970, p. 274) quoted Simons (1948, p. 68):

> ... we may look forward confidently to continued augmenting of the 'free income' of the masses, in the form of commodities and services made available by government, either without charge or with consider- able modification of prevailing price controls. There are remarkable opportunities for extending the range of socialized consumption (medi- cal services, recreation, education, music, drama, etc.).

There is a remarkable contrast between this passage and the positions taker by later Chicago economists such as Milton Friedman.

V THE CHARGE OF PATERNALISM

Such a strategy of equality, underpinning as it does the rationale for the welfare state, has often been subjected to the charge of paternalism Deliberately rather than incidentally, it seems to breach the presumption that an individual is the best judge of his own welfare (assumption (3) on p. 86). The welfare state is thus condemned as damaging to both freedom and efficiency. Paternalism involves the substitution of some external judgement on a particular issue for the individual's own, with the intention being to benefit the individual.

The hold which assumption (3) (p. 86) has exerted over the economics profession is perhaps one reason why, in its literature, the charge of paternalism is usually considered decisive, eliminating the necessity for further analysis. Although philosophers and lawyers (for example: Feinberg. 1971; Dworkin, 1972; Carter 1977) have carefully analysed both the meaning of paternalism and the question of its justification, their own professional concerns have rather narrowed the fields of activity from which their examples are taken: for example, laws which enforce the wearing of safety helmets or belts; regulate sexual conduct, the use of drugs or alcohol; or restrict economic activity through health and safety legislation or profes-

ional licensing. What these examples have in common is that they all relate
to the regulatory rather than the service-providing or redistributive activities
of the state. Despite these different contexts, such discussions bring out very
clearly the difficulties facing an attempt to construct a general theory of when
paternalism might be justified. However strong their presumption against
paternalism might be, most authors operate in practice very much on a case-
by-case basis. For example, Feinberg commended publication of the hazards
of smoking, with 'no softening of the gory details' (p. 116); considered that
he 'state might even be justified' in using taxation to make smoking less
attractive; but deplored any outright ban. Whatever the merits of his policy
conclusions, each of these alternatives must be regarded as paternalist,
though the form and degree differ.

Most philosophical discussions of paternalism go back to John Stuart
Mill's distinction between 'self-regarding' and 'other-regarding' actions
Mill, 1859). He ruled out intervention, whether by other individuals or by
he state, in the case of self-regarding actions, defined as those which only
affected the 'interests' of that individual. However inadvisable a particular
action might appear to others, the individual is the best judge of his own
interests and should not be prevented from carrying out his own wishes.
Where 'other-regarding' actions damaged the interests of others, the pros and
cons of intervention must be considered, weighing heavily the infringement of
liberty this would involve. It has been argued that Mill's distinction simply
cannot hold: few non-trivial actions do not affect others. For example, X may
be distressed by Y's suicide, or offended by his sexual conduct, or feel his own
economic security threatened by Y's revolutionary views. Furthermore,
choices made by one individual in the market-place help to shape the
alternatives available to others, and good performance in any form of
competition, whether in examinations or sport, diminishes the chances of
others. Rees (1960) argued that this difficulty stems from Mill's failure to
sustain the distinction between 'affecting others' and 'affecting the interests
of others'. Social and economic interdependence mean that most actions
affect others' but 'affecting the interests of others' is a more stringent
condition, implying that the individual has a certain protected area in which
others have no standing. By only admitting the possibility of overruling the
individual's choices in cases of 'harm to others', Mill can readily be fitted into
the role of enemy of paternalism. Yet despite his profound distrust of the
state, his practical policy judgements were more complex. For example, he
enthusiastically supported compulsory education, to be partly state financed
but not state provided. This view prompted Acton (1972, p. xxiv) to observe:
'Legislation is not, and education is, the proper means for promoting
morality.' Mill also spelt out his view that the state would be justified in
preventing the marriage of people who could not demonstrate the means for
supporting a family: the resulting lives of 'wretchedness and depravity'
(p. 163) harmed both offspring and third parties.

The arguments which Mill used to reject paternalism were often used to counter the development of the welfare state. There are, however, the separate questions of whether the welfare state is paternalist, and, if so, what justifications might be advanced. At a fundamental level, it would be argued by Nozick that all continuous systems of redistribution are inherently paternalist. If the desired distribution of property rights were to be imposed prior to market exchange commencing, it would not survive that process. To re-impose the initial distribution is paternalist as it is thus limiting what can be done with property holdings, without stimulating a further round of redistribution. The opposing view would be that redistribution has to be continuous because the unequal distribution of natural endowments, and their relative scarcity, is morally arbitrary.

Weale (1978) has challenged the conventional view that redistribution in kind is necessarily more paternalist than redistribution in cash. The usual argument hinges around whether individuals or the state decide upon the way in which the money is spent. Although paternalist motives may be present there may be other reasons for adopting the in-kind form. Individual needs for medical care are both variable and unpredictable: enormous practical problems would accompany the design of a system of cash benefits intended to reflect differential need. Similarly, the prohibition on the sale of places in waiting lists can be defended on non-paternalist grounds (creation of deceptive practices) as well as paternalist ones (the patient's assessment of his medical condition might be seriously in error). In other cases, however, the paternalist intent will be explicit: clothes vouchers or direct payment of rent instead of cash. There is a further point not considered by Weale which is highly relevant. To the extent that cash benefits represent redistribution within an individual's life cycle, rather than between rich and poor or employed and unemployed, they are particularly open to the charge of paternalism, as also are compulsory contributions into private occupational pension schemes and the encouragement to certain forms of saving provided by tax expenditures.

The reasons for the undeniable paternalist streak in the welfare state should be made clear. By not challenging directly the underlying distribution of property rights and by thus retaining an albeit modified market economy, the welfare state is forced back on something like the strategy of equality. Simply by delineating which goods are to be removed from the market, judgements about the relative importance of specific opportunities and forms of consumption have to be made. Their source is from the judgements of individuals, but mediated through the political system rather than expressed directly in the market-place. There are important differences between the factors which are relevant to the forms of paternalism exhibited by public expenditure on welfare from those identified in cases of legal paternalism. Of the six categories identified by Hodson (1977), three are of no relevance: the emotional stress relevant to suicide; the undue influence of third parties; and

nental illness. The three categories relevant to such public expenditure are
gnorance, non-rationality and serious harm. Each of these has been argued
as relevant to the provision of medical care, characterized as it is by the
doctor/patient relationship of unequal knowledge, long timescales, uncertainty and potentially disastrous outcomes.

Philosophical discussions of the circumstances in which paternalism might
be justified emphasize the importance of consent, whether prior, subsequent
or hypothetical. In examples revolving around paternalist behaviour between
individuals, it is possible to illustrate those forms of consent which might be
acceptable. An individual may have instructed a friend to deny him the
whisky bottle, or be delighted that he pushed him out of the way of the
runaway lorry, or that the doctor performed major surgery after he had been
taken unconscious into hospital. The issue is less easily resolved when it is the
state and the individual. Again taking the example of medical care, individuals may be willing to give their consent to public provision by voting for
it. Motives would in practice be mixed: a concern for some measure of equal
access for all as well as a recognition that their own ignorance and non-
rationality in this specific context would make the results of market allocation sub-optimal.

However, such mechanisms for consent suffer from obvious drawbacks.
First, individuals are unlikely to be unanimous in giving consent: some will
vote against public provision. Second, to the extent that public provision has
a redistributive element, the free rider problem will provide incentives for
some individuals either to refuse consent or subsequently to behave strategically. Their own contribution to the redistributive impact is minimal even if
they do support redistribution in principle. Selective use of the private
market may provide a means for evading non-price rationing mechanisms
such as queueing and may even facilitate more advantageous access to
expensive forms of treatment in the public sector. Moreover, some individuals may leave the public sector completely, possibly encouraged by tax
expenditures or by remuneration packages designed to counter progressive
income taxation, and then oppose all public provision for which they are
continuing to pay.

The maintenance of public provision is thus likely to involve paternalist
behaviour towards those who refuse to give consent for non-strategic reasons
and some coercion of those who behave strategically. The latter is not
properly regarded as paternalism as it is not designed to benefit those
individuals but to maintain the integrity of the public system for the benefit of
others. This inevitably raises the issue of what is to be judged 'harm to the
interests of others'. Paternalist intervention, whether in the form of compulsory private insurance or public provision, could be advocated on the
grounds that it would be considered wrong to allow a poor uninsured patient
to die for lack of medical attention.

VI POLICIES FOR REDUCING INEQUALITY

The appropriate set of policy instruments, and hence the role for public expenditure, is sensitive to the precise choice of objectives. An analysis of this issue both assists the design of appropriate policies and proves helpful in providing a framework for evaluating the free-market critique of the welfare state. According to the objectives chosen, public expenditure may play a greater or lesser role as an instrument. Two issues are therefore considered in this section: whether policy is directed towards changing endowments or towards modifying outcomes; and whether redistribution should be in cash or kind.

Tackling unequal endowments versus mediating subsequent inequalities

Unequal endowments which can be a powerful source of inequality might be tackled directly. For example, capital taxation could eliminate large inherited fortunes, and land reform, with or without full compensation, could have a profound social and economic impact in those agrarian societies still characterized by extreme concentrations of landholding. Both these policies rely much more upon the state's law-making function, with the attendant powers of coercion, than upon spending money. Levelling-down policies usually fit this mould. Where taxation is involved, they will generate revenue for the Exchequer. However, the net impact depends upon whether such policies damage or improve the functioning of the economy.

Levelling up usually does involve public expenditure and often extremely large sums. It is difficult to devise counterparts to capital taxation. Because the rich are typically a very small proportion of the population, what is taken away from them as capital would be spread so thinly across the rest of the population that it would be treated as income. Several of the most expensive services of the welfare state, notably education and health care, can be viewed in part as a method of achieving a more equal distribution of human capital.

Sometimes, however, sharp conflicts may develop between different views of the objectives of the educational system. These are most clearly seen in the case of higher education with the tension between the development of the economy's human capital and the achievement of a more equal distribution of human capital. The first might imply devoting resources to the most able despite their already being highly privileged, whereas the second implies devoting resources to the least able and responsive. This is a very explicit conflict between efficiency and equality.

An alternative approach is to mediate the inequalities of income resulting from the operation of a market economy when unequal endowments constitute the starting point for exchanges. It therefore involves some degree of equalization of outcomes rather than of starting points. Redistributive activity will have to be continuous as an important source of inequality has been left untouched. Furthermore, as the focus is upon outcomes, the inequalites which emerge through the process of market exchange themselves demand attention.

Many of the income maintenance programmes of the welfare state fall into this category. Unemployment pay and social security benefits are payable to those who meet certain statutorily defined criteria of eligibility. They are designed to provide relief from certain symptoms of social distress, not to remove the underlying conditions. Such programmes have typically been amongst the fastest growing for a mixture of demographic and economic reasons. The population of most industrialized societies is ageing, and older groups make much higher than proportionate claims. Much higher levels of unemployment have also dramatically increased the proportion of people of working age dependent upon the state for their primary source of income. Some of these transfers are poor substitutes for income derived from the sale of factor services in the market. Few commentators or recipients are likely to view higher public expenditure on unemployment pay as welcome in itself, however necessary this might be given unemployment levels and 'desirable' benefit scales.

Cash versus kind redistribution

It is now appropriate to return to the fourth conclusion characteristic of IEA publications (see page 90): that whatever redistribution is deemed desirable should be effected through cash transfers rather than services in kind. This argument has been a key element in the overall attack on the welfare state as it provides a counter to those critics who allege that IEA writers want no redistribution at all. However, it is a policy conclusion with a wider appeal. For example, those annual reports of the former Supplementary Benefits Commission (for example, 1977) which reflected the hand of its chairman, Professor David Donnison, contained powerful advocacy of cash in preference to kind in the specific context of poverty relief.

Both the strengths and weaknesses of the formal analysis upon which such conclusions are based are illuminating. An examination of them helps to structure ideas about the form of redistribution appropriate to particular egalitarian objectives. The economist's tool of indifference curves can be used to demonstrate the superiority of cash redistribution, given the framework of assumptions on p. 86. After developing the analysis on this basis, more will then be said about the assumptions.

The standard case for cash redistribution. The individual's indifference map describes his preferences. The slope of the budget line indicates relative prices and its position the individual's income. He maximizes his utility by choosing

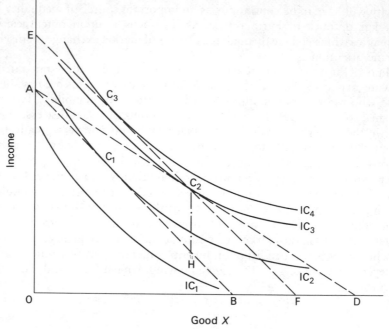

Figure 6.1 The superiority of cash redistribution

the highest attainable indifference curve, given the constraint of the budget line. At this point, this indifference curve is tangential to the budget line. This means that his marginal rate of substitution between the two goods (the slope of the indifference curve) is equal to the price ratio (the slope of the budget line).

In Figure 6.1, such a point is C_1, where IC_2 is the indifference curve and AB is the budget line. If the government wished to improve the welfare of this individual, it might subsidize good X, resulting in a new budget line, AD. The individual now chooses C_2 where IC_3 is tangential to AD.

The cost of this subsidy to the government is measured by HC_2. For the same cost, however, the individual's income, shown on the vertical axis, could be increased from 0A to 0E. This induces a parallel outward shift of the original budget line AB to EF. The individual now chooses C_3, where IC_4 is tangential to EF. Whilst facing the original price ratio, the individual now has a higher income. For the same exchequer cost, cash redistribution has achieved a greater increase in the individual's utility: from IC_2 to IC_4 rather than only to IC_3.

Redistribution in cash only involves income effects whereas redistribution in kind involves both income and substitution effects. Redistribution in kind means that the recipient chooses his consumption package by equating his marginal rate of substitution to the subsidized price ratio. If the unsubsidized price ratio accurately measures opportunity cost, the recipient is responding to a biased price signal. The lower price of the subsidized good X encourages the recipient to consume more of it than he would do at the 'correct' price ratio. Subsidizing good X influences the pattern of spending rather than simply redistributing purchasing power. The conclusions from this example where a particular good is subsidized apply even more forcefully to cases of provision free of charge.

This analysis provides a powerful case for cash rather than kind. It is, however, a far more contingent case than is acknowledged when it is used against state provision of education and health care. Where the Paretian value judgements are upheld, it is persuasive. Assumptions (2) and (3) on p. 86 are crucial to this: that there can be a complete separation of the economic from the non-economic factors affecting an individual's welfare and that he is always the best judge of his own welfare.

Whether these assumptions are to be upheld clearly depends upon philosophical judgements. It appears, however, that they are much less contentious in certain areas than in others. For example, the case for old-age pensions in cash rather than kind is overwhelming, though there may still be disputes over the margins (such as concessionary travel). Drawing a cash pension enables the recipient to choose that consumption package which generates the highest level of utility from the available resources. Instead of paying cash pensions, it would be possible to issue a set of non-tradable vouchers, each redeemable only for a specific consumption activity. The administrative difficulties would be horrendous and the value of each voucher extremely small, given that each pensioner would have a voucher for each activity. Moreover, pensioner A might be a vegetarian and not eat meat, pensioner B might dislike chocolate, and pensioner C might prefer football to the theatre. The fixed consumption package would be far inferior in the eyes of pensioners than ones they could each construct from the same resources but which reflected their own tastes and relative prices. More than the quota of certain preferred activities would be purchased, offset by less of others. The purpose of pensions is not to impose certain consumption profiles but to enable recipients to maintain in old age at least a minimum level of consumption. Much the same argument applies to both unemployment pay and to supplementary benefit. In such cases cash seems much preferable to kind.

Qualifications. There are two fundamental reasons why this conclusion should not be extended to all the in-kind programmes of the welfare state. First, there may be other differences in the way in which recipients respond to cash rather than kind. One possibility, about which folklore exceeds evidence by a vast margin, is the impact upon incentives to supply factor services. It is widely believed that income taxes, unemployment pay and social security benefit are a major disincentive to work. Whatever the reality, the image can be highly influential and constrain the actions of policymakers. The Supplementary Benefits Commission identified such popular attitudes as a major obstacle to achieving the benefit scales it felt justified for its long-term claimants. In contrast, it is much less frequently argued that the availability of free education and health care have comparable effects (but, see Acton, 1971, pp. 48–9). If labour supply is more sensitive to redistribution in cash rather than in kind, or is widely thought to be, there may be practical constraints on a switch from kind to cash.[2]

Second, the analysis assumes that the objective is simply a more equal distribution of utility. Cash is preferable to kind because the recipients derive more utility from a given amount of resources redistributed in this way. Apart from Tawney's objections to reliance upon cash redistribution (see p. 129) nothing has yet been said about the preferences of the donors who finance this redistribution. The conclusion in favour of cash depends crucially upon the assumption that donors are indifferent to the form of redistribution.

Collard (1978) and Culyer (1980) have spelled out clearly the implications of introducing donor preferences into the analysis. Donors might support redistribution because there exists interdependence between utility functions. Their utility might depend not only upon their own consumption and factor supply decisions but also upon the welfare of another group (the 'poor'). This interdependence can take two forms, with the utility of donors depending upon: (a) the utility level attained by the poor; or (b) the poor's consumption of particular goods. On formulation (a), it is the preferences of the poor with respect to their own consumption packages which still count. Cash transfers are the most efficient way of bringing the poor up to some minimum level of utility.

On (b), the donors' concern is not that the poor attain some minimum level of utility on their own evaluation but that they consume at least some minimum amount of certain goods (which might be education, fuel, health care and housing). The donors consider that such goods are more beneficial to the poor than they themselves recognize. As regards the disposal of these transferred resources, the relevance of the poor's preferences is challenged. The willingness of donors to make these transfers may be contingent upon the form of redistribution. For example, donors may suspect that the poor would in practice spend the cash upon alcohol rather than upon medical care. If the poor did spend it on medical care, the donors would support a transfer if its marginal impact on their utility exceeded the marginal loss from the necessary reduction in their own consumption. If spent on alcohol, both might be negative: drinking by the poor at the donors' expense may be worse than at their own!

Being the best judge is not the same as being a perfect judge. Therefore, it is ıot sufficient to show that individuals make mistakes about their own nterests: it must also be established that the state is a better judge. But the ssue is even more complex because donors establish their standing in such natters by virtue of conditionally supplying the resources in question. However, it is very difficult to envisage how either the existence or form of such utility interdependence could be authoritatively established. It is far from being an operational tool of analysis which could generate definitive conclusions about the proper scale and form of redistribution.

The model of utility interdependence emphasizes that confident assertions about the inherent superiority of cash over kind are heavily dependent upon a strong assumption which was previously not made explicit. Rather than automatically assuming that existing forms of provision are misguided, there s obvious scope for teasing out the implied objectives of particular programmes. There appears to be far wider commitment to ensuring reasonably equal access to certain goods than to equalizing money incomes. There are a number of separate routes with this common destination: for example, Tawney's strategy of equality; Rawls's liberal theory of justice; and this literature on interdependent utility functions.

VII   HAS THE STRATEGY OF EQUALITY FAILED?

With the adoption of Tawney's strategy of equality, the idea of the 'social wage' gained currency. It is widely believed that the welfare state has both reduced economic inequalities and eliminated many of the attendant social consequences. This view has been challenged by Le Grand (1982a) in a book which reviews not only his own work (1978, 1982b) but other studies of the distributional impact of public expenditure (including the annual calcu- ations of the Central Statistical Office: for example, 1981). He concluded that equality has not been achieved in any of the four major spending areas which he examined in detail: health, education, housing and transport. In recognition of the complexity of equality as a concept, he considered five alternative formulations.

(1)   Equality of public expenditure: all relevant individuals (or groups) receive equal per capita expenditure.
(2)   Equality of final income: inequalities in private incomes are in part offset by public expenditure.
(3)   Equality of use: equal treatment for equal medical need, or equal educational opportunity.
(4)   Equality of cost: each individual faces the same private cost per unit of service where costs are defined to include non-financial (for example time) costs as well as money.
(5)   Equality of outcome: for example, equal health states or educational attainments.

Whichever of these criteria is adopted, Le Grand concluded that little has been done to reduce inequality and in some cases public expenditure has made it worse.

He calculated that per capita expenditure on the NHS is roughly equal across socio-economic groups but that the pattern favours higher groups when expenditure per patient is considered. He explained this paradox with reference to the higher demands placed upon the system by the more articulate and resourceful and to the class images which medical professionals bring to their jobs, leading, for example, to more time being spent with patients from higher socio-economic groups and a greater willingness to refer them to hospitals. Free provision does not guarantee equal access, particularly when non-financial barriers may be important. There is a clear class gradient for both mortality and ill-health, with such differences having changed little over the past 50 years, despite the establishment of the NHS (Black, 1980). Furthermore, doubts have been expressed about the importance of health care expenditure to such health inequalities, relative to income, environment and life style.

The position in education is even less favourable to the achievement of equality. Whereas public expenditure on compulsory education slightly favours lower socio-economic groups, the reverse is marked for the post-compulsory sector, most noticeably for universities. The result is that:

> On average, households in the richest fifth of the original income distribution receive nearly one-and-a-half times as much public expenditure on education as the mean, and nearly three times as much as households in the poorest fifth (Le Grand, 1982a, p. 57).

However, this conclusion must be qualified a little because of differences in age structure and the size of households. Despite extensive educational reforms, there has been no improvement in the distribution of educational qualifications (such as a degree) and the best predictor of occupational status remains the occupational status of the father. Although the earnings dispersion has reduced over time, the contribution of education is much disputed. Le Grand (1982a) concluded that:

> ... it seems that public expenditure on education has failed as a means of achieving equality (p. 77).

> ... there is a strong case on egalitarian grounds for reducing the subsidies to education beyond the school-leaving age (p. 78).

> ... by and large public expenditure on education is not really an effective tool for promoting equality (p. 79).

nstead, he would favour selective reductions in expenditure, with the money being diverted into cash redistribution.

Le Grand's important study should be compulsory reading for all those on the political left who automatically assume that non-market methods of allocation are automatically more favourable to lower income groups than the market. In reality, much depends upon the circumstances in each case. However this did not prevent the Greater London Council's cheap fares policy being promoted as redistributive when knowledge of the facts (for example socio-economic composition of users and travel-to-work patterns) pointed decisively in the opposite direction. Whatever the arguments on efficiency grounds for subsidized urban public transport, the distributional impact will often be regressive. By driving home the need for scepticism about the distributional impact of public expenditure, Le Grand has emphasized a much neglected truth.

Unfortunately, however, Le Grand then overstated his case, thereby providing dangerous and unnecessary ammunition to those who oppose equality, not just the strategy of equality. There are five criticisms which can be levelled against his book. The first two points are a mixture of method-ology and presentation. First, the study focused solely upon the expenditure side, neglecting how that expenditure is financed. It is obviously exception-ally difficult, if not impossible, to link expenditure on the NHS to particular revenue sources. But this difficulty should urge caution when conclusions are drawn about whether the impact of non-market allocation is 'pro-poor' or 'pro-rich':

> Most public expenditure on the social services in Britain (and else-where) is thus distributed in a manner that broadly favours the higher social groups, whether 'higher' is defined in terms of income or occupation (Le Grand, 1982a, p. 128).

He referred to the fact that expenditure on the NHS by occupational group is distributed roughly equally per person but that the top socio-economic group receives up to 40 per cent more expenditure per patient than the bottom group. However, such a strong conclusion about the distributive impact of the tax-financed NHS entirely neglects the issue of who pays the taxes to finance that expenditure. For example, the distribution of expenditure might be much more equal than the distribution of tax payments.

The second criticism relates to another part of the evidence for that conclusion. In housing expenditure, he included tax expenditures on owner occupation. In assessing the overall impact of public policy, tax expenditures are clearly relevant. But the quotation above runs the serious danger of being misunderstood, encouraging the view that a reduction in (narrowly-defined) public expenditure on social services would have a favourable distributional impact. Tax expenditures have been more a mechanism for disarming the strategy of equality than for implementing it.

The third and fourth criticisms relate to Le Grand's interpretation both of the rationale underlying the strategy of equality and of the implications of his own evidence of its failure. Le Grand (1982a) too readily assumed that the strategy of equality was advocated for reasons of tactics rather than of principle.

> A major reason why the strategy of equality . . . took the form that it did was because of a reluctance by some of its proponents to confront the ideology of inequality. As a result, a system was established that aimed to promote equality within a limited sphere. But, by leaving basic economic inequality relatively untouched, it sowed the seeds of its own failure (p. 150).

An alternative view is that the domain of equality is limited. However, the warning that the interaction of causally-linked domains may frustrate the strategy of equality should be taken seriously.

The fourth criticism is of Le Grand's insistence that the strategy of equality was misconceived rather than just badly implemented.

> Overall, it is difficult to avoid the implication that the strategy of promoting equality through public expenditure on the social services has failed (p. 132).

> Many will no doubt conclude from the above [evidence] that public expenditure on the social services should be reduced, or even eliminated (p. 133).

> There is so much evidence from so many different areas that, almost regardless of the method of provision, the better off will always be able to make more effective use of even a freely provided service than the less well off. In that sense, the strategy of attempting to create equality through the provision of services that are free, or at a subsidised price to all, seems fundamentally misconceived (p. 137).

The strength of Le Grand's work is his emphasis on the non-price barriers which may impede the access of lower income groups to a free service such as the NHS: for example, reliance on public transport, fewer telephones and the difficulty and cost of arranging time off work. To highlight such factors draws attention to a lack of imagination in implementing non-market allocation, rather than to flaws in the concept itself.

Fifth, the resigned tone in which Le Grand discussed the inevitable failure of the strategy of equality contrasts with his clarion call for an assault on the 'ideology of inequality', with policies being directed towards the reduction of inequalities of income and wealth. Le Grand seriously underestimated the practical as opposed to merely ideological obstacles to making cash redistribution carry the weight he would assign to it, namely substituting for (some) existing redistribution in kind and taking the process further. Given the existing strains on the tax/transfer system, both of administration and of consent, it is misleading to refer to a 'legion' of available policy instruments (Le Grand, 1982a, p. 141). Having skilfully dissected the problems of implementation facing the strategy of equality, Le Grand did not apply the same scepticism to his own alternative strategy. After stressing that: 'The supposed trade-off between equality and economic growth is one of the major weapons in the non-egalitarian's armoury' (p. 148), he made strong presumptions about the absence of adverse incentive effects, concluding that: '. . . a degree of economic inequality well below that which currently obtains is desirable, because to get there would involve relatively little cost in terms of other objectives' (p. 149). Whilst the popular debate on the impact of the tax/transfer system on incentives is brimful with nonsense, Brown's survey (1981) of the existing empirical evidence urged the need for caution on all sides. It provided no basis for Le Grand's confidence that the amount of extra reliance he would place on the tax/transfer system could be achieved at 'relatively little cost in terms of other objectives'.

The evidence surveyed in Le Grand's book should therefore deliver a rude shock to all those who presumed the success, whether for good or ill, of the strategy of equality. It is especially disconcerting for supporters of that strategy, arriving at a time when both the commitment to equality and to the public services which have been one of its major manifestations are facing an unprecedented challenge. There is an understandable fear that Le Grand's evidence will be used by those without his egalitarian commitment as a further justification for running down public provision. It has been demonstrated above that his transition from evidence to policy is seriously defective. Yet the dismal picture revealed by his evidence again highlights the extent to which the strategy of equality was disarmed.

Such evidence demonstrates that a professed egalitarian commitment is no guarantee of egalitarian outcomes. Even where non-market methods of allocation are a necessary condition for their achievement, they are not sufficient in themselves. The egalitarian objectives might be frustrated by the political and bureaucratic processes necessarily linking objective and execution. Interest groups, whether defined in terms of income, territory, class or function, can exert powerful influences over non-market allocation. Obvious examples include the influence of large private suppliers of military hardware on the development of defence policy and that of public employees on the form of social programmes. Wolf's (1979) fourth category of non-market failure, *distributional inequity,* incorporated cases where inequities have a non-market rather than a market origin, often being indexed upon access to political power rather than directly upon income. In a society characterized by extensive inequalities, the implementation of an egalitarian policy is fraught with difficulties.

Supporters of the welfare state have been too willing to assume that inequality has been reduced and have paid far too little attention to gathering the evidence necessary to confirm or disprove that belief. Despite the huge scale of redistributive programmes, the effort devoted to statistical monitoring has been derisory. Even relatively sophisticated studies, such as the annual Central Statistical Office estimates, prejudge the issue being investigated by apportioning benefits from many welfare state services on a uniform per capita basis. Such complacency has afforded easy targets for the critics of the welfare state who have advanced two alternative lines of argument.

(1)   That the redistributive impact is perverse, as asserted in Stigler's (1970) exposition of 'Director's Law': 'Public expenditures are made for the primary benefit of the middle classes, and financed with taxes which are borne in considerable part by the poor and rich' (p. 1). Such a view is often supported with reference to the median voter model. As the median voter is likely to belong to the middle-income group, redistributive activity will be organized for the latter's benefit.

(2)   That the costs of running the redistributive machinery will consume all the resources intended for redistribution. Such costs are not just administrative ones but those of compliance, avoidance and of the politicization of economic decision-making (David Friedman, 1980).

It is ironical that the two most sophisticated attempts to tackle the methodological problems involved in assessing redistributive impact should relate to Colombia and Malaysia. As part of its strategy of meeting 'basic needs', two pilot studies were undertaken by the World Bank: Selowsky (1979) on Colombia; and Meerman (1979) on Malaysia. These pilot studies openly acknowledged the conceptual problems about incidence[3], the data deficiencies and the limited resources available. A major objective was to stimulate improvements in the practices of national governments, both in regular monitoring of redistributive impact and in the form of government accounting systems on which such calculations have to be based. These studies bring home the methodological problems and the complex redistributive impact of public expenditure, possibly owing much to the political environment in which programmes are implemented. For example, Meerman concluded that Malaysia had been exceptionally successful in directing its social welfare programmes towards the poor, with much of this success being attributable to the fact that the politically dominant Malays were typically rural and poor whilst the Chinese were urbanized and better-off. In other words, the racial cleavage dominated any tendency for those who are urbanized and have higher incomes to benefit disproportionately. What is required in all countries is careful evaluation of redistributive impact, neither untested faith nor assertions of inevitable failure.

VIII CONCLUSION

The idea of equality is an extremely complex one, with there being severe conflicts between alternative formulations. Rae's grammar of equality (Rae, 1981) provides a coherent structure for analysing its various components and for understanding why such conflicts emerge. Similarly, it is clear that at different points in time particular formulations may command varying degrees of public support. For example, during the 1970s, as the commitment to equality between persons appeared to diminish, equality between sexes acquired a new political salience. Because of the multi-dimensional nature of equality it is seen as an ideal to be strived for rather than as a destination to be reached. Over-enthusiastic commitment to one particular formulation may involve severe costs in terms of others. For example, a society which did achieve complete equality of opportunity might have so elevated the importance of success according to its own criteria that it sacrificed that equality of consideration for all human beings, irrespective of status, which is at the heart of the idea of equality (Williams, 1962).

The strategy of equality has played an important role in stimulating the growth of non-market provision. Le Grand's attack on that strategy raises three crucial issues. First, there is a question of objectives: is the aim to reduce inequality on a broad front or merely to limit its domain? Second, there is the question of tactics: did the strategy of equality accept a limited domain on grounds of principle or because this appeared to command greater chances of political support? The answer is relevant to Le Grand's proposals that public provision of certain goods and services should be withdrawn in favour of an explicit assault on inequalities of income and wealth. Third, there is the question of efficacy: did the strategy of equality fail because it was misconceived or because of a lack of sustained commitment? Similarly, would Le Grand's alternative strategy not be faced by the danger that the intended elimination of income and wealth inequalities would not accompany the withdrawal of the state from certain activities?

Finally, the rhetoric about the merits or otherwise of equality should not disguise the fact that what is often at stake is not the idea of equality but the domain over which it should operate. This point is neatly captured by Rae (1981).

Market liberals . . . are not so much *anti*egalitarian as they are *narrowly* egalitarian. Milton Friedman, Murray Rothbard, and Robert Nozick do not oppose equality, for the very heart of their appeal is a universal — that is, equal — distribution of formal property rights and certain civil and political rights. But they oppose the *broadening* of equality beyond the narrow limits of this domain (p. 47).

Writing about various strands of opinion on the 'right', he concluded that they:

. . . all demand that domains of account be reduced. They also resist the tendency of the state and its bureaucracy continually to expand the domain of public allocation and diminish the range of market decision. But this century-long expansion is a response to the crisis-generating disjunction between narrowly equal citizenship and broadly, often devastatingly, unequal subjection to unregulated market allocation (p. 58).

APPENDIX: COMBINING THE PARETO CRITERION WITH A SOCIAL WELFARE FUNCTION

Figure 6.2 provides valuable insights into how the objectives of efficiency and equity relate to each other. So that two-dimensional geometry can be used, the case of a two-person world is adopted, simply for expositional ease. The horizontal axis plots the utility of individual I and the vertical axis that of individual II. Both these scales are ordinal and not cardinal. Although it is possible to say that one point denotes a higher level of utility than another, no numerical value can be attached to this superiority (such as, twice as much).

The line ZZ′ denotes the utility possibility frontier. Each point on it represents an overall Pareto optimal allocation of resources. If a particular allocation of resources meets all the efficiency conditions, the utility frontier will be reached. If, however, some of the efficiency conditions are broken, the frontier will not be attained. All points in the area 0ZZ′ are feasible and all points to the north-east of ZZ′ are infeasible. Each point on the frontier satisfies all the necessary conditions for efficiency but corresponds to widely differing distributions of utility between I and II.

The (arbitrarily numbered) contours W_{10}, W_{20} and W_{30} are but three of the contours representing a particular social welfare function, a mechanism for making interpersonal comparisons of utility and thus able to define the social optimum. The Pareto criterion has defined the frontier but provides no basis for choice between the different points on it. The social welfare function performs this task.

Before proceeding any further, it must be stressed that the difficulty is not really resolved so easily. The social welfare function used in Figure 6.2 is subject to enormous technical and conceptual objections. Tremendous ingenuity and mathematical elegance have been expended in efforts to overcome them. The results have been disappointing and massive problems still confront any attempt to turn the social welfare function into an operational policy instrument. Nevertheless, there are no objections to its use here solely as a tool for elucidating conceptual issues.

The social optimum is at S^* where the contour W_{30} is tangential to the utility possibility frontier ZZ′. Society is able to reach W_{30} which represents a higher level of utility than W_{20}, itself higher than W_{10}. The fact that S^* is

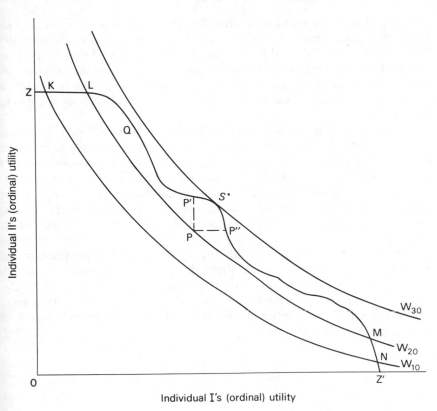

Figure 6.2 Reintegrating equity with efficiency

chosen is a result of the shapes of ZZ' and W_{30}. The shape of the latter embodies a 'social judgement' about the importance or otherwise of distribution. If W_{30} was a downward-sloping straight line which formed an angle of 45° to both axes, distribution would have no significance. The social optimum would always be the most north-easterly point on the utility possibility frontier.

As I's utility rises relative to II's, successive equal increments in I's utility can only be offset by successively smaller reductions in II's utility, if aggregate social welfare is to remain unchanged. Exactly the same point applies if all references to I are read as II and vice versa. This assumed shape for W_{30} denotes that there is a trade-off between efficiency and equity. Although K and N are efficient points on ZZ', they are only on W_{10}, not W_{30}. This social welfare function attaches lower values to points characterized by such unequal distributions of utility.

All points on ZZ' are efficient on the Pareto criterion and all points below it, like P, are inefficient. It is obvious from Figure 6.2 that a social welfare function, embodying aversion to inequality, may rank some inefficient points higher than some efficient ones. P is on W_{20}. A move to anywhere on the P'S*P'' segment of ZZ' will clearly satisfy the Pareto condition: at P', II is better off and I no worse off; anywhere between P' and P'', both are better off and at P'', I is better off and II no worse off. Given that there is a contour through each point, all these points on P'S*P'' are on some contour W_n, where $20<n<30$.

A move from P to a point on either of the segments ZP' or P''Z' of the frontier will not be sanctioned by the Pareto criterion. On the former, I is made worse off than at P: on the latter, this applies to II. It is interesting to note how these points are ranked by the social welfare function. Any point on LP' (such as Q) or on P''M is ranked as high as, or higher than, P: they are on either W_{20} or a higher contour. This difference stems from the social welfare function not being constrained by the starting position as is the Pareto criterion.

Even more interesting are the ZL and MZ' segments of the frontier. All points on these, excluding L and M themselves, are on a lower contour than P. Similarly, moves to them from P do not satisfy the Pareto criterion. Social welfare is higher at the inefficient point P, which is characterized by a 'reasonably equal' distribution of utility, than at these efficient points, where distribution is highly unequal.

PART THREE

Mechanisms

In an economy where public expenditure accounts for a large proportion of GDP, complex issues of accountability and control arise. However justified in the context of achieving social and economic objectives, the removal of a function from the market does not resolve all problems. It generates a new set of problems through its suppression of the systems of control characteristic of the market. The public sector must devise its own systems of accountability and resolve a diverse range of technical issues of planning and control. Because of the multi-dimensional objectives lying behind many of the public sector's activities, the search for accountability, efficiency and equity is an elusive one. Yet this is not a task which can be evaded. Running the public sector badly is an excellent way of alienating support for its underlying objectives.

The mechanisms of accountability in the public sector have been deficient. Elected bodies have failed to adapt themselves to the dramatic enlargement of state activities and to the professionalization of the public service. In the UK, the all-pervading climate of official secrecy has inhibited the development of effective mechanisms of scrutiny. Furthermore, the interaction of technocratic systems of planning and control of public expenditure with the wider political system have been imperfectly understood. The perceived failure of these control systems has played its own part in fostering disillusionment with the substantive activities of the state. Simultaneously, a dramatic deterioration in the climate of public sector industrial relations has accentuated the problems of running a coherent planning and control system, further alienating support for the public sector. These developments have encouraged reliance upon blunt instruments for planning and control, diverting attention from the distinctive characteristics of public sector activities which demand more sophisticated and sensitive evaluation and control systems.

The sheer complexity of activities in a welfare state has imposed severe strains upon the political system at the centre. Despite the centralizing tendencies released by the commitment to the welfare state, the design of systems of decentralization within the public sector has acquired a new

151

practical significance. However, the claims of decentralization have to be reconciled with those of equity, itself often conceived of in a territorial sense. Decentralization thus complicates the achievement of equity objectives and produces a complex network of intergovernmental relationships. Yet i provides alternative mechanisms of accountability within a complex public sector, by dispersing power within the state and by extending the opportunities for participation in the decision-making process.

CHAPTER 7

Public accountability

I THE NEED FOR ACCOUNTABILITY

Although the exact figure depends critically upon definitions, roughly half of GDP passes through the hands of the state. This consists of both exhaustive public expenditure (for which public institutions decide the pattern of final output) and transfer payments (which represent the redistribution between households of the ability to make private expenditures). The extent of the resources at the state's disposal in these two distinct senses is clearly massive. The efficiency and equity with which such activities are conducted are of profound importance, both to the efficiency of the economy and to the nature of the society. Herein lies the necessity for proper systems of public accountability.

For those activities remaining within the market sector, a form of accountability is provided through the market itself. Provided that there is competition, the consumer has a choice of supplier so that, in cases of dissatisfaction, his custom can be transferred elsewhere. This latent threat is a powerful force in ensuring that the producer is responsive to the consumer's wants, provided that they are backed by the ability to pay. Subject to a number of stringent conditions about market structure and about the absence of externalities, the profits earned by a firm provide a measure of the value of its activities. Given that the primary motive in the private sector is financial, the attainment of an appropriate level of profitability constitutes the main mechanism of accountability from the firm to its ultimate owners, the shareholders. As their part ownership is itself a tradable financial asset, shareholders have the option of divesting themselves, though perhaps at a loss, if they are dissatisfied with performance.

Although the foregoing is clearly an idealized account of the functioning of the private sector, it contains an important germ of truth which provides helpful insights into the nature of the problem of accountability in the public sector. One sense in which it is idealized is that production in the private sector is far more dominated by leading firms than the idyllic picture of autonomous producers would suggest. Nevertheless, the choices made by individual households and firms do provide a complex mechanism fo matching resources and preferences: the analogy of a continuous series o referendums on the pattern of output has been suggested. The informationa content of the price signals emanating from the process of market exchange i obviously high.

This argument is often used as a launching pad for the view that the marke is inherently superior to the state. In view of what has been said in earlie chapters, this stance is rejected without further discussion. However, it i essential to understand which mechanisms of accountability are attenuatec by the transfer of an activity from the private to the public sector. Part of tha market chain is not necessarily broken. The link between consumer anc producer depends not just upon ownership but upon whether the product i marketed and upon market structure. If vehicle manufacturing moved intc the public market sector, the consumer would retain his choice of car. I electricity supply were to be transferred into the private sector, domesti consumers would still have no choice of supplier. Although it has been arguec that public ownership is likely to lead to pressures for protection from imports, counter examples can easily be cited: much more has been done ir this way to safeguard (private) textiles than (part-public) vehicles. The part o the chain which is broken is between the firm and its shareholders. Govern ments do not hold shares in a firm merely for financial motives. Divestment a a response to discontent with existing management is an unlikely response privatization schemes are undertaken primarily for ideological and budget ary reasons (Heald and Steel, 1981a, 1982).

The form of accountability provided through the market is narrow in tha it strictly delimits relevant parties as those participating in market trans actions in those goods and services. For better or worse, accountability in the public sector is interpreted in a much wider sense. Its mechanisms mus therefore not only substitute for those market mechanisms which have been eroded but also extend the domain of accountability. This extension takes place along two dimensions: the definition of relevant parties is enlarged; and the range of issues deemed to be legitimate is broadened. For example, the efficiency with which the NHS uses the resources placed at its disposal becomes the proper concern of a much wider group than just current patients and employees. Moreover, the equity of such non-market allocations o resources, derived from explicit political and administrative decisions, is likely to be more vigorously questioned than if they were simply the consequence of a myriad of separate decisions in the market-place.

II   THE MECHANISMS OF ACCOUNTABILITY

Accountability involves an obligation to explain or justify specific actions. Stanyer (1974) has stressed that there is always a precise logical structure involving the form and substance of the account; the occasion in terms of time, place and audience; and the consequences. Such a logical structure attaches to the exercise of accountability in any context. There are, however, specific features of accountability in the public sector deriving in part from its non-market context and its articulation through the political system. The line dividing those issues subject to political decision and those reserved for private decision has become blurred with the result that, in the face of demands from citizens to be heard and answered, it is difficult to exclude almost any subject matter. Furthermore, both the presentation of the account and the consequences which flow from it are inevitably affected by the existence of conflicting values. The contrast with the private sector's use of a simple criterion such as profitability is obvious.

Given the critical importance of public accountability for the functioning of a democratic political system, its analysis raises issues wider than the immediate concerns of this book. Here, the focus is upon the duty of public institutions to explain and justify the ways in which they have used the resources placed at their disposal. Nevertheless, this must be located within its wider context. When systems of accountability for public expenditure are being devised, three broad issues must be considered: (a) the type of accountability; (b) the techniques of measurement; and (c) the institutions to which account is rendered. This framework provides a helpful structure for organizing discussion although there are interactions. For example, the type of accountability may determine both techniques of measurement and audience.

The type of accountability

The growth of the public sector, both in terms of its scale and the diversity of its activities, has overstretched the traditional machinery of public accountability, heavily dependent upon the formal relationship between the executive and the legislature. There have emerged alternative views of what accountability entails, involving different answers to both the substance and form of the account. The conceptions of accountability which now dominate debate are *political* accountability, *managerial* accountability and *legal* accountability. Each of these, however, is capable of further sub-division, with nine types of accountability being analysed below.[1]

Political accountability. Within political accountability three types can be distinguished: constitutional, decentralized and consultative. *Constitutional* accountability has been the hallmark of parliamentary systems but its institutions and mechanisms developed in the era of the minimal state. Its effectiveness has atrophied with the growth of a large public sector. An air of unreality has attached to constitutional doctrines such as that of ministerial responsibility when the resources under the control of a minister are so massive and diverse. However, this doctrine is more subtle than is implied by the view that the litmus test is whether ministers actually resign for errors in their departments. The fact that the minister may have to explain and justify his actions to Parliament may stimulate concern with both standards of administration and the maintenance of equitable treatment. Nevertheless such doctrines may generate administrative burdens which hinder the achievement of other objectives and the pursuit of other types of account ability. For example, the necessity to defend and protect the position of the minister may encourage methods of administration characterized by exces sive caution and delay. Johnson (1974) advocated placing less reliance upon such political modes of accountability as that between ministers and Par liament, redirecting attention towards achieving control over public authori ties by diversifying modes of control.

Whereas accountability is exerted *ex post*, control is exerted *ex ante* Controls are basically of two types: general rules established in advance of decision-making, to which conformity is required; and the insistence upon specific approval being secured at the time of decision-making before action can be taken. Whichever form of control is operated, an important aspect of accountability will be the monitoring of whether these controls have been respected. Any system of accountability must therefore pay attention to the design of mechanisms of control appropriate to the particular activity. Given the diverse nature of public activities, from declaring war to making cars considerable diversity in the structure of the systems of control and account ability is to be expected.

Despite such warnings about the limitations of traditional forms of constitutional accountability, the control over the state's expenditure and revenue by an elected body remains a key democratic principle. Attention is directed in Section III of this chapter towards the underlying reasons why the role of the legislature in fiscal and expenditure issues has become so diminished. The elected representatives, to whom account is due, are few in number compared with the permanent bureaucracy. Moreover, they have remained amateurs whilst the bureaucracy has been professionalized. Members of Parliament are singularly ill-equipped to perform a scrutiny role in relation to the executive branch of government. Few have backgrounds which would provide them with the necessary expertise: being specialists in politics does not necessarily help them to run the machinery of account ability. The internal organization of the House of Commons, which keeps backbench MPs remote from decisions, equips them neither for the managerial demands of ministerial office nor for a scrutinizing role as backbenchers. The political and constituency role of MPs demands an enormous breadth of knowledge, thus denying most elected politicians the opportunity to develop specialist knowledge. Despite drawing its legitimacy from the elected status of the politicians, the bureaucracy often appears rather contemptuous of their role. Legislatures throughout the world have often allowed the accountability of the executive for its expenditure to become a charade. There is, however, nothing inevitable about such shortcomings: they owe much to the failure of legislatures to undertake the necessary institutional and procedural innovation to match the growth of the public sector (Robinson, 1978).

The decentralization of certain of the activities of the public sector is one response to the overload of the constitutional machinery at the centre, thus emphasizing the importance of *decentralized* accountability. By establishing elected bodies, whether in the form of local authorities or regional assemblies, power and responsibility in the political system can be dispersed. Decentralization thus involves some gains in control and accountability but introduces problems of conflict between the centre and the locality. Such issues are so important in the context of a large public sector that they are considered separately in Chapter 10.

In most industrialized democracies, *consultative* accountability has acquired importance. The presumption that the bureaucracy is solely accountable to representatives submitting themselves to periodic elections has itself been challenged. It has been argued that representative democracy is not sufficient: forms of participatory democracy have gained their adherents. The decisions of elected bodies on planning issues (such as road alignments and new industrial developments) and on service management (such as the organization of schools and of housing provision) are monitored by interested parties who claim the right to be consulted, and sometimes to have a policy veto. Such groups claim legitimacy as spokesmen for their communities, whether they be residents adversely affected by planning applications, tenants wanting a better repair service or anti-nuclear groups disputing a policy of building nuclear power stations. Their relationship to the formal political process is ambivalent: they claim their rights to represent the community whereas, unlike the elected bodies, their spokesmen are not subject to election by universal suffrage.

Whatever their suspicions, elected representatives have felt some obligation to account for their decisions to a wider group. Furthermore, the growth of pressure group activity has occurred simultaneously with the decline in the membership of political parties. The resources, expertise and vigour of one-issue pressure groups now exceeds the policy competence of political parties and, on occasion, of the relevant public authority. Consequently, politicians have been unable to ignore articulate pressure groups, typically well-versed in media management. In opposition, the politician can draw useful information from them for which he has few alternative sources. In government, he can negotiate directly with them, as a strategy both for using their expertise and for drawing their public fire. Pressure groups clearly differ, ranging from those prepared to accept such incorporation into the policy process and those committed to public opposition. Which style is adopted will owe much to the nature of the policy issues and the clientele of the pressure group. Some groups have acquired substantial policy influence despite the narrowness of their own constituency and their remoteness from the resource constraints facing elected representatives.

The state and its various agencies thus find it necessary to consult organized interests on matters of policy, a development reflecting the growing importance of functional representation. In turn, the power of pressure groups is legitimized through their involvement in formal advisory and consultative bodies. Pressures for more open government and greater public participation have led to the innovation of consultative Green Papers, supposedly published in advance of a final decision. Inevitably, however, pressure groups are much more equipped than individual citizens both to organize appropriate responses and influence the final decision.

Managerial accountability. The growth of the public sector has necessarily bureaucratized it, in the technical not pejorative meaning of that word. The conduct of the state's extensive and diverse business can no longer be a part-time occupation, as it could be for the justices of the peace of the eighteenth century. Civil servants, local government officers and public enterprise managers are members of career occupations. This professionalization of the public service, however essential on managerial grounds, creates a number of serious difficulties for the relationship between the permanent bureaucracy and the typically ephemeral political leadership. After all, much of the legitimacy of the former stems from its supposed subordination to the latter.

Within managerial accountability three separate types can be distinguished: commercial, resource and professional. *Commercial* accountability applies when publicly owned organizations, financed by user charges and not by budgetary appropriations, are controlled on the basis of their commercial performance. Public corporations are supposedly free to make commercial decisions in response to market pressures and have consequently been distanced from ministerial and parliamentary control. The formidable practical problems of establishing and then maintaining such a framework are outside the scope of this book (but see Foster, 1971; Heald, 1980b; Heald and Steel, 1981b).

Resource accountability, the counterpart in the public non-market sector, is directed towards the adoption of managerial practices which will promote efficiency. Much attention has been directed towards the need to develop both systems of accountable management and improved planning and management control techniques. Given the large scale of many public institutions, attempts at centralized management would lead to rigidities and slow decision-making, both criticisms which have been levelled at them. The Fulton Report of 1968 (Fulton, 1968) on the management of the civil service was enthusiastic about managerial reform, with stress being placed on the establishment of accountable units for which individual managers could be held responsible. The idea of transferring certain activities from government departments to special-purpose agencies subsequently gained popularity as a device for improving efficiency and managerial accountability. A number of organizations with varying legal statuses were established at this period: for example, the Manpower Services Commission (a public corporation whose staff are classified as civil servants) and the Property Services Agency (a departmental agency). It should be stressed that these changes involved a move away from direct ministerial control but the new agencies, loosely described as 'quangos', remained firmly within the public sector. Such 'hiving off' was considered appropriate for work of a non-political, technological or managerial nature. Although hiving off was taken in the early 1970s to include, as an extreme form, the transfer of public activities into the private sector, this interpretation was subdued until the 1980s when the term became frequently used as a synonym for privatization.

Resource accountability is thus concerned with ensuring that the budgetary control framework exists which will permit proper decentralization of managerial decision-making, coupled with systems for evaluating managerial performance. It is on issues such as this that the public sector requires to be alert to best private sector practice. The pace and direction of change within the civil service have disillusioned the reformers connected with the Fulton Committee (Garrett, 1980; Kellner and Crowther-Hunt, 1980). Over a decade later, management accounting and information systems still remain inadequate (Rayner, 1982).

Professional accountability raises very different issues because it involves self-regulation by professional groups employed in the public sector. For certain public activities, the problems of output measurement make elected bodies highly dependent upon the judgement of service providers. In the NHS, professional autonomy has been endorsed in the name of clinical freedom and thus the medical profession, rather than any democratic body, has been allowed to dominate resource allocation decisions. Furthermore, this example illustrates the frequent unwillingness of employees to accept the implications of being part of the public sector. When the taxpayer provides the resources, the management and priorities of a service become a legitimate area for public concern. The British Medical Association (BMA) has consistently disputed the role of outsiders in the management of the NHS. Indeed, the organizational structure of the NHS, from its origins in 1947 through the reorganizations of 1974 and 1982, owes much to the effective veto of the BMA over its integration into the broader framework of local government.

The *ad hoc* nature of health authorities has been consistently criticized, notably for the absence of any directly elected membership (for example, Regan and Stewart, 1982). By ensuring that lay participation has no base, the BMA has gained a formidable influence over the direction of NHS policy. Successive governments have felt unable to challenge its dominance, partly because of the mystique and prestige surrounding the medical profession in the eyes of the general public, and partly because of the way in which the

BMA's equivocation about state medicine has left delicate issues unsettled. The entrenched position of doctors has wider implications. Maynard and Ludbrook (1980a) have stressed that the respect for the clinical freedom of individual doctors has imposed substantial costs by allowing the perpetuation of inefficient treatment practices.

A further example can be drawn from a markedly different part of the public sector (Keating and Rhodes, 1981; Gray, 1982). In the water supply industry there is strong opposition from the dominant professional group of engineers to being part of local government and hence subject to elected politicians. They perceive their own role as being public servants, objectively interpreting the needs of the public in a technical area. Any democratic control, except at far remove through the responsible ministry, would be intrusive as politicians would inject irrelevant partisan controversy. Gray questioned just how exclusively technical many of the decisions about, for example, investment really are, especially when the links to other infrastructural investment undertaken by local authorities are considered. Unlike most public enterprises, water authorities are mainly financed by a tax (the water rate) rather than by charges. There is obviously a temptation to wish to enjoy the advantages of being in the public non-market sector (such as protection from competition and reliance on tax revenues) but to resist claims of accountability over the resources employed.

Legal accountability. The executive actions of government agencies often embody substantial elements of administrative discretion. The growing extent and complexity of state activities has stimulated the development of controls of a legal and quasi-legal nature. Within the broad category of legal accountability three types can be distinguished: judicial, quasi-judicial and procedural. *Judicial* accountability is exercised through judicial review of executive actions at the instigation of aggrieved citizens. The decisions and actions by public bodies should not be *ultra vires* and those required by statute should be undertaken. *Quasi-judicial* accountability involves the control of administrative discretion through the use of specialist tribunals set up to review, especially in the taxation and social security fields, whether relevant law has been appropriately administered in particular cases. *Procedural* accountability involves the review of decisions by an external agency, usually an ombudsman, testing for maladministration in the sense that standards of reasonable administration have not been met. All these mechanisms enhance the importance of conformity and consistency and impose costs in terms of workload, delay and rigidity. What such cases have in common is that they vitally affect the individual interests of the citizen.

The techniques of measurement

Accountability requires a quantitative element. Otherwise, it is impossible to answer questions about whether the resources at the disposal of the public sector have been used efficiently and equitably. Systems for recording how public money is spent are well developed. The UK's system of public accounting provides extensive safeguards, not only against fraud but also against money being spent by the executive on different purposes from those voted by Parliament. But it is difficult to draw conclusions about efficiency or equity until there is a specification of objectives and some method of measuring output. For example, the financial link between consumer and producer is breached in the NHS by the almost complete absence of prices. Other mechanisms are therefore required to ensure the efficient allocation of resources, both in the X-efficiency sense and in terms of injecting practical meaning into rhetoric about responding to needs. If prices are suppressed, there must be devised non-market mechanisms which will allocate resources in the face of competing demands.

Complete reliance on private medicine would ensure that those who valued medical care most would receive it. These valuations would be shaped by ability to pay and the resulting distribution of care would bear little relationship to any measure of need. The problem with need as a concept is that, although it has a powerful appeal as a guide to allocation in such contexts, it is profoundly difficult to produce operational measures. At an intuitive level, it is possible to say that the need of a mother for ante-natal care which will save the life of her baby constitutes a higher need than someone's need for cosmetic surgery. Although such stark comparisons are relevant to decisions as to whether medicine should be public or private, the operational choices within the NHS, once established, are much more difficult (Culyer, 1976). For example, the claims of potential heart-transplant patients and of those with cancer have to be set against those of accident victims, of geriatric and psychiatric patients and of preventive medicine.

The public sector's objectives are therefore far more complex and multi-dimensional than those of the private sector where profitability is a key objective. Private firms take market prices as given since these determine their revenues and costs. In contrast, the government is also concerned that existing market prices may be a misleading guide to resource allocation decisions: for example, because of externalities or of the existence of unemployed factors. The pollution arising from the activities of a private firm does not appear as a cost when it calculates its private profitability. The public sector, however, is concerned about the social profitability of its activities, rather than just the private profitability.

The choice of techniques of measurement is crucial to the evaluation of public sector activities and therefore to the exercise of accountability. To take an extreme example, the cash costs of regional policy are substantial. However, several studies by economists, notably those of Moore and Rhodes (1973, 1976), have concluded that regional policy may be a resource-creating, not resource-consuming policy. If this conclusion is correct, Parliament would be seriously misled if it focused exclusively on the cash costs which appear in the accounts. When the economy is near full employment, regional policy brings into utilization resources which would otherwise be unused by restraining activity in congested areas and redirecting it to those with idle resources: market prices are not reflecting true opportunity costs.

This example provides a warning that none of the cash costs may be proper measures of the resources being used. In principle, it is possible to calculate a set of shadow prices which reflects social opportunity costs much more accurately than market prices. There have been attempts to develop systems of shadow prices for implementation but the conceptual and practical difficulties are immense and some of the short cuts adopted in practice are alarming. Nevertheless, it is clear that some of the activities undertaken by the private sector which are profitable at market prices may be unprofitable at shadow prices: heavily polluting industries are possible examples. In contrast, some public sector activities which are unprofitable at market prices might be profitable at shadow prices: urban public transport might be an example. Private profitability can no longer be relied upon as a valid test.

Although there are profound implications for public policy towards the private sector and for the control framework for public enterprises, they will not be pursued here (but, on the latter, see Heald, 1981). Restricting the focus to public expenditure, the analysis casts doubt on some of the valuations placed upon the inputs. A major reservation relates to the valuation of labour in circumstances of widespread unemployment. Employing people who would otherwise be unemployed can be resource-creating, though imposing financial costs upon the state. Even at the level of financial costs, the cash costs of particular programmes can be seriously misleading if there are offsetting savings on other programmes such as unemployment pay.

The measurement of output generates even greater difficulties. In the government's accounts, no attempt is made to evaluate output. In principle, when there are multiple objectives, a weight or shadow price must be placed upon each so that the multi-dimensional output can be evaluated. However, specifying the objective function to be maximized is a formidable, if not utopian, task. Nevertheless, such a recognition of practical difficulties does nothing to alter the fundamental point that the measurement issues facing the public sector are far more complex than for the private sector. It is necessary to provide safeguards so that the public sector cannot explain away all adverse results at market prices with reference to what the position would be if all calculations were to be done at shadow prices. There is a danger that such shadow prices would be calculated with the explicit intention of justifying existing practices! If shadow prices are to influence decisions, they should be calculated and published ahead of those decisions. Reporting systems need to be designed with care. Decisions are sometimes taken using shadow prices but results are later reported at market prices, thus provoking (possibly unjustified) criticism of the original decision.

Despite the enthusiasm with which British economists have encouraged developing countries to use project appraisal methods incorporating shadow prices (for example, Little and Mirrlees, 1974), practice in the UK is relatively undeveloped. After some initial enthusiasm for output measurement and shadow pricing, it rapidly waned. As criticism of public expenditure as inherently wasteful has mounted, shadow pricing, which might portray 'inefficiency' at market prices in another light, has become distinctly unfashionable. The traditional emphasis upon inputs rather than outputs must play some part in perpetuating the widespread belief that public expenditure is unproductive, a burden upon the market sector. This view reserves the terms 'productive' or 'wealth-creating' for those activities which are profitably marketed, with prices thereby being attached to consumption. It embodies a very narrow view of the nature of wealth, limited to the building up of financial wealth, itself implicitly backed by physical assets. It incorporates many implicit assumptions about the valuation of both inputs and outputs: for example, that the market prices of inputs properly measure opportunity costs; and that there are no externality or public good characteristics causing output valuation problems.

If a proper framework of analysis is adopted, public services such as the NHS clearly produce outputs, however difficult to measure and value. McLachlan and Maynard (1982) dismissed as false the proposition that health care is a productive 'wealth-creating' industry only if private and marketed. Quite apart from any of its other purposes, the NHS provides medical care for which, under other institutional arrangements, individuals would be willing to pay. Removal from the market eliminates a ready measure of output, though not necessarily the most appropriate one.

The institutions to which account is rendered

A crucial aspect of the differentiation between the various types of accountability relates to the assumptions made about the identity of the institutions to which account must be rendered. Contrasting assumptions constitute a potent source of tension amidst this rich diversity of types of accountability, partly determining whether the latter's claims are complementary or contradictory. Of the nine types, both constitutional and decentralized accountability emphasize the pivotal role of elected representatives. However, the growth of the public sector has resulted in such mechanisms of representative democracy being insufficient in themselves to secure accountability. Both commercial and resource accountability are concerned with the internal managerial processes for securing the desired outcomes. Although there are conflicts of interests between representatives and the bureaucracy, it is open, at least in principle, for representatives to establish the objectives which will be pursued. All three types of legal accountability are primarily concerned with providing protection for the individual against administrative discretion. They do not in themselves constitute a challenge to the standing of the legislature in a parliamentary system because it can subsequently alter the framework of law if it disapproves of specific decisions.

The challenge to the role of elected representatives comes from two sources. First, consultative accountability relates to the role of groups independent of the representative body and to participation in the policy process by individuals other than representatives. The tension between such competing accountability claims is increased by the probability that there will be systematic biases: for example, that producers will be stronger than consumers, groups stronger than individuals, and some individuals stronger than others. Second, professional accountability usually involves self-regulation and sometimes extends to the definition of the objectives themselves. It is the fact that the public sector faces resource constraints which accentuates the inevitable tensions between these competing claims and contributes to the dilemma of public accountability.

Given the scale and diversity of the public sector, there can be no simple blueprint which would serve as a model for securing public accountability. As the relative significance attached to the nine types varies through time, the mechanisms must themselves respond if they are not to atrophy. For example, the claims of consultative accountability have been asserted with a growing vigour, producing major consequences for the style of political and bureaucratic decision-making, even though the relative weight of these claims remains unsettled. With such a combination of change and uncertainty, the overall design of systems of public accountability must secure both adaptability and robustness. No single type of accountability will be sufficient on its own. The key task is therefore to harness together these divergent types of accountability, whilst recognizing that there are occasions and contexts in which their respective claims openly conflict. The scope for disagreement both about the relative weights to be attached to these types of accountability, and about the nature of the trade-offs between them, is obviously extremely wide. Whilst stressing the ultimate pre-eminence of the democratic link as the validating mechanism for the public sector's activities, this book seeks to demonstrate the vital contribution which must be drawn from other types of accountability. Although constitutional mechanisms will hold sway at the macro level, at which decisions on the size and scope of the public sector must be taken, the sheer complexities of managing, controlling and monitoring such a diverse set of organizations enhance the appeal of harnessing other types at the micro level, but in support of the macro objectives.

III   THE FAILURE OF ACCOUNTABILITY

Because the chain of accountability from the executive to the legislature is so crucial, this section concentrates upon the reasons why constitutional accountability is in practice so ineffective in the UK. In constitutional theory, arliament exercises control over public expenditure: in reality, this is a hollow myth. It does not even perform a proper scrutiny function. Parliamentary financial procedures, operating through supply estimates, votes, supplementary estimates and excess votes, are far removed from the realities of expenditure decision-making on levels and on priorities. It generates a morass of boring information, irrelevant to the needs of a modern legislature. The House of Commons does not take the financial procedures on the floor with a modicum of seriousness, using every available opportunity for general and topical debate when the nominal business is financial.

The emphasis upon propriety alone which runs throughout parliamentary procedures has its origins in the granting of supply to Charles II. It was well-suited to ensure that money voted by Parliament for war was not spent on royal mistresses. As Charles, who died without an heir, had twenty-two illegitimate children, Parliament's concern was perhaps well-founded. The problem has changed but not many of the procedures: the present task is to monitor the effectiveness of the vast expenditure programmes undertaken by the executive, much less to ensure that ministers and civil servants do not fill numbered Swiss accounts.

To stress that there must be proper mechanisms of public accountability is not to assent to the proposition that public expenditure is either inherently or currently wasteful. An important obstacle to improving defective and decayed mechanisms can be found in divisions among the advocates of reform (Heald, 1979). They subscribe to two positions: those who regard reform of parliamentary procedures as a method of eliminating extensive waste in the public sector, in order to reduce its size; and those who regard it as a means of securing more effective public accountability and better directed, not less, public expenditure. Two separate issues are involved even though they are often, and sometimes deliberately, confused: the desirable size of the public sector; and the role of the legislature in exercising financial control over the executive. Confusion between them would defeat reform if any new machinery were simply perceived to be giving weapons to the opponents of public expenditure *per se*.

Four major reasons for the parlous state of parliamentary financial procedures are now examined in turn: the growth of party government; the plight of official secrecy; the divorce between parliamentary approval of expenditure and taxation; and moribund parliamentary financial procedures.

The growth of party government

This is an environmental factor, outside the control of either executive or legislature. Over the hundred years since the procedures in their present form were introduced, an immensely important development has been the growth of party government. Members of Parliament are rarely elected as individuals, in isolation from a party ticket. As members of a party wishing to form a government, they have commitments both to their party and to the policies outlined in the election manifesto. Although an individual MP may disagree with some of those policies, rebellion or dissent has to be carefully rationed as too much will both hinder advancement and diminish influence. The main channels of influence are through party organizations, both those of the parliamentary group and those outside Parliament. Real power over decision-making is thus diverted still further away from the representative chamber. If the backbench MP finds that his influence over policy exerted through parliamentary work is small, he faces even tighter restraints with regard to expenditure. Within the context of a secularly growing public sector, votes on financial matters have become crucial to the credibility and survival of a government working within a parliamentary system. In contrast, the US Congress frequently transforms the shape of presidential budgets.

The convention within the UK is that decisions on public expenditure and taxation are issues of confidence, even at the level of fine detail. However, the parliamentary weakness of the 1974–79 Labour Government not only encouraged backbenchers to flex their muscles but also caused some revisions to these unwritten rules (Higgins, 1978). In 1976, the Labour Government's public expenditure White Paper (Treasury, 1976a) was the subject of a take-note motion which was lost on the abstention of several left-wing Labour MPs. The following day, however, the House of Commons passed a motion of confidence in the Government which then proceeded to implement the plans contained in the White Paper, a document which did not require parliamentary approval, even though it would govern subsequent decisions. Jeffrey Rooker and Audrey Wise, two left-wing Labour MPs, defied their Government and allowed through a Conservative amendment to the 1977 Finance Act, compelling future Chancellors to introduce an order if they wished to negate the otherwise automatic indexation of income tax thresholds. This clause, which owed its success to their abstention, became known as the Rooker–Wise amendment. Although shaken by such defeats, the minority Labour Government shrugged its shoulders and claimed that the normal rules could not apply in an abnormal parliamentary context. An indication that greater backbench assertiveness might be expected in future was provided when the subsequent Conservative Government had to withdraw its 1981 Budget proposal for higher petrol duty. An incipient backbench rebellion made it clear that the Government's comfortable majority would not save it from defeat unless the proposal was withdrawn at report stage.

Despite these incidents which reflect a trend towards greater dissension (Norton, 1980), governments control their parties extremely tightly on financial matters, never neglecting to warn that the alternative would be an election at an inopportune time. Economic policy is so much at the heart of a government's existence that frequent defeats cannot be inflicted by its own backbenchers unless they are prepared to mount an insurrection. This inhibition stretches as far as preventing them from taking their disagreement with particular items anything like as far as voting them down. Through such conventions, and the party pressures against an opposition MP raising financial points on supply days and hence blunting his party's political attack on the government, MPs have little impact. It remains to be seen whether the innovation in the 1982/83 session of having three estimates days (with the other supply days being replaced by opposition days) will make any difference.

There does exist a form of accountability of the executive to the public by virtue of its earlier election on the basis of declared policies and its exposure to future elections. It would be possible to emphasize this direct chain and to downgrade the role of individual MPs. Such an argument would stress the role of manifestos in shaping the alternatives open to the electorate. Once elections have finished, it could be argued that it is the task of the elected government to proceed with its programme. Much clearly depends upon the constitutional relationship between the executive and the legislature. Whereas the traditional complaint in the UK has been the powerlessness of the House of Commons, criticism in the USA has been directed at the inability of the Presidency to respond to the issues of the day as a result of the constraints imposed by Congress.

Although the necessity for speedy decision-making has implications for the structure of systems of accountability, this is a practical point about costs rather than one of principle. There are, however, conflicting views about the extent to which the executive should be responsive to, or insulated from, political pressure. Many of the constitutional proposals of the radical right are explicitly designed to reduce responsiveness because of the alleged deleterious consequences of democratic politics (see also Chapter 11). Littlechild (1978, p. 77) considered that a major reason for the continuation and extension of the mixed economy stems from 'the political problem of democracy'. He considered it necessary:

... to design a constitution to *protect government against special interest groups*. This might be done by more clearly separating the legislative (law-making) function of Parliament from its executive (day-to-day government) function. The legislature would comprise democratically elected members, only a proportion of whom would be elected each year, with each member holding office for a long period, thereby avoiding the need to respond to party or political pressures (Littlechild, 1979, p. 12).

Such a desire to reduce responsiveness contrasts sharply, not only with pressures for a more participatory style of democracy, but also with proposals, particularly within the Labour Party, for much greater control

over the actions of governments to be exercised by the party machinery
outside Parliament. There are clearly conflicting views about whether
detailed forms of accountability are desirable and, if so, the identity of the
group to which account should be rendered: to Parliament, to interest groups,
or to party.

The blight of official secrecy

The British obsession with official secrecy impedes the development of
systems of accountability. Without information, neither the House of
Commons nor the public can make a proper evaluation of the performance of
the public sector. It is not necessary to subscribe to the view that all the inner
thoughts of government should be continuously exposed to the public gaze.
Organizations and individuals need the security afforded by privacy if policy
ideas and practice are to develop coherently. It is not fruitful to be in a
position in which every tentative idea or proposal raised internally has to be
instantly justified or disowned in public. There are stages in the policy
formulation process which require protection, quite apart from the restrictions necessary for national security, commercial confidentiality and information about individuals.

Official secrecy in the UK extends far beyond such limitations. The ability
to scrutinize expenditure decisions depends upon the background information which is released. In its absence, firm conclusions cannot be drawn,
particularly about whether decisions which, with hindsight, seem to have
been wrong, were reasonably based on evidence when they were made. The
tradition of pervasive official secrecy inhibits open examination of policy
options and programme performance. Successive governments refused to
publish the Programme Analysis and Review (PAR) studies, initiated in 1971.
On one occasion, this degenerated to the level of farce. The Expenditure
Committee (1976b) was denied access to a PAR study on educational
planning which had been made available to OECD and referred to at length in
a published report (OECD, 1975). Parliament, the press and the public are
thus denied the information essential to a proper assessment of executive
actions. Much can always be learned from the policy options which are
rejected.

A major consequence of such attitudes has been the development of a
system of government by leaks. It is never easy for those outside the policy
process to assess the information made available in this way. One fact is
always certain: someone believes that there is some advantage to be gained by
making selected items of information public. Examples are easy to find. Parts
of a memorandum from Sir Douglas Wass, the Permanent Secretary at the
Treasury, to Sir Peter Carey, the Permanent Secretary at the Department of
Industry, were reproduced in the *Guardian* of 28 February 1979. This
memorandum stated that, in the last four months of 1978, the then Labour

Government had initiated seven job-saving projects which would involve losses of up to £800 million. Just before the 1981 Budget, the major national newspapers led on the story that, unless the Cabinet agreed to a new package of expenditure cuts, tax increases were inevitable. No source was cited but other journalists attributed it to a Downing Street dinner given by the Prime Minister for selected journalists. Shortly after this incident, Mr Keith Speed, Parliamentary Under Secretary at the Ministry of Defence, with special responsibility for the navy, was sacked for a speech opposing navy cuts. This speech was the culmination of a series of inspired leaks, believed by the Prime Minister to originate in the Ministry of Defence. On several occasions, it has been leaked that the Treasury was pressing for the introduction of hotel charges in the NHS. On each occasion, there have been ministerial denials (for example Fowler, 1982).

Such examples illustrate that leaks are now systematically used by various groups within government in order to try to win internal arguments. The source of the leaks, and the reliability of the information, are often difficult to establish: prime ministers flying kites; ministers who have lost arguments in Cabinet; departments in conflict with their minister; and disaffected individual civil servants. Such leaks have undermined the credibility of certain stated government positions but never provide the basis for the examination of policy options. The tradition on the revenue side is of even greater secrecy but of more success at preventing leaks. The aura of Budget secrecy is pervasive: not only are MPs excluded from the formulation of revenue proposals but so are most members of the Cabinet (Treasury, 1979d). The process is entirely dominated by the Treasury and its ministers. Despite the extensive round of pre-Budget representations by bodies such as the CBI and TUC, the emphasis upon secrecy still precludes outside expertise being used at the preparatory stages. Once the Budget package is unveiled, too much of the government's credibility hinges upon securing acceptance of the Budget resolutions, and their subsequent incorporation in the Finance Act, for it to be easy for any major change to be accepted, whatever its merits.

The divorce between parliamentary approval of expenditure and of taxation

An underlying problem for systems of accountability is the complete divorce between parliamentary approval of expenditure and that of taxation. A proper budget of expenditure and revenue is never presented to the House of Commons: the processes for authorizing expenditure are separate from those for approving the raising of revenue. Such a system breeds compartmentalized minds: enthusiastic spenders can urge higher expenditure without simultaneously considering how it would be financed; and enthusiastic tax cutters can advocate sweeping reductions without specifying comparable expenditure changes. On occasions, the same person does both.

Consequently, none of the difficult choices are ever explicitly posed. To avoid the worst manifestations of the temptations above, the individual MP has been hemmed in by restrictive standing orders on financial matters. Only the government can move a resolution which would incur expenditure or increase a tax. An individual MP can only move a reduction, not an increase, in any item of expenditure and a reduction, not an increase, in any tax (Treasury, 1983a). The consequences are far-reaching. If either the Opposition or Government backbenchers wish to alter the documents upon which they vote, their options are severely limited. It is not possible, for example, to move a reduction in NHS expenditure on hospitals matched by a comparable increase on preventive medicine: only the first part can be done. Similarly, it is not possible to move an increase in tobacco duty offset by higher income tax thresholds. Both these examples show the constraints which are imposed by this divorce between the systems for authorizing expenditure and revenue.

Moribund parliamentary financial procedures

Budget day is pure theatre, more suited to the talents of parliamentary eccentrics than to a serious appraisal of alternative policies. It is primarily concerned with revenue, much less with expenditure, though more recognition of the links has been forthcoming recently. The melodrama directs attention towards what are frequently minor tax changes, sometimes solely maintaining the real yield of excise duties. On the expenditure side, parliamentary procedures run in parallel to the real decisions, being peripheral, though constitutionally necessary. The estimates cycle produces massive quantities of paper, characterized by a morass of fine detail and little overall coherence. Moreover, it suffers from its lack of integration into the system through which governments take decisions on public expenditure levels and priorities. It merely constitutes the formal process of securing annual parliamentary approval for decisions which were taken much earlier. By the time the House of Commons is called upon to approve the supply estimates, the Cabinet's attention has switched to later years. Whether the context is one of growth or cutbacks, the choices faced by the Cabinet are strategic, about levels and composition. The estimates cycle does not provide MPs with a mechanism for articulating their priorities. Nevertheless, such procedures have promoted high standards of 'regularity and propriety', not always enjoyed by other countries.

Although the documentation produced by the estimates cycle is of limited value for policy debate, it is well suited to conventional auditing. Despite the recent criticism of the narrowness of public auditing in the UK, the work of the Comptroller and Auditor General has contributed to the effectiveness and prestige of the Public Accounts Committee. Established by William Gladstone in 1861, the Public Accounts Committee is deeply embedded in the financial procedures of the House of Commons. Unlike other select committees whose resources have been minimal, it has always been able to rely upon the staff of the Exchequer and Audit Department. It deserves credit for impressing high standards of stewardship over public money upon the executive: its comments upon lapses can be caustic and brutal.

Nevertheless, such *ex post* examinations of the appropriation accounts limit the notion of accountability for public money into a narrow mould and play down wider questions of policy and of 'value for money'. Compared to the breadth of the inquiries of the General Accounting Office in the USA, those of the Exchequer and Audit Department are limited in scope (Garrett, 1978; Normanton, 1978). Although select committees have been convinced of the need to revitalize public auditing (for example, Expenditure Committee, 1977; Procedure Committee, 1978; Public Accounts Committee, 1981a; Treasury and Civil Service Committee, 1982a), successive governments have remained unconvinced about the merits of thoroughgoing reform. The standard defence has been that the Comptroller and Auditor General has in practice been moving towards the 'value for money' studies advocated by his critics and that his relationship with the Treasury does not produce the inhibitions which are alleged. The 1979 Conservative Government's White Paper on the role of the Comptroller and Auditor General (Treasury, 1981f) comprehensively rejected select committee proposals for, *inter alia*, a dramatic extension of the bodies subject to his audit (for example, local authorities, nationalized industries and private sector recipients of grants and loans). Given the establishment of two separate inquiries into the financial procedures of the House, by the Procedure (Supply) Committee (1981) and the Procedure (Finance) Committee (1982), the Government's decision will not be accepted as final. Select committee members are likely to use the other channels available to them as a means of sustaining the pressure, such as the private member's Bill introduced by Norman St John-Stevas to extend the remit of the Comptroller and Auditor General (St John-Stevas, 1983).

Narrow interpretations of financial accountability can themselves be a source of difficulty. 'Regularity and propriety' in the use of public funds is an extremely important objective, but not the only one. Two examples emphasize that its achievement always involves costs which might sometimes prove too high. The Manpower Services Commission (MSC) has been rebuked by the Public Accounts Committee (1980a), following reports from the Comptroller and Auditor General that its financial control over job creation programmes had been below the necessary standards. However, the purpose behind the establishment of MSC was to move away from a cautious, civil service style of administration towards more innovative management. The other side of the flexibility and speed with which MSC has launched its programmes has been the willingness to cut corners, notably about the financial control systems of some of the bodies to which it has granted funds. Similar criticisms of the Housing Corporation's supervision of housing associations (Public Accounts Committee, 1978, 1979, 1980b, 1981b) can be countered in the same way. This is not to defend such lapses, simply to note that flexibility, informality and speed will only be attained at the risk of them.

A belief that the House of Commons must recover some of its former financial initiative has been one factor in explaining the development of support for an extended role for select committees. None of the earlier experiments with select committees had been wholly successful: no new creation had ever matched the influence of the Public Accounts Committee. A report from a Procedure Committee (1978), which called for sweeping reform, was enthusiastically endorsed by the Conservative Opposition and by Labour backbenchers, even though the Labour Government was luke- warm. On the return of a Conservative Government in 1979, fourteen select committees were established, twelve covering functional areas and two having territorial responsibilities (one each for Scotland and Wales).

It is too early to make a balanced assessment of this reform. It would appear to be a step in the right direction if the House of Commons wishes to scrutinize government actions more effectively. As action usually involves expenditure, the potential usefulness of these new vehicles is obvious. However, a number of weaknesses remain. Compared to government departments, their resources are minimal, making them heavily dependent upon part-time specialist advisers. Few of the reports are ever debated on the floor of the House of Commons. The question of who reads the reports and evidence has never been answered. Although they contain invaluable infor- mation, much of it unavailable elsewhere, the sheer volume is an obstacle to their use in policy debate. Reading these reports could be a full-time occupation!

Furthermore, the status of select committee work, amidst all the other pressing claims on an individual backbencher's time, has never been clarified. Much effort is expended on a major inquiry but the political rewards are unclear. Except on glamorous enquiries (such as on the financial conse- quences of the sale of council houses (Environment Committee, 1981)) or prestigious committees (notably, the Treasury and Civil Service Committee), the MP's efforts might pass entirely unnoticed. The career incentives of MPs are completely different from those facing members of the US Congress. It is not usually possible to build a career in the House of Commons on the basis of select committee work. Even the one obvious exception, Edward Du Cann, successively the chairman of the Public Accounts and Treasury and Civil Service Committees, partly owes his formidable prestige to his party role as chairman of the 1922 Committee of Conservative backbenchers. An indi- cation of the low standing attached to select committee work by the Labour Opposition was the resignation in 1980 of Donald Dewar from his position as chairman of the Committee on Scottish Affairs in order to take up the offer of a very junior opposition post. To have refused that offer would have prejudiced his chances of obtaining a ministerial post in a future Labour Government.

No informed debate can proceed without information. Until the automatic reflex of covering decisions in a shroud of official secrecy is finally broken, select committees will have to probe away, patiently and methodically. Their performance will probably disillusion their enthusiastic advocates but that should not prevent recognition of the role they can perform in opening up the policy process to wider scrutiny. Much of the work will be unglamorous, planting seeds for others to reap.

However, select committees should not be envisaged as a means of depoliticizing public expenditure decisions and of undermining party government in favour of a consensus style of government. Such a development would provoke antagonism from other MPs towards their role. Furthermore, select committees cannot be insulated from the growing political divisions over the role of the state. Although matters of fact can be established and areas of disagreement narrowed, different value judgements will lead to different conclusions. Too much emphasis upon the consensus-generating role would be misguided. The investigative and information-gathering roles can themselves provide valuable inputs into the party political conflict, by raising the quality of the debate. That wider debate, whether in the House of Commons or in the media, is now typically of an extremely poor quality, mirroring prejudice rather than reasoned argument.

IV CONCLUSION

Establishing the scale of public expenditure and the priorities within it ought to be at the heart of the democratic political process. It ought not to be undertaken in the recesses of executive secrecy nor should the ability to contribute informed criticism be restricted to a few 'technician' MPs who have served on specialist select committees. Reforms to parliamentary procedures are essential if the mechanisms of constitutional accountability are to be revitalized. The importance which should be attached to realizing the potential of other types of accountability does not detract from the urgency of this task. With confusion reigning at the macro level, it becomes more difficult to establish and sustain the mechanisms of other types of accountability and to reconcile the inevitable conflicts between them. Moreover, institutions and procedures for securing accountability cannot function effectively unless proper regard is taken of the way in which decisions are reached. The formal parliamentary processes have become moribund because of their increasing isolation from the realities of decision-making. Before any comprehensive plan for restoring accountability can be devised, it is first necessary to examine the parallel system of public expenditure management and control.

CHAPTER 8

Managing and Controlling

I THE DISTINGUISHING CHARACTERISTICS OF THE POST-PLOWDEN SYSTEM

The Plowden Report (Plowden, 1961) exercised a dominating influence over the development of the Public Expenditure Survey (PESC) as an executive process independent of the supply procedures. Although the system was substantially modified in the mid-1970s, with the introduction of cash limits, its objective of establishing a comprehensive planning system remained influential.

The fierce criticism to which PESC has been subjected since the mid-1970s has dimmed awareness of how much the post-Plowden reforms did in fact achieve. They detached the planning and control of public expenditure from the cumbersome and inappropriate supply procedures and established many of the necessary features of an effective system. The report of the Estimates Committee (1958) which preceded the establishment of the Plowden investigation convinced most observers and participants that the procedures inherited from earlier generations with a minimal public sector were now inadequate and chaotic. Decisions were taken within a framework which stressed a single financial year without regard to the momentum or profile of expenditure commitments. Only supply expenditure was ever presented to Parliament, meaning that no comprehensive picture of the size, composition or trend of public expenditure was made available. There was no explicit linking of the claims to be made by public expenditure with the resources likely to be available. Not only did PESC establish a new framework but it also encouraged an extension of some of the techniques of appraisal and multi-year planning which had already been initiated, mainly on the defence side.

The initial assessments of PESC were favourable, not just those of its architects (Clarke, 1971; Goldman, 1973) but also of academic observers vith experience of budgetary reforms in other countries (Galnoor, 1974; Heclo and Wildavsky, 1974). The reasons why PESC's reputation was ransformed from that of model child to delinquent monster are taken up ater in this chapter.

The distinguishing characteristics of the PESC system can themselves be raced to the recommendations of the Plowden Report. Unlike some other attempts to reform the machinery of government, the Report's recommendations were faithfully implemented, perhaps owing much to the strength of commitment of key Treasury officials, such as Sir Richard Clarke who had himself been a member of the Plowden Committee (Clarke, 1978; Pliatzky, 1982a). Some of its subsequent flaws can also be detected, notably hose relating to the interface between technocratic planning systems and the ealities of political decision-making.

Multi-year framework

The PESC system adopted a multi-year framework. One year's public expenditure is heavily predetermined by previous decisions. Change is possible only at the margin, though ideas of what constitutes a margin expanded in the 1970s. There is a time lag before programmes can be expanded, or reduced, or priorities changed. Consequently, attention must be focused beyond the immediate year, when the room for manoeuvre is necessarily limited, towards later years in which it is much greater.

This 'forward look' was explicitly linked by the Plowden Report to the medium-term assessment of the growth of resources available within the economy, out of which public expenditure growth would be financed. The projected growth in output assumed in successive White Papers was usually too optimistic whereas planned growth in public expenditure was usually achieved. This led to unintended increases in the public expenditure/GDP ratio, followed by panic efforts to cut programmes at short notice. Heclo and Wildavsky (1981) convincingly argued that such a planning framework, when operated in the closed world of Whitehall insulated from external criticism, established a bias in favour of public expenditure growth. Outsiders could never compare plans and outturns as programmes were rolled forward on to a different price basis.

Comprehensive coverage

The post-Plowden system attempted comprehensive coverage. If the objective was to secure an overall picture of the size of public expenditure in relation to available resources, such coverage was essential. For example, it involved considering the large spending programmes of local government, whereas the supply procedures limited themselves to central government grants to local authorities.

The objective of comprehensive coverage is worth sustaining. Thre difficulties to which its implementation has given rise should, however, b noted. First, such a move in the UK was not followed in other countries leaving the UK with an untypically wide official definition of public expendi ture. When used in international comparisons, this practice resulted ii misunderstandings and, on some occasions, outright misrepresentation.

Second, local government expenditure, even that part financed by loca taxes, has been included within the public expenditure totals on whic Cabinets make decisions. The fact that these decisions are taken withou reference to elected local authorities has played its part in generating sever strains in central–local relations.

Third, the commitment to comprehensiveness has never extended either t tax expenditures or to coerced private expenditures. The 1979 White Pape (Treasury, 1979a) was the first to produce an official costing of tax expenditures. These have remained as supplementary tables, accompanied b strong warnings that they are subject to considerable margins of error an that individual estimates cannot be added. There is no programme attri bution. Negligible resources have been devoted to improving such estimate and there have been frequent ministerial denials of significance. Even les attention has been devoted to quantifying coerced private expenditures.

Comprehensiveness thus has some dangers which only a clear understand ing of the structure of the public sector and careful international comparison can overcome. Nevertheless, the case for greater comprehensiveness remain compelling, especially at the margins where public expenditure blurs into ta expenditures and coerced private expenditures.

Volume planning

Programmes were planned in constant prices. It is virtually impossible t interpret a time series of expenditure over an inflationary period if this i expressed in current prices. The question 'has the level of service provisior increased or decreased and by how much?' can never be answered. Meaning ful answers can only be given using a constant price series. The clumsy jargor and mechanics of 'constant prices' ('funny money') is an essential supplemen to data in 'current prices' or 'cash'. Just as for the interpretation of pas trends, projections of future spending must be in constant price terms if ther is to be serious analysis of resource implications and options. It is unneccessar to complicate the forward planning of public services by the introduction o forecasts of inflation which are inevitably subject to a wide margin of erro and to frequent revision.

The plans of successive public expenditure White Papers were presented ir volume terms, being expressed in 'survey prices'. For example, the 197 White Paper (Treasury, 1975) summarized plans for the period 1974/75 t 1978/79 in 1974 survey prices (broadly speaking, those ruling around the enc of 1973). The following year's White Paper (Treasury, 1976a) rolled these plans forward one year, taking in 1979/80, revised them in the light of new decisions and revalued the programmes to 1975 survey prices. Such a revaluation procedure was thus an essential part of the multi-year planning system.

Broad categories of expenditure were revalued according to actual movements in costs. There are two objections to this procedure, if the resulting volume series is allowed to stand on its own. First, it means that the public sector is automatically fully compensated for wage and price increases, however large these might be. Second, the managers in the public sector should be responding to changing relative input prices by substituting now cheaper for now more expensive inputs. However, revaluation procedures implicitly assume fixed input proportions and therefore provide overcompensation if managers are acting as cost-minimizers.

Before this crucial area of weakness is analysed, another defect should be noted. Until the changes introduced in 1976, the planning system diverted attention from cash figures (Godley, 1976; Heald, 1976a; Wright, 1977). This was a consequence of how the Treasury presented the figures, particularly to outside audiences, rather than of an inherent characteristic of the system. There was no logical reason why readily comparable data, facilitating transition from the moving constant price base to cash, could not have been available. The main practical reason probably was the existence of primitive management information systems. However, the failure to establish a link between the constant price and cash figures did much to discredit volume planning.

The relative price effect

The critical weakness of pure volume planning is to be found in the tendency of public sector costs to rise through time at a considerably faster rate than private sector costs. The alternative explanations for this phenomenon, namely Baumol's disease and growing X-inefficiency, were considered in Chapter 5. Whatever the underlying causal mechanism, the result is that even a constant volume of public services costs steadily more to finance, pushing up the public expenditure/GDP ratio and imposing strains on the taxation system. Over a period of years, the relative price effect takes a dramatic toll. If the relevant cost index had risen from 1948 to 1981 at the same rate as the GDP deflator, general government final consumption would have increased in money terms eighteen-fold rather than the actual thirty-fold. Any comparison over such a long period is necessarily subject to a large number of caveats, such as the absence of quality adjustments, the inclusion in the government consumption index of import prices which are excluded from the GDP deflator, and the distortions introduced by the base-weighting system when the composition of expenditure has shifted markedly over the period. Nevertheless, the broad trend is unmistakable.

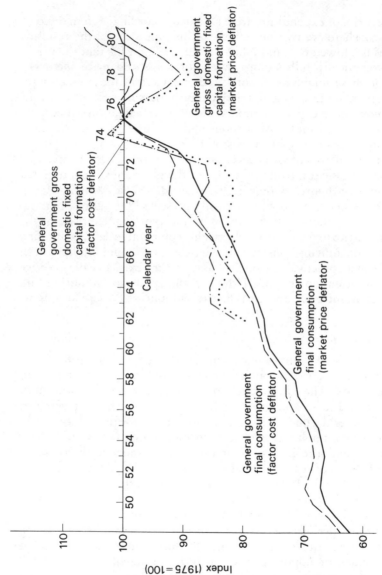

Figure 8.1 Public sector costs relative to GDP deflators, 1948–81

Source: Central Statistical Office (1982b).

Notes: The Treasury used the factor cost deflator (see the methodology handbook, Treasury, 1972, p. 25) but has switched to the market price deflator (Treasury, 1983b, Vol. I, p. 17). The pattern of relative price effects, on a year-on-year basis, is clearly sensitive to the choice of deflator.

Figure 8.1 plots the relative cost indexes for general government final consumption for the period 1948–81 and for general government gross domestic fixed capital formation for the period 1962–81. Over 33 years, the real cost of general government final consumption rose by roughly two-thirds relative to costs for the economy as a whole, whether measured by the market price GDP deflator (solid line) or by the factor cost GDP deflator (dashed line). Until the mid-1960s, deviations from the trend were subdued. Although the two GDP deflators move together over the medium-term, they can give different answers for any particular year as to the size and sign of the relative price effect. Neither are the relative price effects in successive years entirely independent: years of negative (that is favourable) relative price effects tend to be followed by years of large positive relative price effects which see the trend reassert itself. The relative price index for general government domestic fixed capital formation, only available for a shorter period, shows even more volatility in the 1970s. The effect on this index of general economic conditions is dramatic: there was a positive relative price effect of 18.6 points in the two years 1972–74 and then a negative relative price effect of 13.3 points in the four years 1974–78 (using the market price deflator).

The existence of a trend relative price effect, itself subject to measurement problems, complicates the task of interpreting the expenditure record in a way which was deliberately sidestepped in Chapter 2. In order to establish the rate of growth of 'real' government expenditure, adjusted for the relative price effect, it is necessary to select appropriate deflators. The difficulties facing such adjustments are illustrated by the work of Beck. In his original article (Beck 1976), he concluded that:

> In real terms government's share of gross domestic products declined between 1950 and 1970 in a majority of thirteen developed countries studied (p. 15).

> ... government's share of the GDP in Great Britain shrank from 30% to 25% over the two decades (p. 16).

However, Beck (1979) later retracted these conclusions:

> Calculations of public-sector size [in Beck, 1976] were based on an unweighted deflator – the only one then available. As will be demonstrated in this report, which employs a *weighted* price index for *total* government expenditure, the growth curve for government spending has turned negative for collective consumption ... but not for transfer outlays. ... Over the study period [now 1950–77] size of the public sector expanded in real as well as nominal terms (p. 314).

> A total of seven countries, including the UK, reduced the proportion of resources allocated to general public services while enlarging the overall public sector (p. 319).

At 36% of real GDP, the total public sector of the UK in 1977 was considerably larger than in 1950, but well below the 41 percent level suggested by undeflated data (p. 320).

The reason for such dramatically different answers lies simply in the choice of deflators. In the 1979 study, Beck used separate deflators for exhaustive expenditure and for transfer payments: for the first using an index of government costs and for the second using the implicit price deflator for private consumption expenditure derived from the national accounts. In contrast, the earlier 1976 study had, entirely inappropriately, used a government cost index to deflate total expenditure. Although it is easier to criticize than to do better, the transformation of Beck's earlier well-publicized results emphasizes the need for much greater caution.

The discussion so far has focused exclusively upon the difficulties created for the interpretation of the historical record. Of much greater practical importance are the consequences for the planning and control system. The Plowden Report (1961) made no reference to the relative price effect. It was referred to, but only in a footnote, in a public expenditure White Paper published in December 1963 (Treasury, 1963, p. 10). The first of the series of annual public expenditure White Papers was published in 1969 (Treasury, 1969). From then until 1981, there were two constant price series: the volume series and a cost series, described as 'in cost terms including the relative price effect'. Although there was growing recognition in the Treasury of the significance of the relative price effect, the form of presentation of the annual public expenditure White Papers directed attention to the volume basis on which functional programmes were analysed and diverted it from the summary table on the cost basis. The reason for this emphasis is understandable, even if the consequences have proved damaging. A Treasury publication on methodology (Treasury, 1972, para. 70) noted that:

> The net effect of the RPE adjustment is to increase the growth rate of total public expenditure by some 0.6 per cent per annum; it thus adds nearly 2.5 per cent to the figures for the final year of the Survey.

It warned that this was only a trend allowance and the actual relative price effect fluctuated from year to year. Given such volatility, it would have been more difficult to use the cost rather than volume series as the main planning figures.

Despite its technical sophistication, PESC was undermined by two factors concerning the relative price effect. A glance back at Figure 8.1 confirms the much greater fluctuations around the long-term trend which accompanied the much higher rates of inflation of the 1970s. This development exposed the weaknesses of the control system which had not developed a similar sophistication to the planning system. Even more significantly, there has been

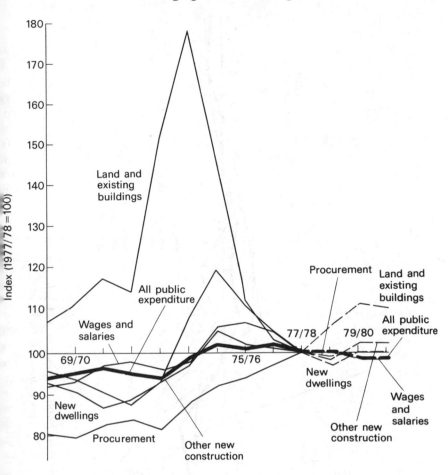

Figure 8.2 Relative price indexes: public expenditure by selected economic categories, 1968/69 to 1980/81

Source: Redrawn freehand from the graph in Treasury, 1979a, p. 235.
Note: The solid lines relate to outturns and the dashed lines plot the projected relative price effect planned for in the 1979 public expenditure White Paper.

a political refusal to recognize the practical realities of the relative price effect. Governments have dissembled, or perhaps deceived themselves, that it can be suppressed. Price (1979, p. 71) attributed the expenditure cuts introduced by the Conservative Government in 1979 to the assumption made in the Labour Government's 1979 White Paper (Treasury, 1979a) that there would be no relative price effect over the planning period:

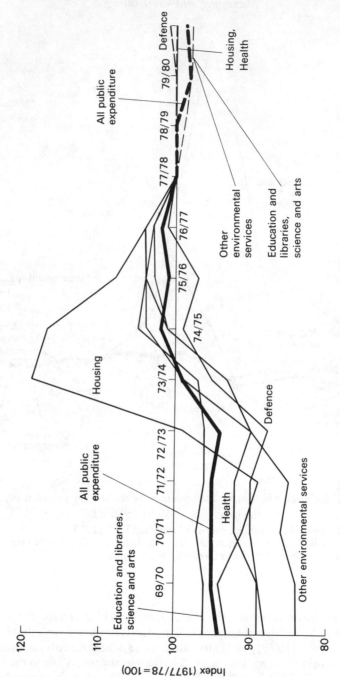

Figure 8.3 Relative price indexes: public expenditure by selected programmes, 1968/69 to 1980/81
Source and note: See Figure 8.2.

The current crisis is explicable in terms of the re-emergence of the relative price effect in general government consumption of goods and services category of spending ... after a number of years when it has been suppressed.

The annual public expenditure White Papers have provided limited analysis of the relative price effect. Nevertheless, the data which are available indicate that during the 1970s the relative price effect was not just volatile but varied dramatically by economic category. A proper analysis can therefore only be undertaken at a disaggregated level. The relative price effect is not restricted to wages and salaries, with other economic categories making a major contribution. The 1979 White Paper (Treasury, 1979a) provided a diagram, redrawn as Figures 8.2 and 8.3, which showed relative price indexes for the period 1968/69 to 1977/78 by selected economic categories and programmes, and projected relative price indexes for the years 1978/79 to 1980/81. Price's criticism is easily understood when the negligible projected changes in the indexes (broken lines) are compared with the volatile historical record (solid lines). The most remarkable feature of Figure 8.2 is the behaviour of the indexes for 'land and existing buildings' and for 'new dwellings': dramatic rises in the period 1971/72 to 1973/74 were followed by falls. Over the period the index for 'procurement' rose significantly. The impact on individual programmes reflects their composition by economic category: for example, the housing index reflects the sharp rise in property costs in the 1971/72 to 1973/74 period. Unfortunately, no other White Paper has ever provided such an informative diagram over a similar period.

The late 1970s were a period in which the relative price effect was suppressed but then reasserted itself dramatically in 1980/81. Figures 8.4 and 8.5 are consistent with Table 4.13 of the 1981 White Paper (Treasury, 1981d). It should be stressed that such analyses by economic category and spending authority are very approximate and that not too much significance should be read into the precise values. Nevertheless, they demonstrate that, the greater the degree of disaggregation, the picture which emerges becomes more complex. The solid lines again relate to the historical record and the broken lines to the projected years. Taking volume spending measured in 1979/80 average prices as the base, the two figures show the percentage additional/reduced cost for each of the years 1975/76 to 1981/82 relative to that base. Figure 8.4 disaggregates by economic category and Figure 8.5 by spending authority, though the latter also distinguishes wages and salaries. Not only does the volatility of public sector pay emerge dramatically but the variations by spending authority are themselves marked: contrast the paths of central and local wages and salaries. Yet it must be stressed that the relative price effect is not a phenomenon just restricted to pay. To its credit, the 1981 White Paper did recognize the re-emergence of the relative price effect, although it underestimated its size.

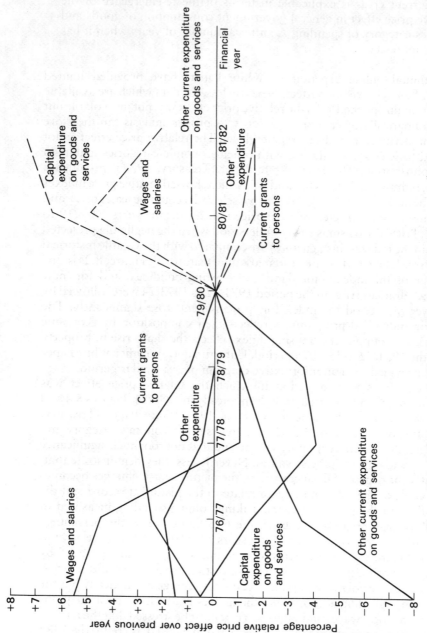

Figure 8.4 *Relative price effect by economic category, 1975/76 to 1981/82*

Source: Treasury (1981d, p. 217).

Note: These figures should be regarded as rough approximations, less reliable than the standard usual for public expenditure

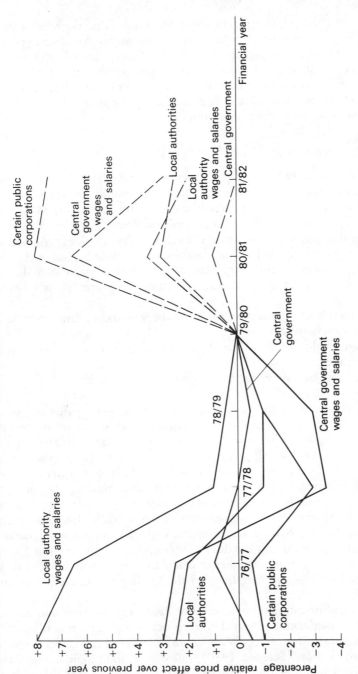

Figure 8.5 Relative price effect by spending authority, 1975/76 to 1981/82

Source: Unpublished data supplied by HM Treasury.

Note: See Figure 8.4.

In 1979, the Labour Government wished to believe that the relative price effect had disappeared, whereas what was just coming to an end was a period in which it had been suppressed. From 1982, the Conservative Government's abandonment of planning in constant prices means that the data are no longer collected which would facilitate further analysis along the lines of this section. A belief that the relative price effect can be suppressed by the rigours of cash planning is yet another delusion.

The neglect of evaluation

The public expenditure White Paper, despite its undeniable merits, remains primarily a document about resource inputs. It provides invaluable information about the resources used in public expenditure programmes but says little about the outputs which are purchased with them. It is likely that there will never be unequivocal measures of the value of the output of programmes as diverse as operating nuclear submarines, performing hernia operations and teaching economics. But if the issue of output measurement (Williams, 1967) is neglected, three types of question cannot be properly answered:

(1) How far should public expenditure be expanded, thus sacrificing private expenditures?
(2) Can better value for money be obtained by switching resources between programmes?
(3) Is it possible to achieve the same output with fewer inputs?

Question (1) leads to the condition that the marginal value of public expenditure should be equal to its marginal cost in terms of private expenditures foregone. Question (2) leads to the condition that marginal benefit should be equal for all programmes. However, more progress can be made on question (3) than on the first two in the absence of measures of output. Cost minimization requires that the marginal product of each input should be equal to its marginal cost. When undertaking cost minimization exercises in the absence of output measures, it is often difficult to ensure that output does, in fact, remain unchanged. A good example is alternative methods of providing care for the elderly, in hospitals, old people's homes or in their own homes. It is much easier to calculate the resource costs of these options than to assess the variations in the quality of life (Williams and Anderson, 1975).

Despite its sophistication on other counts, PESC neglected evaluation. The early attempts (Bridgeman, 1969, 1970) to develop programme budgeting frameworks, notably for police (Wasserman, 1970) and education (Department of Education and Science, 1970), failed to sustain their momentum. Much was then made in the early 1970s of the potential of Programme Analysis and Review (PAR) which originated out of the enthusiasm of the

Conservative Government of Edward Heath for introducing businessmen and their methods into government. It was intended that a regular system of PAR studies would be synchronized into the annual PESC survey, with a number of sub-programmes being scrutinized each year. The unhappy fate of PAR reveals much about the workings of British central government: it promised much but only burned dimly, then flickered on for several years before expiring in 1979 (Gray and Jenkins, 1982).

The Public Expenditure Survey was built upon the assumption that collegiate decision-making by Cabinet ministers on public expenditure plans would lead to a willingness to forswear departmental loyalties and take a broader view. In practice, however, the tendency to evaluate the ability and competence of a minister in terms of how effectively he advances his department's interests, or protects it in hard times, is deeply ingrained in British political culture. Furthermore, ministers proved reluctant to join the Treasury in an attack on other ministers' programmes for various reasons: fear of subsequent retaliation, personal friendships and the diversion from 'more urgent' business which briefing for such a venture would involve. In such a climate, PAR had no clients. Departments viewed evaluation as a threat and the Treasury was mainly concerned with totals.

The reasons for the failure of PAR remain instructive. First, as an outside initiative, it inevitably was regarded with suspicion by the civil service, and the 'irregulars' who were its initial moving force were outside established networks and critically dependent upon sustained political support. Although prime ministerial support was given in the early stages, it did not survive the changed preoccupations of the Heath Government after 1972.

Second, PAR had no coherent body of techniques. Although advantages were claimed for such eclecticism, this characteristic reflected the lack of detailed thought as to how and where business techniques could be applied in the public sector. A certain naivety about the real differences between public and private sector decisions, notably over the definition of relevant costs and benefits, provided legitimate counter arguments, perhaps even where the criticisms were substantively correct.

Third, the machinery through which PAR was operated left it exposed to almost every budgetary trick. Departments could volunteer for study either their strongest programmes or ones of extreme political sensitivity, thus protecting their weak programmes. The energies of PAR could thus be misdirected or led into political traps in which it would be discredited.

Fourth, PAR succumbed to Whitehall's greatest defence mechanism, that of official secrecy. Businessmen dislike publicity about their own affairs and such advisers would be only too anxious to keep out of the public limelight. However, the effect of decisions behind closed doors in Whitehall is different. Whereas in business, this means that decisions can be taken in isolation from outside pressures, the effect in Whitehall is to ensure that such external pressures are exercised in a secret, unaccountable way.

Programme Analysis and Review was so shrouded in secrecy that not even a list of topics being examined was publicly available. The results were never published, or at least not identified as PARs. Initially, it was implied that public references to them could not be made because they were so penetrating and that they would cease to be so forthright if available for other eyes. Later, the lack of reference seemed to mean that PARs were really not of significance, in comparison with some of the major policy reviews undertaken by the Labour Government, notably on energy, housing and transport.

The announcement by the 1979 Conservative Government that PAR had been formally abandoned neither surprised nor distressed anyone. Its attempts to apply business methods to government took a different form. Sir Derek (later Lord) Rayner, who had been a member of the panels of businessmen set up by Edward Heath, returned to Whitehall on secondment from Marks and Spencer PLC in order to act as adviser to the Prime Minister on a part-time, unpaid basis. The main thrust of Rayner's work has been directed towards question (3) on p. 186: using less inputs to achieve the same output. There has been little of the type of evaluation which would satisfy the microeconomist interested in efficient resource allocation in the public sector. To emphasize this crucial deficiency is to urge the need for a proper evaluative framework, not to dismiss the potential of Rayner's methodology for curbing X-inefficiency in the public sector. Some of the areas which have been examined clearly involve managerial problems common to the public and private sectors. Attempts to instil into the public sector the cost consciousness of the best parts of the private sector are wholly admirable.

Rayner's approach subsumed two separate kinds of activity: 'scrutinies' which are short (that is ninety day) investigations of particular aspects of the work of central government, each undertaken by an 'examining officer' from the affected department, operating on the basis of ground rules established by Rayner; and 'lasting reforms' designed both to alter managerial styles and to clarify responsibilities for the management of resources (Allen, 1981; Likierman, 1982b). There are annual programmes of departmental scrutinies, with responsibility for accepting and introducing the proposed changes resting with the relevant minister. Emphasis has been placed upon eliminating obsolete activities; terminating those activities whose benefits are not worth the costs involved; and simplifying administrative procedures. The lasting reforms have included a review of administrative forms (Cabinet Office, 1982a) and the improvement of inadequate management accounting systems. In strengthening the latter, great stress has been placed upon the introduction of recharging for goods and services hitherto supplied free of charge to departments, such as those of the Central Computer and Telecommunications Agency, Her Majesty's Stationery Office and the Property Services Agency.

Rayner's undoubted impact has stemmed from sustained political support in a climate in which deep ministerial hostility towards the civil service has pushed it back onto the defensive. The spending areas subjected to Rayner scrutinies have been publicly identified, with progress reports given, listing the expenditure and manpower reductions secured (for example, Rayner, 1982). Supported by a small unit, Rayner has reported direct to the Prime Minister, thus acquiring a political backing denied to PAR which had to be cleared through the top hierarchy of the affected department. His emphasis upon cost cutting and the elimination of unnecessary activities has struck a chord with a Prime Minister who has developed a deep distrust of the public sector and its employees. Manpower and expenditure reductions have become part of prime ministerial machismo, a tangible sign of her determination to curb the size and scope of the public sector. Recognizing the obstacles confronting such a transformation, she was reported early in her period of office to be concerned about the need to alter the structure of ministerial incentives, towards cutting rather than expanding or defending programmes. Although meeting with mixed success in the case of departmental ministers, a series of judicious appointments to key Treasury and other economic posts, backed up by special machinery such as Rayner's, has enabled her to retain the initiative in an area where previous efforts have petered out lamely. With such support, Rayner's work, even where disliked, had to be taken seriously. Moreover, her enthusiasm for almost any measure which could be described as privatization opened up new policy options and provided a background threat, capable of being used as a sanction against non-compliance or obstruction. Given the role which such political backing has played in establishing Rayner's standing, there must be serious doubts as to whether the impetus will be maintained now that, after his departure from Whitehall, his unit has become part of the newly established Manpower and Personnel Office, itself created out of the ashes of the ill-starred Civil Service Department.

Despite his admirable success at ruffling civil service attitudes, Rayner's activities should themselves be subjected to close scrutiny. Although political backing has been crucial, it may have reinforced his own inclination to view the tasks of government in an excessively narrow light, responding to the Prime Minister's desire to publicize expenditure savings and manpower reductions. But cutting expenditure is not synonymous with increasing efficiency. Such preoccupations may distort policies, especially in areas where benefits are intangible but costs are tangible, or where costs hitherto borne by government can be off-loaded. Similarly, the climate in which his work has been undertaken has polarized attitudes, with the result that there is no convincing source of independent expertise capable of evaluating Rayner's work. Well-defined positions have been struck by those involved: either Raynerism is about 'strengthening civil service management' (according to a member of his staff; Allen, 1981) or about 'securing manpower cuts in disguise' with little concern for either equity or the effect on output (according to a civil service union official; Christie, 1982). Whilst 'savings' are trumpeted, counter claims flourish, with discrimination between then being an elusive task: the apparent insensitivity of Rayner to fundamenta issues concerning the nature of the managerial task in the public sector i counterposed with union denials that improvements can be made.

Issues of efficiency and equity are both involved. The principles illustrated by the examples below are more important than the cases themselves, with their expository power stemming from the way in which they focus the issue: sharply. What is disturbing about the Rayner exercises is that they are no always sensitive to the point at which genuine public/private differences d emerge. Whereas Chapter 5 revealed just how complex is the issue o efficiency in the public sector, many of those subtleties seem to be ignored Three interesting examples illustrate this neatly. First, Rayner has pressed fo the government statistical services and Ordnance Survey to be placed on more commercial basis, equating a move towards profitability with greate efficiency. An unsigned article in *Public Money* (1981a, p. 3) quoted at lengtl from Rayner's proposals for the government's statistical services, comment ing that these: '. . . typify only too well the narrowness of the Rayner vision o what government is about'. Rayner's advocacy of the rapid curtailment o subsidy did not even consider the public good properties of the informatio generated through such services. Because of the unenforceability of copyrigh laws prohibiting photocopying, any supplier, whether government or not can in most cases only reap part of the potential revenue. Furthermore, the government is, for reasons of confidentiality of sources, often a monopol supplier of economic and social statistics without which informed debate within a democratic society is impossible.

The second example relates to industrial training. The standard economi argument for public subsidy is that, as training develops general human capital as well as specific skills, it is impossible for the employer, in the absence of slavery, to appropriate these benefits fully. The individua employer will fear that the workers whom he trains will be poached by othe employers, leaving him carrying the cost. In a world characterized by imperfect capital markets and by collective bargaining, such effects will no be reflected in the wages paid to trainees. The prediction is that, if left entirely to private decisions, there will be an undersupply of training. However Rayner proposed, and the government has largely accepted, that the cost o industrial training should be transferred from the Exchequer to employers.

Third, the Education, Science and Arts Committee's (1982) report on the museums scrutiny which urged abandonment or privatization of the pro posed national theatre museum should be read for its sheer entertainment value. The retired civil servant who undertook the scrutiny obviously enjoyed the opportunity to pronounce on a subject of which he had no prior knowledge, but rather less the roasting subsequently delivered by backbench MPs. The fashionable formula of higher charges and privatization found little support on this occasion. Whereas part of the difficulty stemmed from the startling superficiality of the scrutiny, the much deeper problem that managerial scrutiny can rarely be separated from matters of policy emerged with striking clarity.

In addition to subscribing to an unsustainably narrow conception of efficiency, Rayner's scrutinies inevitably raise difficult problems of equity. Procedural equality is an important requirement in, at least, certain parts of the public sector whereas it is rarely explicitly considered in the private sector. If a Marks and Spencer's shop in a depressed community such as Clydebank in Scotland would be unprofitable, there will be no shop, thus depriving citizens of this facility. Whereas Marks and Spencer PLC feels no sense of obligation in this context, the Manpower Services Commission is widely believed to have obligations to run job centres, even where the odds might appear hopeless. On equity grounds, the state must often provide facilities in unpromising circumstances, where 'profitability' would indicate otherwise.

There remains, of course, scope for debating the particular equity objectives chosen and for ensuring that these are achieved at minimum cost. But the latter exercises must be undertaken with both sensitivity to the equity objectives and careful monitoring of output changes when cost-reducing measures are implemented. Otherwise, value judgements about the relative importance of equity are camouflaged as technical judgements, and cost reductions may reduce both expenditure and efficiency. The accusation by civil service unions that Rayner has downgraded equity is given some support in the following question, one of a set which departments were instructed to ask themselves as they prepared for another round of Rayner scrutinies: 'Is too much attention given to the wishes of individuals and to equity, and not enough to the needs of departments?' (Cited in the *Guardian*, 26 August 1982 and 2 September 1982.) There is nothing wrong in asking such questions, provided that the converse is also considered. The state's relationship to the individual is always a delicate one, an awareness of which seems to be lacking unless that question is to be taken as self-parody. Although union officials obviously have corners to fight, Christie's (1982, p. 8) warning is apposite.

> Reducing control of government finances by cutting checks on grants or reducing staff on the collection side weakens efficiency as money is lost or revenue due not received. It also raises the important issue of equity, or the duty of government to uphold and apply the law across the whole population, evenly and comprehensively. Once again we are drawn back to considering the appropriateness of private sector analogies in making decisions about governments.

If ministers did not appear to value Rayner scrutinies primarily for their ability to generate loudly-acclaimed savings (albeit very small in relation to public expenditure) and for contributions to independently chosen targets for reductions in the size of the civil service, it would be possible to give two cheers rather than one.

Separate systems of executive planning and parliamentary authorization

There has been a clear separation between the system used by the government for planning, managing and controlling public expenditure and the system for securing parliamentary authorization for that expenditure. Although they came together in places, two distinctive systems were in operation, often without much harmony between them. Over the years, several attempts have been made to move them closer together, without full integration ever being attempted.

The separation of expenditure from revenue decisions

Just as parliamentary discussion of expenditure and taxation has been split, there has never been an integrated executive framework for expenditure and revenue decisions, with the cycles being quite separate. Whereas expenditure planning moved on to a multi-year basis, revenue has remained on an annual basis. Such a procedure tends to provoke in outside commentators a reaction of disbelief, tinged with outrage. Public expenditure is planned over the planning period against macroeconomic forecasts of output growth. But the implications for tax rates if such assumptions are realized are never spelled out. Not until the 1980 White Paper (Treasury, 1980b) and the 1980/81 Financial Statement and Budget Report (Treasury, 1980a) was there a published forecast of total taxation and the PSBR.

Setting the overall levels of public expenditure and revenue ought to be a simultaneous decision. It is essentially a question of comparing the marginal benefits from extra expenditure against the marginal costs of revenue, whether this comes from taxes, borrowing, or money creation. Despite the conceptual simplicity of such a formulation, the measurement problems involved make it a difficult decision rule to make operational. Such a recognition does not mean that expenditure planning should be allowed to proceed with a life of its own, entirely removed from such financing questions. In practice, governments have had to make expenditure cuts because the taxation consequences as they unfolded have proved unacceptable. Given a system which does not automatically generate such figures, governments have tended to conceal the tax implications of White Paper plans, fearing the political criticism which 'premature' release of such information would generate. Expenditure and revenue decisions only come together as a single problem for the central policy units in the Treasury. Even most parts of the Treasury are exclusively concerned with one side. The published documents provide irresistible incentives for self-deception, encouraging blindness about the necessity for choice.

II THE END OF PLANNING?

The Public Expenditure Survey promised so much and has been widely judged to have failed. The preceding assessment, broadly sympathetic to the system but stressing the need for more openness, more evaluation and better control systems probably mirrors the orthodoxy of academic commentators. However, the defects of PESC, real and imagined, have produced strong anti-planning views, notably amongst economic journalists and Conservative politicians. In many circles, controlling public expenditure has become synonymous with cutting it: this is particularly apparent in discussion of whether public expenditure is 'out of control', a phrase with both technical ('does the system work?') and political ('is it too high?') overtones.

In the changed climate towards public expenditure, the planning system has attracted much criticism which in reality is more directed at substantive decisions than at procedures. But there were undeniably technical weaknesses, most notably in the failure prior to cash limits to bring together the planning figures (in constant prices) and the actual cash expenditures. When inflation soared in 1974/75, such weaknesses were dramatically exposed (Heald, 1976a). The public sector pay explosion irretrievably damaged the credibility of volume planning. This in turn led at first to cash limits and then to the abandonment of volume planning. Instead of greater sophistication in the form of output measurement being grafted on to the PESC system, blunt instruments reacquired popularity. It is evident from Pliatzky's account (1982a) that there were those in the Treasury, like himself, who had limited commitment to PESC and welcomed such developments. Furthermore, another insider account, that of Joel Barnett, the Chief Secretary to the Treasury in the 1974–79 Labour Government, reveals the continuing weaknesses in ministerial decision-making (Barnett, 1982). Despite the objective of collegiate decision-making on public expenditure priorities, much in the last resort depends upon the political weight and skill of the ministers in charge of particular spending departments. There is a refusal, in the Cabinet just as outside, to acknowledge that explicit choices have to be made, both between public expenditure and taxation, and between competing expenditure programmes.

The introduction of cash limits

Substantial modifications have been made to the post-Plowden system. Cash limits were developed as a mechanism for ensuring that the major public expenditure cuts announced during the budgetary crises of 1976 were in fact achieved. Introduced in financial year 1976/77 and gradually extended in coverage, cash limits structurally altered the entire public expenditure system (Else and Marshall, 1981; Likierman, 1981). The implications of their introduction as an appendage to a volume-based system will now be considered before attention is turned to the subsequent abandonment of volume planning in 1982/83.

In the autumn before a financial year began, revaluation factors had to be set with which to convert the planning figures for that year (expressed in survey prices which were those prevailing during the preceding autumn) into estimated outturn prices. Such a procedure involved two stages.

(1) Automatically applying the *actual* inflation rates applicable to sub-groups of expenditure as revaluation factors, thus converting the price base from year t's survey prices to year $t + 1$'s.
(2) Forecasting *allowable* price increases from year $t + 1$'s survey prices to outturn prices.

Stage (1) was essentially a routine exercise, though disputes did arise about the choice of revaluation factors. Stage (2) was, however, quite different. Forecasts, targets, wishful thinking and even deceit all entered into such calculations.

The Treasury clearly needed to make forecasts of the relevant inflation rate as this influenced cash expenditure, with ramifications for taxation and borrowing. The cruel dilemma was that any honest published forecast was likely to be exceeded, because of the impact it would have on price and wage expectations, with the wages forecast becoming both an effective floor to settlements and a target which union negotiators would seek to exceed. Consequently, the figures adopted for stage (2) were typically targets, on which some slippage was expected, rather than forecasts in the best-estimate sense. These issues represented real difficulties for the Treasury. There was, however, a temptation for it to use for stage (2) figures which were entirely implausible, representing either wishful thinking or an attempt to conceal intended volume cuts. By setting cash limits incorporating stage (2) factors which were much below actual inflation rates, the volume of expenditure could be squeezed without ever making explicit how large cuts were planned.

Whenever the actual inflation rate exceeded the stage (2) factor, cash limits squeezed volume expenditure. It has been widely believed that the parallel existence of a formal incomes policy limited the extent of cash limit squeeze compared with the situation in which there was no such policy. However, recently available evidence qualifies that judgement by showing that the issue is more complex. The Treasury (1982f) has estimated that the lower than actual inflation forecast embodied in cash limits reduced the volume allowed by 3 per cent in 1976/77, by a negligible amount in 1977/78, by 3 per cent in 1978/79, and by 4 per cent in 1979/80 (the years of formal incomes policy). In 1980/81 and 1981/82, years with no formal incomes policy, the comparable figures were 2 per cent and 1 per cent (estimate) respectively. As well as this squeeze on volume from cash limits, there was extensive shortfall (that is less actual volume spending than allowed) in the early years of cash limits, as managers adjusted to the new system (Imber, 1980). Nevertheless, the existence of the Labour Government's 'voluntary' incomes policy, enforced fairly tightly in the public sector, meant that the calculation of stage (2) factors had clear rules on which to work. Once this policy collapsed, cash limits became an implicit public sector pay policy. For 1981/82, cash limits allowed for pay increases of 6 per cent and increases in other costs of 11 per cent. Such a use of cash limits forged a link between the institutions of collective bargaining and the machinery of public expenditure control, a development which is the subject of Chapter 9.

The move to cash planning

From 1982, the White Paper plans have no longer been published in volume terms, but in cash terms, incorporating the Treasury's inflation assumptions. The 1982 White Paper (Treasury, 1982a) used the following revaluation factors from one year's average outturn prices to those of the next: from 1981/82 to 1982/83, 7 per cent; from 1982/83 to 1983/84, 6 per cent; and from 1983/84 to 1984/85, 5 per cent. The switch to cash planning therefore involves the Treasury making assumptions about inflation over the survey period and revaluing programmes on that basis: the implicit volume plans are thus highly contingent. If these assumptions remain unchanged, the volume is a residual, given by the actual inflation rate. The implications of cash planning can best be illustrated by contrasting how it tackles the problem of inflation with that of earlier systems. Three distinct stages in the development of PESC can be identified: (a) pure volume planning (as existed from 1961/62 to 1975/76; (b) volume planning with cash limits (as existed from 1976/77 to 1981/82); and (c) cash planning (as from 1982/83). For each case the effect on volume of a higher than forecast rate of inflation is now examined.

Under *volume planning*, there was no volume squeeze as full compensation would automatically be provided, a practice which led Heclo and Wildavsky (1981, p. xxvii) to conclude that '... PESC indexed the public sector'. Whether such a tolerant system is acceptable depends upon how high, volatile and unpredictable is the rate of inflation. When inflation was low, slowly rising and predictable, the ensuing difficulties were not too serious. For such a system of automatic revaluations to operate, there must be an independent system for monitoring public sector costs, since such a PESC revaluation process is a passive facilitator. Because of recent changes in the climate of public sector industrial relations, the public sector is a generator in inflationary pressures at certain stages of the pay cycle. Pure volume planning is now only feasible with a strictly enforced pay policy. In no other circumstances could volume plans be regarded as sacrosanct.

Under *cash limits*, volume spending would be squeezed if the cash limit factors were lower than the appropriate inflation rates. However, a crucial characteristic of the cash limit system was that such shortfalls in revaluation factors were not cumulative. Subsequent years in the survey period were fully revalued when the transition was made from one year's survey prices to the next. Whether such a reversion to the earlier spending plans is a reasonable procedure or not depends crucially upon the cause of the revaluation shortfall. If public sector costs have gone 'out of control', it is not. If, however, the cash limit had been deliberately set too low, the procedure has some merit in that a modified form of volume planning is still possible. However, such a procedure generates abrupt year-on-year changes: from squeezed volume back to original planned volume for the next year, though this might in turn be subject to cash limit squeeze.

Cash planning makes revaluation shortfalls cumulative in their impact. Revaluation only takes place at the predetermined cash limit factors. The method through which major volume cuts can be secured is quite clear: the revaluation factors set in the 1982 White Paper (Treasury, 1982a) indicate that this is likely to happen unless they are, in the event, revised. This switch to cash planning provides an excellent illustration of how views on technical questions become interwoven with broader judgements about the desirable level of public expenditure. Cash planning, even more so than cash limits, is a blunt instrument of great appeal to those attaching priority to *less* rather than *better* public spending.

III RESCUING THE SYSTEM FROM DESPAIR AND CYNICISM

There is much despair around, and not a little cynicism. After earlier enthusiasm for planning, blunt instruments have many advocates, not least Wildavsky (1980) with his proposed US constitutional amendment limiting government expenditure. For those who believe that public expenditure is both excessive and inferior to private expenditure, blunt instruments have obvious merits. But what can those rejecting both propositions learn from past events and how can the system be reformed to achieve their objectives? Indeed, what should such objectives be? The answer is that there should be a proper framework for taking decisions on the level and composition of public expenditure. Crucially, it is a question of careful examination of benefits and costs. Far more rhetorical splendour can be achieved advancing either the proposition that public is always bad, or its converse, than performing such painstaking and inherently difficult calculations.

There is no shortage of proposals for reform but much resistance on the part of successive governments to implementing them. After generations of neglect, MPs (or at least those manning the key select committees) have been won over, but the practical achievements so far are limited. Although there exist some differences between the various proposals, the similarities are striking. Recently, the report of an unofficial committee established by the

Institute for Fiscal Studies and chaired by the late Lord Armstrong (1980), a former Permanent Secretary at the Treasury and head of the home civil service, has provided a focus for debate. Although largely ignored by the Government, it stimulated the recent bout of select committee inquiries into the budgetary and financial procedures. The Treasury and Civil Service Committee (1982b) endorsed many of the Armstrong proposals and more support is likely to accrue from the specially established Procedure Committee on financial procedures. Rather than evaluate the Armstrong proposals or any variants, this section sets out an agenda designed to re-establish a coherent framework for decisions. No claim as to originality is made for most of its constituent proposals, even where no acknowledgement is given, though these are differences of both emphasis and detail from the Armstrong proposals. More important than the precise detail is that the lessons of past failures are perceived correctly and that the retreat from planning is reversed. Otherwise, the efficient management and control of public expenditure programmes is unattainable. The agenda's nine elements are each discussed in turn.

Integration of revenue and expenditure decisions

There should be a single budget document, subject to a reformed parliamentary procedure. Outsiders have consistently argued for a single document, a view supported by the Armstrong Committee which advocated the publication three months ahead of a provisional tax and expenditure budget, to be subjected in that time to detailed scrutiny by specialist select committees. Negligible progress has been made. Owing to delays in securing agreement to the 1981 White Paper (Treasury, 1981d), it was published on Budget day. Perhaps making a virtue out of necessity the Government announced its intention to adopt such a practice in future years. The tokenism of this change was roundly criticized by the Treasury and Civil Service Committee (1982b) which argued strongly that, prior to thoroughgoing reform, the public expenditure White Paper should be published as soon as decisions are taken, not held back until Budget day. Acceding to this view, the Government published the 1983 White Paper (1983b) at the beginning of February. In response to strong criticism of the inadequacy of the information provided in the regular autumn announcement by the Chancellor of the Exchequer of the final public expenditure plans for the year ahead, the Treasury (1982g) published in 1982 the first issue of the Autumn Statement, a more comprehensive document paralleling the Financial Statement and Budget Report.

Although there may be some timing problems to be resolved, the case for unifying the expenditure and revenue sides is overwhelming. Because final decisions are now taken so late against printing deadlines, there are already some discrepancies between the White Paper, the Financial Statement and Budget Report and the supply estimates. The counter argument has been that an attempt to produce a unified document, supported by supplementary detailed volumes, would run into the difficulty that the latter could not be printed until the former had been agreed. The way to resolve this problem is to recognize that there might have to be a two-stage procedure, with the broad expenditure and taxation strategy being released in advance of the detailed volumes. Reading supply estimates is not the favourite pastime of many MPs: their publication could be delayed provided that summaries were provided. What is required is a fully integrated document which is presented to Parliament as the starting point for parliamentary debate and for subsequent processing through approval procedures.

More openness in the policy system

The existing combination of rigid official secrecy, punctuated by a series of leaks, some of which look inspired, is thoroughly damaging to the cause of establishing a calm and open dialogue about the future of public expenditure. Not only must more information be published but it should take a form which facilitates external monitoring and stimulates meaningful debate. Although both the quantity and quality of published information has markedly improved, mainly thanks to the promptings of select committees, much remains to be done. Not least, comprehensive and accurate handbooks on methodology and sources should be published and systematically updated. The 1972 handbook on methodology (Treasury, 1972) was never updated, nor has there been an update of the excellent 1979 guide to sources of public sector financial information (Treasury and Central Statistical Office, 1979). Although the explanatory and technical notes contained in the annual public expenditure White Paper (for example, Treasury, 1982a, Vol II, pp. 101–9) are partial substitutes and valuable in themselves, the greater sophistication and quantity of published information requires a more ambitious guide.

Greater comprehensiveness

All tax expenditures should be identified, costed and attributed to programmes, being explicitly treated as revenue foregone. A rather longer-term development would be to provide supplementary tables quantifying coerced private expenditures, also with programme attribution.

Revitalize multi-year planning

The PESC system has gradually become more short-term, with the later years of each survey being treated as less and less firm. From the 1981 White Paper (Treasury, 1981d), the survey period was reduced from five to four years. Cash planning has accelerated this erosion of the planning horizon. This

etreat back to the present owes much to the difficulties, both psychological
nd practical, caused by earlier planning within a framework characterized
y over-optimistic macroeconomic forecasts. Yet it has become clear that the
ressures generating public expenditure growth are partly medium-term
recession) and partly long-term (demography). Current developments can
nly be assessed when set in context.

The logic of the planning exercise requires time horizons longer than five
ears, not shorter. Such is the timescale over which demographic change
mpacts in different ways upon health and educational provision, as well as
pon transfers. Policy options can look different. The indexation arrangements of the 1970s appear to have been inadequately costed. The option of
tunnelling through' the peak of demand for places in higher education,
ather than expanding provision for a short period (as in teacher education),
merges much more clearly when the horizon is lengthened. Although such
ssues are probably best dealt with in linked reviews, rather than in the main
nnual document, the difficulties generated by this shortened horizon are
vident. Indeed, by the time it is now published, the first year of the White
Paper's four-year period has almost ended.

The integrated Budget document should provide expenditure plans for five
ears, with the first year starting on 1 April after publication. The first three
ears should provide clear sub-programme detail whilst for the last two years,
he extent of this would depend upon the nature and predictability of the sub-
programme. A chapter in the document would consider the momentum
ehind different programmes over ten and twenty years, so that, for example,
he interaction of demography and current decisions to bequeath expenditure
vould be made explicit.

Within the five-year plan, the planning total for public expenditure would
e determined against the resources available. A new mechanism is required
o prevent over-optimistic macroeconomic forecasts validating extra expen-
liture even when the projected extra output fails to materialize. There can be
o absolute guarantees against such events. The best deterrent is to open up
he system so that any further lapses are made fully explicit. Nevertheless, a
mall technical change would help. One of the beneficial consequences of
udgetary stress has been the development of the contingency reserve as an
ctive instrument. A small part of the planning total is not attributed to
programmes but held by the Treasury. During the year, ministers wishing to
ncrease expenditure must make bids, to be weighed against those of other
ministers, for the money remaining in the contingency reserve (Treasury,
1982e). This is one part of the PESC system in which genuine competition for
esources, and hence explicit choices, has emerged.

The detailed proposal is that the Treasury should set three macroeconomic
orecasts: low, best-estimate and high. The overall level of public expenditure
vould be set against the best-estimate forecast but the total attributed to
programmes would be based on the low forecast. The contingency reserve

would therefore be higher for each successive year of the survey. It would be divided into two elements: triggered release and discretionary release. If the best-estimate output forecast is achieved in year t, the first element would be attributed to programmes for year $t+1$ on a predetermined basis. If output growth falls short in year t, the triggered release for year $t+1$ is cancelled. No triggered release would occur for any subsequent year until the cumulative output growth has recovered, unless explicit revisions to volume figures were announced. The discretionary release element would be operated in the same way as the existing contingency reserve.

Return to volume planning, albeit 'reinforced'

Volume planning is essential but it can no longer stand alone. There should be a return to a modified version of the cash limit system as operated from 1976/77 to 1981/82. Pure volume planning is vulnerable to sudden surges in public sector costs, often, but not always, originating in the industrial relations system. When roughly 30 per cent of the employed population work in the public sector, some form of incomes policy is inevitable: that being so there is much to be said for one which is explicit and subject to monitoring. However, this is not to deny either the practical or political obstacles. With an effective incomes policy, cash limits do not independently squeeze volume expenditure. In its absence, cash limits become a surrogate policy, sometimes biting deeply as they take the full strain. Too often, they are used as a substitute for explicit volume cuts and in an attempt to secure a negative relative price effect.

Explicit planning for the relative price effect

The long-term trend for public sector costs to rise faster than the GDP deflator is well-documented. Regardless of which of the alternative explanations for this phenomenon is accepted, it would be foolish to assume that it will suddenly disappear. If suppressed for a number of years the financial implications of its re-emergence are likely to be dramatic. Differential relative price effects both for programmes and for economic categories will influence the preferred composition of expenditure. Overall, it is likely to diminish the attractiveness of exhaustive expenditure relative to transfer programmes (for which a price index for private consumption is appropriate).

Writing about one of the earlier 'forward looks' into particular areas of public expenditure, themselves the precursors of PESC, Clarke (1978, p. 22) noted:

> Before this [relative price effect] was understood, all forward projections of public services at 'constant pay and prices' significantly underestimated how the charge on resources would appear in five years' time.

Although the technical practice became more sophisticated, the significance of the relative price effect was frequently ignored. It is a reality of which policymakers must be consistently reminded. If not, the public expenditure/ GDP ratio will steadily rise, even when this is not planned. Attempts to suppress the relative price effect will lead in turn to industrial conflict in the public sector; dramatic increases in expenditure during 'catching-up' phases; and hasty and ill-advised cuts in volume expenditure during the resulting budgetary crisis. For this reason more than any other, the move to cash planning must be reversed. If the relative price effect is 'a necessary consequence of economic growth' (Byatt, 1973), it cannot be so easily abolished.

More evaluation, both internally and externally

There is a clear role for Rayner-type cost-cutting exercises, provided that the subtleties of costs and benefits in the public sector are understood. More permanent, and more ambitious, evaluation machinery is nevertheless required. Every sub-programme should be subject to review on a ten-year cycle, with the sequence set in advance and independent of the latest panic or fashion. When the time for an appraisal is approaching, overlapping programme evaluations should be commissioned from the Treasury, the departments and outside specialists. Control of the evaluation budget should be held by the Treasury and Civil Service Committee. Although outside researchers face disadvantages through being outsiders, they are much less likely to be intimidated, and hence to tone down criticism. Their involvement should stimulate internal work, in the knowledge that it will have to stand external comparison.

Proper identification of inter-programme spillovers

The existing information on programmes can be misleading as a guide to policy. For example, higher charges on the housing programme may generate expenditure on another programme, such as social security. Even where it is difficult to integrate such calculations into the formal system, it is essential that such effects are highlighted. Without this information, flawed perceptions of the available trade-offs can lead policy down blind alleys. Cutting public employment during a recession in order to reduce the PSBR may prove counter-productive because of offsetting expenditure on other programmes.

Better management information systems

Budgetary stress has exposed this aspect of public sector management as exceptionally weak, with documentary evidence to this effect being most readily available for the civil service. Until the development of the Financial

Information System (FIS) in the mid-1970s, the Treasury's internal information about spending in the current year was both unsophisticated and out-of-date (Butler and Aldred, 1977; Aldred, 1979). Although the initial steps were prompted by the earlier problem of shortfall, the introduction of cash limits emphasized the need for good, prompt management information. Of particular importance was the development of monthly programme profiles as the basis for monitoring in subsequent years.

In the civil service, the problem of poor management information is reflected in the limited role of professional accountants, whose number and impact have been relatively small. Resistance to such expertise can be detected in the slow pace of developments since the Melville and Burney Report (1973) criticized the civil service's lack of accountancy skills. But it is essential that such skills are applied within a framework giving full recognition to distinctive public sector characteristics. An example of how not to approach such questions is provided by the decision of Michael Heseltine, then the Secretary of State for the Environment, to send in private sector accountants to review the 1981/82 charges of water authorities, securing much-publicized reductions through devices entirely alien to the required move to current cost accounting (McMillan, 1981). To be valuable, accountancy skills should not be confused either with those of the axeman or of the beautician.

Although there are no simple answers, it is possible to improve the financial management of the public non-market sector if such tasks are approached with imagination as well as dedication. However, the Management Information System for Ministers (MINIS) in the Department of the Environment has again emphasized the importance of ministerial commitment if any managerial reforms are to be effective. Likierman (1982a) attributed much of the credit for the implementation of MINIS to Michael Heseltine's enthusiasm to transfer best private sector practice into his department (Heseltine, 1980). This judgement gains credibility from the extraordinary lengths to which officials from other departments have gone to deny the relevance of MINIS to themselves.

The enthusiasm of the Treasury and Civil Service Committee (1982a) for an extension of the MINIS principle, if not detailed practice, throughout the civil service and other parts of the public sector was obviously not shared by departments. It will be difficult to improve the financial management of the public sector if political support is either missing or not sustained. The financial management initiative launched in May 1982 as a method of securing much needed improvements in management accounting and financial information systems is an excellent illustration. But for the personal intervention of the Prime Minister, the Government's response to the wide-ranging Treasury and Civil Service Committee inquiry (1982a) might have been as lame as the earlier White Paper on civil service efficiency (Cabinet Office, 1981), a document brutally parodied in *Public Money* (1981b). The

White Paper (Cabinet Office, 1982b) which finally emerged, for all its shortcomings, made an unprecedented effort to respond constructively to criticisms levelled by a select committee against the efficiency and effectiveness of the civil service. This report has not yet suffered the fate of being scrupulously ignored as experienced by an earlier inquiry undertaken by the Expenditure Committee (1977).

This new-found emphasis upon better management information systems in the civil service has been stimulated by policies of cuts in public expenditure and employment. Parallel weaknesses can be found in other parts of the public non-market sector (for example, Perrin's (1978) study for the (Merrison) Royal Commission on the National Health Service (1979)). Improvements in the financial management of the public sector are just as relevant in the context of public expenditure growth. Recent initiatives should therefore be evaluated on their merits and not rejected because of their origins.

IV CONCLUSION

Crucial parts of this chapter's agenda will be resisted by the Treasury on the grounds of administrative impracticality. Such a claim can be confidently rejected because the practices of other countries (Treasury and Civil Service Committee, 1982b) reveal it to be a camouflage for deeper objections. The UK is exceptionally centralist in its fiscal affairs, with the Treasury and its ministers being opposed to all changes (whether budgetary reform or devolution) which would relax its grip. The crux of the matter is revealed by Pliatzky's (1982b) comment on the Armstrong proposals: '. . . such a move would entail conceding more to Parliament than has so far been conceded to Cabinet' (p. 164). Sustained pressure over a long period offers the best prospect for achieving reform, especially as select committees have helped to build cross-party support. There is, however, a vital issue on which there is far less sign of light. As has emerged from this chapter's discussion of management and control, changes in the climate of public sector industrial relations have exerted a profound influence over developments in the planning and control system. No constructive system, such as advocated in the preceding section, can now operate unless explicit attention is paid to the nature of collective bargaining in the public sector. Unless certain difficulties which have emerged in the industrial relations system can be resolved, blunt instruments, rather than coherent planning, will become increasingly dominant.

CHAPTER 9

Collective Bargaining

I THE GROWTH OF PUBLIC EMPLOYMENT

Initially almost imperceptibly, but later with dramatic force, the much enhanced economic role of the state has brought certain issues to the centre of the political stage and forged unexpected links between them. The desire of governments to combine a large public non-market sector with pursuit of the objective of full employment has made the planning and control of public expenditure inextricably linked to the conduct of public sector industrial relations. During the 1970s, such issues not only became more intransigent but began to dominate the entire economic and political agenda.

The state's role as an employer has increased dramatically with the emergence of the welfare state. Many of its major services are extremely labour intensive. In 1901, only 5.8 per cent of the working population in the UK were public employees (Abramovitz and Eliasberg, 1957), but by 1982 this had reached almost 30 per cent. The Central Statistical Office has compiled a statistical series for UK public employment which extends back to 1961, distinguishing between central government, local authorities and public corporations (Semple, 1979; Lomas, 1980; Briscoe, 1981; Morrison 1983). Caution is required for detailed interpretation because of transfers between the public and private sectors and reclassifications within the public sector.

The broad trends are clear from Figure 9.1. Over just two decades, the public sector proportion of the employed labour force increased by 6 percentage points: from 23.9 per cent to 29.9 per cent. The major expansion was in the core services of the welfare state: the contribution of the NHS and local authority, education, health and social services went from 6.3 per cent to 13.3 per cent of the employed labour force and from 26.2 per cent to 44.4 per cent of public employment. The available evidence on the detailed growth of public employment has been helpfully brought together by Parry (1980) and Wilkinson and Jackson (1981).

The UK's ranking among OECD countries on employment is much higher than on expenditure, reflecting its emphasis on direct provision of health and

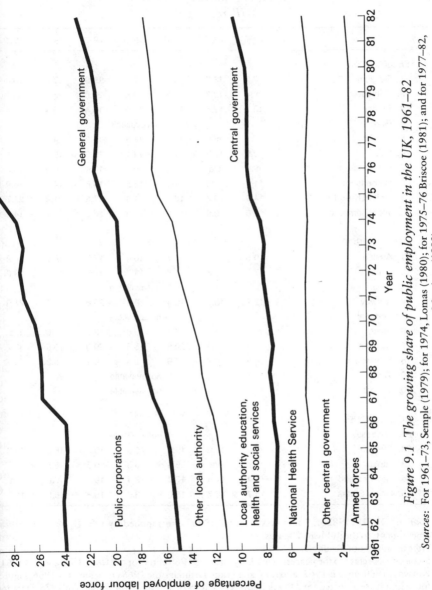

Figure 9.1 The growing share of public employment in the UK, 1961–82

Sources: For 1961–73, Semple (1979); for 1974, Lomas (1980); for 1975–76 Briscoe (1981); and for 1977–82, Morrison (1983).

Notes: The original sources should be consulted about both definitions and reclassifications. The figures are mid-year estimates.

Table 9.1: The share of general government in total employment in OECD member countries, 1960–80
(Percentage)

	1960	1965	1970	1975	1978	1979	1980
A. EEC-EUROPE							
1. Belgium	12.2	13.2	13.9	15.2	16.9	17.6	18.0
2. Denmark	n/a	13.2	16.8	23.6	25.8	26.9	28.1
3. France	13.1	12.5	13.4	14.9	15.4	15.4	15.5
4. Greece				not available			
5. Ireland	n/a	n/a	11.2	13.4	14.2	14.3	n/a
6. Italy	9.0	10.9	11.8	14.1	15.0	15.1	15.1
7. Luxembourg	n/a	n/a	9.4	9.8	10.4	10.6	10.8
8. Netherlands	11.7	11.5	12.1	13.5	14.6	14.7	14.9
9. United Kingdom	**14.9**	**15.7**	**18.0**	**21.0**	**21.3**	**21.4**	**21.7**
10. West Germany	8.0	9.8	11.2	13.9	14.5	14.7	14.8
B. OTHER EUROPE							
11. Austria	10.5	11.6	13.7	16.4	17.7	18.0	18.2
12. Finland	7.8	9.3	11.8	14.7	17.8	18.1	18.2
13. Iceland				not available			
14. Norway	12.7	13.8	16.4	19.2	20.8	21.1	21.6
15. Portugal				not available			
16. Spain	n/a	6.6	7.1	10.0	12.3	12.6	n/a
17. Sweden	12.8	15.3	20.6	25.5	29.0	29.8	30.7
18. Switzerland	6.3	6.7	7.9	9.4	10.1	10.2	10.2
19. Turkey				not available			
20. Yugoslavia				not available			
C. NON-EUROPE							
21. Australia				not available			
22. Canada	n/a	17.6	19.5	20.3	19.8	18.9	18.8
23. Japan	n/a	n/a	5.8	6.5	6.5	6.5	6.6
24. New Zealand	17.4	17.4	17.7	18.4	19.2	n/a	n/a
25. United States	15.7	16.7	18.0	18.0	16.8	16.5	16.7

Source: OECD (1982b), Table 1. Values for 1980 were supplied by OECD, as were certair amendments to the published figures.
Notes: n/a = not available.
Some entries relate to the nearest available year: thus 1960 entry for the United Kingdom is 1961 Norway, 1960 entry is 1962; and for Canada and Denmark the 1965 entries are for 1966. Figure for Belgium are adjusted for a break in the series in 1970 and those for Canada in 1975. Data for both Netherlands and Norway are in person-years.

educational services. Table 9.1 shows for selected years over the period 1960–80 the share of general government in total employment in OECD member countries. The UK comes second in EEC-Europe in 1980 after Denmark, with an employment share markedly higher than that for countries such as the Netherlands which have higher expenditure shares. It should be stressed that this ranking is a result of explicit decisions on the form taken by public provision, a point made by Tait and Heller (1982). However, it means that the problems of establishing a stable framework for collective bargaining in the public sector are of particular importance in the UK.

Governments are profoundly concerned about the cost of public employment, much of it within the public non-market sector, having to be financed by taxation, borrowing or money creation. Wages, salaries, and associated employment expenses and taxes accounted for 29 per cent of total public expenditure in 1981. The behaviour of wages and salaries therefore has major repercussions for public expenditure totals. It is this fact which has forged the link between public expenditure planning and public sector industrial relations. When the inflation rate was low and public sector industrial relations were quiet, explicit recognition was unnecessary. Yet the full significance was slow to be appreciated even when both factors changed decisively: Thomson and Beaumont's book (1978) was a pioneeering study when it appeared as late as 1978.

II THE CHARACTERISTICS OF UK PUBLIC SECTOR INDUSTRIAL RELATIONS

This growth in public sector employment has been the counterpart of conscious policies to expand services. Some of the consequences have, however, been far from intended. This employment growth has been paralleled by the emergence of a complex system of collective bargaining arrangements, designed to regulate the relationship between the state and its employees. There are five special characteristics of public sector industrial relations which have contributed to their mounting importance.

The clash of roles of the state

The state has a dual role with regard to its own employees, as employer and as sovereign, a relationship generating incompatible pressures. For example, it cannot employ roughly 30 per cent of the working population without becoming embroiled, as employer, in the practices and problems of industrial relations. It is no longer possible for the state to stand aside and leave collective bargaining to the management and workforce in those parts of the economy where it is itself the employer and must subsequently pick up the bill both for the dispute and the settlement. A referee or adjudicator role in the conflict between management and workforce becomes less viable: the state's self-interest as employer is too evident. Its relationships with such a large and diverse workforce raise a host of complex issues, the settlement of any one having potential spillover effects on to the others. Furthermore, extensive public employment is the counterpart to the pursuit of many of the objectives of the modern welfare state. Consequently, actual or threatened action by its own employees can frustrate so many policies.

Furthermore, the traditional conflicts of industrial relations are interpreted as being between capital and labour. In the private sector, such roles can easily be ascribed to participants. However, in the public sector the private capitalist has been displaced, a demise which was often thought to remove a major source of industrial conflict. Rather than being seen as action by employees against an individual capitalist, industrial conflict in the public sector is quickly interpreted as a challenge to the state itself. Whereas strikes in the private sector rarely raise explicitly constitutional issues, however severe the wider economic damage might be, those in the public sector almost always do.

Public sector industrial relations erupted in the 1970s with an unsuspected venom, following a long period of comparative quiet in which industrial conflict in the private sector was the focus of both public concern and the inquiry of the Royal Commission on Trade Unions and Employers' Associations (Donovan, 1968). By the end of the decade, however, all participants in public sector industrial relations felt bitter, frustrated and unable to devise satisfactory mechanisms to resolve the underlying problems. Paradoxically, both state and unions have much to lose from such developments for, whatever the historic antagonism implicit in their roles as employer and employed, they are, together, the central targets of the radical right. In their respective ways, both are considered to subordinate the freedom of individuals to the power of collectivities. The policies of the radical right mean a much reduced level of public expenditure and employment coupled with a direct challenge to the monopoly power of trade unions.

Greater unionization in the public sector

The degree of unionization in the public sector is much higher than that in the private sector. Bain and Price's (1980) statistical volume charted both the overall growth of union membership and the dramatic variations in union densities between different parts of the economy. Bain and Price calculated union densities as the actual number of union members divided by the potential number of union members where the latter includes both the employed and unemployed.[1] Using what was recognized to be an imperfect dividing line between the public and private sectors, they constructed from their disaggregated figures a series for the public sector from 1948 to 1978. Figure 9.2 shows that for the entire period the public sector union density has

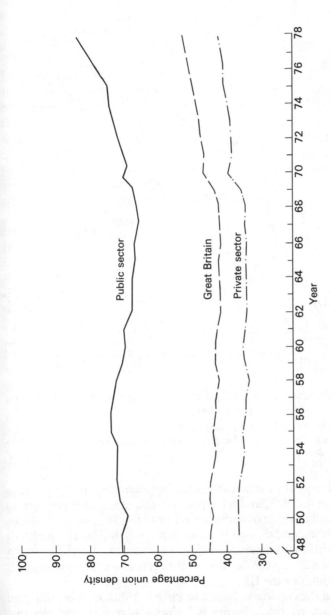

Figure 9.2 Comparison of union densities in the public and private sectors, 1948–78

Sources: Bain and Price (1980) and Price and Bain (1983).

Notes: See the original sources for a careful explanation of both coverage and the limitations inherent in the available data. Unsurprisingly, there are severe difficulties confronting a statistical exercise such as this as to how the public sector should be defined. Bain and Price's working definition of the public sector comprised national government; local government and education; health services; post and telecommunications; air transport; port and inland water transport; railways; gas, electricity and water; and coal mining; but excluded iron and steel.

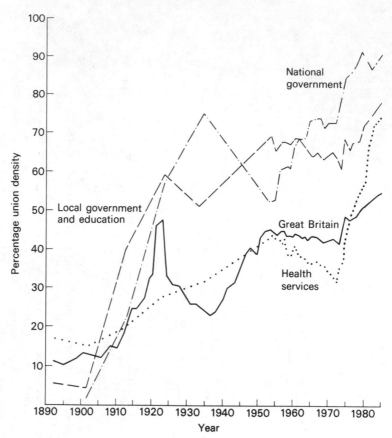

*Figure 9.3   Union densities in selected parts of the public non-market sector,
1892–1979*

Sources: Bain and Price (1980) and Price and Bain (1983).
Notes: See the original sources for a careful explanation of both coverage and the limitations
inherent in the available data.

been roughly double that for the private sector: for example, 70.7 per cent as
against 37.3 per cent in 1948, and 81.5 per cent as against 43.0 per cent in
1978. After only small changes over the period 1948 to 1968, union densities
rose steadily in both sectors, though from very different levels. The width of
the public/private differential is reflected in the way in which the much
smaller public sector pulls up the density for the economy as a whole (figures
relate to Great Britain, not the UK).

For many parts of the economy, Bain and Price's (1980) membership and
density series go back to 1892. Figure 9.3 plots union densities over this
period for three important parts of the public non-market sector: national

government; local government and education; and health services. Until the figures became continuous in 1948, they are available at ten-year intervals. Even within the public sector, there remain considerable variations in densities and the time profiles are markedly different. The most remarkable aspect of Figure 9.3 is the rapid growth of unionization in health services, an area hitherto lagging not just behind the rest of the public sector but also behind the economy-wide density. From only 32.2 per cent in 1966, this density surged to 73.7 per cent in 1979. By the end of the period, the differences between the densities recorded in these three parts of the public non-market sector were less pronounced than at earlier periods. In the public market sector, densities are even higher, with the major nationalized industries recording over 90 per cent, sometimes nearly 100 per cent (Price and Bain, 1983).

The reasons for higher union densities in the public sector are complex but certainly include the historically much more favourable attitude of the state, away from the spheres of external and internal security, towards the development of trade unionism and of collective bargaining institutions. Indeed, when certain activities have been transferred from the private to public sectors, explicit injunctions to recognize trade unions and promote consultative and collective bargaining machinery have been included in the legislation.

In the absence of explicit employer hostility, union membership has prospered in all grades, but dramatically so in managerial ones. Recognition, traditionally an important barrier in the private sector, has never been an obstacle. Much more recently, however, a completely different factor has stimulated increases in public sector union density: the almost universal belief among public employees, whether substantiated or not, that they were being treated in a discriminatory way. Some of the cherished fringe differentials of public sector employment (for example pensions and sick pay) have been eroded, if not reversed, by the growth of the remuneration package in the private sector. However, the customary allegation has centred upon the more rigid enforcement of incomes policies in the public sector, even when a blind eye has been turned to breaches elsewhere in the economy. The relevant empirical evidence on pay outcomes has been the subject of conflicting assessments. Whereas Clegg (1982) and Robinson (1982) argued that there has been discrimination against public employees, Elliott and Fallick (1981) judged otherwise. What is indisputable is that the feeling of being unfairly treated has stimulated unionization as a defensive response and weakened earlier inhibitions against taking industrial action.

The public sector as the new fulcrum of industrial conflict

Whatever the underlying reasons, the fulcrum of industrial conflict in the UK economy has transferred from private sector manufacturing into the public sector, both its market and non-market components. Despite frequent appeal to the old rhetoric, much of the conflict is not between labour and capital but between labour and the state. Over issues such as nurses' or teachers' pay, it is somewhat stretching the point to see demands for higher wages as an attack on the capitalist class when, whatever is eventually conceded, will have to be extracted from the bulk of the population, either through higher taxes or worse services.

Paradoxically, this change has not made such conflicts any less bitter or intractable. In contrast, individual groups of public employees have demonstrated themselves willing to pursue sectional objectives with unprecedented vigour. Yet each public employee has a dual role: as employee, and as taxpayer and voter. A major problem has been that the increased willingness to use all available instruments in advance of one's own pay claim has been matched by rising intolerance of inconvenience caused by other people's industrial disputes. As taxpayer and voter, the individual public employee may wish the state to get tough – with other public employees!

The Donovan Commission's (1968) neglect of public sector industrial relations can be understood in terms of their comparative quiet, a feature which did not survive the 1960s. The available analyses of industrial disputes by sector cover only a limited number of years and are subject to serious classification problems. No analysis at all is available for years earlier than 1966 so that the transformation of public sector industrial relations cannot be properly documented. The two official sources providing the required analysis cover the periods 1966–76 (Smith *et al.*, 1978) and 1973–81 (Waddington, 1982). In Figure 9.4, these are described as 'series A' and 'series B' respectively, so that their entries for the overlapping years can be distinguished. The main defects in these statistics relate to the procedures for classifying whether a dispute is in the public or private sector and for recording small disputes. Figure 9.4 graphs two different measures of industrial conflict, plotting both the public sector's share of industrial stoppages and of working days lost. On the definitions of the public sector underlying these figures, a public sector share of roughly 25 per cent would be par. Although the year-to-year variations are pronounced, the broad pattern is for the public sector to account for less than its proportionate share of stoppages but more than its share of working days lost (Clegg, 1979). In the years in which there are major public sector disputes, the public sector's share of working days lost can be exceptionally high, far out of line with its share of employment: for example, 50 per cent in 1971 and 82 per cent in 1980.

The importance of disaggregating such broad data is emphasized by Figures 9.5 and 9.6 which examine the record of the component parts of the public sector. Unfortunately, these series can only be taken back until 1973. Figure 9.5 records stoppage frequency, expressed as the number of stoppages per 1000 employees. Similarly, Figure 9.6 records working days lost per 1000 employees. On both these measures, the most troublesome part of the public

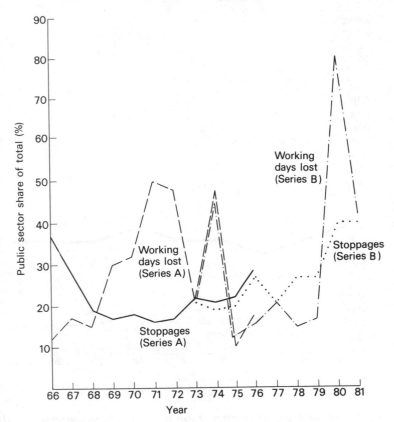

Figure 9.4 The public sector's share of stoppages and working days lost, 1966–81

Sources: Smith *et al.* (1978) and Waddington (1982).
Notes: The procedures for classifying disputes as located in the public or private sectors are imperfect and a considerable margin of error attaches to them. Over the period covered by Smith *et al.* (1976), the proportion of employment in the public sector equivalent to these procedures was between 24 per cent and 28 per cent. Data are not available prior to 1966. The series in Smith runs from 1966–76 and is called Series A above. More recent work by the Department of Employment (Series B) can be extended back to 1973 but is not consistent with Smith. However, the overlaps shown above indicate that the discrepancies are not large.

sector is public corporations which exhibit a stoppage frequency far higher than for any other part of the economy and a pattern of working days lost in which relative calm is punctuated, as in 1974 and 1980, with massive losses. In sharp contrast, both central government and local authorities emerge as less prone to industrial conflict than the private sector. All three figures reveal

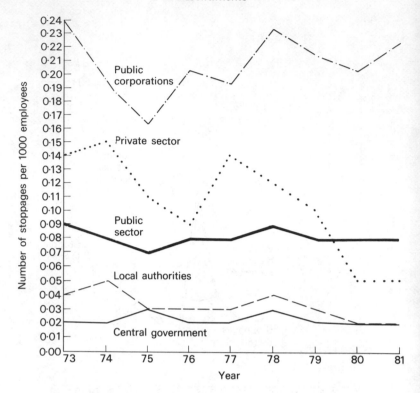

Figure 9.5 Frequency of industrial stoppages for component parts of the public sector, 1973–81

Source: Waddington (1982).

Notes: These series which can only be taken back to 1973 are not comprehensive or fully comparable because of difficulties in ensuring full recording of small disputes and because stoppages involving workers in both the public and private sectors have been allocated to the sector more affected.

that the present recession has been associated with a lower rate of stoppages and working days lost in the private sector, thus contributing to the public sector's increased share.

If the centre of conflict had simply shifted from the private to the public sector, this would of itself raise many difficult issues. However, most parts of the public sector are profoundly different from the old battleground of private manufacturing (Thomson and Heald, 1979). These public producers often enjoy a monopoly or near-monopoly of a good or service, with this sometimes being secured by statutory protection. It is therefore rarely easy for

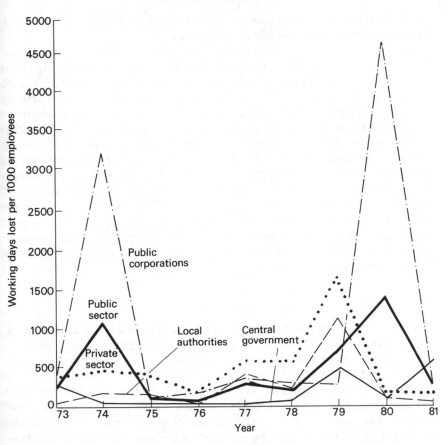

Figure 9.6 Working days lost through industrial stoppages for component parts of the public sector, 1973–81
Source: Waddington (1982).
Notes: See notes on Figure 9.5

consumers to find alternative supplies during an industrial dispute. The monopolistic feature is reinforced by the predominance of services, consumption of which is time-specific. As far as manufacturing products are concerned, it is usually possible to advance or delay purchases in response to an industrial dispute: indeed, distributors may still hold substantial stocks. In contrast, a dispute of electricity supply workers, nurses or railwaymen takes effect immediately and can cause major disruption and extensive hardship to the public. Such a difference in impact is not revealed by figures showing number of disputes or working days lost. There have not been any sophisticated efforts to measure the full cost of industrial disputes but the switch to the public sector may have increased the unit cost.

The public also pays the cost of public sector disputes in other ways through the claims upon social security of strikers' families; and through their subsequent share in the extra funds required to repair the financial damage to the public service or enterprise. What does not emerge from summary statistics is the profound political and constitutional significance which has attached to some of the largest disputes. Industrial conflict in the public sector contributed to the downfall of three successive governments: the 1964–70 Labour Government was faced by increased public sector militancy after the collapse of a formal incomes policy; the 1970–74 Conservative Government lost an election it had called to vindicate its position over a miners' strike; and the 1974–79 Labour Government was discredited by the disputes of the 1978/79 winter of discontent, which erupted in the face of its attempt to impose a 5 per cent pay policy. There are clearly substantive grounds, political as well as economic, for disquiet about the troubled climate of public sector industrial relations.

The centralized collective bargaining system

When roughly 30 per cent of the working population are public employees, themselves organized by typically specialist public sector unions which have achieved high levels of density, the processes of establishing rates of pay are inevitably of profound economic, social and political importance. A labour market continues to operate but it is highly structured with, for many occupational groups, a monopsonist employer facing a monopolist union. Cases of bilateral monopoly are notoriously unstable, not least in the labour market. It is scarcely surprising that both sides have recognized the advantages of a heavily structured, well-ordered and centrally dominated pattern of collective bargaining.

British public sector industrial relations have developed in this way, with a tradition of national agreements, negotiated at a very senior level. Both sides are prepared to risk severe temporary unpopularity with their own members if this should be the necessary price for maintaining the integrity of national agreements. There are cases of the national unions standing aside and allowing local action by their members to be defeated, even, as in the case of the Glasgow dustmen's strike of 1975, tacitly accepting the introduction of troops. In turn, the local authority employers have applied pressure upon their members not to pay below the level of national agreements, even where local labour market conditions would make this possible. These examples highlight the extent of the fear that the collapse of an ordered system of national bargaining would degenerate into local anarchy. There is a marked contrast with the private sector in which company and plant bargaining has grown at the expense of national bargaining.

Table 9.2: The greater coverage of public sector collective bargaining in 1978

Type of Employee	National Agreement Only	National plus Supplementary Agreement	Company, District or Local Agreement	No Agreement
	Percentage of public sector male employees in 1978 covered by:			
Managers	76.7 (7.7)	11.3 (8.5)	2.7 (10.5)	9.3 (73.3)
Professionals	80.0 (7.4)	12.9 (11.1)	0.9 (15.8)	6.2 (65.7)
Intermediate Non-Manual	82.7 (10.6)	12.8 (8.8)	1.1 (18.3)	3.3 (62.3)
Junior Non-Manual	86.8 (12.9)	9.7 (18.7)	1.1 (14.9)	2.3 (53.3)
Foremen	70.0 (20.8)	19.3 (21.0)	5.5 (18.5)	5.2 (39.7)
Skilled Manual	65.1 (24.8)	27.4 (33.1)	3.5 (15.3)	3.9 (26.7)
Semi-skilled Manual	78.4 (19.1)	17.1 (30.5)	1.1 (18.2)	3.4 (32.2)
Unskilled	66.6 (29.6)	28.2 (23.0)	2.0 (14.7)	3.1 (32.7)

Source: Gregory and Thomson (1981) based on Department of Employment (1979, Part F, pp. 45–56).
Notes: Entries in parentheses give the equivalent figures for the private sector. The question in the New Earnings Survey on which the table is based was only asked in 1973 and 1978. See Gregory and Thomson (1981) for the definition of public sector employees used in this table.

Greater coverage. The centralized bargaining system is characterized not just by the predominance of national agreements but also by the much greater coverage of employees by collective agreements (Gregory and Thomson, 1981; Beaumont and Leopold, 1982). Using the answers to a question now asked in the New Earnings Survey at five-year intervals, the extent of these differences can be tabulated for 1978, the latest year available. Table 9.2 shows for the different grades of public sector male employees the arrangements under which pay is determined, distinguishing between cases in which there are only national agreements; where national agreements are supplemented locally; where there are company, district or local agreements and no national agreement; and where there are no agreements at all. Directly underneath each public sector entry appears a figure in parentheses giving the equivalent percentage for the private sector. The dominant arrangement in the public sector is for there only to be a national agreement, with very few cases where there is no agreement at all. In contrast, there are many cases of no agreement in the private sector, with a national agreement alone being a much less frequent arrangement. The other striking contrast between the public and private sectors revealed by Table 9.2 is the dramatically higher coverage of managers and professionals in the public sector. Managers in the public sector are ten times more likely than their private sector counterparts to have their pay settled by a national agreement alone and only an eighth as likely to be covered by no agreement at all. There is obviously a complex relationship between these arrangements for settling pay and the high union densities, coupled with deep penetration into managerial grades, character- istic of the public sector.

The 'good employer' obligation. Aware of the costs, both direct and indirect, of conflict with their own employees, governments have favoured a struc- tured system. Uncomfortable about becoming too identified with capital, in a way which would impair their mediating role elsewhere, they have been prepared to accept a 'good employer' obligation, with regard both to pay and other conditions of employment. Beaumont (1978, 1981a) has traced the evolution of this idea in both official publications and pronouncements. This approach had great appeal, particularly to governments sympathetic both to the expansion of public employment and to trade unions. The ministers of Labour Governments, often men with long personal, sometimes painful, experience of being trade union activists and negotiators, had no wish to transplant what were perceived to be the bad practices of the private sector. As the counterpart, however, this notion of being a 'good employer' also allowed governments to defend their practices to a wider audience. They could assure industrialists, private sector unions and taxpayers that public employees were not unduly favoured, being treated in accord with good, but not the best, private sector practice.

Unsurprisingly, being a 'good employer' has its disadvantages, notably that it costs money. It implies that not every opportunity is taken in the short term to minimize labour costs though, of course, there might be offsetting advantages in the longer term through the retention of better quality employees and higher performance. During periods of budgetary crisis, these alleged long-term advantages may seem insubstantial in the face of the immediate costs. The private sector may allege that public employees are a privileged class who have conspired to manipulate the system in their own favour. The 'good employer' tradition can thus be interpreted as favouritism. Towards the end of the 1970s, claims to this effect abounded, frequently centring upon the issue of indexed public sector pensions.

The comparability principle. The public sector faith in national negotiations is closely linked to the primary system for settling pay: namely, the appeal to comparability with the private sector. However, there are many occupations in the public sector which have few, if any, exact counterparts in the private sector: for example, doctors, firemen, policemen and teachers. Given the structure of the labour market for these occupations, the idea of a market-determined wage encounters severe difficulties. The state decides how many of each of these occupational groups it will employ and frequently also controls the rate of entry into the occupation. Although it is possible to examine whether there are 'shortages' of policemen or 'surpluses' of teachers, such answers are extremely sensitive to decisions by the state. For the individual, certain career decisions are only partly reversible and even then at substantial cost. Such factors enhance the attractions to employees of a structured pattern of collective bargaining which provides some safeguard against decisions damaging to their interests.

Even in its heyday, comparability was never an easy principle to make operational. Ironically, the problem stemmed from one of the factors which constituted its appeal: the domination of certain occupational labour markets by the state. As successive attempts to apply the principle of comparability discovered, there are few direct comparators in the private sector to ambulancemen, nurses or primary teachers. The Standing Commission on Pay Comparability, chaired by Professor Hugh Clegg throughout its short life from February 1979 to August 1980, was fully aware of this problem and assessed alternative methods of comparing individual jobs through an analysis of their component parts (Clegg, 1980a). But neither the Labour Government which established it nor the subsequent Conservative Government which eventually abolished it, was prepared to recognize the timescale involved. Rather than allow the Clegg Commission to develop an overall approach to the underlying issues, both governments wanted swift answers to the latest dispute.

Moreover, the motives of the Labour Government had been inauspicious: to resolve the proliferating public sector disputes of the winter of 1978/79, even if this only meant delaying the bill until after the impending election. The incoming Conservative Government, with a manifesto commitment to reduce public employment, had no wish to see the relative cost of public employees increase. However, undertakings made during the election period hampered its later freedom of action: in the event, the relative cost of public employees increased sharply in the Government's first year of office (Beaumont and Heald, 1981).

Fragmentation of the employer role. Such a focus on the state as employer diverts attention away from the fact that public employees are separately engaged by a large number of diverse institutions, all classified as being within the public sector. It is frequently difficult to define an unambiguous management interest: there may be profound conflicts of interest on the employer side, between, for example, the Treasury, the central departments supervising local government services, the local authority associations and the individual councils. The Treasury may be concerned about the impact of any particular settlement elsewhere in the economy and may be willing to accept the risk of a damaging strike as a test case. In contrast, local authorities will be much more concerned about the issues relating to the particular occupational group and the services they provide.

In the public sector, there is extensive multilateral bargaining (Kochan, 1977), stemming from the frequent existence of a funding employer separate from the direct employer. Although 40 per cent of public employees were directly employed by local authorities in 1980, roughly half of the latter's gross expenditure is borne by the Exchequer. The potential for division on the management side is further compounded by the ability of public employees to win over their direct employer and to use avenues of political influence as a bargaining tactic.

The operation of such a centralized collective bargaining system, however inevitable it might be, can be a source of serious obstacles to adjustment, thus generating X-inefficiency. Problems which were disguised during periods of steady growth acquire significance during periods of cutbacks in public expenditure. In this environment, resistance to direct job losses through redundancy has become a primary union objective. In many cases this may also become a management objective particularly, as in local government, where there are direct channels of political influence. Such 'no redundancy' policies are understandable when the rationale for the cuts is itself disputed. But there is clearly a danger that there will be an attempt to shuffle off the costs of adjustment on to outsiders. Examples include concentrating the cuts on capital and on non-pay items and by relying on natural wastage which protects existing jobholders at the expense of the unemployed and of new entrants to the labour force.

Quite apart from doubts concerning the equity of such an allocation of costs, these strategies can only be pursued so far without importing serious inefficiencies into public services. The danger of double standards, whereby redundancies are accepted in the private sector and in the public market sector but not in the public non-market sector, is undeniable. Such attitudes make it more difficult for service provision to respond sensitively to changes in needs: defending the jobs of primary teachers who have no children to teach whilst being unable to afford to recruit the social workers to attend the elderly might be understandable but is certainly damaging (Bailey, 1980).

Another microeconomic issue is that the operation of the national pay scales which emerge out of centralized bargaining means that employees in slack local labour markets are 'overpaid' and that those in tight local labour markets are 'underpaid'. Depending upon the circumstances, this may or may not be a reasonable price to pay for an orderly system of industrial relations. Nevertheless, in the latter case, the problem with recruitment can be severe, leading to profound strains upon the quality of local services. Signs of this kind of stress have been seen in the past, particularly in labour-intensive services in central London.

'ublic/private pay desynchronization

)uring the 1970s, the traditional linkages between public and private sector
›ay have been broken: the loss of such an anchor has been both a cause and a
:onsequence of industrial conflict and budgetary stress. This development
:an be illustrated by the behaviour of the public/private sector pay relatives.
)ata in this field are not entirely satisfactory but are sufficient for the present
›urpose. Figure 9.7 is based upon the calculations of Dean (1981). It plots
›ublic sector pay as a percentage of private sector pay for four groups:
nanual men; non-manual men; manual women; and non-manual women. It
s not the absolute values of the indexes which are important but changes in
hem. For example, the high values for non-manual women reflect, *inter alia,*
he much greater job opportunities for women in the public sector. There is
herefore no reason why the absolute value should be 100. Caution is also
·equired in interpreting changes over a long period as occupational compo-
ition itself changes. For the period 1950–69, data are only available for
nanual men, based on inquiries in each April into manual workers' earnings.
=rom 1970, the New Earnings Survey provided data for the four groups. It
hould be noted that the percentages shown in Figure 9.7 are based on raw
:omparisons, with no adjustments for differences in composition (such as by
›ccupation, age, length of service and region) or in performance (such as
ours worked and efficiency).

For the period until 1970, the earnings of the two sectors moved closely
ogether but there was a cyclical difference with the private sector gaining
luring expansion and the public sector pulling back during the down-turn.
After 1970, the relationship between public and private sector pay became
lesynchronized, with distinct cycles emerging. Although the turning points
or the four groups are not always the same, the period 1973–75 represented
ı period of large public sector gains relative to the private sector. These were
hen eroded over the period 1976–79 with another upwards swing starting in
1980 and ending in 1982. Such short-term fluctuations can under no circum-
itances be accounted for by skill or occupational changes.

The main caveat which should be attached to graphs of the pay relatives
·uch as those in Figure 9.7 is that the public sector is so diverse that
:omparisons at such an aggregated level may be concealing vital clues
·hrough the process of averaging out. Figure 9.8 distinguishes pay relatives
·or male manuals for the three component parts of the public sector, revealing
ı tendency for the three to move broadly together. However, the relative for
›ublic corporations far exceeds those for central government and local
ıuthorities, being responsible for pulling up the public sector relative above
100. These discoveries re-emphasize that disaggregation is essential if the
›rocesses of pay determination and desynchronization are to be analysed and
ınderstood. The cycles which developed in the pay relatives in the 1970s are

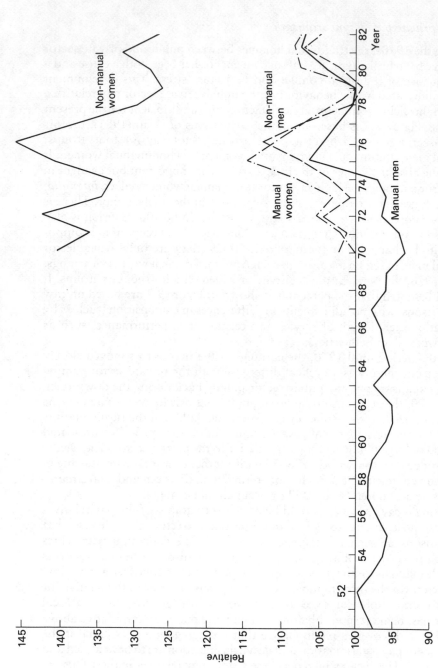

Figure 9.7 Public/private sector pay relatives by employment status and sex, 1950–82
Sources: Dean (1981, pp. 47, 53); Department of Employment (1980, p. 1092; 1981, p. 446; 1982, p. A17)

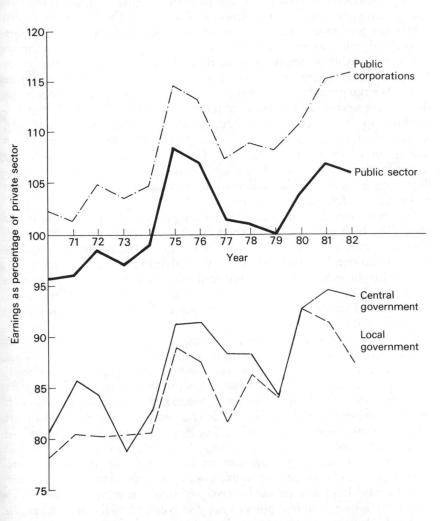

Figure 9.8 Public/private pay relatives by component parts of the public sector: male manuals, 1970–82

Sources: Department of Employment (1977, p. 1340; 1978, p. 1143; 1979, p. 972; 1980, p. 1092; 1981, p. 446; and 1982, p. A17).

Notes: The 1980 New Earnings Survey does not give results for central government and local government separately, only a single figure for 'public services'.

vividly illustrated in Figure 9.9. For each of the three components of the public sector, it plots the annual rate of increase in earnings as a proportion of that in the private sector. The extent of desynchronization is brought home most clearly when a comparison is struck between rates of change in earnings.

The uncertainties stemming from these, sometimes sharp, year-on-year fluctuations, have generated severe discontent on all sides. Public employees remember the periods in which their relative position deteriorated whereas the private sector and outside commentators remember the periods of catching-up. The fact that catching-up often involves numerically large settlements for many groups just as the private sector's difficulties mount makes these periods extremely difficult for the latter to swallow. For example, the florid criticism of Clegg settlements typically cited only the difference between public and private settlements for a particular year without any reference to this wider context.

Teachers provide a good example of the problems of pay desynchroniz ation. The high point of the teachers' position in the pay hierarchy was in 1965 at a time of widespread teacher shortage. Subsequently, this position deteriorated steadily until 1975 when the Labour Government's acceptance of the Houghton Report (1975) restored this position. Their position again deteriorated until 1980 when the Clegg Commission, though rejecting a return to the Houghton reference point, conceded a major catching-up award (Clegg, 1980b).

Three points should be noted about this example. First, conditions in the labour market for teachers had dramatically changed between 1965 and 1975: instead of shortage there was substantial excess supply. Nevertheless, the 1965 relative position still exerts a major influence in negotiations as it has become a legitimized aspiration level. Second, the chronology was one of steady deterioration followed by sudden recovery: the predominant experi ence was thus one of falling behind. The short recovery phase was on both occasions the culmination of increasingly bitter resort to forms of industrial action hitherto considered inappropriate for the teaching profession. Third, governments find it almost impossible to sustain a refusal to set up an inquiry into the pay claim of a particular group of public employees. Once estab lished, the inquiry rarely reports to the disadvantage of the affected group: unstable relativities make it extemely easy to provide an 'objective' base for favourable proposals. There are major problems of dynamic instability when different groups each use selected phases of their own cycle as the basis for claims.

If public employees feel both unfairly treated by their employer and abused by the media, governments for their own part feel powerless to reconcile the many conflicting pressures upon them. In consequence, public policy is often shortsighted and counterproductive. However ill-advised certain measures may appear, the underlying dilemmas are real. Superimposed upon the structural factors have been two further ones: the pressure of external

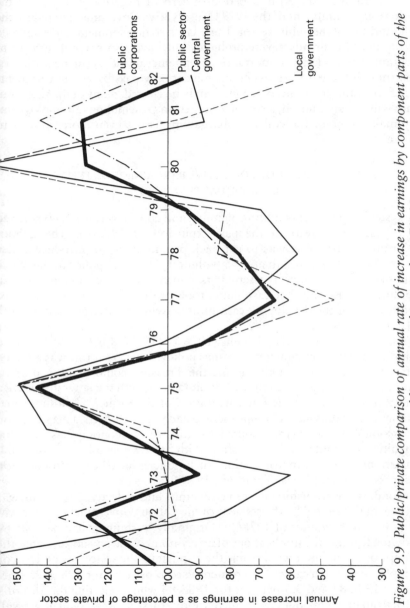

Figure 9.9 Public/private comparison of annual rate of increase in earnings by component parts of the public sector: male manuals, 1970–82

Sources and notes: See Figure 9.8.

economic events which has ended the long period of steady public expendi
ture growth and ushered in a period of zero or negative growth; and th
ideological commitment of the 1979 Conservative Government to reduce th
scope and size of the public sector. These last two developments have not onl
accentuated the already severe problems but have also made it difficult t
disentangle the relative importance of ephemeral and permanent factors
Even though the world recession may eventually pass by and government
more favourable to public expenditure may be elected, many of the structura
issues will remain. Indeed, a return to something resembling full employmen
may make some of the collective bargaining issues even more difficult t
resolve.

III THE IMPACT OF COLLECTIVE BARGAINING ON PUBLIC EXPENDITURE PLANNING

The system of public expenditure planning and control was severely criticize
for its failure to restrain the pay explosion of 1974/75. The Labou
Government's response was to cut back programmes, to introduce a nev
system of cash limits and to apply a 'voluntary' incomes policy to the whol
economy. The Treasury reasserted its control over the amount of cas
spending by ensuring that cash limits took precedence over volume plans
Two aspects of the developing cash limit system emphasized its links wit
collective bargaining.

First, the initial years of cash limits (1976/77, 1977/78, 1978/79) coincide
with the Labour Government's incomes policy. Given that this was adhere
to fairly closely in the public sector, the Treasury could build well-base
assumptions about pay into the cash limit factors, with the latter providing
non-arbitrary basis for the implementation of the former. Cash limits an
incomes policy thus neatly complemented each other. Indeed, a major reaso
for incomes policies being adopted for the whole economy has been th
difficulties encountered by the state with its own employees: to avoi
accusations of discriminatory action, such policies have been introduced o
an across-the-board basis (Thomson, 1979).

Second, the relationship between cash limits and collective bargaining wa
fundamentally altered by the collapse of the Labour Government's 5 per cen
pay policy in the winter of 1978/79. Originally, cash limits had been set b
following through the implications of an economy-wide pay norm. Later, th
assumptions built into them became the implicit public sector pay policy. Fo
example, the Conservative Government used 6 per cent for 1981/82, 4 pe
cent for 1982/83 and 3.5 per cent for 1983/84 whilst rejecting the idea of
return to an incomes policy. Settlements above these figures would now resul
in offsetting reductions in volume spending, unless the cash limits wer
relaxed. The contrast with 1974/75, when volume spending could b
maintained irrespective of current settlements, is complete.

The setting of cash limits therefore occupies a central position in recent
ttempts to control public expenditure, especially in periods without a formal
1comes policy. The inflation allowances implicit in the cash limits have been
requently criticized as being consistently too low. This has been interpreted
s a 'back door' method of securing expenditure reductions: no announce-
1ent has to be made when volume is squeezed by a deliberate underestimate
f inflation (Convention of Scottish Local Authorities, 1981, 1982). Never-
heless, the Treasury faces a dilemma when it sets cash limits. Any forecast
vhich it adopts is likely to become a target to be exceeded in collective
argaining, a fact which encourages it to use underestimates since use of the
est-estimate would in the event guarantee that this turned out to be too low.
The introduction of cash limits has been one policy response to the
mergent problems of public sector industrial relations (Bevan, Sisson and
Vay, 1981). It has involved retreat from other objectives, such as the
levelopment of a system of public expenditure planning sensitive to the
eeds of programme objectives, through resort to the blunt instrument of
ash limits. The subsequent move to cash planning has ended volume
lanning and downgraded the multi-year framework. Such changes have
een motivated not only by a desire to cut programmes but also by the
ncertainties and frustrations generated by the collective bargaining system.

IV   POLICIES TOWARDS PUBLIC SECTOR INDUSTRIAL RELATIONS

he emergent difficulties of public sector industrial relations have not only
aised intractable policy issues but also magnified their political salience. A
ange of proposals has been advanced, their tone varying according to the
nderlying attitude towards public expenditure and employment. The most
mportant sets of proposals are now surveyed.

Veaken public sector unions

he turbulent climate of the 1970s has raised the long-muted issue of the
roper role of trade unions in the public sector, especially the question of the
ight to strike. There have been several proposals to institute legal restrictions
n public employees, including making trade union membership illegal,
emoving the legal immunities for strike action in the public sector and
estricting the voting rights of public employees. Although often linked to
nore general proposals to curb the power of trade unions, specific measures
or the public sector have been advocated because of the damaging nature of
ts disputes.
Beaumont (1981b) evaluated the three justifications advanced for such
roposals: the sovereign employer argument; the strong union bargaining
ower argument; and the high cost of strikes argument. He considered that
ppeal to the first is typically an attempt to win over public opinion against

the strikers: in contrast with those in the private sector, the outcome o
public sector disputes is seen to depend crucially upon which side wins publi
sympathy. On the second point, the empirical evidence about the returns i
the public sector to either union membership or collective bargainin;
coverage is limited and inconclusive. On the third, the high costs of publi
sector disputes, though plausible, are much more an assertion than a carefull
quantified assessment.

Even if, however, such arguments were judged to be convincing, there ar
two major obstacles confronting a policy of abolishing the right to strike i
the public sector. First, Beaumont cited evidence from the USA in support o
the view that enforcement would be difficult: even where strikes are illega
they frequently occur without any legal sanction being invoked. Further
more, there are forms of industrial action short of outright strikes available t
public employees: teachers can refuse to supervise school meals; civil servant
to implement a particular measure; and doctors to sign medical certificates
As it would be impossible to frame legislation covering all conceivable form
of such action, a ban on strikes would encourage refinement of suc
techniques.

Second, there would be extensive pressure for procedural substitutes fo
the right to strike, such as compulsory arbitration. However, that arrange
ment might be more expensive than allowing strikes. Neither side would hav
any incentive to settle once the threat of disputes damaging to both wer
removed. Governments may thus lose all control over the pay of public em
ployees and hence over much of public expenditure, assigning the former t
an independent agency which does not have to finance the resulting settle
ment. Furthermore, a problem with all forms of arbitration in the publi
sector is that of maintaining the perceived neutrality of the arbitrator
Suspicions that arbitrators are pressured to conform to government policy o
pay have discredited arbitration in the eyes of public employees and led t
reduced use of the available machinery (Elliott and Fallick, 1981). At th
same time, however, public employers, whether funding or direct, have ofte
considered that arbitrators have paid insufficient attention to the 'ability t
pay' for the arbitration award. Arbitrators have thus made themselve
unpopular with governments: Professor Hugh Clegg was dismissed from th
civil service arbitration machinery and Lord McCarthy criticized for award
allegedly beyond the ability to pay of the ailing British Rail.

Privatization

An alternative, though in part complementary, approach would be to retur
as many public sector activities as possible to the private sector. Part of th
appeal of privatization to the political right is thus to weaken the power o
public sector trade unions. Privatization would reduce the extent of monop
oly for those activities where the barriers to competition are statutory rathe

han natural. It would fragment existing systems of national bargaining and might lead to plant or company bargaining. Furthermore, the services would be distanced from the political pressures which make union recognition difficult to resist in the public sector: explicitly anti-union policies could therefore be adopted in sensitive areas, thus attempting to remove them from the scope of collective bargaining. Finally, the wage elasticity of demand for labour might be increased in the more competitive environment, with the threat of bankruptcy restored.

Such arguments are very appealing to those who, on other grounds, disapprove of many of the public sector's existing activities. In contrast, few advocates of, for example, public provision of medical care would be converted to the case for privatizing the NHS, simply because of its undoubted industrial relations problems. However, the future image and development of the NHS might be highly sensitive to how it resolves these difficulties. Its ability to secure funds from the Exchequer, and its attractiveness to patients *vis-à-vis* the private sector, would be diminished if it became a constant battleground between the unions and both direct and funding employers. Such an outcome becomes more likely under a government which lacks both commitment to continuing public provision and sensitivity to many of the complex industrial relations issues. This danger is reinforced by the desire of certain public sector trade unions to use industrial action as a battering ram against government policy in general.

Reform the bargaining system

Very substantial damage has been done to the interests of both the state and of its employees by the events of the 1970s. At the end, the net changes have been small, with gains and losses often cancelling each other out. This position has, however, only been reached after a decade of damaging conflict which left both sides exhausted and vulnerable to criticism, thus enhancing the appeal of the revival of free-market economics on the political right. The desynchronization of pay relatives has resulted in many incorrect, usually unfavourable, interpretations being placed upon events. The state and its unions have often been accused of conspiring together to subvert the interests of the private sector and the taxpayer.

Extensive reforms to the system of collective bargaining have been suggested. However, even what initially appear as promising reforms can have unexpected and unwanted side-effects. It has often been argued that a synchronization of settlement dates in the public sector would avoid the practice of leap-frogging, whereby the settlement achieved by each group in turn becomes the target to surpass for the next group. In the aftermath of the winter of discontent of 1978/79, such ideas gained currency in trade union circles, with David Basnett, General Secretary of the General and Municipal Workers Union, being a notable exponent. Although the synchronization of settlement dates would mitigate the problem of leap-frogging, the fact tha separate negotiations reach their critical phase simultaneously might general ize the conflict, on occasions producing a public sector general strike Without some consensus as to the appropriate structure of pay differentials or at least about the machinery for settling them, institutional and procedura reform is likely to fail.

Little was subsequently heard about bargaining reforms after the election of the Conservative Government pledged to cut public employment and willing to use its position as employer as a means of signalling to the private sector its determination to hold down wages. Within such a climate, union willingness to co-operate in reforms is likely to be extremely limited Furthermore, the events of 1978/79 exhausted the finances and morale o several unions: ironically, their success at destroying the Labour Govern ment's 5 per cent pay policy has contrasted with their failure to mount coherent response to the Conservative Government's attack on public employment.

A reason for the diminished interest in the reform of collective bargaining arrangements has been the fall in the number of disputes and working day lost since 1978/79. This development must, at least in part, reflect the effect of higher unemployment as well as the more hostile ideological and financia climate for the public sector. Despite the Conservative Government's policies towards public employment, the new downwards phase in the pay relative did not start until 1982, reflecting the delayed impact of Clegg settlements However, the experience of earlier cycles suggests that any gains to the Exchequer accruing from holding down public sector pay may later be recouped, after another round of bitter strife. Public sector unions can be expected to recover from their temporary exhaustion and may subsequently attempt to settle scores arising from this period of weakness. This possibility increases the difficulties which will be faced by any government committed to the restoration of full employment, particularly if it also takes a favourable attitude towards public expenditure.

Restoration or abolition of comparability

Despite the criticism levelled against comparability (for example, Beenstock and Immanuel, 1979), it is difficult to conceive of a public sector industria relations system which did not contain at least an important element o comparability. Free collective bargaining is a mirage in the public sector when the taxpayer ultimately meets the cost of settlements. The amount of explici force which would necessarily accompany any unilateral imposition of pay and conditions by the state would prove unacceptable in most democratic societies. Although 'scarcities' and 'surpluses' in segmented labour market can provide important information, several of them are so dominated by the state that exclusive reliance cannot be placed on such signals.

If comparability is inevitable, it is essential that the system through which it operates is comprehensive, not piecemeal. The only attempt to institute such a system was the Clegg Commission but this was doomed by its origins in the winter of discontent. The necessity for comprehensiveness stems from the well-established tendency of inquiries or arbitrators with a narrow remit to look favourably upon their own charges. But resources are limited: teachers can only be paid more at the expense of some other public sector group, such as nurses, or through reductions in provision, or higher taxes or charges. A permanent body with a comprehensive remit cannot avoid this truth whereas successive temporary, specialized bodies can and do.

The record of institutional innovation and dissolution in this sphere of public policy does not generate confidence in the viability of any long-term policy: the National Board for Prices and Incomes operated from 1966 to 1970; the Pay Board from 1972 to 1974; and the Clegg Commission from 1979 to 1980. Such oscillations in policy have proved damaging. For example, the 1979 Conservative Government's attitude to the Clegg Commission contained serious internal contradictions. Despite its commitment to cut public employment, the Government initially presided over an increase in the relative cost of public employees. It first honoured Clegg settlements and made further references, but then abolished the Commission without establishing any method of resolving the problem of public/private pay desynchronization. It thus paid the price for Clegg in terms of catching-up awards without securing any reforms in collective bargaining procedures. Past events encourage the view that any gains from the rigid application of cash limits are likely to generate pressures in the future for new inquiries and catching-up awards (Beaumont and Heald, 1981).

The difficulties can be illustrated with reference to the pay and conditions of the non-industrial civil service. After a protracted industrial dispute in the summer of 1981, the Government established an inquiry into civil service pay, under the chairmanship of Sir John Megaw (Megaw, 1982). Although this inquiry was prevented by its terms of reference from taking a view about the level of civil service pay, as opposed to the principles by which it should be set, its establishment after an industrial dispute represented a major retreat for the Government. Despite the terms of reference and the packing of the Committee, the Government's challenge to the principle of comparability had only limited success. The report reaffirmed the insistence of the Priestley Royal Commission (1955) that some mechanism is required if civil service pay and conditions are to be removed from the everyday cut-and-thrust of politics, even though it wished to assign to it a more subordinate role.

There is a greater contrast between the language of the two reports than between their substantive proposals, partly a matter of advocacy in different climates. Priestley urged that civil service pay should be based on 'fair comparison with the current remuneration of outside staff employed on broadly comparable work, taking account of differences in other conditions of service' (para. 96), in order to achieve the objective of 'the maintenance of Civil Service recognised as efficient and staffed by members whose remuner ation and conditions of service are thought to be fair both by themselves and by the community they serve' (para. 95). In contrast, Megaw recommended that:

> The governing principle for the civil service pay system in the future should be to ensure that the Government as an employer pays civil servants enough, taking one year with another, to recruit, retain and motivate them to perform efficiently the duties required of them at an appropriate level of competence (para. 91).

Nevertheless, comparability re-emerges in an amended form. Megaw defended the record of the Priestley system against charges of bias in favour of the civil service. Its practical proposals can be seen as reforming the Priestley system rather than abolishing it: the establishment of an independent Pay Information Board; the restriction of comparisons to the private sector and the inclusion for the first time of smaller firms; external audit of the values attached to fringe benefits such as indexed pensions; and switching the focus of comparisons from the median to the range between the middle two quartiles, leaving the precise point to be settled through collective bargaining on the basis of labour market conditions. Furthermore, Megaw concluded that cash limits should be set on the basis of a reasonable outcome from this reformed system of collective bargaining and not as an independently chosen ceiling on pay. In summary, the Government received only limited support for its views on how civil service pay should be set. Much more dramatically, the Scott Committee (1981), established in order to legitimate restrictive measures against indexed public sector pensions, sanctioned such schemes and called for their wider availability in the private sector.

The example of the civil service illustrates wider points. With the abolition of the Clegg Commission, the problem of public sector pay is again being tackled on a piecemeal basis, with comprehensiveness being lost sight of. After unprecedented industrial action in the civil service, there is a return to a modified principle of comparability but only after disputes which are intensely damaging to the image of the public sector. Finally, there is not only the misrepresentation of facts which is perhaps inevitable when industrial disputes become bitter, but there are also elementary gaps in the necessary information for making independent judgements. Megaw expressed surprise at such statistical weaknesses. Furthermore, studies prepared for the Com- mittee by Elliott (1982) and Layard, Marin and Zabalza (1982) demon- strated that the Treasury's own evidence (Treasury, 1982c), claiming that non-manual men had improved their position relative to their private sector counterparts, was based upon a distorted sample. That such a rebuke should be necessary is a measure of the mishandling of the issue of public sector pay.

IV CONCLUSION

The failure to resolve the growing problems of public sector industrial relations has had, and will continue to have, a damaging impact on the image of the public sector. The political attractiveness of policies of public expenditure cuts and privatization has been enhanced by these apparently insoluble problems. At the same time, however, there is real bitterness amongst many groups of public employees about how they have been treated: the fact that this can often be shown to be unjustified does nothing to diminish the consequences. Such developments pose desperate dilemmas for any government which is committed to the public sector and does not view privatization and weakening public sector unions as beneficial in themselves. The comparative quiet after 1979 owes much to the impact of widespread unemployment, as well as to the Conservative Government's deep hostility to the public sector. The present industrial weakness of public sector unions should not disguise the fact that the underlying problems are not being resolved. A return to full employment and to a more favourable climate for public expenditure will cause them to re-emerge. Unless these issues are tackled they will continue to cast a dark shadow over the public sector.

CHAPTER 10

Decentralization and Territory

I INTRODUCTION

The complex issue of designing and enforcing effective systems of account ability for the operation of the public sector was examined in Chapter 7. I was noted there that one possible approach to the problem of accountability is to decentralize responsibility for all public sector activities to the lowes possible tier of government. This injunction has much to commend it provided that it is always recognized that public policy objectives may extend beyond the efficiency of service provision. In some cases, it may prove necessary to centralize provision in order to achieve an objective of equa access to a particular service. This reservation directs attention towards the key dilemma considered in this chapter: the possibility of a conflict between the claims of decentralization and those of equity. The trade-offs are much more complex and subtle than is usually acknowledged, either in the literature or in administrative practice.

After the case for decentralization has been examined, the nature o territorial equity and its links with interpersonal equity are explored. There then follows an examination of policies and practices in the UK, showing no only that objectives are complex but also that there exists extensive confusior about them. The political salience of such issues has sharply risen in the UK with the debates in the 1970s about devolution to elected assemblies ir Scotland and Wales and the deteriorating climate of central/local governmen relationships in the 1980s (Heald, 1976b, 1980c, 1982b).

II THE CASE FOR DECENTRALIZATION

The types of decentralization under consideration here are those relating to the vertical structure of the public sector and involving elected representative bodies whose constituency is territorially narrower than that of the centra government. Outside the present remit are schemes for decentralizing through the market, by privatizing existing public services; and the dele-

234

gation of public functions to appointed bodies, lacking any independent democratic legitimacy.

The presumption in favour of centralization

The economic arguments concerning efficiency which have been used in support of centralization are now reviewed. The first argument is based on economies of scale. Whatever their final recommendations, there is a marked tendency for official reports to see economic factors as pointing towards centralization (Redcliffe-Maud, 1969; Wheatley, 1969). What is interesting is that few economists are as convinced about the existence of major economies of scale over the relevant size range as were these official bodies. Empirical evidence, whether commissioned or independently undertaken, is very thin and has failed to provide convincing evidence in the support of such an hypothesis (Gupta and Hutton, 1968; Page, 1969; Bennett, 1980).

Furthermore, it has been strongly argued that, even if they could be shown to exist, economies of scale do not settle the question of the optimal size for jurisdictions as it is possible for contracting to take place, either from other public bodies or from the private sector (Foster, Jackman and Perlman, 1980). This point is well made, though the costs of decision-making and of control under such a framework would have to be introduced into the problem and might decisively affect the conclusion. There is comparatively little experience in the UK of such a contracting framework, but there was a complex network of joint boards prior to the local government reorganiz-ations of the mid-1970s. Dissatisfaction with these was a notable component of the case for larger units which would enable most of them to be eliminated.

The second economic argument pointing in the direction of larger units relates to intergovernmental spillovers. The advocacy of metropolitan con-solidation has rested in part upon their importance. The territorial incidence of the costs and benefits of local public services is not necessarily contained within jurisdictional boundaries, especially if they pay scant regard to the current economic and social functioning of a city. It is often possible, through judicious choice of residence, to enjoy many of the services of a city without paying for them – the classic free rider problem. An individual living in an independent suburb may work in the city and use its services, notably roads, leisure and cultural facilities. If such use does not incur a price equal to marginal cost, there will be a redistribution of welfare away from the city to the suburb. When interjurisdictional spillovers are not properly priced, they encourage further migration from the city to the suburbs and, on plausible assumptions, lead to an under-provision of services in the city. In addition to free riding on services, residence in an independent suburb may have the additional attraction that many of the social costs of commercial and industrial activity can also be avoided.

Williams (1966) has demonstrated that, in principle, a set of specific grants related to the magnitude and incidence of such spillovers is the most efficient policy response. However, given the problem of measuring them accurately enough for this purpose and the predictable opposition to such explicit transfers, the typical policy response has been to attempt to internalize spillovers by jurisdictional consolidation. This issue is more pressing in the USA, with its much more fragmented local government structure, than it is in the UK.

The efficiency case for decentralization

Having noted these centralizing tendencies, an examination will now be made of the case for decentralization within the public sector. Decentralization has been advocated for many different purposes and in support of conflicting values. For example, it can be portrayed as a method of limiting the worst excesses of democratic politics such as a bloated public sector or as an expression of participatory democracy.

Economists place great emphasis upon the efficiency properties of decentralization. In examining the operation of the public sector, they immediately look for quasi-market mechanisms which will perform for it an analogous role to that of the market for the private sector. The efficiency case for decentralization has been developed by, *inter alia,* Tiebout (1961) and Rothenburg (1970), and is lucidly surveyed by Oates (1972). If the public sector is highly centralized, one of two consequences will result. Either the pattern of service provision will be uniform across all areas, irrespective of relevant differences; or attempts to adjust services in response to variations in preferences and needs will be at least partly unsuccessful because of the informational and perceptual obstacles to implementation.

Decentralization will enable service provision to be more responsive to local preferences, producing an efficiency gain as the same amount of resources will generate more highly valued output. This conclusion rests upon the implicit assumption that these local preferences should count. The question of whether an individual's preferences should count in consumption decisions or whether paternalist preferences, expressed through the state, should be imposed has a clear parallel in the question of whether the preferences of the centre or locality should count. There might be powerful reasons in particular cases for the preferences of the locality to be overridden, particularly if decisions generate important cost and benefit spillovers to other jurisdictions. If, for example, one jurisdiction resolved not to provide public education, the impact on other jurisdictions, directly through migration flows and indirectly through future unemployment pay to the educationally neglected, might be substantial. Local autonomy cannot be absolute and will in practice be heavily constrained by legislation in a unitary state such as the UK.

But to emphasize the limits to local autonomy is not to deny its importance.

There are three reasons why a presumption can be made in favour of a measure of local autonomy in service provision. First, the complexity of the operations of the modern welfare state are such that the centre simply cannot process the necessary information in order to take all decisions. The cognitive limitations on the centre are severe: much of the relevant information may be unstructured, resistant to quantification and heavily dependent on local knowledge. Second, the efficiency gains resulting from local choices, provided that local preferences are judged to be relevant, have already been highlighted. Furthermore, decentralization offers the possibility of more experimentation, and hence learning from differences, than is usually possible in a centrally administered service. Third, there may be positive advantages in the diffusion of power and responsibility, thus facilitating wider participation in the democratic process, for example, through membership of local authorities. Such participation might cultivate both deeper commitment to the democratic process and provide a training ground for those later becoming politicians at the centre.

The economics literature has been powerfully influenced by Tiebout (1956). He was concerned to show that decentralization provided an efficiency-generating mechanism in the public sector. Samuelson (1954, 1955) had proved that the market could not secure an efficient allocation of resources in an economy with both public and private goods. It was defeated by the excludability and non-rivalry properties of the public good. Tiebout countered that, if public goods were 'local', in the sense that benefits were constrained to a defined geographical area, a quasi-market mechanism was restored through the ability of individuals to choose the jurisdiction in which they lived. It is important to stress that Tiebout developed his analysis within very stringent assumptions, the relaxation of which might lead to a weakening of both the normative case for decentralization and of the predictive power of his model in terms of migration patterns (see Aronson, 1974).

Nevertheless, it contains insights of fundamental importance. If individuals (described by Tiebout as 'consumer/taxpayers' in order to highlight their dual role) are self-seeking utility-maximizers, they can be expected to take their residence decisions in response to the package of services and taxes offered by alternative jurisdictions. In Tiebout's model, this is the propelling force behind migration, partly because of the stringency of his assumptions. In the real world, it will not be the sole factor but it might be an important one. Tiebout assumed that consumer/taxpayers live on dividend income which means that place of work has no influence on place of residence. Relocation is costless. There are many, otherwise identical, jurisdictions from which to choose, a more realistic assumption for metropolitan areas in the USA than in the UK. There are no interjurisdictional spillovers. Migration, motivated by differences in preferences about the public service/tax package, is an efficiency-generating process. If, instead, it were motivated by a desire to free ride on the services of other jurisdictions, made possible by the absence of systems for pricing spillovers, it would also be a generator of inefficiencies. The net effect would be ambivalent.

The fact that consumer/taxpayers have a choice of jurisdiction introduces competition between jurisdictions. This competition will improve efficiency in two senses. First, it will introduce pressures for higher X-efficiency. Second, there will be incentives for jurisdictions to offer different packages in order to appeal to different groups, thus making for a higher level of allocative efficiency than if there were a single jurisdiction with a uniform level of provision. The restoration of choice to the consumer/taxpayer, effected through decisions in the housing market, is a quasi-market mechanism for securing the accountability of the providers of public services. The representative basis of these officials is irrelevant to this mechanism: this form of accountability operates through individual decisions in related markets not through any political process of democratic elections. This argument for decentralization is thus likely to appeal most strongly to those with a preference for the market to the state.

Although writing from the contrasting perspectives of economist and political scientist, Oates (1977) and Beer (1977) both stressed:

(1)   The efficiency-generating properties of decentralization and Tiebout-style fiscal mobility which facilitate a closer correspondence between preferences and outcomes.
(2)   The severe constraints this places on the ability of lower tiers of government to redistribute income, coupled with the problems typically associated with social segregation by income and race.

The allocation of functions to different tiers of government will therefore condition the extent of effective redistributive policies. For those who favour redistribution, Tiebout's work on fiscally-induced migration should stimulate a recognition that the main thrust of redistributive policy has to be undertaken, or at least structured, by the central government. It is impossible for them to subscribe to an unqualified case for decentralization. Independent local efforts are likely to be self-defeating. The existence of many jurisdictions provides an important constraint upon the extent of effective redistribution which can be secured at the local level. The 'rich' always have the option to leave and to congregate in homogeneous jurisdictions, there facing little threat of having to make redistributive transfers because they constitute the political majority and in any case have few 'poor' to support. Consequently, either the centre must undertake the redistribution itself as a national programme or design grant systems which offset the higher costs of certain programmes in less affluent jurisdictions, to avoid generating incentives for higher income groups to leave.

In the UK, the main poverty-relief programmes are indeed implemented by the centre which took them over as expenditure on the welfare state increased. The main exception relates to council housing for which rate fund contributions vary markedly, in response to territorially differentiated tenure patterns and rents policies. The resulting differences in rate poundages provide incentives for owner occupiers (who receive their subsidies through different channels) to move to the suburbs which have a much smaller proportion of the housing stock in council ownership and, generally speaking, much less sympathy for subsidizing tenants from the rates. The ability of local authorities to pursue effective redistributive policies is thereby heavily constrained: transfers can be made but, as high income groups leave, they are increasingly paid for either by individuals not much different from the recipients, or by businesses. This example highlights that the structure of the public sector is crucial both to the design and operation of systems of redistribution.

III THE MEANING OF TERRITORIAL EQUITY

It is necessary to establish the relationship between two conceptions of equity. Whilst interpersonal equity relates to the treatment of individuals, territorial equity relates to the treatment of areas. In both cases the conception can have both a horizontal dimension (equal treatment of equals) and a vertical dimension (unequal treatment of unequals). Different analytical tools may be required in order to illuminate these different cases.

Economists, for example, find it much easier to think in terms of interpersonal equity because individuals are the natural focus of their methods of analysis: they find territorial equity a much stranger conception. In contrast, the modes of analysis of political scientists which focus attention upon the activities of groups can incorporate the significance of territory. It is important to them because political jurisdictions tend to be defined territorially. Furthermore, territory can sometimes serve as the basis for political mobilization as groups involved in the political process often themselves have a territorial basis. The difficulty which economists have experienced in handling questions of equity as opposed to efficiency are even more pronounced in the context of a policy concern with territorial equity. Economists tend to adopt one of three responses. The first is to deny the possibility of such a conception as anything but special pleading, and to maintain both that obstacles to market efficiency should be removed and that the state should not attempt to modify the resulting market outcomes. The second response is to attempt to redefine the problem as an efficiency problem so that conventional economic tools can be applied. Whereas non-economists probably regard regionally differentiated unemployment as primarily an equity problem, economists more frequently treat it as an efficiency problem. The third response is to take a synoptic view. There is much greater conflict between efficiency and territorial equity when the latter is defined in terms of the availability of individual services. Such a formulation denies the possibility of responding to varying local cost conditions and for any balancing out of advantages and disadvantages: for example, the open space of rural areas against the cultural facilities of large cities. There appears to be some evidence implicit in the directions which policy has taken that non-economists do not share this synoptic view. Equity concerns seem to be fragmented and incremental.

The breadth of definition of objectives and of available instruments is crucial. The narrower the focus, the more sensitive the policy conclusions will be to the external assumptions. One example is the ease with which tax/transfer policy can be operated. If it is assumed that this method is always costlessly available, different conclusions may be reached on the desirability of a particular policy than if they are compared as alternatives on realistic assumptions. The question always has to be asked about whether the efficiency losses occasioned by the pursuit of an equity objective are justifiable. Ultimately, the answer may depend upon the weights attached to these objectives.

An excellent example of how alternative policies must be compared on realistic assumptions is provided by regional policy. Wilson (1979) has consistently emphasized that relatively small sums are spent on regional policy in comparison with the automatic transfers through the public budget. Any efficiency losses resulting from regional policy are therefore a far from sufficient reason to reject it.[1] If transfers will take place in some form, there is much to be said for those directed towards the convergence of economic performance. However, the policy of the 1979 Conservative Government has been to reduce explicit regional policy expenditure but to leave untouched the implicit transfers.

Such policy issues should stimulate questions about the relationship between territorial and interpersonal equity, including:

(1)   Is territorial equity a direct target in itself, or is it an intermediate target chosen because of a shortage of direct instruments with which to achieve interpersonal equity, itself the real objective?
(2)   Is the simultaneous achievement of interpersonal and territorial equity possible or are the two conceptions contradictory?

The exploration of such questions, together with an examination of their policy implications, is the focus of this section.

Alternative conceptions

A fundamental conceptual issue is whether territorial equity is about actual outcomes or potential outcomes: this emerges as one of the central issues of practical policy. If the focus is upon actual outcomes, territorial equity requires that there *actually are* equal standards of provision in all areas. If, however, the focus is upon potential outcomes, territorial equity requires that there *might be* equal standards of provision. What matters is this potential for equal standards of provision: local choices determine whether standards are, in fact, equal. On the former criterion, equal standards of educational provision are thus necessary. On the latter criterion, they are not necessary because some communities might prefer more spending on, for example, accommodation for the elderly and less on education, or lower levels of public expenditure and lower tax rates.

If the relevant criterion of territorial equity is that each area should have an equal standard of service, the focus appears to be upon actual outcomes. However, it can also be interpreted in the potential sense, particularly when, as in the case of local government, a number of separate services are provided over the same jurisdiction. If this specified territorial equity objective is defined over actual outcomes, it is immediately clear that it is an extremely centralist concept. The desired level of service is specified centrally and pursued uniformly. What counts are the centre's preferences and perceptions of 'need': those of the units below the centre are of relevance only as an obstacle to the attainment of territorial equity. In this model, it is not possible to subscribe to both territorial equity and local autonomy.

If, however, the specified territorial equity objective is defined over potential outcomes, the position is greatly modified. The preferences and perceptions of need of centre and locality both count: a set of intergovernmental tensions may be generated but are themselves regarded as legitimate expressions of contrasting viewpoints and interests. What the centre does is to ensure that each jurisdiction faces the same choice of alternative outcomes. In economic jargon, each jurisdiction faces the same opportunity set but different outcomes will be chosen if there are different utility functions. The centre achieves territorial equity through the payment of equalization grants which can be designed to eliminate the effects of low resources and high needs. It is thus possible to achieve territorial equity whilst maintaining local autonomy. Indeed, it could be argued that the practical value of local autonomy has been enhanced.

Territorial equity does not necessarily demand territorial equality of outcome. Whether this is required depends upon how the conception is defined. When defined over potential outcomes, local preferences can play a role. These may differ from each other, and from the centre, in terms of the relative valuations attached to publicly provided and privately provided goods and between different publicly provided goods. Such variations in preferences will generate both different levels and compositions of public spending but this result does not constitute evidence that there are territorial inequities. For example, jurisdiction A might have a higher level of spending on education but a lower level of spending on housing than B.

If the focus is now switched from the jurisdiction to the individuals comprising it, a potential conflict between territorial and interpersonal equity becomes obvious. The level of public education and housing available to any particular household clearly depends upon the jurisdiction in which it resides. There are markedly different participation rates in the public sector for these two services. The position of an unskilled working-class household wanting public sector housing will be worse in A than in B (in terms of availability and rent levels) to an extent that more educational facilities may not fully compensate. Similarly, the position of a middle-class household will be much worse in B than in A. Given that it probably does not want public sector tenancies means that there is no compensation at all. Although Tiebout-style fiscal mobility is likely to increase the homogeneity of jurisdictions, there is sufficient friction in the system to ensure that this process is far from complete.

The compatibility with interpersonal equity

Interpersonal equity can itself be defined in terms of either actual or potential outcomes. This distinction lies behind much of the debate over the respective merits of redistribution in cash versus kind. There will be a conflict between interpersonal equity and territorial equity unless both are defined in terms of actual outcomes. In this case, an individual, regardless of jurisdiction, will receive equal standards of service. In none of the three other combinations are the requirements of territorial equity and interpersonal equity consistent: these are potential, potential; potential, actual; and actual, potential.

If territorial equity is defined in terms of potential outcomes, the existence of an intermediate level of collective decision-making will result in neither criterion of interpersonal equity being satisfied. The utility level achieved by a particular individual will depend upon the jurisdiction of residence. For example, the access of a school leaver to sixth form or further education facilities will depend upon local decisions, both about the level of expenditure and about its composition. There is no necessary direct compensation for that individual if local priorities in his jurisdiction favour provision for the elderly. Consequently, although each similar individual within that jurisdiction will be treated equally, this does not hold across jurisdictions. Interpersonal equity throughout the state, whether defined in potential or actual terms, has thus been sacrificed.

The actual version of territorial equity requires that there are exactly equal standards of service everywhere. This rules out the potential version of interpersonal equity as any exercise of substitutability, central to the potential version, must be in conflict with it.

The idea of local autonomy is fundamental to the potential version of territorial equity. Through it, public service provision can, it is argued, respond more flexibly to differences in local preferences and needs. Although such adjustments are diametrically opposed to the actual version, they constitute the substance of the potential version. An intriguing set of paradoxes has been developed:

(1) Territorial equity (actual outcome version) is:
—consistent with interpersonal equity
—inconsistent with local autonomy.
(2) Territorial equity (potential outcome version) is:
—inconsistent with interpersonal equity
—consistent with local autonomy.

The fiscal structure of the state

Many fiscal conflicts can be characterized in terms of alternative processes of aggregation. Not only do needs and resources vary between areas, so do preferences and perceptions of need, raising the question of which will count. The fiscal structure of the state, and the associated delineation of areas, is crucial both to the patterns of resources and needs, and to voting and policy outcomes (Ashford, 1980).

The causes of the legendary confusion and inconsistency in political attitudes towards local autonomy, and territorial and interpersonal equity, become much clearer. The lower the importance attached to either form of equity the easier it is to subscribe to an unqualified case for decentralization: resisting the growth of the 'centralized state'/'federal power' has long been a 'conservative' cause. Given the limits on redistribution by decentralized tiers, a fairly strong centre is a pre-condition for effective redistribution of any form. Such controversies are familiar in federal countries such as the USA and Australia. In the UK, Rowley (1979b) espoused the cause of devolution explicitly on the basis that such fragmentation would weaken the state relative to the market. The problem is much more complex for those who subscribe to all three values: local autonomy, territorial and interpersonal equity. The potential for conflict between them has already been illustrated.

Also clearer are the reasons why the centre is so frequently tempted to intervene. The centre has its own perceptions of need and policy preferences. Especially when it has provided the necessary resources, it is likely to cite interpersonal equity as a basis for intervention. In opposition, both the Conservative and Labour parties champion the cause of local autonomy: for example, on selection in education and on housing rents policy respectively. In office, the position changes sharply. Conservative Governments stress the inequity to ratepayers in some areas having to fund the housing revenue account deficits of Labour councils. In turn, Labour Governments stress the inequity of the educational opportunities of children in some areas being reduced by the selection policies of Conservative councils. This alternating emphasis is not just hypocrisy: there is a real dilemma. Few individuals seem to have fully defined preferences over the three values of territorial equity, interpersonal equity and local autonomy.

Equalization grants have developed as a policy response to the problem of reconciling decentralization with territorial equity. They can be a powerful tool for reducing the conflict between local autonomy and territorial equity provided that the latter is defined in potential terms. However, the conditions for interpersonal equity across the state as a whole will be breached, a point recognized in an exchange between Musgrave (1961a, b) and Buchanan (1961). Where they disagreed was on whether the centre should take action (say, in the form of taxes and transfers) to offset this consequence of discretionary fiscal action at the locality. Musgrave rejected Buchanan's proposal to this effect on the grounds that it was entirely alien to the idea of federalism. The same problem also arises in a state which, though unitary, has decentralized much of public service provision to lower tiers of government. In this case, however, Musgrave's reply carries less conviction.

Nothing has been said so far about which characteristics enhance the claim of certain jurisdictions to local autonomy. Jurisdictions can have very different origins. Contrast, for example, one which owes its establishment to expert opinion on the economically optimal size for a set of functions with one which has a clear historical, political and cultural basis. Scotland and Wales may not be immediately appealing jurisdictions on functional grounds, yet it would be foolish to deny that cultural and nationalist factors play a powerful role in legitimizing patterns of decentralization. When attention is turned to issues of territorial equity across a range of jurisdictions, a crucial question is the domain over which the claims of territorial equity will apply. It is generally recognized that Scotland and Wales have a claim over UK resources based on territorial equity. The operation of such a principle is curtailed at the boundaries of the UK despite the fact that, for example, Zimbabwe is unimaginably poorer. The claims of interpersonal equity are often viewed as being similarly constrained. The hesitant steps now being taken by the EEC confirm that there is a perceived link with citizenship: the emerging discussion of fiscal inequalities is seen as a necessary part of the process of political and economic integration (MacDougall, 1977). The contrast between the internal policies of the 'rich' countries, themselves welfare states, and their limited sense of obligation towards 'poor' countries (Brandt, 1980; Gutmann, 1980) is often seized upon by those hostile to the claims of equity.

IV PUBLIC EXPENDITURE AND TERRITORIAL EQUITY

The evidence on expenditure shares

Public expenditure has profound territorial implications. Even a uniform level throughout the UK would generate massive territorial transfers because any given tax structure will have yielded very different sums of revenue from different parts of the UK. The principle of derivation (that is that each area gets back in public expenditure what it contributes in revenue) has been overridden. In practice, the transfers are much greater than this. Those areas which probably generate the least revenue (the regional statistics for which are poor) also have the highest levels of expenditure. The published figures show that Scotland, Wales and Northern Ireland have enjoyed levels well above those in England.

There are three main sources of information about the territorial pattern of public expenditure. The first series, identifiable public expenditure, provides a breakdown of about 80 per cent of total public expenditure by programme and by country. In 1981/82, identifiable expenditure per head in Scotland was 123 per cent of the UK average; in Wales 112 per cent; in Northern Ireland 147 per cent; and in England 95 per cent (Brittan, 1983). During the 1960s and 1970s there was a dramatic improvement in the relative positions of Scotland and Northern Ireland. Although the identifiable public expenditure series does not go back as far on a consistent basis, there is other evidence which confirms this development (Heald, 1980c). Wales, however, despite many problems in common with the other two small countries, did not enjoy such an improvement relative to England. This has been attributed by Rose (1982) to a lack of 'political clout' on the part of Welsh institutions.

The second source of official data became available in the late 1970s as a result of the then Labour Government's plans to establish separately elected assemblies for both Scotland and Wales (Treasury, 1979b). As part of a planning exercise for the block grants which would have financed these assemblies, calculations were undertaken by the Treasury and then published, expressing devolved expenditure as a percentage of English equivalent expenditure on the same services. Although the results for Scotland and Wales were not comparable as devolved expenditure reflected differing responsibilities, it provided new evidence about the favourable treatment, particularly of Scotland. Scottish devolved expenditure was calculated to be roughly 30 per cent above its English equivalent expenditure. Similarly, Welsh devolved expenditure was roughly 10 per cent above its English equivalent expenditure (Heald, 1980c, pp. 32–35).

A third source, but this time unofficial, is Short's work (1976, 1981, 1982) on the distribution of 'regionally relevant' expenditure.[2] The great advantage of this source is that it did not treat England as a homogeneous unit, but attempted to calculate expenditure for the former economic planning regions. It showed sharp differences within England. When expenditure share is divided by population share, the resulting average per capita index for the period 1974/75 to 1977/78 ranged from 88.2 for East Anglia to 112.4 for the North (Short, 1982). He confirmed the favourable treatment of Scotland (122.2) and of Wales where the index (109.2) was higher than for any English region with the exception of the North.

In the UK, the territorial pattern of public expenditure has traditionally generated negligible interest. This is one of the reasons why data, except for the last few years, are so sketchy. Recognition of the major shifts that had taken place during the 1960s and 1970s only dawned fairly late in the devolution debate and raised fears that there would be an English backlash about expenditure differentials (Jackson, 1979).

The determination of expenditure shares

The question of territorial shares of public expenditure provides many insights into the implicit territorial equity objectives being pursued and into the processes through which the UK system of government attempts to handle the resulting tensions. There are a number of methods by which country shares might be established: by pre-set formula, by pseudo-technical means, or through an explicit political bargaining process. These possibilities are not necessarily mutually exclusive.

The Goschen formula of 11/80ths (named after a Chancellor of the Exchequer) was originally established as the basis for calculating the Scottish education grant (Boyle, 1966). It survived long after its original rationale (relative population shares in Scotland and England in 1891) had ceased to have any relevance. Not only did it linger on but it was also extended to public expenditure shares. The practical influence of the Goschen formula is little documented. However, its longevity has been confirmed by William (later Lord) Ross (1977) who has referred to it being used during his early parliamentary career, but then disappearing.

The clearest example of a technical exercise is the work undertaken as part of the Treasury's preparation for the Scottish and Welsh block grants (Treasury, 1979b). Although surrounded by heavy qualifications as to its proper use, this study viewed the problem of expenditure shares as that of calculating the cost of applying English policies to Scotland and Wales. It concluded that Scotland's present expenditure share was too high and Wales's too low. The incumbency of William Ross as Labour Secretary of State for Scotland from 1964–70 and from 1974–76 is widely regarded as a period in which political muscles were flexed to improve Scotland's relative position. The evidence is consistent with the view that the paths of expenditure shares were then heavily influenced by political bargaining.

In 1978, there was a return to a formula. It is some measure of the extent of UK official secrecy that its use was never placed upon the public record until the Committee on Scottish Affairs (1980) elicited this information from George Younger, the Conservative Secretary of State for Scotland. The Labour Government did not reveal the existence of this formula regulating expenditure relatives within Great Britain (thus excluding Northern Ireland), despite its relevance to the debate on the financing of devolved assemblies. Similarly, the debate on how Scotland would fare during the Conservative Government's programme of public expenditure cuts was initially conducted without reference to its operation.

The 1978 formula is known as the Barnett formula after Joel Barnett, the then Chief Secretary to the Treasury with responsibility for public expenditure (Heald, 1980d, 1982a; Committee on Scottish Affairs, 1982).[3] Under it, Scotland and Wales receive respectively 10/85ths and 5/85ths of any changes in expenditure in England on programmes comparable to those in the Scottish and Welsh blocks. These blocks contain that part of the expenditure within the responsibility of the respective Secretaries of State falling within this arrangement: 95 per cent in Scotland and 93 per cent in Wales in 1981/82. In a few cases, such as law and order, where expenditure is not divided between England and Wales, Scotland receives 10/90ths of the change to the joint English and Welsh comparable programme. It thus involves *changes* in such public expenditure being allocated between Scotland, Wales and England in the proportions 10 : 5 : 85. The latest population estimates then available would be those for June 1977 which were 9.57 per cent, 5.10 per cent and 85.34 per cent respectively, rounded to two places of decimals. The new formula looks to be based on population shares.

The formula affects the total size of the Scottish and Welsh expenditure blocks, each of which broadly consists of expenditure within the responsibility of the Secretary of State other than on agriculture, fisheries and industrial support. The Scottish and Welsh blocks serve two distinct purposes.

(1)   The Barnett formula is applied to changes in the expenditure in England (or England and Wales) on programmes comparable to those in the Scottish and Welsh blocks.
(2)   The Secretaries of State for Scotland and Wales have complete discretion as to expenditure switching between programmes within their own blocks.

The system thereby entails the use of a formula to allocate to Scotland and Wales shares of changes in public expenditure on English programmes comparable to those in the Scottish and Welsh blocks and the granting to each of the Secretaries of State of discretion to determine the pattern of expenditure within his own block.

The implicit criterion of territorial equity

The relevant territorial equity criterion therefore focuses upon potential rather than actual outcomes. Little progress has been made on the question of how expenditure shares should be determined. Furthermore, attention has been restricted to those programmes which are subject to the existing institutions of administrative devolution. This narrow focus has avoided the important but intractable questions surrounding the overall territorial impact of public expenditure for which a measure of regionally relevant expenditure is required, covering other programmes such as defence, social security and the nationalized industries. The evidence demonstrates that there are territorial variations in both the level and pattern of public expenditure. Variations in the former are clearly subject to alternative explanations (for example the outcome of political bargaining, or an attempt to allocate public expenditure according to the underlying pattern of need).

There appears to be an emerging consensus that, even when the level of expenditure has been set centrally, the pattern should be the responsibility of the appropriate territorial unit: the Scottish and Welsh Offices. If the devolution proposals had been implemented, this responsibility would have been transferred to the separately elected assemblies. Interpersonal equity is thereby sacrificed to the potential version of territorial equity. Two contrasting examples further illustrate such conflicts.

First, much attention has been paid in recent years to the territorial distribution of resources within the NHS. Despite the 'equal access' rationale of the NHS, the territorial distribution of resources remained markedly unequal thirty years after its establishment, breaching both interpersonal and territorial equity. Even where there is no governmental unit capable of switching resources between, say, health and education, the issue still arises because of intra-NHS allocations between health specialisms. Furthermore, care is required when comparing, say, NHS provision in Scotland and England, as any observed variations may partly reflect different preferences, articulated at the Scottish level, between health and, say, education. What is particularly noteworthy about health equalization is that there have been four schemes, one for each country, and not one (Heald, 1980d). Different factors and weights are used in order to distribute the available funds within each country. Maynard and Ludbrook (1980b) have calculated that if the English formula were to be applied to the UK as a whole, Scotland would lose 14.9 per cent of its budget and Northern Ireland 13.6 per cent whereas England would gain 2.2 per cent and Wales 7.5 per cent.

The Treasury study (1979b) recorded that there were serious disagreements within its specialist group for health about the use of the mortality index as a proxy for morbidity. Taking England as 100, the assessed need index for health and personal social services was calculated as Scotland, 107.1; Wales, 106.1; and Northern Ireland, 107.1. On the minority view, the index would have been Scotland, 118.0; Wales, 112.1; and Northern Ireland, 121.8. The study used the argument that the majority assumption is consistent with the internal allocation procedures adopted in all four countries. However, this raises a fundamental point: is such information about local choices, which reflect preferences as well as needs, legitimate evidence in the central assessment of need?

Second, there would seem to be very different public attitudes towards territorial variations in exhaustive public expenditure and in cash transfers. Whereas the former are considered acceptable, the latter are not. Health and educational services can vary territorially but child benefit and old age pensions cannot. Different versions of territorial equity seem to be applied: the potential to the former and the actual outcome to the latter. If such distinctions are made, they generate a whole set of fiscal problems (for example, in the design of financing systems for decentralization, and in cases where exhaustive expenditure can be substituted for transfers).

V INTERGOVERNMENTAL GRANTS AS A FACILITATOR OF DECENTRALIZATION

Intergovernmental grants raise a number of new issues, most notably that they constitute a transfer of resources between politically separate units of government rather than transfers within the same administrative unit. This is the essential difference between Rate Support Grant (RSG) and health equalization schemes. The political separateness, derived from its different territorial base, of local from central government has been supplemented in the UK by the pattern of strong swings in local government elections against the party in office nationally. Central–local relations have become a major political issue. The pressure for reductions in the rate of growth and then in the level of local government expenditure has stimulated intergovernmental conflict and much greater academic interest.

Paralleling the growing role of the Scottish and Welsh Offices in public expenditure planning, their role in intergovernmental grants has similarly been strengthened. The Scottish RSG, though structured in the same way as the pre-1981 system in England and Wales, has a certain distinctive character-istics and has always been administered by the Scottish Office (Heald 1980e, 1982b). The radical recasting of the RSG in 1981/82, whereby the needs and resources elements were replaced by the block grant (Jackman, 1981), did not extend to Scotland. Indeed, when the Secretary of State for Scotland eventually produced his own legislative changes to deal with 'overspenders', they were markedly different from the measures in England and Wales. In contrast, Wales had been an integral part of a single RSG covering England and Wales. From 1981/82, however, there has been a separate Welsh RSG which, though structured in the same way as the English block grant, is administered separately by the Welsh Office. Administrative devolution has therefore been gathering strength, despite the collapse of the devolution plans in 1979. Consequently, Scotland, Wales and England are being treated as distinct entities, with still different arrangements being made for Northern Ireland. By pursuing the potential version of territorial equity (that is allowing expenditure or grant switching within each separately), interper-sonal equity across the UK as a whole is thus sacrificed. Furthermore, the territorial equity objectives actually pursued may differ between countries: local authorities, identical but for their country, might be treated quite differently.

Although central government does not directly control the revenue expenditure of local authorities, their dependence upon RSG provides an indirect mechanism of control. It is useful to distinguish three objectives of grants policy even though it is possible to pursue combinations of them.

Determining the aggregate level of local government expenditure

Although such an assignment has often been asserted to be a central government responsibility, it has more significant consequences than is usually made explicit. It would be regarded in a federal country as a crucial, and inappropriate, concession. The centre has been given the power to determine the total size of the public sector. In a Keynesian world, there is a macroeconomic rationale for such an assignment: the regulation of the level of economic activity. In a monetarist world, the rationale is much less obvious. If local government expenditure increases, and is financed by an equivalent increase in local taxes, then the PSBR remains unchanged. It is the level of the PSBR which may contribute to the growth of the money supply, not the level of public expenditure itself. What matters is the proportion not financed by taxation.

A decision to restrict the concern of central government to this objective could be taken on the basis of an appeal either to local autonomy or the potential version of territorial equity. The government's sole objective would be to secure its targeted reduction in aggregate local government expenditure. Its concern would be exclusively with aggregates and not with the expenditure of individual local authorities. The refusal of some local authorities to make cuts would be offset by the readiness of others. The government would not be concerned with either the territorial or functional composition of the cuts, though it would possess the power to ensure that local authorities fulfilled their statutory responsibilities.

Central government can thus achieve its targeted expenditure reductions without becoming embroiled in the detailed affairs of a large number of local authorities. Whilst extolling the virtues of local autonomy, it can evade the odium of actually specifying the pattern of cuts. There are disadvantages as well. It abdicates decisions on the territorial and functional pattern to units of government which may be controlled by opposition parties, determined to frustrate the government's priorities. What is worse, certain local authorities may be provocatively defiant, thus generating political pressures for central intervention. Although such actions may involve sums which are irrelevant to the achievement of the targeted expenditure reduction, they may have an important influence upon the perceived fairness of the policy.

Under the RSG system as it existed before the changes of 1980 and 1981, the centre had sufficient powers to control aggregate local government expenditure provided that it was prepared to adjust the level of RSG, perhaps abruptly. In the recent conflict between the central government and local authorities, the latter have disputed the centre's rights to be the sole arbiter of expenditure, as opposed to grant, levels.

Prescribing the functional pattern of local government expenditure

Governments have relied upon persuasion, rather than upon any financial or administrative powers, as their major tool to shape the functional composition of both expenditure growth and cutbacks. For example, the traditional commentary contained in the annual RSG report (for example, Scottish Office, 1982) always qualifies its comments upon the prospects for functional programmes by emphasizing the primary responsibility of local authorities.

There is an inbuilt tension between central priorities (as specified in the public expenditure White Paper) and local priorities. However, local discretion about how an authority will allocate its RSG funds has so far remained intact. Local prerogatives on this issue receive some protection from internal conflicts within central government. On the question of functional pattern, interpersonal equity has so far been subordinated to the potential version of territorial equity. Nevertheless such local discretion might in future be reduced if the conflict over expenditure levels encourages central government to devise more detailed mechanisms of control. The dangers are highlighted by the system introduced by the Scottish Office from 1981/82 whereby the housing capital allocations of local authorities are reduced on a pound- for - pound basis by the amount by which actual rate fund contributions to housing revenue account exceed centrally-prescribed targets (Heald, Jones and Lamont, 1981).

Prescribing the territorial pattern of local government expenditure

This objective takes the central government into much deeper water. The increasingly fraught climate of central–local relations can best be understood in terms of a switching of the focus from aggregate expenditure targets to the budgets of individual authorities. There are two possible approaches to the implementation of this objective. The direct method is to specify the rate poundages, and hence the expenditure levels, of each local authority. This measure would not only be centralist but also would dramatically increase both the workload and the level of political exposure of the central departments. The indirect method is to restructure RSG so that local authorities face marginal incentives/disincentives to spend which are consistent with the government's expenditure targets, both in aggregate and for each local authority. This is exactly what the block grant seeks to do.

Both methods involve the government extending its grant objective beyond the control of the aggregate level of expenditure to embrace the control of the expenditure of individual authorities. In Scotland, where there is no tradition of a formalized methodology for establishing grant distribution, the direct method (that is expenditure and rates ceilings) has been adopted. In both England and Wales, the block grant represents the indirect method. The main innovation of the block grant is not that there will be a systematic pattern of marginal incentives to expenditure, since they were implicit in the existing RSG, but rather that the structuring of the marginal incentives facing individual local authorities has become a focal issue.

By enhancing the visibility of certain parts of the system and by altering the use which is made of them, their significance can be transformed. This point is illustrated by the assessment of spending need. Given a desire to compensate fully for the expenditure consequences of differential need, it is necessary that there should be some form of central assessment of expenditure need. Such information can be used for two distinct purposes. First, it is required so that central funds can be disbursed in accordance with this equalization objective. Second, it becomes a policy objective, to be achieved through the design of the grant system, that each local authority should spend in line with this central assessment. The block grant is designed to achieve both, whereas the previous RSG structure was exclusively geared to the first.

There are fundamental political and constitutional issues lurking behind what seem at first sight to be highly technical decisions. The chosen objectives of grants policy, and the methods through which their achievement is attempted, have profound implications for the nature of accountability in the public sector. In the UK, the central government has asserted its right to make decisions about the aggregate level of public expenditure. This is illustrated by the inclusion within the public expenditure plans determined by the Cabinet of all local government expenditure, even that part financed by local taxes. There has been much criticism of the extremely general form of the powers taken by the 1979 Conservative Government in order to penalize individual local authorities which have disputed central judgements about the desirable level of their expenditure. It has been a feature of its attempts to roll back the state that the position of local government has been weakened relative to that of central government, thereby centralizing power within the public sector.

VI CONCLUSION

The chapter has shown the difficulties of simultaneously pursuing the commonly cited objectives of territorial equity, interpersonal equity and local autonomy. The relationships between them have been shown to be more complex than is usually assumed. It is likely that policymakers' preferences are both volatile and ill-defined, thus greatly reducing the chances of there being a coherent and consistent policy.

Within the context of a large and diverse public sector decentralization provides a means for resolving some of the problems of accountability.

Nevertheless, there are key areas of public policy in which the primary objective of redistribution means that the function has to be centralized. Even outside such areas, decentralization can constitute an obstacle to the implementation of synoptic policies. The extent of the conflict will depend upon the precise formulation of the equity objectives. The contribution which intergovernmental grants can make towards reconciling decentralization with territorial equity has been emphasized.

The formal extent of decentralization can be a misleading guide as to the real location of decision-making power. Despite being regarded as a unitary state there is extensive decentralization in the UK of the provision of public services. Nevertheless, the wider political and economic context limits the extent of local autonomy. It is constrained explicitly by the mechanisms used by the central government in order to secure adherence to its public expenditure plans and implicitly by the domination of local elections by national politics and by the highly centralized collective bargaining system.

The operation of a democratic political system raises the issue of equity in a territorial as well as an interpersonal form. Territory is a key component of political mobilization. Most democratic states have been confronted by heightened perceptions of 'unjustified' differences coupled with demands for greater regional autonomy. Devising mechanisms for achieving territorial equity within the context of a decentralized system is therefore a crucial task if the benefits of decentralization are to be realized.

PART FOUR

The Future

Much of this book has been concerned with understanding the role of public expenditure in an industrialized economy and the reasons why it has recently been subjected to unprecedented challenge. The point has now been reached at which attention must be turned towards substantive policy questions, all relating to the future strategy for public expenditure. The earlier discussions of context, values and mechanisms have, quite apart from their own intrinsic importance, been necessary preliminaries to such a task. Inevitably, a book with such a broad canvas operates at the level of strategy, whereas many of the practical decisions have to be taken in terms of functional programmes and small detail. But without a coherent sense of strategy, policies on public expenditure are liable to be confused and contradictory, frustrating those who are sympathetic to its role and delighting critics by the easy ammunition which is provided.

The first three chapters of Part Four each relate to issues central to the future of public expenditure. One of the themes of this book is that there has emerged a paralysing crisis in the intellectual tradition which facilitated the development of the Keynesian social democratic state. Whereas the book is almost exclusively concerned with the attack on that tradition from the radical right, there are revealing parallels in the attack from the Marxist left. Perhaps the most significant consequence of the latter has been to erode the willingness and ability of many socialist supporters of that tradition to respond to the monetarist free-market critique.

One central weakness in the Keynesian social democratic tradition has been the neglect of how public expenditure is to be 'paid for'. Too many people profess support for the welfare state, but are unwilling to accept the implications for taxation. A modern welfare state cannot be paid for by soaking the rich: the 'burden' has to be borne by the bulk of the working population. The apparently irresistible temptation to evade this fact has allowed severe distortions to emerge in the taxation system which have contributed to the erosion of consent. In response to the alleged deficiencies of the public sector, privatization has gathered momentum as the solution, successfully being transplanted from the writings of free-market economists on to the political agenda. However, it is a term with many meanings and covers a range of policy developments, some concerned more with the form of the welfare state and others with its very existence.

It is tempting to seek simple solutions to complex problems, never more so than in an age of uncertainty. The appeal of both the radical right and the Marxist left lies in their ability to provide clear-cut remedies: 'roll back the state' or 'smash capitalism'. If ever it could, the Keynesian social democratic tradition no longer offers such a confident agenda but that can be interpreted as a strength rather than just as a source of weakness. Although critical of aspects of that tradition, this book has shown that much that is to be valued still lies within it. A more realistic assessment of the problems of running a large public sector does not imply a withdrawal of support for its objectives. This book suggests that the strategy for public expenditure should be one of defence but reform.

CHAPTER 11

The Crisis of the Keynesian
Social Democratic State

I A TRADITION IN DISARRAY

The image of the large public sectors characteristic of the Keynesian social democratic state is now sorely tarnished. Charges of bureaucracy, centralization, corporatism, inefficiency, paternalism and oppression are vigorously levelled against them. Although some of the attacks verge on polemical abuse, they have contributed towards the decisive shift in the climate of opinion towards the public sector. Significantly, the mud has stuck even when it only has been mud. However, no reader could have progressed to this chapter without becoming aware that there has been much to criticize in the way in which public sectors have been run. In part, such defects reflect the greater interest of the architects of the Keynesian social democratic state in the grand design, than in the practicalities of managing an extensive public sector. All too often, then and since, appeal has been made to 'planning', as if it were a panacea, the state's equivalent of the market's invisible hand. The role of planning in the public sector should not be disparaged for, despite fashionable views, it is indispensable. But so is a hard-headed approach to the realities of political processes and to the limits of administrative action. Its absence has set up ready targets for the opponents of the Keynesian social democratic state, thus allowing the latter to fudge the issue of whether the assault is directed not so much at the institutions but rather at the values which they were designed to serve.

The fundamental change in intellectual opinion, especially the counter-revolution in the economics profession, is perhaps even more dramatic a development than the shifts in the political arena. It used to be claimed that the brightest minds were sympathetic to the programmes of the Keynesian social democratic state, echoing Schumpeter's view (1943) that intellectuals were naturally hostile to capitalism. The reverse could now be argued, at least about the economics profession: not so much in terms of numbers as of commitment, vigour and self-confidence. To a remarkable extent, monetarist and free-market economists have been setting the intellectual and political agenda.[1] Fifty years ago, R. H. Tawney's political commitment generated the

257

suspicion amongst his colleagues at the London School of Economics that he was unable to draw a proper line between academic research and political activity (Reisman 1982). What sustained Tawney was his belief that he was right: that his research had demonstrated that the adoption of his policy proposals was the only route to a civilized and humane society. Now, however, the heirs of Keynes and Tawney seem inhibited by self-doubt when faced by confident assertions that there are simple answers to the problems which have subsequently emerged. To reply that economic and social changes have made problems much more complex and difficult to resolve might be true. But it sounds lame, hardly ground on which to stem either revolutions or crusades.

The crisis of the Keynesian social democratic state is in essence the loss of faith in its continuing efficacy as a political accommodation of both universal suffrage and organized labour with a market-orientated economy. For the Marxist left, it is nothing more than another face of the capitalist state, more cosmetically attractive but insidiously distracting the working class from the task of smashing capitalism. Undeniably, the accommodation did not fully satisfy socialist aspirations: for example, most of the means of production in the market sector remained in private ownership. This capitalist dimension created a fundamental dilemma for elected socialist governments as the scope for social programmes and for improved living standards depended upon the economic performance of the very private capitalists to which socialist movements had grown up in mutual antagonism. Yet it did bring a firm commitment to full employment and to use the tax and expenditure powers of the state to mediate the economic and social inequality induced by the distribution of property and ability, the class system, and the market economy. For those on the political right who rejected its inherent value system, the appeal of the Keynesian social democratic state lay in its usefulness as an accommodation which fell far short of proletarian revolution and socialist transformation. Whenever votes are more equally distributed than economic resources, there are incentives for those with high shares of the latter to seek some form of accommodation. Similar incentives are provided by the power of organized labour. These factors lay behind the remarkable similarities between countries despite marked differences in the electoral fortunes of working-class parties. What has differentiated the radical right from the traditional right has been its willingness to challenge that accommodation, re-opening debates presumed to have been settled long ago.

Perhaps the most significant achievement of the Keynesian revolution in macroeconomic thought was that, for a time, it banished the notion that mass unemployment was just an inevitable feature, a mark on the landscape, of economic and social life. It was no longer seen as God-given: enlightened policy could dramatically reduce its extent. The view that it was remediable, rather than part of the remorseless logic of the market economy, also encouraged a more humanitarian outlook towards the unemployed. The less unemployment was interpreted as a badge of individual failure to conform to the signals of the market-place, more attention could be directed towards the needs of the unemployed as less emphasis was being placed upon the social discipline of unemployment. Furthermore, any given level of 'generosity' in the tax/transfer system is much less costly when there is a macroeconomic commitment to full employment. Indeed, Crouch (1981) argued that the commitment to full employment was perhaps the most significant aspect of the welfare state for much of the working class, involving little direct public expenditure but reducing the insecurity of their earnings in the market-place. The abandonment of that commitment has augured in another period in which it is respectable for economists to discuss the therapeutic qualities of unemployment: it is good social discipline which, *inter alia,* quells trade unions (Minford and Peel, 1981; Seldon, 1982a; and Stapleton, 1981).[2] Unemployment is again attributed to individual shortcomings or to the microeconomic maladjustments caused by union power, state regulation and an excessively generous tax/transfer system. The acceptance of much higher unemployment as a necessary consequence of monetarist counter-inflation policy has produced a receptive audience for such views.

Keynesian policies were seen to have 'failed', leaving open terrain for monetarists to occupy. That failure was social and political, rather than economic and technical, originating in the labour market. The commitment to full employment and to a large public sector was made without sufficient attention being paid to the subsequent implications for the nature and role of the state. Furthermore, it was not initially understood the extent to which the early success in combining full employment and growth with only modest rates of inflation relied heavily upon the tacit constraints imposed upon collective bargaining by convention and forbearance. When such inhibitions eroded, a catalogue of contradictory attitudes towards the state was revealed. The supporters of the Keynesian social democratic state were probably the worst afflicted.

The dilemma is simple to state, if not to resolve. The commitment to full employment and an extensive public sector were an accommodation secured at least in part by the activities of the labour movement, acting through both its political wing (the Labour Party) and its industrial wing (the trade unions). Such developments led to three workers out of ten being employed in the public sector, with two out of ten being paid out of taxation. When collective bargaining consisted of trade unions facing private capitalists, the conflict between capital and labour appeared stark. But when the enhanced economic role of the state made it become the major employer of labour, facing a labour force which had achieved much higher levels of union density than in the private sector, the implications of industrial conflict became more ambivalent. The left faced the question of whether all industrial conflict in a public sector which it had done much to establish should be supported as part of the wider class struggle. If so, how could the priority accorded to the expansion of public services allocated on 'need', rather than ability to pay, be squared with unqualified support for industrial disruption of those services by the workers employed in them? For example, strikes in the NHS or in state schools inflict the greatest harm upon those most dependent upon them and with the least access to private substitutes of various forms. In practice, the non-Marxist left attempted to look both ways, claiming the welfare state as its great political achievement, but displaying hostility towards the managers of its services and sympathizing with almost every case of industrial action within the public sector. Attitudes which had seemed unproblematical in the earlier period generated profound contradictions in the context of the Keynesian social democratic state. The non-Marxist left exhibited little grasp of the difficult practical issues of regulating the relationship between the state and its employees, even less of how its failure even to understand the basic dilemma had left both unions and the state exposed to the free-market critique. The Marxist left had one advantage: it had always stressed, with or without qualification, that the actions of the capitalist state were directed towards meeting the needs of capital and that those who believed otherwise were deluded.

To recognize such disarray, and to understand the reasons for it, does not necessarily imply forsaking commitment to the Keynesian social democratic state. Its enemies on both right and left have a good story to tell, tasks made easier by the lack of serious thought within that tradition about the nature and role of the state. But vigour and style are not the same as substance and evidence. Both the radical right and the Marxist left make a few core ideas do an enormous amount of work, constructing a 'view of the world' into which other 'facts' must fit. The 'invisible hand' of the market is a masterful idea, rich in insight. However, admiration at the sheer power of the metaphor can outrun curiosity as to how real-world markets actually function. What can in the hands of the skilful economic theorist reveal much about how economies function and might be improved, can easily degenerate into a slogan. When set against the isolated and timeless individual of economic analysis who acquires his preferences from nowhere, the Marxist analysis of how the emergence of the capitalist mode of production leads to the formation of unequal social classes constitutes a welcome caution against claiming too much for the market. Class struggle, whether actual or potential, possibly does more to limit the forms and extent of economic and social inequalities which are deemed acceptable than all the elegant reasoning of philosophers. However, class struggle imposes costs, the incidence of which can be unpredictable, some certainly falling upon the working class itself rather than upon the capitalist class. If class struggle is envisaged primarily as the means for securing economic and political gains for the working class, some arrangements will have to be made which contain these costs. If the objective is revolution, such mundane considerations can be dismissed as irrelevant.

Given Marxists' renowned lack of interest in what happens after the revolution, non-Marxists find it difficult to establish any dialogue with them, either about the benefits and costs of revolution or about the regulation of conflict in the labour markets of capitalist economies.

Yet both the radical right and the Marxist left have at least thought seriously about the state. Both reject the Keynesian social democratic state, prompting Crouch (1979, p. 24) to observe: 'Reactionaries and radicals alike celebrate the same evidence of discomfiture in the political compromise which has kept them both at bay for so long even if at the end of the celebration they return to opposite corners.'[3] Although their respective vocabularies are markedly different, there are common concerns. Whilst the radical right distrusts the state as the vehicle for collectivism, Marxists view the 'capitalist' (that is pre-revolution) state as an obstacle to socialism. An important parallel is the emphasis upon the role of property rights and relations. For the radical right, property rights make possible the operation of a market economy which promotes economic efficiency and enhances individual freedom. For Marxists, the institution of private property divides society into antagonistic social classes, defined in terms of their relationship to the ownership of the means of production. Marxists switch the emphasis from the behaviour of autonomous individuals to the conflict of social classes. Both schools neglect the fundamental insight of the other: there is just as little recognition of the significance of social class in the literature of free-market economics as of the usefulness of markets in Marxist literature.

II   THE MARXIST CRITIQUE OF THE CAPITALIST STATE

The traditional supporters of the Keynesian social democratic state have failed to mount a coherent defence of their position, either against attacks from the radical right or from the Marxist left. This book is almost exclusively concerned with the former, for highly practical reasons. First, the benefits from the erosion of that accommodation have accrued almost entirely to them, as evidenced by the decisive shifts to the right of both electorates and intellectual opinion. Second, the Marxist literature on the capitalist state is inward-looking, written by Marxists for other Marxists. This characteristic has made it highly inaccessible to others, thereby limiting its influence on the mainstream of political events. Furthermore, as Jessop's (1982) survey explicitly acknowledged, the academic positions adopted by particular authors are intimately related to their views on the correct political strategy for overthrowing capitalism and establishing socialism. It is a literature in which political commitment is explicit, in contrast to the way in which it remains implicit in much of the literature of the radical right. Within the Marxist literature, there are deep and bitterly contested divisions. The unifying proposition, however, is that the capitalist state is subservient to the interests of capital, though there is a wide spectrum of views on how complete is this subservience. Such a proposition sharply differentiates the Marxist left from the non-Marxist left. The latter has been profoundly influenced by the Fabian tradition of identifying in the state enormous potential for beneficial action, to be released by securing political control over its institutions through the electoral activities of a working-class party (in the UK, through the Labour Party). The non-Marxist left has thus stressed the importance of changing the identity of the rulers, less of altering the nature or form of state institutions: commitment to socialist policies and suitable administrative arrangements are what is required. Just as the Paretian welfare economist implicitly looks to the altruistic public official for the implementation of optimal policies, the non-Marxist left implicitly relies upon the good Fabian administrator to chart the road to socialism. Although neither tradition is unworthy, both are vulnerable to satire. Neither firmly locates its decision-makers within the economic and social context within which they must operate. Marxists take a far less optimistic view than the non-Marxist left of the possibilities arising from a left-wing political party winning democratic elections: a change of government does not of itself alter either the nature of the economic and social system nor the role of the state within that.

There is a long tradition of Marxists viewing the capitalist state as an enemy, not as the potential ally envisaged by reformist parties. Indeed, Marx and Engels (1848, p. 5) were emphatic: 'The executive of the modern State is but a committee for managing the common affairs of the whole bourgeoisie.' Nevertheless, there is much greater depth and diversity in their writings than is suggested by this thundering denunciation. Jessop (1977) distinguished six different approaches to be found in traditional Marxist thought:

(1)   The state as a *parasitic institution*: the state becomes the private property of its officials who further their own interests, favouring particular sectional groups at the expense of the common interest.

(2)   The state and state power as *epiphenomena* (that is simple surface reflections) of the system of property relations and the resulting class struggles.

(3)   The state as a *factor of cohesion* with the function of regulating class conflict, using the techniques of repression and of concession, in a way which mediates, though without undermining, the rule of capital.

(4)   The state as an *instrument of class rule* which is often assumed to be neutral, capable of being used by any class.

(5)   The state as a *set of institutions or 'public power'*, developing at a certain stage of the division of labour, and which is characterized by a distinct system of government involving officials who specialize in administration and/or repression.

(6)   The state as a *system of political domination* which conditions the results of class struggle through the forms of state intervention and of political representation which are adopted.

These strands were not combined into a single, coherent theory of the capitalist state. However, they summarize the various ideas, often conflicting, which recur in the writings of Karl Marx, Friedrich Engels and Vladimir Lenin.

Contemporary Marxist theories of the capitalist state combine one or more of these features, but in different ways. A number of distinct schools, each with its own variants, have emerged. There is great diversity in views, emphasis and methodology. For example, Miliband (1969) emphasized the social backgrounds, personal ties and shared values of economic and political élites, stressing that socialization into the ideology of the ruling class is an important source of political power. Such a focus was criticized by Poulantzas (1969) who argued that attention should be directed at the structurally-determined role of the state in capitalist society, rather than at the individuals who man its machinery. The decision of many of the communist parties of Western Europe to abandon the means of proletarian revolution in favour of an electoral strategy has injected new vigour into such controversies. They have been criticized for believing that an election which gives them control over the institutions of the state would suddenly transform the capitalist state into an instrument for socialism. In this sense, they have become almost indistinguishable from the social democratic and labour parties which became reformist at a much earlier date.

A recurrent topic in the Marxist literature is the 'relative autonomy' of the capitalist state, referring to whether it has any independence from capital. This idea has developed from the rejection as much too unsophisticated of the view that the capitalist state is the pliant tool of 'monopoly capital'. The concern, therefore, is with establishing the limits circumscribing its ability to serve interests other than those of capital. Although the capitalist state is not a neutral instrument capable of being turned against capital by the working class, the institutional structure of the state and the ways in which state power is exercised will influence the results of class struggle, thus providing the working class with the opportunity for substantive gains. Such gains are constrained by the functional role of the capitalist state to allow capital accumulation to proceed unhindered. Paradoxically, the working class's gains from class struggle may, by maintaining the social cohesion necessary for capital accumulation, indirectly promote the interests of capital. However, the consequence is that class struggle is imported into the institutions of the capitalist state.

III   THE FISCAL CRISIS OF THE STATE

A number of Marxist writers, notably James O'Connor, Claus Offe and Ian Gough, have applied the tools of Marxist analysis to the fiscal activities of the capitalist state, identifying a set of contradictions which they confidently predict will destroy capitalism. However, these writers are rather eclectic Marxists, drawing upon other traditions. The most influential book has been *The Fiscal Crisis of the State* (O'Connor, 1973). O'Connor's central thesis is that the capitalist state is incapable of resolving its mounting fiscal crisis, itself a symptom of a deeper malaise.

> The fiscal crisis of the capitalist state is the inevitable consequence of the structural gap between state expenditures and revenues. It is our contention that the only lasting solution is socialism. However, the state might be able to ameliorate the fiscal crisis by accelerating the growth of the social-industrial complex (p. 221).

In order to set O'Connor's diagnosis in context, it is first necessary to sketch the central features of his model of the fiscal activities of the capitalist state. Inevitably an exposition of this length loses much of the detail and some of the subtlety, but it does capture the mechanisms generating fiscal crisis. Although O'Connor intended his model to have a wider application, it was developed and discussed almost exclusively with reference to the USA, leading to it having certain features (for example greater hostility to state sector unionism than private) not applicable elsewhere. The economy is assumed to have three sectors:

(1) *The competitive sector* characterized by low capital intensity and small-scale operations; highly competitive markets into which entry is easy; low profitability; slow productivity growth; poor working conditions and low job security; low wages; and weak or non-existent unions.

(2) *The monopoly sector* characterized by high capital intensity and large-scale operations; limited competition stemming from high barriers to entry; high profitability; fast productivity growth; reasonably high job security; high wages; and strong unions with high densities.

(3) *The state sector* with two parts, (a) production by the state, and (b) production by private capital under contract to the state. It is characterized by: high capital intensity and large-scale operations in (b); protection from competition; high profitability in (b) guaranteed by the state which pursues goals other than profit in (a); slow or unmeasured productivity growth; high job security; wages linked in the long run to the monopoly sector; high union densities but unions are inhibited in (a) by the proportion of females, by professional norms, and by state hostility.

State expenditure is analysed in the model in terms of its relationship to the two basic, though often mutually contradictory, functions of the capitalist state: *accumulation* (securing the conditions for profitable private capital accumulation) and *legitimization* (securing the conditions for social harmony). Although almost every item of state expenditure serves more than one purpose, meaning that classification can never be unambiguous, the main purpose of any item can be determined within the following scheme:

(1) *Social capital*: expenditure which is required for profitable private capital accumulation, being indirectly productive in the sense that it indirectly expands surplus value, consisting of:

    (a) *Social investment*: projects and services which increase the productivity of a given amount of labour power and, other things being equal, increase the rate of profit, such as:

        (i) *physical capital*: investment in the infrastructure for transport (for example roads and ports), utilities (for example electricity and water) and urban renewal (for example commercial buildings, car parks and sports stadiums) and which in turn can be divided into:
complementary investments without which private capital projects would be unprofitable; and
discretionary investments designed to provide incentives for new private accumulation but which themselves fail the test of the market, typically being made at times of crisis when profitable opportunities for capital are scarce and being potentially very wasteful.

    (b) *Social consumption*: projects and services which lower the reproduction costs of labour and, other factors being equal, increase the rate of profit in the monopoly sector because of the resulting lower wage level. It consists of:

        (i) goods and services which are consumed collectively by the working class such as suburban development projects (for example roads, schools, recreational facilities and mortgage subsidies), urban renewal (for example housing and commuter facilities); and related services (for example child care and medical facilities); and

        (ii) social insurance against economic insecurity such as workmen's compensation, old age pensions, unemployment benefits, and medical insurance.

(2) *Social expenses*: expenditure which is required to maintain social harmony, thus fulfilling the state's legitimization function, but which are not even directly productive. They consist of:

    (a) *military expenditure*: surplus capital in the monopoly sector creates political pressures for aggressive foreign economic expansion which also inhibits the development of world revolution, thus keeping labour power, raw materials and markets within the capitalist orbit; and

(b) *welfare expenditure*: surplus labour power creates political pressures for the growth of the welfare system in order to control the surplus population and to expand the domestic markets of monopoly capital.

Given this analytical framework, the nature of the fiscal crisis of the state can be established. The monopoly sector is the engine of capital accumulation and economic growth but its productive capacity tends to grow faster than the demand for its output. Workers in the monopoly sector who become redundant, together with new entrants to the labour market, constitute the surplus population. They are compelled to seek work in the competitive and state sectors, thus depressing wage levels in the competitive sector and hence discouraging capital–labour substitution in it. However, the special characteristics of the state sector mean that the existence of this surplus population does not exert downwards pressure on its wage levels. In the monopoly sector, the protection from competition enables monopoly capital to strike an accommodation with its strong unions, granting wage increases linked to productivity growth, in exchange for the co-option of organized labour into the interests of monopoly capital. Rather than being borne by monopoly capital, the costs of the social investments which are prerequisites for profitable private accumulation are socialized and fall upon the state. The growth of the monopoly sector also leads to the growth of social expenses: military expenditure, to develop and protect its markets through the state's foreign policy; and welfare expenditure, to support not just the surplus population but also the increasingly impoverished workers in the competitive sector.

These sources of irresistible expenditure growth are not matched by corresponding increases in state revenues. The financing problem is compounded by the way in which the relative cost of state sector production steadily grows as a result of the combination of low productivity growth with wages linked to those in the monopoly sector. Through both its political power and avoidance devices, monopoly capital successfully resists taxation so that the state must rely upon a tax system based primarily upon the exploitation of the working class, especially the part of it employed in the monopoly sector whose taxable incomes are relatively high. State expenditure designed to benefit monopoly capital must thus be paid for by the working class and by competitive capital. O'Connor derides the conventional view about the redistributive function of the state: 'The most amazing aspect ... is that bourgeois economists actually claim that the distribution of the benefits of state expenditures favor the working class (especially the poor) at the expense of the owning classes' (p. 216, footnote 6). The fiscal crisis is compounded when the working class sees through the concealment and mystification of the taxation system and resists it by using its industrial strength to protect its real income against the state.

Despite the formalities of democracy, the capitalist state is run by a 'class-conscious political directorate' (O'Connor, 1973, p. 67) which responds to the needs of monopoly capital. Whereas too intimate a relationship between capital and the state would arouse opposition, the distance which the political élite has been able to maintain allowed it to satisfy the needs of monopoly capital without sacrificing the legitimacy of the capitalist state. However, the fiscal crisis of the state has imperilled this arrangement. Monopoly capital pressures the state to accelerate the growth of the social-industrial complex by mounting more extensive expenditure programmes which provide subsidized investment opportunities, both directly and indirectly through the enhanced purchasing power of the surplus population. But the capitalist state is now confronted with tax revolts; political mobilization amongst the surplus population, especially ethnic minorities, women and students; and the radicalization of state workers who have achieved consciousness of their role as the agents of social control, on behalf of monopoly capital, over the surplus population and the working class and who now defend themselves against the state's counter-attack against their wages, conditions and autonomy. In this irresolvable crisis, O'Connor saw the opportunity for a transition to socialism.

His account of the mechanisms generating the fiscal crisis of the capitalist state raises many interesting issues, not all of which can be pursued here. Whereas parts of his analysis would command broad assent, others would be vigorously disputed, partly because of the way in which assertion is intermingled with description and evidence is fragmentary and unsystematic. The main contribution of the book is not in producing a compelling analysis of the substantive issues, a task at which it fails, but in focusing attention upon the nature and purpose of the state's fiscal activities and their relationship to the economic and social system in which they are located. It poses disturbing questions which have never been squarely faced by the supporters of the Keynesian social democratic state. Even if O'Connor's answers are to be rejected, the questions remain apposite. Rather than attempt a comprehensive critique of O'Connor's work, five issues are considered below which, taken together, illuminate both its limitations and its significance.

First, there are certain unexpected but striking parallels between O'Connor's crisis-generating mechanisms and the radical right's own critique. The vocabulary is different, not being that of mainstream economics in which the latter is expressed. For example, O'Connor used the term 'capitalist state'; explicitly rejected the adjective 'public' on the grounds of it 'prejudging the question of the real purposes of the budget' (p. 10, footnote 3), using 'state' instead (as in 'state expenditure'); and conducted his analysis in terms of class relations rather than of markets. Nevertheless, whole sections of The Fiscal Crisis of the State could be redrafted to read much like Stephen Littlechild's The Fallacy of the Mixed Economy (Littlechild, 1978). These two authors regard themselves as advocates of, respectively, 'socialism' and of 'free-market capitalism'. Yet they shared a common target, the Keynesian social democratic state, irrespective of whether they described it as 'state capitalism' or 'the mixed economy'. Both ascribe crucial roles to unions, the politicization of economic decisions and uncontrollable state expenditure, in the process of undermining capitalism. It is their different sympathies, rather than their analysis, which prompts one author to applaud such developments, and the other to deplore them.

Second, the image which O'Connor conveyed of the fiscal activities of the capitalist state is unattractive. Although his ambivalent attitude towards state expenditure became evident whenever he ventured near to prescription more detailed than socialism, the impression emerging from his book is of state expenditure being wasteful, counterproductive and directed towards serving special interests. Taxation is interpreted as 'economic exploitation' which the state either attempts to conceal or to rationalize through appeal to principles of equity which divert attention from the reality. Approvingly, he cited criticisms of state expenditure levelled by James Buchanan, Arthur Burns, Milton Friedman and Murray Weidenbaum without any recognition of how their own economic and political philosophies make them naturally hostile to much state expenditure. One reason for such a lack of recognition is that O'Connor divided the economics profession into two groups, Marxist economists and 'bourgeois economists'. All the members of the second group, knowingly or unwittingly, serve the interests of monopoly capital. Instead of the deep schisms on microeconomic and macroeconomic questions which have dominated much of this book, O'Connor portrayed an undifferentiated mass. Another reason is opportunism: all available criticisms are used against the capitalist state. They are counted, not weighed, with no attention being given as to whether they could similarly, or with more force, be levelled against socialism.

Third, O'Connor's analysis was directed towards dismissing as a complete illusion the reformist interpretation of the establishment of the Keynesian social democratic state as the triumph of labour over capital. Rather, it exists not to meet needs but to facilitate the reproduction of labour power necessary for capitalist accumulation and to exert social control over the working class. Almost every state action, in its regulatory, welfare and stabilization roles, which the radical right has ever attacked for undermining capitalism, is reinterpreted by O'Connor as being in the interests of monopoly capital, even if the political representatives of that class do not recognize or admit this fact. The sceptical reader of O'Connor's book is left to wonder at the success of monopoly capital in securing political domination through the capitalist state. Gough's (1979) more qualified position is that the welfare state under capitalism, though directed towards the needs of capital, nevertheless represents a substantive gain for the working class. Even those Marxists who adopt this more qualified position are desperately exposed to the following paradox. If the expansion of state expenditure has been designed to meet the needs of capital and to establish social control over labour, how can it also be the case that its reduction, perhaps leading to the dismantling of the welfare state, now meets the needs of capital? Furthermore, if state expenditure exists not to benefit the working class but to control it, why is the working class exhorted to resist its reduction?

Fourth, it is far from obvious that the class divisions stressed in such accounts are the ones which are relevant in contemporary capitalist economies. The Marxist conception of class is inextricably linked to the ownership of the means of production: the working class, itself without capital, is hired to operate the capital owned by the capitalist class, suffering exploitation because it is not paid the full value of its labour power. However, the ascription of class on such a definition becomes problematical in the context of an extensive state sector and the spread of institutional ownership and managerial control in the private sector. Many individuals do not readily fit into categories such as 'working class' or 'capitalist class'. Class differences, though deeply ingrained in the fabric of such societies, are much more subtly rooted in socio-economic characteristics (such as income and occupational status, family background, educational attainment and housing tenure), deriving more from the division of labour than from the ownership of the means of production. Indeed, even in O'Connor's model, class divisions would be far more complex, owing much to whether an individual is employed in the 'advantaged' monopoly or state sectors rather than in the 'disadvantaged' competitive sector.

Fifth, the increased industrial conflict in the state sector is interpreted as evidence of how the fiscal crisis of the state has imported the conflict between labour and capital inside the state apparatus. The role of class-conscious state employees, being *in and against* the state, has been stressed, not just in O'Connor (1973) and Gough (1979) but especially in the derivative literature concerned explicitly with political strategy (Conference of Socialist Economists' State Apparatus and Expenditure Group, 1979; London Edinburgh Weekend Return Group, 1980). Given the welfare state's function of regulating the working class in the interests of capital, conflict between the state and its employees can be interpreted as stemming from the growing recognition by some state employees of the real nature of the capitalist state and of their own role. Consequently, the radicalization of state employees, manifest in the growth of unionization and the spread of industrial action, is welcomed as part of the working class's response to capital's increased reliance upon the state. State employees resist the introduction of capitalist norms of efficiency into the state sector which threaten their autonomy; defend their living standards against the state's attempt to break the links between wage levels in the state and monopoly sectors; and attempt to protect their clients against the withdrawal and restructuring of services in the interests of monopoly capital. Yet, despite the emphasis placed upon the struggles of state employees being part of the class struggle of labour against capital, there remain glaring ambiguities. If state services do benefit clients, industrial action by state employees must hurt them. If they do not benefit clients, state employees must instead be solely defending their own interests when they resist cutbacks. Furthermore, the portrayal of almost every attempt to reorganize the delivery of services and to improve working practices as an offensive by the state on behalf of capital is neat, but unconvincing. In O'Connor's model, state employees enjoy several advantages, notably the link with wages in the monopoly sector. Moreover:

> ... state sector unions are actually dysfunctional from the standpoint of regulating production relations – their wage demands are inflationary and they play little or no role in maintaining labor discipline (p. 240).

> ... there is no general understanding of the function of the state in capitalist society, and especially of the fact that state employees are not employed by the 'people' but rather by the representatives of private capital as a whole (p. 240).

Despite the surface confidence of these quotations, there is real ambiguity in O'Connor's view of the struggle of state employees. Furthermore, an increasingly important cleavage in contemporary capitalist economies, cutting across class lines, is the sector (state or private) from which an individual derives his livelihood (whether wage or benefit) (Dunleavy, 1980).

IV CONSTRAINING THE LEVIATHAN STATE

Whereas labour is exploited by capital in the Marxist portrayal of the capitalist state, an important section of the radical right (notably Virginian public choice theorists) depicts citizens being exploited by the state in a political democracy. The citizen is exploited by a Leviathan state, represented either as a budget-maximizing bureaucracy or as a rapacious revenue maximizer. Leviathan, a sea monster, often symbolising evil, has been adopted as the image chosen to convey the dire consequences resulting from an expansion of the fiscal activities of the state.[4] The Leviathan model of government has been described as a 'monopoly theory government' (Brennan and Buchanan, 1977, p. 264). Once granted the coercive power to tax, Leviathan will exploit that monopoly power, indulging to the full his natural appetites for expenditure or proclivities for revenue. In one formulation, Leviathan is a budget-maximizing (Niskanen-type) bureaucracy. In the other, he is represented as a 'king', wishing to maximize the excess of revenue over expenditure on the goods he provides for the citizenry so that the surplus can be used for his own purposes. Once Leviathan has acquired the power of taxation, the citizen (voter/taxpayer) possesses no effective mechanism which

:an prevent himself being exploited by Leviathan. Neither electoral processes
n a political democracy characterized by majority rule nor moral constraints
leriving from a notion of public duty will constrain Leviathan. The citizens'
only prospect for limiting such exploitation is at the constitution-setting stage
when the form and extent of the power to tax is decided and the constitu-
ional constraints upon that power are established. The task therefore
becomes one of establishing 'a tax constitution for Leviathan' (Brennan and
Buchanan, 1977).

Within what Brennan and Buchanan claimed is a more realistic interpreta-
ion of the motivation of politicians and bureaucrats than any alternative
model, they considered the limitations on the power to tax which citizens
might agree to embody in a constitution. It would be drawn up behind some-
hing approaching a Rawlsian 'veil of ignorance' (Rawls, 1972) so that the
citizen would know neither his future position in society nor his taste for pub-
ic goods. In such a context, they argued that the tax powers granted to
Leviathan would look very different from the prescriptions derived from
normative public finance theory. Instead of a comprehensive tax base, the
citizens would restrict Leviathan to a narrow base as a method of limiting the
extent of exploitation. Restrictions upon the tax yield for a given base would
be achieved by insisting upon the rate structure being progressive. Furthermore, a rule that certain taxes were earmarked for a particular publicly
provided good or service which was complementary to the tax base (such as
motor vehicle taxation for roads) would induce Leviathan to choose a pattern
of expenditure closer to the preferences of citizens (Brennan and Buchanan,
1978). These conclusions in favour of a narrow tax base and earmarking are
diametrically opposed to the conventional prescriptions which are concerned
with minimizing the economic costs (including compliance and excess
burden) associated with raising a predetermined amount of revenue for
public expenditure. Leviathan theorists maintain that levels of expenditure
are not independent of the taxation structure: restricting the power to tax
limits Leviathan's capacity to spend and exploit.

The same group of public choice theorists wish to reimpose a balanced
budget rule, developing their argument in the following way. Without such a
rule, there will be no fiscal discipline over the government which will be
encouraged by the expenditure-generating biases of political competition to
spend without taxing, thus generating inflation either through borrowing or
printing money. In the nineteenth century, in which ideas of *laissez-faire* and
of the minimal state held sway, the unwritten convention of the balanced
budget held firm. The discipline exerted by this convention was destroyed by
the misleading macroeconomic doctrines of John Maynard Keynes which
exposed the stable market economy to disruption from both ill-judged
interference and the manipulation of the economy for political profit
(Buchanan and Wagner, 1977). Keynesian doctrines, therefore, introduced a
bias towards persistent budget deficits and hence inflation. Keynes's illusion

of macroeconomic policy being implemented by public-spirited official
contrasts sharply with the reality of self-interested politicians and bureau
crats. Keynes's legacy of 'Folly in a Great Kingdom' imperils democracy
'How long British democracy and the Mother of Parliaments will surviv
under the corruption of Keynesianism is an open question. Without consti
tutional reform their ultimate crumbling can hardly be in doubt (Burton
1978, p. 74).

Constitutional reform is advocated as the means to re-establish fisca
control. Buchanan, Burton and Wagner (1978, p. 82) proposed the adoptior
of a written constitutional rule embodying the principle of the balancec
budget: 'The House of Commons must adopt a new Standing Order: "Thi
House requires that total government expenditure does not exceed tota
government revenue from taxation and charges".'[5] This rule would b
accompanied by an automatic adjustment procedure which would take effec
if the budget went out of balance and there would be a transitional stage o
five years in which the previous year's deficit would be reduced by not les
than 20 per cent of the original figure. The balanced budget rule could b
waived in national emergencies, such as wars or financial crises by a two
thirds majority of all MPs (not just those voting). Alongside these fisca
provisions, the Bank of England would be granted statutory independenc
from the government and there would be a fixed and specific rule for the rat
of growth of the money supply.

Although Leviathan theorists present their case in an unusually dramati
form, all sections of the radical right emphasize constitutional reform. Th
differences lie less in the concrete proposals (except on the question of th
balanced budget rule) and more in the source of the danger to be guardec
against. For example, Littlechild (1979) urged constitutional reform as
method of protecting government from the demands of interest groups. Bu
the interest in constitutional reform is not restricted to those who subscribe tc
the full vision of the radical right. The most distinguished recruit is Aaroi
Wildavsky who has been converted to the view that constitutional limitatior
on expenditure is the only method of halting the inexorable growth of bi
government. Wildavsky (1980) is different, not just because his vocabulary i
that of a political scientist and that he talks in terms of 'conservatives' (fo
limitation) and 'liberals' (for big government), but also in that he wishes onl
to halt, rather than reverse, the growth of government. However, he becam
actively involved in the campaign for constitutional limitation and was
member of the drafting committee convened by the National Tax Limitatior
Committee. Many of his colleagues on that committee, such as William
Niskanen, hoped for a sharp reduction in the size of government.

Whereas public choice models portray the government as the enemy of th
people, Wildavsky depicts the people as the enemy of themselves. Th
central problem for Wildavsky is not the appetites or self-interest o
politicians or bureaucrats, but that citizens favour the individual items o

public expenditure but oppose the resulting totals. He argued that all the incentives of the political process point towards expenditure growth: forbearance by one interest group will not be matched by others, meaning a sacrifice unrewarded by the lower taxes or inflation resulting from lower public expenditure. Constitutional limitation is advocated 'not to replace the political process but to perfect it' (Wildavsky, 1980, p. 101), ensuring that interest groups and individual parts of the bureaucracy must fight each other. Constitutional limitation on expenditure is therefore designed to allow citizens to agree to restrict public expenditure in the knowledge that the restriction will apply to everyone. Both the National Tax Limitation Committee's (1980) proposed constitutional amendment and Niskanen's (1980) shorter amendment, preferred by Wildavsky, linked the percentage increase in federal government expenditure in any fiscal year to the percentage increase in GNP in the previous calendar year. A ceiling would thus be placed on the relative size of government, one which would be lowered automatically either if actual expenditure fell below the maximum allowable in any fiscal year or, through a penalty mechanism, if inflation exceeded a certain rate. This ceiling could only be raised through a difficult and complex procedure, for example, by a three-quarters majority of both Houses of Congress and approval by the legislatures of a majority of States. However, there would be an emergency procedure to provide for national emergencies, such as a major war.

As a thorough discussion of such proposed constitutional reforms would require a separate book, it must suffice here to explain briefly why they should all be rejected. First, it is taken as a starting assumption that big government is bad, a view which has been vigorously disputed throughout this book. Similarly, budget deficits are portrayed by both Wildavsky and the Virginian public choice theorists as the cause of inflation, even though a careful reading of Friedman (for example, 1980) would not lend support to that view. Underlying such proposals can usually be found a bleak image of representative government: democracy is valued provided that the results of the electoral process can have no impact upon the market economy. Anyone who does not share the presumption that big government is bad is likely to note with wry amusement the exceptions which are always proposed in order to allow the same untrustworthy politicians and bureaucrats to undertake major wars.

Second, it is another measure of the intellectual realignment that scarcely concealed ideology can now wear the clothes of positive economics. Musgrave's observation (1981, p. 88) cannot be improved upon:

> While claiming to offer a positive approach, this literature reflects the consequences (derived neatly and on occasion, gleefully) from a preconceived model of behaviour, designed so that it cannot but result in the demonstration of government failure.

Sophistication and elegance in deriving the logical properties of models of budget, revenue or vote maximization may command professional esteem and reassure those opposed to public expenditure of the justice and wisdom of their cause. Although potentially helpful as a source of insight into political and budgetary processes if they are interpreted with care and modesty, such models can easily degenerate into vehicles for ideological reinforcement.

Third, the potential distortions introduced into the budgetary process by such limitations would be of profound significance. For example, governments would respond to limitations on public expenditure by making greater use of existing policy substitutes and by devising new ones. Tax expenditures and enforced private expenditures would grow. Furthermore, the practice already common in the USA of the government giving loan guarantees to private borrowers would be copied. There would only be a charge on public expenditure in cases of default but the cost of the guarantee would be hidden in the higher borrowing costs of other private borrowers forced to pay more for their loans because of the pre-emption of funds by government-guaranteed loans. In the case of the balanced budget rule, devices such as coerced private expenditures would be supplemented by a search for new revenue, such as from the substitution of taxes for standards. Given that the Buchanan, Burton and Wagner (1978) balanced budget rule would preclude borrowing to pay for capital expenditure, loan guarantees would be adopted as an escape route. Often advocated, at least in part, as a means of improving efficiency in the public sector, such reforms would introduce a host of new rigidities, distortions and inefficiencies.

Fourth, constitutional limitation is designed to allow existing politicians and citizens to circumscribe severely the discretion of future politicians and citizens. Ironically, Wildavsky justified his conversion to constitutional limitation by commenting that the present is very different from the 1950s and 1960s: the 1990s might be very different still in quite unpredictable directions. Constitutional expenditure limitation would deliberately introduce a profound asymmetry into the political process, with the ceilings established at the level of a particular year which in itself owes much to choices in the past: contrast, for example, the USA with industrialized Europe. The election of governments of the political right, such as those of Margaret Thatcher and Ronald Reagan, indicate that political mobilization against the public sector is quite feasible within the present constitutional framework. It is difficult to imagine either as a budget-maximizer: politicians can themselves subscribe to ideologies antagonistic to big government. Indeed, a number of members of the radical right, more in the USA than in the UK, have enthusiastically accepted jobs in such governments, presumably without becoming budget-maximizers.

V   IN DEFENCE OF THE KEYNESIAN SOCIAL DEMOCRATIC STATE

Beleaguered by enemies, the Keynesian social democratic state deserves a defence: this book is intended to provide just that. Part of any defence must be based upon countering the prosecution's claims, another part in analysing the weaknesses which have been exposed and how they might be remedied, and a third in restating the positive case. The Keynesian social democratic state must repel enemies on both left and right. On fiscal issues, the similarities between their charges are often uncanny. Take, for example, the impact of high public expenditure levels and growth. For the Marxist theorists of 'fiscal crisis', the capitalist state fails to resolve the tension generated by it being called upon to perform functions (maintain social harmony through expanded state expenditure) which conflict with its main function (maintain the conditions for profitable private accumulation of the surplus value arising from economic activity). The crisis is accentuated by the outcome of class struggle in which the working class, strengthened by full employment and more effective trade union organization, is able to make political and industrial gains at the expense of capital. Yet, paradoxically, the expenditure won by the working class is needed by capital: the 'over-expansion' of welfare expenditure is thus interpreted as a 'contradiction of capitalism'. Nothing more requires to be said about the hostility of the radical right to public expenditure nor about the damaging effects attributed to it. Unsurprisingly, writers on the non-Marxist left (for example, Crouch, 1979) tend to react with disbelief when such a mechanism is presented as a Marxist notion. They consider that Marxists have argued too frequently in the past that capitalist crises of under-consumption could only be resolved by massive public expenditure on armaments for them to be able to claim parentage of the view that public expenditure on social programmes has undermined capitalism. Such a claim, both logically and historically, fits far more convincingly into the free-market tradition.

Transcending the differences in ideology, methodology and vocabulary, the shared hostility of the radical right and the Marxist left towards the Keynesian social democratic state provides striking parallels. On policy, they diverge. For Marxists, the problem is the contradictions of capitalism: the solution is to smash capitalism. For the radical right, the problem is democracy: the solution is to insulate capitalism from democracy. These two apparently disparate bodies of literature can be characterized in terms of convergence of analysis but conflict of values. Both carry clear ideological overtones. Both are hostile to the pre-revolution state: the radical right hopes that the socialist revolution will never come and Marxists look forward to the withering away of the state after capitalism has been smashed. Richard Wagner (1975) portrays the state as a parasitic institution, just like some Marxists (see p. 262). Moreover, Jessop (1982, p. 27) refers to the 'fundamental insight' in:

Lenin's remark in *The State and Revolution* that the bourgeois democratic republic is the best possible political shell for capital and that, once it has gained possession of this shell, capital establishes its power so securely that no change of persons, institutions or parties can shake it.

Exactly the same idea, and especially its corollary that capitalism is the best safeguard of democracy, is fundamental to the intellectual and moral case for capitalism articulated by Milton Friedman. Both emphasize how full employment has strengthened labour against capital. Both sets of literature describe the public sector as 'unproductive'. Although the meanings attached to this word are very different, the vocabulary clearly communicates a view of the public sector as a burden. There is a shared contention that the present strain engulfing Western societies (whether described as the 'failure of the mixed economy' or as the 'crisis of capitalism') can only be resolved through radical action (respectively the rolling back of the state or socialist revolution).

Although such calls to action are diametrically opposed, the similarities between their criticisms of the Keynesian social democratic state have made them mutually reinforcing, inducing a crisis of confidence in the efficacy of state action, a belief central to that tradition. Such an impact is full of irony. In reality, both the Marxist left and the radical right depend upon a strong and effective state: the former to ensure that, after the revolution but before the state has withered away, capitalism cannot re-emerge; and the latter to sustain the framework for the market economy in the face of encroachment from the polity. The solutions of revolution or withdrawal have the attraction of simplicity. Yet both involve matters of faith: namely, that the revolution will lead to justice, equality and fraternity and not to totalitarianism bureaucracy and inefficiency; and that the pursuit of self-interest can be commended as the code of behaviour, secure in the knowledge that it can still be reconciled by the invisible hand. Nevertheless, this two-pronged attack has achieved such a measure of success that the erstwhile supporters of that accommodation have found themselves on the defensive, with responses ranging from recantation, discomfort and persistence.

One of the main purposes of this book has been to assess how much irreparable damage has been inflicted upon the intellectual foundations of the Keynesian social democratic state. Deciding how much ground to concede, and where to hold the line, is an exceptionally difficult task for any tradition under assault. Even more, too long spent solely on the defensive can impair the capacity to respond constructively to both intellectual challenges and developing events. What has emerged from this book is that, battered though that tradition may now appear, a coherent and vigorous defence of the essentials, if not of many details, can be mounted. The tradition's debilitating weakness has been its crisis of confidence, stemming in part from its image of being a rejected intellectual fashion. However, the advocates of free-market capitalism who have commanded the stage in the 1970s and early 1980s stand as living testimony to the fact that no issue is ever settled for all time. The supporters of the Keynesian social democratic state must regroup, learning from the criticisms levelled against the policies they advocated and the institutions they embraced, modifying where necessary but remaining loyal to its values.

In reality, the irreparable damage is modest, though the incidental damage is extensive and will require patient reconstruction, perhaps assuming a somewhat different shape. The macroeconomic component of the Keynesian social democratic state was the explicit commitment to full employment, much less the presumption in favour of the use of certain policy instruments or styles of macroeconomic policy. What mattered about the switch from fiscal policy to monetary policy was not the switch itself but that it was accompanied by a weakening, then abandonment, of the commitment to full employment. Mayer's (1978, p. 2) eleventh proposition about monetarism is worth repeating: 'a relatively greater concern about inflation than about unemployment compared to other economists.' Laidler (1978, p. 134) commented:

> Though he may be right in the context of American debates, British monetarists have always shown as much concern for the maintenance of high employment as have their 'Keynesian' opponents. . . . Even so, differences of opinion about appropriate policies towards inflation and unemployment are extremely sharp in Britain. They reflect fundamental differences over economic theory and facts, however, not over social values.

Although this response can be accepted as a statement of Laidler's own position, and also that of some other academic monetarists, it reveals a lack of awareness of how monetarism was being embraced as part of a political doctrine. Whatever its validity and the ethical positions of its academic proponents, the monetarism of economists such as Laidler inflicted severe damage upon the credibility of the Keynesian social democratic state, opening the door for both politicians and other monetarists who discounted the importance of full employment. But if such monetarists are to be blamed for not properly distancing themselves from the politicians of the right who seemed to offer the best opportunity for having their policies implemented, so should those Keynesians who had forgotten that it was full employment which mattered, not particular policy instruments. The task of reconstruction involves rebuilding a political consensus which places a high value on full employment whilst retaining an open mind, willing to be moved by the evidence, on the best techniques of macroeconomic control.

In a similar vein, commitment to the values underlying the welfare state should not preclude a willingness to recognize deficiencies in the public sector. It is essential that the current presumption of 'public bad, private good' is not rebounded into 'public good, private bad'. Commitment alone is inadequate: the welfare state needs critical friends, not apologists. Whatever governments are in power in the 1980s and 1990s, the spectacular growth of public expenditure and of manpower which took place in the 1950s and 1960s will not be repeated. Improvements in provision will be heavily dependent upon making more effective use of existing resources. Too many supporters of the welfare state react with something approaching horror when economists begin to discuss the efficiency of the social services. Efficiency and compassion are not in implacable conflict: efficiency is a vital cog in the process of making compassion an attainable goal. To reject modern management techniques on the grounds that they inject alien capitalist values into the welfare state is not just misguided: it is thoroughly dangerous as it concedes so much territory to the opponents of the welfare state.

Although the charge that the UK public sector is endemically inefficient (or, more so than the private sector) is based on assertion rather than evidence, it must be recognized that parts of it have been very badly managed. Ambivalence about the importance of efficiency has been one factor leading to inefficient practices being tolerated. Where goods and services have been removed from the market, the efficiency with which inputs are combined and directed towards the attainment of policy objectives is of crucial significance, meaning that proper attention must be given to questions of cost effectiveness. Moreover, the managerial reforms of the 1979 Conservative Government (such as Michael Heseltine's MINIS and Sir Derek Rayner's reviews) must not be rejected out of hand, simply because of the anti-public sector rhetoric of that government or because they have played a role in promoting privatization, frequently more as a numbers game with public employment than as a genuine search for efficiency. It is the supporters, not the detractors, of the welfare state who stand to gain most from improved efficiency in the public sector. They cannot afford to concede the cause of efficiency, not least because their opponents often bring to such issues an exceptionally narrow and unsustainable notion of efficiency. Similarly, they have ignored for too long the question of how public expenditure is to be financed, thus contributing through neglect to the backlash against the high levels of taxation which are the necessary counterpart to the welfare state. The next chapter briefly considers the financing of public expenditure. Subsequently, attention turns to 'privatization' in order to evaluate the claims which have been made for it as the remedy for both public sector inefficiency and excessive taxation.

But, to repeat, the essentials of the Keynesian social democratic state are worth defending: not just because the alternatives are unappealing, rather for the values it seeks to uphold.

CHAPTER 12

Paying for Public Expenditure

I INTRODUCTION

The resources used in the public non-market sector have, using the term loosely, to be 'paid for'. Although this statement sounds platitudinous when put so baldly, one of the most remarkable features of public debate is the willingness of otherwise sophisticated people to wish away this uncomfortable reality. Such myopia has extremely damaging consequences. There has developed a major contradiction between popular aspirations for better public services and popular resistance to the financing mechanisms open to governments. Expenditure plans are formulated under strong pressure from public opinion, potential beneficiaries, producers and from other interest groups. The cumulative total of such public expenditure then outruns the willingness of the same citizens *qua* taxpayers to accept the necessary reduction in their command over private goods and services. Although this is not a book about taxation, for its coverage is wide enough already, it would be inappropriate not to consider, albeit in rather general terms, the question of how public expenditure is to be financed. The provision of services in the public non-market sector can only be effected if the necessary resources are diverted from the private sector. Paying for public expenditure is a necessary evil, which has to be taken into account when decisions are made about its scale and composition. The benefits of public expenditure have to be balanced against the costs of securing the resources required.

There are, however, two important preliminaries. First, although there may be circumstances in which higher public expenditure is possible without any offsetting loss in private expenditure, they are exceptions: for example, when there is a large amount of unused resources in the economy, the context within which the rationale for Keynesian policies was originally developed. Fortunately, such a context is not typical. The amount of spare capacity in the UK economy is usually very small indeed when compared to the public sector's claims on output. The notion that private expenditure need not be sacrificed to provide the major programmes of the welfare state is an illusion. Second, public expenditure cannot be financed solely be squeezing the rich. If

279

Table 12.1: Taxation/GDP ratios on a standa
(Expr

	1960	1961	1962	1963	1964	1965	1966	1967	19
A. EEC-EUROPE									
1. Belgium	27.5	28.4	29.2	29.4	30.0	30.7	32.4	33.2	33
2. Denmark	27.3	26.6	28.2	29.9	29.7	31.2	33.5	34.1	36
3. France	34.9	36.2	36.3	37.1	38.0	38.4	38.4	38.2	38
4. Greece	21.1	22.0	23.2	23.2	24.0	23.7	25.3	26.2	27
5. Ireland	24.8	25.7	25.2	26.1	26.9	27.9	30.0	30.6	31
6. Italy	28.8	28.2	29.1	29.5	30.6	30.1	30.1	31.0	31
7. Luxembourg	32.5	34.1	33.5	33.6	33.5	35.2	35.8	35.7	34
8. Netherlands	33.9	34.9	34.4	35.6	35.7	37.3	39.2	40.6	41
9. United Kingdom	**30.3**	**31.5**	**33.1**	**31.7**	**31.7**	**33.4**	**34.5**	**36.5**	**38**
10. West Germany	34.8	35.9	36.2	36.5	36.0	35.3	35.9	36.3	36
B. OTHER EUROPE									
11. Austria	31.0	33.1	34.0	33.6	37.8	38.5	39.3	39.1	38
12. Finland	30.0	28.9	30.1	29.5	31.2	32.1	33.4	35.3	35
13. Iceland	36.4	27.3	27.5	28.7	28.4	29.3	31.0	33.6	33
14. Norway	33.1	34.2	35.5	35.5	36.0	36.8	38.3	40.5	41
15. Portugal	17.6	18.4	19.3	19.0	19.3	20.4	20.8	21.0	21
16. Spain	18.1	17.6	17.5	16.8	18.8	19.3	19.4	21.4	21
17. Sweden	32.2	33.6	35.5	36.5	36.7	39.6	41.2	42.6	45
18. Switzerland									
19. Turkey	—	—	19.1	19.1	19.4	19.9	19.9	22.1	21
20. Yugoslavia									
C. NON-EUROPE									
21. Australia	25.4	25.1	24.2	24.4	25.8	27.0	26.2	27.0	26
22. Canada	26.0	26.6	27.0	26.8	27.8	28.1	29.4	31.0	32
23. Japan	20.7	20.9	21.6	21.4	20.5	19.5	19.1	19.2	19
24. New Zealand									
25. United States	27.4	27.4	27.5	28.0	27.0	27.0	27.9	28.4	30
D. TOTAL OECD	28.3	28.7	29.0	29.2	28.9	29.0	29.6	30.2	31

Source: Table R9 of OECD (1982c).
Notes: n/a = not available.
The data in this table are measured according to the standard definitions of the OECD–UN system of accounts. The definition of taxation is 'current receipts of government', consisting

OECD *member countries, 1960–80*
ges)

71	1972	1973	1974	1975	1976	1977	1978	1979	1980	Increase in percentage points 1960–1980
.7	35.5	36.4	37.7	40.4	40.3	41.7	42.5	43.3	43.3	+ 15.8
.4	45.9	46.8	48.4	46.1	46.9	47.6	49.6	51.4	51.9	+ 24.6
.3	38.2	38.6	39.4	40.3	42.5	42.4	42.3	43.7	45.4	+ 10.5
.6	26.6	25.4	27.0	27.4	29.5	29.9	30.1	30.6	30.5	+ 9.4
.3	34.9	34.5	35.2	35.2	38.5	37.7	36.8	38.2	—	n/a
.1	30.9	30.4	30.6	31.2	32.9	34.3	36.0	35.7	37.5	+ 8.7
.7	38.2	38.3	40.3	49.0	50.3	54.8	55.4	51.5	57.4	+ 24.9
.3	47.4	49.2	50.0	52.5	52.8	53.9	54.6	55.8	57.5	+ 23.6
.6	**37.0**	**36.3**	**40.1**	**40.7**	**39.8**	**39.4**	**38.2**	**39.0**	**40.4**	**+ 10.1**
.3	38.7	41.2	41.5	40.8	42.3	43.5	43.3	42.9	42.8	+ 8.0
.5	41.1	41.9	42.5	42.8	42.4	43.7	46.2	45.6	45.9	+ 14.9
.5	36.3	36.9	36.7	38.7	42.3	41.6	39.5	38.0	37.9	+ 7.9
.0	34.5	36.4	34.2	35.6	35.4	34.0	—	—	—	n/a
.6	48.4	49.6	48.5	49.6	50.9	51.0	52.0	52.3	54.3	+ 21.2
.5	23.4	22.7	23.0	24.8	28.1	—	—	—	—	n/a
.6	23.0	23.7	22.8	24.3	25.3	26.5	27.1	28.3	28.6	+ 10.5
.6	49.7	47.9	48.9	50.7	55.3	58.4	57.9	56.9	57.1	+ 24.9
.7	27.1	—	—	—	—	—	—	—	—	n/a
.4	27.2	28.4	30.0	31.0	31.9	32.2	31.3	32.5	33.5	+ 8.1
.3	35.9	35.6	37.8	36.9	36.5	36.8	36.6	36.1	37.1	+ 11.1
.6	21.5	22.4	24.4	24.0	23.6	24.8	24.6	26.6	28.2	+ 7.5
.6	30.7	30.9	31.9	30.4	31.5	31.8	32.3	32.5	32.7	+ 5.3
.8	32.2	32.7	33.9	33.7	34.5	35.0	35.1	35.9	36.8	+ 8.5

t.)
direct and indirect taxes, and social security contributions paid by employers and
It is given on line 12 of Table 9 of OECD (1982a, Vol. I). The entry for 'Total OECD'
ed average for those countries for which information is available.

all taxable income (that is income after allowances) over £11250 had been confiscated in 1981/82 through 100 per cent tax rates, the yield would have financed under 7 per cent of public expenditure in that year. Similarly, if all wealth over £100000 had been confiscated in 1978 (the latest year for which data are available), the proceeds would have financed only a third of that year's public expenditure (Ridley, 1982). Without any reference to subsequent economic effects and the inability to repeat any such capital levy, it is therefore obvious that public expenditure has to be financed through taxes and charges upon ordinary taxpayers and beneficiaries. Whatever the merits of steeply progressive taxation, making a major contribution to the cost of the welfare state is not one. There has been a general unwillingness to face this fact, and to argue for public expenditure whilst acknowledging the implications for taxation. Such illusions have afforded easy targets for the opponents of the Keynesian social democratic state and their inevitable puncturing has contributed to the backlash against taxation which has been sweeping the industrialized democracies.

The main financing mechanism for public expenditure is taxation. The three other mechanisms, namely borrowing and printing money, and charges, are considered elsewhere in the book (in Chapters 3 and 13). However effective are public expenditure programmes or well-designed are tax systems, people will complain about taxes. Carping about them is a well-established pastime in almost all societies where this activity is safe, and in some others too. Taxes are not there to be liked but as means to certain ends such as providing services and altering the allocation of resources, redistributing income and wealth, and regulating the level of economic activity. The issue is whether these programmes, especially at the margin, are worth the cost. Nevertheless, it is also clear that tax systems must command, if not enthusiasm, at least popular consent. Otherwise, serious difficulties will emerge in their administration, notably avoidance and evasion. Myths about how the system works may also influence the way individuals respond to the perceived and true incentives. Furthermore, a tax system which has lost consent may provoke a political backlash, leading to electoral successes for parties pledged to cut taxation, often without explaining what activities would have to be reduced. All of these happened in the UK in the 1970s, as in many other industrialized countries.

The level of taxation in the UK has risen dramatically since 1900, matching the rise in public expenditure. However, it should come as no surprise, following the international comparisons of public expenditure shares summarized in Chapter 2, that the UK has a middle ranking on taxation among OECD countries. Table 12.1 summarizes taxation/GDP ratios in a similar format to Table 2.3. Despite such evidence, there is a widespread and deeply resistant belief that the UK is a much more heavily taxed country than its competitors.

There have been various attempts to specify the limits of taxation, often in the form of a ceiling taxation/GDP ratio which can only be breached with dire consequences for efficiency and freedom. Clark (1945, 1954) set this at 25 per cent of national income, above which taxation was a direct cause of inflation.[1] Later, after it had reached much higher levels, he remained committed to this figure as the maximum tolerable percentage and considered that post-war experience had supported his judgement (Clark, 1964, 1977). However, not only is his analysis of the inflationary process unconvincing but also his choice of 25 per cent is arbitrary, even if it were conceded that there is some such limit. Moreover, there is an obvious reply to the view that many of the contemporary problems of the UK economy stem from excessive taxation: West Germany has a similar fiscal history but remarkably different economic performance. Picking target or threshold percentages out of the air seems a particularly fruitless activity. Such figures can take no account of many relevant factors: for example, the danger of war; the demographic structure of the population; the extent of inequality; the level of economic activity; or the use of policy substitutes for public expenditure. But this is not to deny that there has been growing support for the view that the level of taxation is too high, matched by electoral support for parties articulating it. The existence of the welfare state means high taxation which, having existed for a generation, is now subjected to far sharper criticism. Opinion polls have consistently shown majority support for cuts in taxation, coupled with support for most expenditure programmes. Ironically, over the period during which resentment at existing levels of taxation has mounted sharply, taxation as a percentage of GDP has in fact stabilized.

II THE DISTORTION OF THE TAX STRUCTURE

The search for explanations for the undeniable discontent must focus upon the structure of taxation, not just its level. The tax burden can be analysed in a number of different ways, each providing distinctive insights. However, a relatively simple analysis, based upon the same set of OECD comparative statistics (OECD, 1981a, 1982d), is sufficient to support the conclusion of this section, namely that there have been major changes in the composition of tax revenues which have taken place without being consciously planned. Unprecedented rates of inflation have distorted the tax structure, shifting the burden in ways not intended by policy makers, but which, for various reasons, they have felt unable or unwilling to resist.

Table 12.2 serves two purposes. First, it records changes in the percentage composition of UK tax revenues over the period 1955–80, initially at five-year intervals and then annually from 1965. The percentage share of personal income taxes rose sharply in the early 1970s, then fell back in the second half of the decade: from 31.08 per cent in 1970, up to 38.24 per cent in 1975, then down to 30.02 per cent in 1980. Although not separated out in Table 12.2,

Table 12.2: The structure of UK taxation, 1955–80 (Percentage of total)

Taxes	1955	1960	1965	1966	1967	1968	1969	1970	1971	1972	1973	1974	1975	1976	1977	1978	1979	1980
Personal income	40.6	37.5	29.82 (21.55)	30.52 (23.93)	30.32 (24.15)	30.14 (24.04)	30.74 (23.89)	31.08 (23.18)	32.72 (24.81)	31.53 (24.89)	32.34 (25.36)	33.44 (26.76)	38.24 (27.24)	38.18 (27.10)	35.08 (27.56)	32.92 (27.53)	31.38 (27.73)	30.02 (28.38)
Corporate income	—	—	6.97 (6.77)	6.29 (6.77)	8.25 (6.73)	7.67 (6.82)	7.54 (7.76)	9.17 (7.33)	8.12 (6.52)	7.52 (6.49)	8.64 (7.07)	9.63 (7.84)	6.20 (6.43)	5.11 (6.45)	6.45 (6.65)	7.46 (7.18)	7.61 (6.95)	7.69 (6.73)
Social security contributions	10.4	12.6	15.40 (24.36)	14.90 (23.96)	14.51 (24.08)	14.43 (24.58)	13.20 (24.18)	13.91 (25.20)	14.04 (25.61)	15.54 (25.90)	16.96 (26.18)	17.09 (26.62)	17.41 (28.10)	18.61 (27.84)	18.47 (27.60)	18.05 (27.38)	17.37 (27.48)	16.87 (27.38)
Payroll taxes	—	—	— (0.70)	2.49 (0.96)	3.27 (1.05)	4.11 (1.13)	4.76 (0.85)	4.42 (0.80)	2.75 (0.66)	2.03 (0.59)	0.05 (0.60)	-0.01 (0.40)	— (0.44)	— (0.47)	1.65 (0.65)	2.83 (0.77)	4.43 (0.93)	4.15 (0.86)
Taxes on property	12.9	15.2	14.54 (7.98)	14.39 (7.52)	14.14 (7.36)	13.77 (7.25)	13.34 (6.92)	12.46 (6.79)	13.31 (6.82)	14.72 (7.12)	13.63 (6.63)	12.59 (5.92)	12.65 (5.82)	12.12 (5.72)	11.98 (5.74)	11.96 (5.60)	12.10 (5.48)	12.09 (5.38)
Taxes on goods and services	35.8	34.5	33.00 (37.92)	31.18 (36.27)	29.23 (36.09)	29.72 (35.60)	30.18 (35.82)	28.76 (36.16)	28.72 (35.06)	28.46 (34.50)	28.20 (33.74)	27.10 (31.80)	25.38 (31.36)	25.79 (31.40)	26.17 (31.23)	26.56 (31.02)	26.96 (30.94)	28.81 (30.76)
Other	0.3	0.2	—	—	—	—	—	—	—	—	—	—	—	—	—	—	—	0.38

Source: The entries for 1955, 1960, 1965 and 1970–80 are from OECD (1982d) and those for 1966–69 are from OECD (1981a).

Notes: The main entries in the Table are for the UK, with the figures in parentheses immediately below being those for EEC-Europe. 'Other' relates to revenues which have not been classifiable on the OECD scheme. The figures for 1955 and 1960 are less reliable than those for later years. There is a small discrepancy in the case of EEC-Europe (but not for the UK) between the percentage accounted for by the sum of personal and corporate income taxes and the total for taxes on income and profits, again owing to classification problems.

there have been opposing trends within the category of taxes on goods and services: general consumption taxes rose after the introduction of VAT, more than offset by the continuing decline in the share of specific taxes on goods and services.

Second, the figures in parentheses below each UK entry give the equivalent percentage for (what is now) EEC-Europe. A number of major differences clearly emerge from these figures. The UK's personal income tax share is much higher but this must be interpreted in the light of the far smaller percentage accounted for by social security contributions. Taking these with payroll taxes, the UK's percentage in 1980 was 51.04, compared with 56.62 per cent for EEC-Europe. The most striking difference is the UK's much greater contribution from taxes on property which account for roughly twice the EEC-Europe percentage, a feature attributable to the reliance of local authorities upon rates as their sole tax. For all the controversies which it has generated, capital taxation, included here, has yielded a small and diminishing percentage. Yet despite both such distinctive UK features and the considerable variations between OECD countries, the broad trends diagnosed in an OECD study (1981b) of the same period are closely paralleled in the UK. Within a rising taxation/GDP ratio, there has been a decreased reliance on consumption taxes and an increased reliance upon income taxes and social security contributions. Whereas the share of consumption taxes has been falling, the reduction in the percentage accounted for by specific taxes has been dramatic, reflecting not only the switch to broader-based systems such as VAT, but, more fundamentally, the failure to maintain the real yield of specific taxes owing to the absence of formal indexation provisions. However, there were important changes in the UK in the second half of the 1970s (notably the falling back of the personal income taxes percentage) whereas the OECD study observed that the long-term trends had slowed down after 1975, with the 1980 structure being virtually identical to that of 1977.

Fiscal drag

Many of the parameters of the tax system such as the various thresholds and rate bands for income tax are set in nominal terms. Without regular adjustments to allow for inflation, there will be a marked drift towards existing taxpayers paying a higher proportion of their income in income tax and towards the creation of new taxpayers as the nominal incomes of hitherto untaxed individuals cross the unchanged threshold. During periods of high and accelerating inflation, this drift can become a stampede. Governments are ambivalent about such fiscal drag. In principle, it is bad as it distorts the policy-determined tax structure and is typically regressive in its distributional impact. In practice, hard-pressed Chancellors usually welcome the cash, asking few questions.

Figures 12.1–12.4 provide a devastating indictment of tax policy in the UK. Figure 12.1 plots the real value of income tax thresholds over the post-war period, taking 1949/50 as 100. Four different 'tax units' are shown: single person (solid line); married man without children (dashed line); married man with two children (dotted line); and married man with four children (dot-dashed line). These comparisons should be regarded as illustrative as demographic change over the period means that such households cannot be regarded as representative of the whole population. For the reasons to be discussed below, the tax threshold for married men with children loses much of its significance as an indicator from 1976/77. The path of real thresholds is startlingly erratic: sharp upwards adjustments were repeatedly followed by a number of years in which the real value depreciated. Despite such volatility, there was not much difference between the real value of thresholds in the mid-1970s from that in 1949/50. In the later period, single persons and married men without children fared better than households with children. Figure 12.2 plots 'break-even' points for net liability to tax for households with children. The switch over from child tax allowances and cash family allowances to the new system of child benefits makes it necessary to treat tax payments and income transfers simultaneously. The break-even points are calculated as the level of income at which net liability to tax arises (that is tax payments exceed benefit receipts). Figure 12.2 confirms that households with children have fared relatively badly, with the transition to child benefits merely restoring the erosion of the early 1970s.

However, these comparisons have merely removed the effect of inflation, providing a measure of the purchasing power of threshold income, but have ignored the large growth in real incomes. Figure 12.3 records the dramatic reductions in tax thresholds over this period, when expressed as a percentage of average male manual earnings: for example, the percentage roughly halved for both a single person and a married man without children. As exactly the same difficulty with the switch over to child benefit again occurs, Figure 12.4 relates earnings to break-even points. The march of the tax burden down the income hierarchy is striking. No longer is income tax an imposition mainly paid by the well-off: it now takes a sizeable chunk out of the gross income of most families.

There is a curious paradox. Income tax is a progressive tax because of its thresholds and rate-band structure. But the evidence above shows quite clearly that recent increments in income tax revenue have accrued in a profoundly regressive way. The individual making the marginal payment in this sense might be considered to be one with a low income who now crosses the threshold into tax liability. The failure to adjust the higher thresholds and bands has a similar impact on high earners, but the total revenue involved is far smaller. These considerations raise three questions. First, how does the distributional impact of such marginal increases in income tax revenues compare with those for other taxes such as VAT? Second, how does the

287

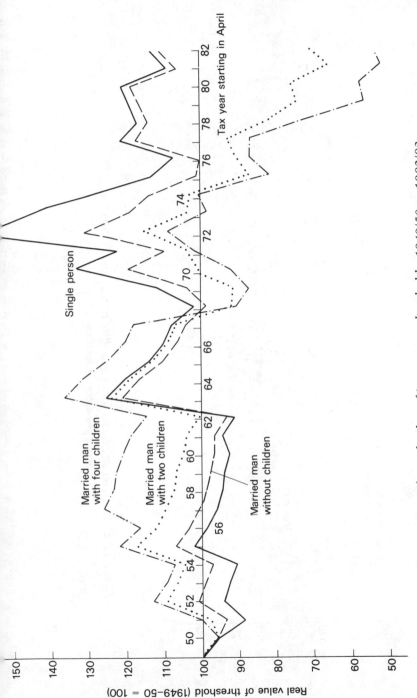

Figure 12.1 The real value of income-tax thresholds, 1949/50 to 1982/83

Source: For the statistics, Board of Inland Revenue (1982). For the method, Board of Inland Revenue (1980).
Notes: It is assumed that, in the household with two children, both are under 11 and, in the household with four children, two are under 11, one 11–15 and one 16 or over (but entitled to child benefit). The wife is assumed not to be working. The figures for 1981/82 and 1982/83 are provisional, dependent upon an assumed inflation rate.

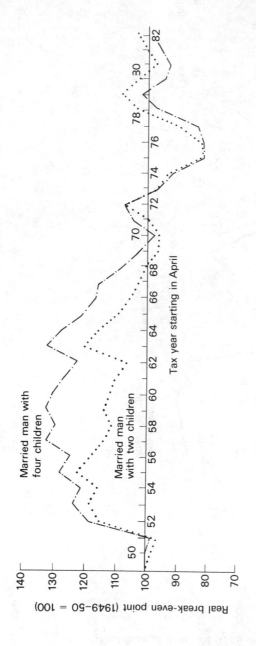

Figure 12.2 'Break-even' points for net liability to tax, 1949/50 to 1982/83
Source and notes: As for Figure 12.1.

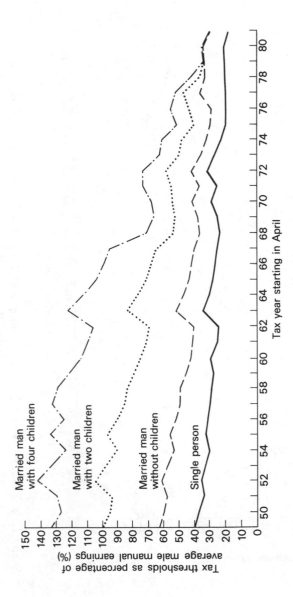

Figure 12.3 The relationship between earnings and tax thresholds, 1949/50 to 1981/82
Source and notes: As for Figure 12.1

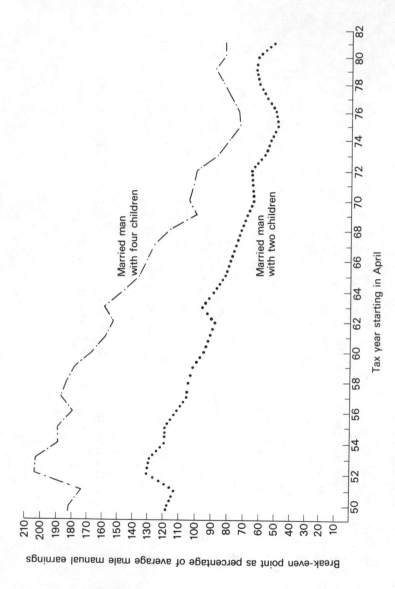

Figure 12.4 The relationship between earnings and 'break-even' points for net liability to tax, 1949/50 to 1981/82

Source and notes: As for Figure 12.1.

distributional impact of marginal public expenditure compare with that of tax revenue? This distributional test for programmes is much tougher than if it can be safely assumed that the marginal tax burden is automatically progressive. Third, how could such a development have occurred?

Only the third question will be considered here, with the answer revealing much about the formation of tax policy in the UK. Tax legislation is a highly specialized affair of interest mainly to the tax authorities and to those who advise taxpayers on how to minimize their liabilities. Few MPs maintain much interest in broad principles: it is either involvement in the minutiae of Finance Bills or nothing. There is negligible debate about strategy or even about the impact of one year's changes on the system as a whole. Until the Rooker-Wise amendment in 1977, Chancellors of the Exchequer never indicated the extent to which thresholds had to be revalued each year in order to take account of the previous year's inflation. Indeed, they would some-times take credit for reducing taxes in Budgets in which the increases in thresholds were below this figure. The constraints on individual MPs are extremely tight: Rooker and Wise severely embarrassed the minority Labour Government and their principled stance earned them the wrath of ministers, colleagues and party members. In this context, it becomes much easier to understand how the tax system could have developed, even during periods of Labour Government, in directions which ought to have been profoundly disturbing to it.

Erosion of the real yield of specific duties

If Chancellors have been willing to dissemble on tax thresholds, one of the reasons has been their failure to maintain the real value of many excise duties. Roughly 90 per cent of the yield from excise duties now comes from duties which are specific rather than *ad valorem,* notably those on alcohol, tobacco and petrol (Bruce-Gardyne, 1982). Unless such specific duties are either indexed or regularly revalued, their real yield will fall. Both the theatre of Budget day and the media's sense of 'news' have combined to make discretionary revaluation of specific duties highly unpopular with Chancellors. Such changes are interpreted as tax increases even when they are only maintaining the real yield. In contrast, *ad valorem* taxes on expenditure, such as VAT, generate extra revenue in nominal terms as an automatic by-product of inflation. Allowing this process to take its natural course is not interpreted as increasing taxes. Frightened of properly revaluing specific duties and stealthily accepting the bonus of fiscal drag, successive Chancellors have presided over a major shift in the tax burden. Such duties have never been converted into *ad valorem* rates nor indexed which are alternative methods for protecting the real yield. There are articulate and well-financed lobbies opposed to any increases in these duties on particular forms of consumption which, it should be stressed, remain highly taxed. Nevertheless, there exist opposing pressure groups which have criticized the erosion of real levels of duty and have called for higher rates. In the case of tobacco, the Royal College of Physicians of London (1971, 1977) has published studies on the effect of consumption on health. Indeed, it is possible that uncertainty about the level of real duty is one factor which stimulates such a fierce response from the manufacturers and associated pressure groups when nominal rates are, sometimes sharply, increased. Planning would be easier for them if the real yield of duty were more predictable but the recognition that such a move would inevitably mean higher levels leads manufacturers to reject such proposals (Tobacco Advisory Council, 1982). The choice between index-ation of specific duties and the conversion to *ad valorem* rates raises, *inter alia,* issues of EEC tax harmonization (on which see Kay and Keen, 1982).

III   EROSION OF THE TAX BASE

There are two other ways in which the erosion of revenue has produced distortions in the tax structure: the growth of tax expenditures and the apparent growth of avoidance and evasion. As a result of the rapid growth of tax expenditures, a given level of public expenditure will have to be financed by higher tax rates on a narrower base. If such offsets are more readily available to those on higher incomes, the effective degree of tax progression can be substantially less than the nominal degree. Given the nature of many tax expenditures in the UK, favouring, *inter alia,* owner occupation, occu-pational pensions and life insurance, this clearly happens. Their contribution to the erosion of the income tax base has intensified the shifting of the tax burden down the income hierarchy. Furthermore, serious problems of horizontal equity and of efficiency emerge because an individual's tax liability can crucially depend on his pattern of consumption. The poor quality of data, and even that only of recent origin, hinders a proper assessment of this effect. Nevertheless, there can be no doubts about either their dynamic or resistance to elimination.

The apparent spread of avoidance and evasion has more ambivalent distributional effects. Avoidance, which is legal, means that the individual organizes his financial affairs in particular ways so as to reduce his tax liability. Taxpayers with large liabilities can obviously afford to employ tax lawyers and accountants to exploit any loopholes. A modern tax system requires complex sets of rules and this, of itself, inevitably generates possibilities for avoidance. The most important question is whether the tax authorities are sufficiently vigilant in closing old loopholes and in anticipat-ing new ones. The obvious danger is that too many successful avoidance schemes may discredit the tax system as a whole in the eyes of the vast majority of taxpayers whose opportunities for avoidance are relatively limited. However, part of the growth of tax expenditures can be interpreted as avoidance as individuals take advantage of the implicit incentives to adjust consumption patterns. Similarly, high marginal income tax rates have stimulated the growth of the remuneration package. For many high earners, the non-salary component can be quite high, thus eroding both the effects of high nominal rates and creating severe problems of horizontal equity.

Evasion is illegal: it means that the individual does not declare his full income to the tax authorities. It is widely believed that the black economy, which operates mainly in cash, has expanded but there is no agreement as to its extent. On closer examination, all of the much-publicized estimates are based on either faulty methodology or guesswork (Dilnot and Morris, 1981; Blades, 1982). Participation in the black economy is open to all social classes though casual empiricism would suggest that, unlike avoidance, the working class might be heavily represented through home tradesmen such as electricians, joiners and painters. Uncertainty about the scale of the black economy makes some of the aggregate economic indicators more difficult to interpret, especially if it is thought to have been growing rapidly. The co-existence of taxed and untaxed sectors will divert resources into the latter even when these would have been more usefully employed in the former. Redistributive policies become much more difficult to operate when major uncertainty begins to attach to the declared incomes of many individuals. This is a genuine difficulty and should not be confused with the view that unemployment causes little hardship as the unemployed are all really employed in the black economy. These developments have been interpreted by some commentators (for example, Seldon, 1979) as a response to excessive levels of taxation. The appropriate policy is therefore a sharp reduction. However, attempts to draw direct links between the level of taxation and compliance underestimates the role of cultural factors. For example, France and Italy have long been believed to suffer far more severely from non-compliance than the UK even though their overall levels of taxation were broadly comparable. If the apparent deterioration in tax morality in the UK over recent years does reflect a change in cultural norms, the problem is likely to be more complex. It is unlikely that any feasible reduction in levels would of itself have any decisive impact.

IV THE DEGREE OF PROGRESSION AND THE DEFINITION OF THE TAX BASE

Two entirely different concepts are frequently confused in popular debates about taxation: the degree of progression and the definition of the tax base. The tax base defines the activity taxed and falls into one of three categories: income, expenditure or capital. The degree of progression can be calculated both for individual taxes and for the tax system as a whole, though the existence of alternative measures indicates that there are no completely unambiguous answers. A progressive tax takes a higher proportion of an individual's income as that income itself increases; a neutral tax takes a constant proportion; and a regressive tax takes a declining proportion. As tax changes are incremental, it is not surprising that the policy debate usually focuses upon the degree of progression of a particular tax. Nevertheless, what really matters is the degree of progression of the tax system as a whole: there may be good reasons for accepting certain regressive taxes (for example those on alcohol and tobacco) within a progressive tax system. Much of the advocacy of a major switch from direct to indirect taxation blurs together these quite different concepts. Direct taxes are typically thought to be progressive taxes on income and capital whereas indirect taxes are neutral or regressive taxes on expenditure. The switch to indirect taxes is therefore not only taken to mean an expenditure base but also a lower degree of progression, even though such a connection is not logically necessary.

The rationale of progression

The proper degree of progression of the tax system has generated much academic interest and fierce political debates. During the development of the progressive tax system, the sacrifice theories of taxation dominated academic discourse and provided a justification for such policies. On the assumption that marginal utility of income is a diminishing function of income, it can be argued that a progressive tax system involves the least total sacrifice of utility. Amongst the many difficulties associated with this argument are that it involves cardinal measures of utility and interpersonal comparisons of utility. As soon as these were discarded as illegitimate, this particular route for justifying progression disintegrated. But, even before this, the exponents of the sacrifice theories were careful not to force the argument to its logical conclusion. If every individual's utility function were identical and marginal utility of income a diminishing function of income, incomes ought to be equalized. Instead, they posited various principles not so much based on the internal efficiency logic but on ideas of distributive justice. Equal absolute sacrifice and equal proportional sacrifice are tax rules which must be derived from considerations of justice: only equal marginal sacrifice could be derived from either efficiency or justice. Although used to justify some measure of progression, the sacrifice theories were indeterminate about its proper extent. The reason for this nervousness in accepting the policy conclusion inherent in the sacrifice theories is straightforward. They entirely abstract from the existence of factor markets. Even on an intuitive level it is obvious that the equalization of post-tax incomes will have profound consequences for, *inter alia*, the labour market. At the level of high theory, the optimal taxation literature, inspired by the seminal work of Mirrlees (1971), has explored the desirable properties of an income tax when social welfare is maximized subject to a labour supply function. Although important insights have been derived, this literature still remains far removed from practical questions of tax policy.

The soundest case for progressive taxation is one based upon the objective of limiting the inequality of money income. This involves an explicit value judgement against excessive inequality and does not rest upon spurious or unsustainable efficiency arguments. The degree of progression will therefore depend upon cultural values, especially the extent of commitment to this form of equality, and to the costs in terms of reduced economic efficiency arising from such modifications to the market-determined pattern of rewards. It is upon the latter where economic analysis can play a role in specifying the available trade-offs.

The disincentive effects of progression

The gap between popular myth and academic evidence about the incentive effects of the UK tax system is astonishing. The UK income tax has been characterized by a low threshold, a very wide basic rate band, and exceptionally high marginal rates on high incomes. It is this third feature which has created the impression that progression is high by international standards. Given that these higher rates have never generated much incremental revenue, their myth-creating capacity is a powerful argument against them. Furthermore, well-publicized avoidance schemes create a widespread impression of inconsistency and unfairness: some, such as government stock issued at a discount, have even been devised by the Treasury itself. The 1979 reduction of the higher marginal rates, however welcome if combined with an effective purge on accumulated avoidance devices, gave substantial increases in post-tax incomes to high income groups without grasping that nettle.

More than a decade of his own work is summarized in Brown's (1981) review of the evidence about the disincentive effects of the UK income tax. He suggested that the effects are relatively limited, although there has been a detectable shift in his own position in the direction of giving more credence to them. A questionnaire-based study of major companies, designed to investigate the belief that high levels of taxation discouraged senior managers from accepting promotion or moving to new jobs, found no evidence to support it (Fiegehen with Reddaway, 1981). Acknowledging the technical problems in designing proper tests, this academic evidence nevertheless justifies a sceptical, if not disbelieving, response to the claims that the new incentives provided by tax reductions will prove a major force towards rejuvenating the economy. The political right is probably correct that there is now less philosophical commitment to equality but their claims about the economic consequences of reversing past policies are grounded in little evidence.

The tax base

Frustrated by the way in which official policymakers were preoccupied with piecemeal, stop-gap measures, the Institute for Fiscal Studies established an unofficial committee to examine the structure of direct taxation under the chairmanship of the Nobel prize winner, James Meade (1978). The membership of the Meade Committee included some of the most distinguished younger British economists with interests in this field – Tony Atkinson (though he resigned before the publication of the report), John Flemming, John Kay and Mervyn King. The result was a long, detailed and sophisticated document which eloquently advocated a switch to an expenditure base for personal taxation and a revamping of the income maintenance system. It devoted great energy and ingenuity to the task of devising an expenditure tax combining an expenditure base with progression. That the Meade Report eventually had so little impact on policy probably owed less to substantive doubts about the proposals than to the general political climate and to the way in which UK tax policy is made. Although it received extensive and favourable press coverage, it was a difficult document to read, even for the economist. A much shorter resumé was badly missed. Despite the claim that its proposals would appeal to parties with very different objectives, it mirrored the rather narrow ideological range of the Committee's membership. Whatever their voting affiliations, their Report had a distinctly centrist ring, taking as unquestioned the role of private enterprise and of the welfare state. If the process of selecting members had been so designed to ensure that a report could be agreed, the price was paid subsequently in that no members of the incoming Conservative Government of 1979 had any commitment to the document.

It is impossible to do justice in a few words to such a complex document. The Meade Report based its advocacy of an expenditure tax partly on the inherent attractions of expenditure as a measure of taxable capacity and partly upon the fact that all attempts to devise a measure of income, which was both conceptually and operationally satisfactory, had failed. It argued that the use of the income base and the particular defects of the existing UK income tax have produced massive distortions in the capital market which it is probably impossible to remove without a shift to an expenditure base. As Peacock (1978) noted in an admiring but sceptical review, the Meade Report tended to stress the importance of removing imperfections in the capital market but paid much less attention to the possible consequences for the labour market. The narrower base of an equivalent-yield expenditure tax would necessitate higher marginal rates than for an income tax. Although further consideration of this issue goes beyond the scope of this book, it should be noted that the Meade Report has suffered the unkind fate of being ignored rather than disputed.

V CONCLUSION

Unsurprisingly, all methods of paying for public expenditure themselves produce problems for public policy, especially if one particular method is pressed too hard. The expansion of public expenditure during periods of relative prosperity diverted attention away from financing issues towards expenditure issues. Advocates of public expenditure must accept a substantial part of the responsibility for this neglect. During periods of public expenditure growth, such financing issues seemed less than pressing. However, such a tradition of neglect left both practice and prescription seriously exposed to the criticisms directed from the free-market right.

Ironically, when the recognition that public expenditure has to be paid for has been painfully dawning upon its advocates, there have been claims from sections of the political and academic right that major cuts in levels of taxation can be effected without any loss of revenue. Freed from the inhibiting consequences of regulations and taxes, a thousand flowers will spontaneously flourish with the higher levels of GDP induced by these new incentives resulting in lower tax rates producing the same revenue yield. The Laffer curve (Laffer and Seymour, 1979) is predicated upon the proposition that, as tax rates of both 0 per cent and 100 per cent will produce zero revenues, there is an aggregate tax rate which will maximize revenues. Higher rates than this will produce less revenue through the substitution of leisure for work and untaxed activity for taxed activity. Any given tax revenue can thus be produced by two different tax rates, a high one and a low one. The confident policy prescription is therefore major tax cuts to move the economy away from the counterproductive position in which tax revenue is generated by the higher of these two rates.

Although there is no empirical evidence to sustain this belief in such incentive effects on output (as opposed to any Keynesian multiplier effects), that is not allowed to detract from the vigour with which the proponents of 'supply side economics' promote such policies (for example Wanniski, 1979). Although such views have exerted much more influence over Ronald Reagan than over Margaret Thatcher, nevertheless major claims have been advanced for the Laffer curve analysis. For example, Beenstock (1979) claimed that reduction of the taxation/GDP ratio from 40 per cent to 35 per cent would increase GDP by 15 per cent and that the 1979 reduction in the top marginal rates would result in no loss of revenue. As Atkinson and Stern (1980) forcefully countered, such claims, based upon a single equation model for GDP, are at odds with the accumulated microeconomic evidence on the disincentive effects of taxation. It is therefore difficult to know whether to take such propositions seriously or simply to regard them as elaborate cover for a political strategy recognizing that less revenue must ultimately mean less expenditure. Faced by the difficult realities of budgetary stress, more revenue from lower taxes is a convenient, if implausible, story.

CHAPTER 13

Privatization

I INTRODUCTION

The inbuilt dynamic of public expenditure programmes and the growing difficulties of financing them have stimulated the search for alternative policies which would relieve the budgetary stress on the Exchequer. The potent combination of demography and recession has encouraged the view that the existing level of expenditure commitments will be unsustainable in the future. Linked to such budgetary pressures which would confront governments of any political persuasion has been the growing antagonism towards the state, matched on the political right by a new willingness to embrace market solutions. Whereas the Conservative Party had never before been an unequivocal supporter of free-market capitalism, the 1979 Conservative Government articulated in a coherent and vigorous way a political and economic philosophy remarkably close to that of Milton Friedman. This transformation, set in the context of inflation and budgetary stress, illustrates the formidable power of ideas when they are carried by a persuasive vehicle and capture the mood of the time.

'Privatization' is a new word, scarcely heard before 1979, which has quickly gained popular currency as an umbrella term for very many different policies, loosely linked by the way in which they are taken to mean a strengthening of the market at the expense of the state. Given the diverse policies so described, the potential benefits and costs accruing from privatization must be specified and then evaluated carefully. It is a measure of the quality of the policy debate that so much of it is conducted in the terms of 'private good, public bad: so privatize' or of its converse. However, a number of the policies now described as privatization have been discussed and adopted in the past, with discussion being couched in technical, and not exclusively ideological, terms. The public sector has been a major market for the private sector and the lines between production in the public sector and purchase of private sector production by the public sector have never been neatly drawn. Indeed, there will often be a large number of technical and cost considerations to be taken into account in any particular case, independent of

298

whether direct production by the public sector is considered inherently good or bad.

There are four separate components which have been grouped under the term 'privatization':

(1) Privatization of the financing of a service which continues to be produced by the public sector: the respective roles of taxes and charges for public services is, of course, an age-old issue but there is now vigorous advocacy of charges playing a much more significant role.

(2) Privatization of the production of a service which continues to be financed by the public sector out of taxation: there are many proposals for contracting out work to the private sector and for educational vouchers which could be redeemed with either public or private sector suppliers.

(3) Denationalization and load-shedding, meaning respectively the selling off of public enterprises and the transfer of hitherto state functions to the private sector, both thus involving transfers of activity from the public to private sectors.

(4) Liberalization, meaning a relaxation of any statutory monopolies or licensing arrangements which prevent private sector firms from entering markets previously exclusively supplied by the public sector.

These four components are examined in separate sections of this chapter. Both the elements of continuity and the radical departures encouraged by budgetary stress and renewed commitment to market solutions are examined. Each of these components is capable of being reversed, if there were to be a new phase of 'publicization' following the present phase of 'privatization'. Although deep ideological significance is assigned to the precise line drawn between the public and private sectors, any careful analysis quickly cautions that attitudes which can be summed up as 'privatization good' or 'privatization bad' miss many of the most important and practical issues which have to be resolved. Within the broad framework provided by a political and economic judgement about the respective roles of the market and the state, detailed decisions have to be taken about the appropriate policy instruments in highly diverse sectors. Otherwise, policies of privatization or publicization are likely to be pursued with great vigour but little insight. Tellingly, Victor Keegan (1982) observed: '. . . Ministers are now considering privatising practically everything that is run by the State short of the Falklands task force'.

II CHARGES

Levying charges on the users of public services is an alternative to financing them through taxation. Such a method has different implications both for the efficiency of resource allocation (see Chapter 5) and for income distribution (see Chapter 6). Charges play a relatively minor role in financing the services of the welfare state. A major extension of the scope of charges, together with a sharp upwards revision of the level of existing charges, has been one of the major themes of the Institute of Economic Affairs. Its eloquent advocacy over a long period has both won new adherents and stimulated others to argue for such an extension. Although its case was developed primarily in terms of freedom and efficiency, the appeal of such measures has been enhanced by the onset of budgetary stress. Nevertheless, whatever views are held about the desirable scope and level of charges for public services, the design and operation of charging systems raises a number of crucial policy issues.

Yet given existing public expenditure conventions and the statistical data which have been collected and published, it is surprisingly difficult to establish the current numerical significance of charges or the historical trends. The main difficulty relates to the accounting treatment of charges when public expenditure figures are calculated. The usual practice, though not consistently applied, is to net charges off against gross expenditure rather than to regard them as a source of finance. Consequently, tables purporting to show how public services are financed can give rather different impressions, depending upon whether the focus is upon gross or net expenditure. An example makes these points neatly. Gross expenditure on services A and B is £10 million in each case. However, charges cover 50 per cent of the cost of A but only 5 per cent of B, the rest in both cases being met from taxes. Net expenditure is £5 million on A and £9.5 million on B. If the financing of net expenditure is examined, both are 100 per cent financed by taxes, but B looks a much larger public service. What produces even more confusion is when some charges are netted and others treated as a source of finance. The programme totals in the annual public expenditure White Paper are presented net of certain charges, without the extent of such charges being identified. Existing conventions, explained by the Treasury (1978; 1982a, Vol. II, p. 106), mean that:

> ... current expenditure on goods and services is shown net of charges when:
> (i)   there is a clear and direct link between the payment of the charge and the acquisition of specific goods and services (including the testing of an ability or level of performance or the establishment of standards): and
> (ii)   the charge is related to the cost of providing the goods and services, and the Government is not using its power to make the charge an instrument for raising revenue.

Consequently, prescription and dental charges are netted, whereas national insurance contributions are treated as a source of revenue.

It is exceptionally difficult from the currently available information to obtain a coherent picture of the significance of charges as a source of revenue. Table 13.1 provides for 1981/82 an analysis of charges for each of the main public expenditure programmes. This type of analysis does not appear in the annual public expenditure White Papers but was provided in the answer to a written parliamentary question (Brittan, 1982a). Because of the difficult issues concerning accounting conventions, it should be treated as indicative rather than complete, highlighting both informational deficiencies and substantive policy issues. The netting convention leads to current expenditure being 'understated' in the 1982 White Paper (Treasury, 1982a) by 4.8 per cent. Moreover, the absence of any entry for charges under 'housing' highlights another difficulty. For public sector activities which are classified as trading services (for example rather than rate fund services in a local authority context), a different netting convention applies. Public expenditure on such local authority services is calculated as the net expenditure to be financed from grants, rates and balances. Not only are rents thus netted but also loan charges are charged to revenue account, prior to this figure being struck. Accounting conventions are thus crucially important in determining the level of 'declared' public expenditure, meaning that any set of published figures must always be interpreted extremely carefully, with a sensitive understanding of the underlying conventions. The charges included in column 2 cover only a very small proportion of gross current expenditure and, partly for the reasons considered above, the expected variations between programmes fail to materialize. Furthermore, the main programme structure represents a high level of aggregation in the context of examining the role of charges. The diverse activities contained in some programmes inevitably mean that variations in the extent of charges will be masked. Taken together, these deficiencies highlight the absence of suitable data which might form the starting point for a debate upon the desirable extent of charges in the public non-market sector.[1]

Nevertheless, it is clear that the existing scope, level and structure of charges owes far more to history and administrative convenience than to an application of economic principles. Tables showing the proportion of gross expenditure covered by charges have one crucial limitation: economists do not merely view prices for goods and services as a method of financing their costs of production. For them, the central idea is that prices are a crucial factor in shaping the allocation of resources. Utility-maximizing individuals adjust their consumption decisions in response to changes in relative prices. Therefore economists will probably be less interested in what proportion of the costs of a particular public service is met from charges than in whether the structure of existing or proposed charges is conducive to efficiency in resource allocation.

In the public non-market sector, especially in the social services which are mainly private goods publicly provided rather than pure public goods, the

Table 13.1: The significance of charges and asset sales by public expenditure programme, 1981/82 (£m cash, estimated outturn)

Main programme	Current				Capital				Total
	1 Gross expenditure (i.e. before netting off charges)	2 Charges	3 Expenditure as in Cmnd 8494	4 Charges as a percentage of gross expenditure	5 Gross expenditure (i.e. before netting off asset sales)	6 Asset sales	7 Expenditure as in Cmnd 8494	8 Asset sales as a percentage of gross expenditure	9 Charges plus asset sales as a percentage of gross expenditure
				(%)				(%)	(%)
Defence	13727	1213	12513	8.8	193	73	120	37.8	9.2
Overseas aid and other overseas services	1365	17	1348	1.2	298	1	298	0.3	1.1
Agriculture, fisheries, and food and forestry	1135	7	1128	0.6	442	13	428	2.9	1.3
Industry, energy, trade and employment	4681	245	4438	5.2	1176	12	1164	1.0	4.4
Transport	2906	144	2762	5.0	1167	7	1161	0.6	3.7
Housing	1797	—	1797	—	2983	1460	1523	48.9	30.5
Other environmental services	2812	481	2331	17.1	1454	314	1140	21.6	18.6
Law, order and protective services	3834	288	3546	7.5	213	12	201	5.6	7.4
Education, science, arts and libraries	12589	859	11730	6.8	661	29	632	4.4	6.7
Health and personal social services	12745	730	12015	5.7	767	19	749	2.5	5.5
Social security	28597	3	28594	—	23	—	23	—	—
Other public services	1373	87	1286	6.3	47	—	47	—	6.1
Common services	1583	46	1537	2.9	68	5	62	7.4	3.1
Scotland	4700	216	4485	4.6	1351	114	1238	8.4	5.5
Wales	1875	112	1764	6.0	622	97	525	15.6	8.4
Northern Ireland	2810	44	2766	1.6	558	49	509	8.8	2.8
Government lending to nationalized industries	—	—	—	—	1816	—	1816	—	—
Total	98528	4492	94040	4.6	13841	2205	11637	15.9	6.0

Source: Brittan, (1982a).

key issue is whether existing or potential charges possess efficiency-generating properties. The neglect of such questions is illustrated by the example of prescription charges since the establishment of the NHS. Figure 13.1 plots both the nominal value of prescription charges and their real value expressed in 1980 prices. For two periods, there were no charges: 1947–52 and 1965–68. When prescription charges existed, they remained at a given nominal value for a number of years: for example, at 5p from 1952–61 and 20p from 1971–79. Increases in the nominal charge were abrupt: for example, 100 per cent in 1961 and 60 per cent in 1971. Between such sharp increases the real value of the charge was steadily eroded: for example, by 66 per cent from 1971–79. Unwillingness to increase nominal charges seems to be the explanation for this erratic behaviour of real charges. Such a curious path highlights major confusion about the purpose of prescription charges. Symbolic opposition to them has always been strong as they are seen to represent a small but potentially dangerous move away from the principle that health care is allocated on the basis of need and is free at the point of consumption. What Figure 13.1 does not show is the extent to which patients are exempt from the payment of prescription charges. Roughly three quarters of prescriptions in England in 1981 were dispensed without the patient facing the charge per item: 68 per cent were to exempt patients and 6 per cent to season ticket holders (Finsberg, 1982a). Such a high proportion of exemptions is clearly relevant to an evaluation of the efficiency and distributional consequences arising from the sharp increases in both nominal and real charges after 1979. Although the gains in revenue are unambiguous, there might be complicated feedbacks on the demand for unpriced NHS treatment and interactions between the exemption rules and the tax/transfer system. Both the erratic fluctuations in the real charge and the small proportion of patients paying the charge[2] reveal the extent of confusion about what role charges should play in a predominantly tax-financed service.

Proposals for an extended range of charges in the NHS provide excellent illustrations of the issues involved. Both the British Medical Association (1977) and John Banham (1977) of the management consultancy firm of McKinsey & Co. proposed in their evidence to the (Merrison) Royal Commission on the National Health Service (1979) that there should be hotel charges for overnight accommodation in hospitals and charges for each visit to a general practitioner. It was envisaged that this extra income would be used to increase gross expenditure. These particular proposals were for a piecemeal extension of charges within the still predominantly tax-financed NHS. However, such policies would be predicted by economists to influence the behaviour of doctors and patients. Prices are now being attached to some inputs but not to others. What will worry economists interested in the efficiency of the NHS is the likelihood that unpriced inputs will now be substituted for these newly-priced inputs. This substitution would not be based upon true opportunity costs but upon the implicit relative prices

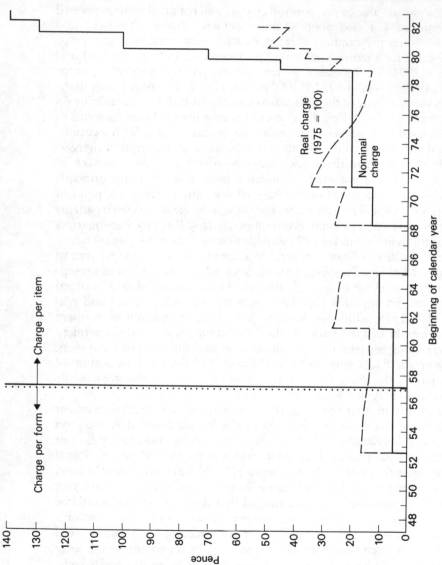

Figure 13.1 The nominal and real value of prescription charges, 1947–83

Source: Finsberg (1982a) and Central Statistical Office (1982b).

Note: No allowance is made for the switch on 1 June 1957 from a charge per form to a charge per item.

established by such charging practices. For example, the introduction of hotel charges would encourage individual doctors and patients to make a greater use of out-patient clinics, ambulance services and local authority residential accommodation. This would occur even in those cases where the minimization of all relevant costs would be achieved by the use of in-patient facilities. On occasions, reluctance to use such priced facilities would be clinically damaging, perhaps by inducing delays before proper treatment was sought. Similarly, consultation fees at general practitioners' surgeries would encourage direct approaches to hospitals if these had no comparable charges; requests for much larger prescriptions; and delays in seeking attention which might eventually create the need for much more expensive treatment.

The common theme of all these cases is that an inappropriate set of relative prices can encourage resources to be wasted, in the sense that costs are not minimized. If an activity is to remain in the public non-market sector, very great care has to be taken when introducing piecemeal charging in order to ensure that this does not have side-effects at odds with programme objectives. It is upon such points that Maynard (1979,a, b) is now carefully distancing himself from the Institute of Economic Affairs. It is impossible to read its pamphlets without being struck by the extent to which charges are deemed to be good and taxes bad. Although Maynard retains his commitment to the market, and favours the extensive use of charging, he rejects the presumption in favour of *any* charges. Much of the current advocacy of charges rests upon the proposition that the services in question should not be in the public non-market sector, indeed often that they should not be in the public sector at all. The substitution of charges for tax finance is thus seen partly as a move towards complete privatization, perhaps as far as can practically be achieved at the present time. The first policy conclusion of the Institute of Economic Affairs (page 90) is usually advanced in this spirit. Its very success in securing a place for its views on the political agenda has polarized opinion sharply. Many socialists and social administrators, stung by this attack on the fabric of the welfare state, are tempted to respond by claiming that all charges are bad and all taxes good.

What emerges quite clearly from the evidence on the structure and scope of charges within the welfare state is the complete absence of any coherent philosophy about their role. This was noted by the Layfield Committee (1976) in the context of local government services. The internal Department of Environment review, undertaken following one of the Committee's recommendations, was never published and appears to have had minimal impact. Given the prevalence of crude pro- and anti-pricing views, it becomes more difficult for supporters of the welfare state to accept any of the proposals contained in the prodigious output of the Institute of Economic Affairs, without appearing to compromise their broad stance. Over most of the major services of the welfare state, decisions to remove certain services from the market have eliminated much of the normal significance of prices which do not fulfil their usual role in shaping the allocation of resources. But, if some remain as unconsidered residuals, they have side-effects which may run counter to policy objectives. Nevertheless, there may be cases where the introduction of pricing can be supportive of the policy objectives underlying the welfare state. Examples might be road pricing (Walters, 1969) and water pricing (Herrington, 1979; National Water Council, 1980). Prices by themselves are neither good nor bad: their desirability depends upon the objective being pursued. If the aim is equal access to health care, the existing NHS has much to commend it. If the aim is to protect the fabric of cities from motor vehicles or the countryside from new reservoirs, there is much to commend the use of pricing as a rationing mechanism, provided that the distributional implications are squarely faced. It is the suspicion that advocates of pricing frequently are not much concerned about distribution which makes it so difficult to secure assent to pricing in such cases. An excellent example is the policy of raising UK energy prices, at least in part, as a conservation measure. Webb (1980), who supports this policy, has sharply criticized the lack of offsetting adjustments to other policies, both for the distributional impact and for the obstacles which the absence of such policies thereby erects to prices being set at allocatively efficient levels. But if the advocates of pricing are often careless of the distributional implications, many of the supporters of the welfare state become too preoccupied with charges as the only obstacle to allocation according to need. Access to health care does not solely depend upon whether there are charges for consultations or for prescriptions.

III CONTRACTING OUT

The decision to provide a service through the public budget does not require its production to be undertaken by the public sector. There exists a range of organizational alternatives, of which that is just one. Even though ideological passions are aroused by the question of whether such production, and hence employment, should be public or private, there are important practical and managerial considerations, the most important being the relative costs. A number of American economists, heavily influenced by public choice models (for example, Spann, 1977; Orzechowski, 1977; Savas, 1982) are prepared to assert without qualification that private production is inherently superior: public services should therefore be 'contracted out'. Such a prescription has been enthusiastically taken up in the UK by free-market pressure groups such as the Adam Smith Institute (Butler and Pirie, 1981; Forsyth, 1980, 1982) and by business organizations such as the Institute of Directors and, with more restraint, the Confederation of British Industry (1981). As its term of office progressed, ministers in the 1979 Conservative Government (for example, Brittan, 1982b) placed increasing stress on privatization, in both the contracting out and load-shedding senses, as the means of cutting public expenditure.

Contracting out therefore forms part of an overall strategy. The issues raised by the adoption of such a policy on an extensive, rather than piecemeal, scale are far more complex than its protagonists acknowledge. First, contracting out only shrinks government if the new arrangements do prove to be cheaper in the long run than direct production. For a given level of services, public expenditure will be reduced (increased) by the savings (additional costs) accruing from the switch. Unless spectacular projected savings are claimed to be possible (as indeed they sometimes are), it would be wrong to expect that the effect on the public expenditure/GDP ratio would be anything but modest, either way. Irrespective of whether financial savings are achieved, the size of government would appear to shrink on an employment measure (that is the proportion of the workforce employed in the public sector). Indeed, even if the new arrangements turned out to be more expensive, leading to a higher public expenditure/GDP ratio, it would look smaller on the employment measure. A government committed to roll back the public sector may therefore be tempted to play a numbers game, contracting out services in order to achieve targeted reductions in public employment, rather than on the merits of the particular case. The available evidence suggests that this version of the game has taken over from the techniques used (at least in part) in order to disguise the earlier growth of public employment (see, for example, Hood (1978) on the growth of quangos performing similar tasks to central government but whose employees were excluded from counts of civil servants). The Civil Service Department (1980), when justifying its decision to privatize 11 000 civil service jobs, in areas such as building supplies, maintenance and cleaning, stated that no tasks would be contracted out at the sacrifice of efficiency, reliability or cost, yet was unable to quantify the net (as opposed to gross) financial savings. A proper assessment of the relative cost of direct production and external contracting would automatically generate figures for savings. The Conservative Government's desire to be seen to be taking an axe to the bureaucracy (meeting its target of a reduction in the civil service from 732 000 in May 1979 to 630 000 in April 1984) seemed to have taken precedence over the objective of cutting public expenditure. The civil service, though accounting for only a relatively small proportion of public sector employment, is rich in symbolic value (Beaumont and Heald, 1981).

Second, the public sector is already a mammoth consumer of the goods and services produced by the private sector, relying upon it for almost all its capital expenditure and for innumerable types of goods and services. The dividing line between direct production (involving public expenditure on wages and salaries) and external contracting (involving public expenditure on goods and services) is in practice a blurred one, dependent at least in part upon historical accident. There is nothing sacrosanct about that line which might require adjustment, in either direction. Public employees and public sector unions will resist this form of privatization, just as business lobbies will vigorously canvas it and resist moves in the opposite direction. But if public sector unions were as powerful and malevolent as some of the advocates of contracting out portray them, they would never have tolerated the development of the existing hybrid arrangements. If greater efficiency is the objective, to be obtained by exposing parts of the public sector to more competition, there are a number of prerequisites for a balanced assessment of direct production against contracting out. Much improved systems of cost accounting in the public sector, required in any case for managerial purposes, are necessary if the alternatives are to be compared in an even-handed way. Such comparisons are impossible if the issues are clouded by arbitrary public employment targets or by restrictions designed to prevent the public sector from competing on equal terms. It is important both to take a reasonable time-scale and to understand the reasons for the superiority of contracting out over direct production, or vice versa. In a serious recession, private contractors may be able to reduce costs in a number of ways less open to the public sector: for example, by taking on part-time employees who work just below the number of hours at which eligibility to various forms of statutory protection take effect; by paring on safety precautions; by paying lower wages; and by refusing to recognize trade unions. In such a macroeconomic context, such private employees, conscious of the existence of the 'reserve army of the unemployed', have far less bargaining power than their public sector counterparts, afforded protection by the collective bargaining system. Although many proponents of contracting out would welcome these effects as advantages, less committed observers may wish to distinguish between them and savings from improved working practices. In the past, the public sector's concession of equal pay before it was statutorily enforced would have disadvantaged it. As for the present, it would be wrong not to take seriously the Council of Civil Service Unions' (1982, p. 348) warning, even though it is not disinterested, about the extent of the black economy in certain areas considered for privatization (such as building, cleaning and catering). When the economy is more buoyant, the more stable framework of public sector employment may bring advantages: private contractors might be far less interested in such contracts. Especially if its own capacity to undertake such work has been relinquished, the public sector might then find contract prices escalating sharply.

Third, the amount of systematic evidence on the relative efficiency of public and private production is extremely limited. The combination of little evidence and acute ideological significance makes for a heady brew: universal generalizations are drawn on the basis of a few empirical studies and impressionistic examples. One of the obstacles to illumination is the open hostility to the public sector of most of the authors using a public choice framework. Given Spann's (1977) opening comparison of the inherently inefficient public sector with the efficient private sector consisting of firms of optimal size, it would be truly remarkable if he had concluded his survey of the empirical evidence with anything other than an overwhelming vote for private enterprise. Although Savas's comparisons of alternative arrangements for refuse collection (for example, 1980) are among the best designed and most careful studies, his book (1982) sought to apply his conclusions of private superiority to the entire public sector and demonstrated a willingness to make great play with flimsy and impressionistic evidence. His presumptions are quite explicit:

> It is evident that with few exceptions, little rigorous research has been done to evaluate and compare public and private provision of services. . . . Nevertheless, while no universal and generalizable conclusion can be drawn from the evidence presented in this chapter, it is safe to say, at the least, that public provision of services is not superior to private provision, while those who believe on *a priori* grounds that private services are best can find considerable support for their position (pp. 110–11).

Yet the policies advocated by his book are predicated upon private being superior to public across the whole range of goods and services now provided through the public sector. However, Millward's (1982, p. 83) reading of the same evidence is very different from that of either Spann (1977) or Savas (1982), probably reflecting in part his much greater sympathy for the objectives of the public sector: 'In summary there seems no general ground for believing managerial efficiency is less in public firms.' It should be noted that Millward's survey mainly covered the public market sector which is exposed to varying degrees of competition. Furthermore, he stressed the narrow basis on which provisional assessments have to be struck, owing both to a surprising lack of professional interest by economists in comparative performance and in the segregation by sector of public and private ownership, meaning that outside the USA there is relatively little overlap. Pryke's (1982) comparisons of the peripheral activities of major UK nationalized industries (for example, electricity and gas showrooms, and British Rail's shipping subsidiary, Sealink) with their nearest private competitors, concluded in favour of overwhelming private superiority. Although neither of these cases reflects any credit upon the parent enterprises, Pryke's determination to read general lessons into such comparisons of activities peripheral to the main business of the public enterprise but central to that of the private enterprise is unfounded. His conversion from being the foremost defender of the UK nationalized industries (Pryke, 1971) to being an equally committed critic (Pryke, 1980, 1981) has been remarkable.

Fourth, Millward raises a fundamental question, often neglected, of what is the proper basis of comparison. If organizations in the public sector have multiple objectives which involve trade-offs between each other, they will fare relatively badly when their performance is evaluated on a single criterion, whether that be profitability or cost levels. At various times, public sector organizations are used as vehicles for other policies such as regional development, employment maintenance, support for domestic industry through purchasing policy, income redistribution, and counter-inflation policy. There are a number of different responses which can be made to this phenomenon. Such departures from the pursuit of efficiency (as measured by costs and profitability) might be attributed to the folly of having such activities within the public sector, inevitably subject to the whims of vote-maximizing politicians: either the policies, or at least these instruments, are dismissed as illegitimate. Alternatively, the policy objective might be supported but the choice of instrument questioned. Or, the problem might be viewed as one of establishing the relative cost of alternative methods of achieving a predetermined objective. If the first view is adopted, the public and private sectors can be compared without reservation on the basis of relative cost and profitability. However, if either the second or third view is accepted, then the problem of evaluation becomes far more complex. If multiple objectives are pursued, whether they be explicit or implicit, shadow prices must be attached to each of them so that a composite measure of output can be constructed. Similarly, if the public sector adjusts its production decisions in response to market failure of either the microeconomic or macroeconomic variety, inputs must themselves be shadow priced. Subsequent performance evaluation must be conducted on the basis of shadow prices, not of market prices. The formidable difficulties confronting such an exercise should not be underestimated: a tightrope has to be walked between the contrasting pitfalls of comprehensively loading the dice against the public sector so that it could never win, and of excusing anything it does. The significance attached to such issues will hinge upon the view adopted about the relative importance of market failure and of state failure.

Fifth, the establishment of a framework for assessing the appropriate delivery mechanism for particular goods and services is essential. Savas's (1982) discussion of the available alternatives, once stripped of his presumption in favour of universal privatization, is helpful. He distinguished eight alternatives to direct production: intergovernmental contracting; contracting with the private sector; the award of franchises; the payment of grants to private suppliers; the distribution of vouchers to consumers; private purchases by consumers; supply through voluntary arrangements; and self-service by consumers. He analysed goods according to their location along the rival/non-rival and excludable/non-excludable dimensions, distinguishing four polar cases: private goods (rival and excludable); common pool goods (rival and non-excludable); toll goods (non-rival and excludable); and collective goods (non-rival and non-excludable). Rejecting the supply of private goods by the public sector, Savas (1982, p. 125) ranked the alternatives judged to be feasible for the other three types of goods, giving the bottom mark to direct production in each case: the privatization of the Falklands Task Force could therefore proceed after all! Although each of his alternative mechanisms can be found to varying extents in the UK, the core welfare state, in its interface with consumers rather than its own suppliers, generally follows the direct production model. Perhaps the greatest obstacle to a balanced assessment of the relative advantages of alternative delivery mechanisms in the core services of the welfare state is the interdependence, stressed by proponents as well as by opponents, between any such changes and 'load-shedding', the abandonment of functions by the public sector.

IV   DENATIONALIZATION AND LOAD-SHEDDING

Denationalization refers to the transfer of an activity from the public sector to the private sector through the sale of public sector assets. In its usual meaning, it is taken to refer to the sale of public enterprises, belonging in the public market sector by virtue of the fact that their primary source of revenue is from the sale of their output rather than from budgetary appropriations. The denationalization of major public enterprises has been an important component of the 1979 Conservative Government's privatization programme. There were four major strands in the case advanced by the Government in support of this programme: the reduction in economic freedom inherent in public ownership; the superior efficiency of private enterprise; the greater discipline exerted over trade unions by the threat of bankruptcy which exists in the private sector but not in the public sector; and the budgetary gains, both directly in terms of the proceeds of asset sales and indirectly in terms of disentangling the financing of these enterprises from both public expenditure and public sector borrowing statistics. (For an evaluation of these arguments and for an analysis of the extent of the programme, see Heald and Steel (1982).)

If the arguments for denationalization are valid, its potential scope is far-reaching. However, much of this book has been devoted to countering the assumptions underlying the view that the economic activities of the state destroy freedom and are inherently inefficient. Little systematic evidence has been produced to justify the sweeping assertions which have ushered in such measures. In particular, the arguments about the advantages of denationalization to the public expenditure and public sector borrowing figures are spurious and misleading, conveniently using the distortions introduced by inappropriate accounting conventions in order to justify policies promoted on other grounds. Furthermore, the disposal of public sector assets on almost any terms in order to reduce public expenditure and public sector borrowing is a strange contribution to economic efficiency. If the public sector is inherently bad, denationalization is appropriate. Otherwise, it misdirects attention from the complex task of managing the public sector more efficiently, not least by leaving it in an extremely unbalanced form, with 'unsellable' and 'unshuttable' activities prominent.

The 1979 Conservative Government's concentration upon the privatization of the public market sector owes much to convenience and history,
notably the ease of selling an already independent unit and through the much
greater hostility of Conservative MPs to the nationalized industries than to
the public non-market sector. Nevertheless, if the arguments advanced for
privatization were accepted, there would seem to be almost no limit to the
possible extent of denationalization and load-shedding until the minimal
state has been reached. There have been clear indications that, if the
Conservative Government secured another term, influential ministers would
then turn their attention towards the privatization of the public non-market
sector, involving the dismantling of much of the core welfare state. The
leaked summary of the Central Policy Review Staff's options for radical cuts
in public expenditure (*The Economist*, 1982) contained a number of specific
proposals as to how public expenditure might be contained. Its proposals
were supported by Treasury ministers, fearful of how present welfare state
policies, if combined with the worst assumptions about economic growth,
would lead to a public expenditure/GDP ratio of 60 per cent by 1990, even if
still under a Government committed to roll back the public sector. The
Central Policy Review Staff's document recognized that the only method by
which public expenditure could be contained would be to introduce fundamental changes in the policy areas accounting for that expenditure. Given the
high priority attached to defence, this requires extensive load-shedding of
welfare state activities. Major cuts in public expenditure could be effected
through the following measures: the ending of all public funding for
institutions of higher education; the abolition of indexation of all social
security benefits; and the abolition of the NHS, to be replaced by private
insurance (possibly with a compulsory minimum cover) with higher prescription charges and the introduction of consultation charges as an interim
measure. When the document was tabled at the Cabinet in September 1982,
the majority of the members were so outraged by its proposals that they
successfully resisted discussion. No reference to this matter was contained in
the Cabinet minutes and the motive and identity of the person leaking the
document to *The Economist* is unsettled but subject to speculation. The
Prime Minister subsequently refused a request by Christopher Price, the
Chairman of the Education, Science and Arts Committee, to publish the
document in full.

The merit of the Central Policy Review Staff's contribution is the recognition that load-shedding is the only viable method of containing the public
expenditure/GDP ratio in an unfavourable economic environment, let alone
of reducing it. Although improving the efficiency, properly defined, of the
public sector is a crucial task, such gains are unlikely to offset the powerful
expenditure-generating pressures. If the public expenditure/GDP ratio is
regarded as an index of sin, then the only hope of redemption is to abolish the
welfare state. Otherwise, the tendency of the ratio to rise in recession should

be explicitly recognized: the most desirable, and least painful, method of cutting the ratio is to return the economy to full employment. Furthermore, the fact that abolishing the welfare state would cut the ratio means that such a policy scores well on that count but says nothing about its impact on freedom, efficiency or equality. Such a policy would be predicated upon assertions that public expenditure destroys freedom, undermines efficiency and, either fails to reduce inequality or, if successful, achieves an undesirable objective. The vigorous advocacy of the free market by the radical right has reaped its reward in the privatization programme of the Conservative Government, composed of lawyers and others who have accepted the package without any of the qualifications which the more careful members of the economics profession would attach to the case for the market.

The presumption that privatization is the panacea for the various ills of the public sector should be rejected. Given that the Central Policy Review Staff envisaged saving £3–4 billion out of the 1982/83 health budget of £10 billion, the NHS provides a convenient example which highlights some of the issues involved. McLachlan and Maynard (1982, p. 555), the editors of a Nuffield Provincial Hospitals Trust study of the public/private mix in health care in a number of industrialized countries, summarized their own position in a postscript to their conclusion, the ringing tone perhaps inspired by growing ministerial references to the privatization of the NHS:

> After reviewing the evidence we have accumulated over these past months, as well as from our collective experience and observations, we both feel that despite its faults, the variety of complex services which is termed the 'National Health Service' constitutes a unique and precious national asset which provides basic services of a high standard at a very low proportion of GDP compared to other countries. According to OECD data it has a relatively low cost of administration too. . . . Above all, it still retains a vital core of the ideal regarding equity in service, with which it was launched in 1948 and the importance of this should not be overlooked.

A series of contributors (such as Culyer, 1982; Maynard, 1982; McLachlan, 1982) stressed that the complexities of the health care market resulted in all countries, regardless of both the ownership of health care institutions and the method of financing, facing similar problems: the containment of costs; the problem of access; the monopoly power of providers; the limited information of consumers; and the failure to evaluate therapies. All stressed the error of setting up an idealized, perfectly competitive health care market as an alternative to the existing imperfect NHS, and the opposing error of an idealized public system against the reality of an uncompetitive market system. All systems lack effective mechanisms for securing efficient resource allocation. Private health insurance systems, although often advocated as a means of confronting consumers with prices, in practice do not: once insured, patients face zero prices, just as in the NHS, unless compelled to pay a proportion of charges, thus limiting their cover. Whatever the extent of charges, the impact upon the utilization of other health care resources must be given proper attention. Maynard (1982) concluded that the specific characteristics of the health care market meant that regulation was inevitable: privatization would mean growing regulation and there was no evidence that such an arrangement would be more efficient than the existing system.

Furthermore, there is a strong element of illusion in the reductions in the public expenditure/GDP ratio consequent upon any prospective load-shedding of core welfare state activities. Advocates of such an approach frequently presume that such private expenditures would be tax-deductible, thus creating a new range of tax expenditures neglected by the public accounting system. For example, the Central Policy Review Staff's proposals for the abolition of the NHS would generate both extensive tax expenditures and, through any legal requirement for a minimum level of cover, heavy coerced private expenditures. Such provisions would be regressive in their impact: tax allowances are worth more to those paying tax, and especially higher rate taxpayers, and any minimum cover requirement would obviously absorb a higher proportion of lower incomes. Until there is a proper system of accounting for such policy substitutes for public expenditure, any proposals for major reforms involving the substitution of these for explicit expenditure should be subjected to the most searching scrutiny.

If privatization of the core welfare state were to be implemented, vouchers might play a significant role, notably in education (Kent County Council, 1978). Ironically, the enthusiastic advocacy of educational vouchers by those who would prefer complete privatization, if that were considered feasible (such as Sir Keith Joseph and Dr Rhodes Boyson), has guaranteed polarization. If there were no serious disputes about continued public financing and provision of education, the possible advantages of vouchers as a simulator of competitive pressures for the public sector might be discussed in an even-handed manner and then weighed against the effects upon other objectives. But it is obvious that, in a context in which such disputes are becoming more important, supporters of continued public financing and provision will vehemently resist voucher schemes irrespective of their detailed characteristics. Although the distributional impact of voucher schemes is crucially dependent upon their detailed design, it is obvious that a government, wishing to privatize education completely, would find its task immeasurably easier if vouchers, rather than direct provision, were already the dominant mode. For example, the value of vouchers could be sharply cut back so that they covered a smaller proportion of average cost; any restrictions upon parental supplementation of vouchers from their own incomes could be abolished; and any restrictions upon redemption of vouchers with private sector suppliers could be relaxed.

Neither should it be presumed that privatization measures would necessarily lead to cheaper administration: just like direct provision, the alternatives involve costs. The public sector as a bureaucrat's paradise may have entered the popular imagination but it is an image unsubstantiated by hard evidence. The cacophony of criticism directed against the post-reorganization NHS as bursting at the seams with unproductive administrators stands in remarkable contrast to the view, based on OECD (1977) evidence, that it is 'cheap to run' (Maynard, 1982, p. 493) and that much of its alleged inflexibility *'might be because of false economy in administration'* (McLachlan and Maynard, 1982, p. 543). The fact that privatization would mean that administrative costs were less visible is not to say that they would be lower, or that resources would be managed more effectively. Rather than the public sector living up to its popular image, there is other evidence (for example, Kogan (1978) on the NHS and Page and Midwinter (1980) on local government) which heavily discounts criticisms of the level of administrative costs. There is more evidence to support the view that one of the real difficulties of the public sector is that key parts of it have been 'undermanaged'.

V LIBERALIZATION

Another dimension of privatization is the removal of statutory barriers which prevent the private sector from competing for markets against the public sector. The most significant cases of liberalization have been in the public market sector: for example, the repeal of many of the statutory provisions which reinforce the natural monopoly enjoyed by the electricity, gas and telecommunications industries; and the relaxation of transport licensing which protected the businesses of publicly owned bus operators. Although the practical consequences of such relaxation may be relatively insignificant in some cases, they represent an attempt to expose hitherto protected parts of the public market sector to greater competition. In terms of public expenditure, the consequences of such measures may prove paradoxical. The existing statutory protection had enabled bus operators to maintain a much more extensive network, particularly in rural areas, than could be justified on commercial criteria, through the practice of cross-subsidization. To an extent, liberalization is envisaged as a method of eliminating cross-subsidization, judged to be damaging because of the way that it produces a distorted tariff structure with prices unrelated to costs. Yet if governments feel unable, for a mixture of social and political reasons, to witness the entire collapse of rural bus services, they may have to incur much higher levels of public expenditure on subsidies in order to sustain the desired network. A higher level of public expenditure can thus be a consequence of liberalization. Similar considerations can apply to other goods and services such as posts, telecommunications and public utilities.

Liberalization is one aspect of a wider move towards the deregulation of the economy, meaning less state intervention in the private sector. The rolling back of the regulatory state is just as important an objective for the radical right as the rolling back of its welfare and stabilization activities. Deregulation would cover not just civil aviation and road transport but regulatory activities such as health and safety, environmental standards and consumer protection. There is a fundamental conflict between those on the radical right such as Cheung (1978) who interpret growing regulation as a symptom of bureaucratic expansionism paralleling budget overexpansion, and those such as Baumol and Oates (1975, 1977) who identify the escalation of externalities associated with urban and industrialized living as the most significant allocative problem and which requires the adoption by the state of a set of well-designed and co-ordinated instruments. The controversy therefore hinges upon the question of whether there should be a wave of deregulation sweeping the economy or whether the arguments for more or less regulation should be assessed on a case-by-case basis. Paradoxically, both contracting out of the production of public services and denationalization may lead to a substitution of regulation over the private sector for production within the public sector. This process is already visible in the context of the proposed privatization of British Telecommunications and would become much more evident if such measures were extended to significant parts of the public non-market sector such as health and education. Unless the state effectively disowned responsibility for costs, tariffs and standards in such activities, the demise of public production would be accompanied by the rise of regulation.

VI   CONCLUSION

The various policies embraced by the term 'privatization' have been shown to be extremely diverse. Consequently, an evaluation of specific acts of privatization will depend heavily upon which particular sense of the word is involved and how such a step affects the achievement of the various policy objectives. It is yet another measure of the public sector's loss of consent that privatization as a slogan has acquired such currency and that resistance to it has been so sporadic and ineffective. In the rhetoric of the 1979 Conservative Government, privatization is depicted as the route to increased efficiency and the way of making 'the public sector for the public' (Treasury, 1982d). Once the central message is accepted, privatization has few logical bounds: not only where performance is judged to be unsatisfactory but also to prevent now satisfactory performance deteriorating in future through the manifold inherent deficiencies of the public sector.

When privatization is advocated in this way, few of the real complexities concerning the concept and measurement of efficiency in public sector activities are even contemplated, let alone resolved. Some of the economists who contributed to the developing prestige of the Institute of Economic Affairs, such as Tony Culyer, Alan Maynard and Alan Peacock, were and are fully conversant with such issues. But once market solutions secured a place on the political agenda, the care and qualifications attached to their advocacy of the market are entirely lost. The more Culyer and Maynard have written about the economic and managerial problems of the NHS, the less willing they have become to embrace simple market solutions to economic problems and the more they argue that the specific characteristics of the health sector must be carefully considered when designing public policy. If such economists of justifiably high professional prestige are meticulously careful, that cannot be said of others. For Seldon (1982b), it is simply a matter of the public sector getting out of activities such as housing, health and telecommunications. For the Adam Smith Institute (1982), the policy agenda would be universal privatization, through mechanisms such as tax incentives for private health, vouchers for education, and the disposal of public sector housing. However ill-advised some economists might have been in believing that 'the market plus redistribution' was likely to be delivered by the political right, all the support which is available should now be mustered to counter the view that anything the public sector does the private sector can do better.

CHAPTER 14

Reflections

Writing this book has been like a long arduous journey, full of surprises, twists and turns, and plain drudgery. Now the destination has been reached, the prospect of mapping out a 'Grand Conclusion' is too forbidding. The arguments and conclusions of the various parts of the book must therefore stand on their own. But from this vantage point, I should answer a question often asked by long-suffering colleagues and friends, on being told that completion was near at hand. What they wanted to know was less what conclusions I had drawn, more how the process of writing such a book had made me revise my views. Reflecting back over the evolution of the typescript, that is a question striking a chord. I wrote in Chapter 11 that the key dilemma facing an intellectual tradition under attack was knowing where to hold the line, delineating what could safely be conceded and what must be defended as important. Writing this book has confronted me, both as an economist and as a citizen, with that dilemma in a particularly explicit form. Without launching into intellectual autobiography, it is worth recounting briefly how my views have changed. These changes have been modifications, not Damascus conversions: the book was conceived as, and will see daylight as, a vigorous defence of the Keynesian social democratic state. Yet some of the modifications are important, representing not only my own attempt to map out the territory to be defended but also revised judgements about what constitute the crucial political and economic obstacles to the attainment of the underlying policy goals.

Starting with the 'negative' count, I am now much more troubled than before about a number of aspects of the operation of the UK public sector which I have come to view as critical faults, obstructing the achievement of policy objectives and potentially fatal to consent for the policies themselves. The three main worries, each of which has emerged powerfully from the preceding chapters, are the efficiency of the public sector, the conduct of public sector industrial relations, and the structure of the tax/transfer system. Whilst I can with conviction dismiss the wild allegations often emanating from free-market economists and right-wing politicians about the inherent inefficiency of public sector organizations, I view with dismay the all-too-

318

available evidence that X-inefficiency is not only a problem in the public sector but one which has been too willingly tolerated. I believe that McLachlan and Maynard's (1982) judgement upon the NHS contains important insights which may have a wider application. They concluded that the NHS stands up well internationally in terms of 'value for money' but nevertheless exhibits chronic problems of allocative and X-inefficiency which can only be reduced through a painstaking search for cost effectiveness, not through dramatic solutions such as major reorganizations or privatization. The structure of the incentives facing decision-makers in the public sector is a matter of paramount importance which must engage the attention of policymakers. I have become increasingly sceptical about the wisdom of establishing unitary organizations possessing a monopoly of a particular sector. Proposals to this effect should be scrutinized much more carefully than in the past in order to verify that forms of decentralization, perhaps involving parallel organizations covering geographical areas, are not a more suitable model. To be repetitive, it is those who support the programmes generating public expenditure who have the most to gain from increased efficiency in the public sector: to surrender the cause of efficiency to our opponents is unforgivable folly.

The deteriorating climate of its industrial relations has obstructed efficiency in the public sector. From being regarded at the time of the Donovan Commission (1968) as one of the few jewels in the crown of what was seen as a much-troubled system, public sector industrial relations have become its bed of thorns. This transformation has not only impeded efficiency but also has sorely damaged the public image of the public sector. If privatization of the core welfare state were ever to acquire momentum, the public sector's reduced esteem would be a significant factor, both in encouraging the adoption of such policies and in softening public opposition to them. The lack of any effective response to the 1979 Conservative Government's programme of privatizing nationalized industries, extending far beyond the relatively modest proposals of its election manifesto, should be heeded as a warning bell. The omens are not propitious: bewilderment and outrage are now the standard emotions of all sides of the public sector industrial relations system. Insight and foresight are sadly missing, attributes without which the stubborn dilemmas analysed in Chapter 9 will never be resolved.

Public sector trade unions have to reconcile their immediate industrial objectives, including the safeguarding of their members from discriminatory treatment, with a recognition that existing forms of public provision, central to their political objectives, are only sustainable in the long term if industrial relations are regulated in a manner which minimizes the disruption of monopoly services. Internally, those unions are experiencing dislocating tensions, fired by widespread disenchantment on the part of their membership with their perceived maltreatment by the state as employer, and by radicalized activists encouraged by the Marxist left to view industrial conflicts in the public sector as the new trenches against capitalism. Even more threatening are the implications of the public sector being run by governments hostile to its existence. A foretaste of the potential consequences was provided during the protracted 1982 NHS dispute: Conservative ministers responded not just by promoting the privatization of ancillary services, on which a draft circular was distributed at the height of the dispute, but also by talking about dismantling the NHS (Brittan, 1982b). The reform of the public sector collective bargaining system need not be a high priority for a government lacking commitment to the public sector, willing to use cash limits, threats of privatization and the fears generated by high unemployment as methods of disciplining public sector unions and employees. But any subsequent government, attaching high priority to both the welfare state and reduced unemployment, will reap a harvest of bitterness if procedures are not reformed. On this issue, more than on any other, hinges the future of the welfare state.

The final worry relates to the tax/transfer system, an issue less central to the main themes of the book but which has inevitably recurred throughout it. The interactions between its two components, the system of personal taxation and the social security system, have generated substantive problems such as the poverty trap and contributed towards the tax/transfer system's loss of public consent. Through the neglect of such issues, ammunition has been abandoned in the field, to be marshalled in the scrounger theory of unemployment, whether in the hands of Iain Sproat or of Patrick Minford.

But it would be wrong to end the book on notes of such pessimism. I am not surprised to discover that the problems of modern economies are complex, not capable of simple solutions. Economists have to live with the fact that others seek the solace of imagining them. Unlike a civil engineer designing a suspension bridge, we have no protected area of expertise. The temptation for those in public life is to trivialize the real complexity. Roy Jenkins (1976) contemplates 'frontiers of social democracy' defined by figures not just of incredible plasticity but so ephemeral that the numbers for the 60 per cent calculation have since been lost; Margaret Thatcher (1982) wishes to run the economy like a family budget; and Michael Foot readily commits a future Labour Government to implement an uncosted 'pensioners' plan'. Yet I reject entirely the view that life would be peaceful, just and efficient if only intrusive ideology could be excluded. For me, ideology is not a dirty word: it must play a crucial role in defining goals, involving complex trade-offs between the values considered in Part Two. History is not made by the anguished but by those combining determination with direction, characteristics possessed both by the original architects of the welfare state and by those who would now dismantle it. But ideology, though indispensible, is insufficient on its own, requiring an accompanying willingness to enquire and adjust. Otherwise, the determined charge is just as likely to be down a blind alley as through a tunnel affording light. Economists have a major technical contribution to make in detecting which is which, though the controversies surveyed in this book have illustrated the persistent uneasy combination of ideology and expertise which is the lot of the economics profession.

What writing the book has done has been to cement my personal commitment both to full employment as a policy objective of the highest importance and to the broad structure of the existing welfare state. I come back to the values espoused by Keynes and Tawney, not necessarily all their mechanics. Brought up in the 1950s and 1960s, I listened to parental stories about the 1930s with incomprehension and perhaps too little tolerance, as about a world as far removed from my experience as the Spanish Inquisition. Though safely protected myself, the return of mass unemployment is again blighting lives, not as severely in a financial sense but possibly more so in other ways, so much had full employment become taken as part of the legitimate expectations of a generation. For a mixture of economic and social reasons, full employment will never so easily be achieved again, an unpalatable conclusion I reluctantly accept, being willing to argue through why that should be the case and to explore the implications for policy. What I react to with something approaching moral outrage is the pretence that unemployment, even on its present scale, is a voluntarily-chosen condition. Of the alternatives on offer, I much prefer the version explicitly based on class politics, viewing it either as evidence of a lack of moral fibre or simply good for social discipline, to the attempt to wrap it up in an abuse of the concept of the natural rate of unemployment, that rate being conveniently judged to have moved along with the actual rate, whatever that might be.

Nor should the new-found confidence of the political right, succoured by the present ascendancy of monetarist and free-market economics, remain unchallenged in the wider arena of political debate. Tendentious propositions have been allowed to stand as incontrovertible truths, unfailingly presented as 'common sense'. What has made developments within the economics profession so profoundly damaging is that the political right has been able to lift ideas and policies on a selective basis. Amongst monetarist and free-market economists can be found those who take a consistently libertarian position on the relationship between the state and the individual. The political right has been delighted to receive their intellectual support for its rekindled antagonism towards the Keynesian social democratic state. Unsurprisingly, there is no willingness to follow through that libertarianism to some of the most difficult areas of the individual's relationship to the state. Instead, appeal is made to morality, order and patriotism, with libertarian views receiving short shrift. 'Getting the state off the backs of the people' might be the public credo of the resurgent political right but the issue is far more complex and subtle than the implied move along a unidimensional spectrum.

The dismantling of the Keynesian social democratic state would certainly reduce public expenditure but greater state power would be required to effect such a transformation, not least through a dramatic centralization of the public sector in order to neutralize opposition and through the substitution of repression for concession. Occasionally, a right-wing politician who embraces market solutions makes explicit appeal to the link between the free market and the strong state. In a lecture, Margaret Thatcher (1980) argued that the extended role of the state had meant:

> . . . its authority is not enhanced, it is diminished. In our Party we do not ask for a feeble State. On the contrary, we need a strong State to preserve both liberty and order, to prevent liberty from crumbling and to keep order from hardening into despotism. The State has, let us not forget, certain duties which are incontrovertibly its own: for example – to uphold and maintain the law; to defend the nation against attack from without; to safeguard the currency; to guarantee essential services. We have frequently argued that the State should be more strongly concerned with these matters than it has been. . . . What we need is a strong State determined to maintain in good repair the frame which surrounds society. But the frame should not be so heavy or so elaborate as to dominate the whole picture. . . . We should not expect the State to appear in the guise of an extravagant good fairy at every christening, a loquacious and tedious companion at every stage of life's journey; the unknown mourner at every funeral.

The scene is thereby set for rolling back the public sector on which 'too much is spent' and which 'produces little real wealth'. Ironically, despite repeated series of public expenditure cuts, the Thatcher Government presided over a sharp increase in the public expenditure/GDP ratio in the first four years of its term, a powerful reminder that the ratio also depends upon what happens to GDP. Yet there can be little doubt that its re-election for a second term would herald in an unprecedented attempt to dismantle the core welfare state.

Those like myself who support the welfare state should be alert to its faults, prepared to listen to perceptive critics. But there are two fundamental reasons why proposals to dismantle it should be rejected, even when they are couched in terms of an extensive substitution of cash redistribution for existing in-kind services. Pragmatically, I simply do not believe, whatever the intentions of the advocates of such policies, that cash redistribution would take the place of an abolished NHS or public education: so acute already is the tax/transfer system's crisis of consent. More fundamentally, the existing shape of the welfare state, however ragged and ill-defined the edges might be, represents the most suitable model for achieving the egalitarian objectives to which I subscribe in the context of an affluent market economy. When pressed to explain what 'equality' in such a context means to me, I reply, much more emphatically than before, that the central component must be 'limiting the domain of inequality', an attainable and far more relevant objective than any precise equalization of incomes.

Although I have written this book with reference to institutions and developments in the UK, I suspect that much of my argument will strike chords with readers concerned with other economies: the problems associated with running large public sectors are probably universal. Indeed, at an OECD seminar on 'The Welfare State in Crisis', its Secretary-General, Emile van Lennep (1981, p. 11) contended that '. . .rigour is the best defence of the Welfare State in the hard economic circumstances of today'. If this book has a central message, it is that the Keynesian social democratic state has not failed, its temporary eclipse as a prevailing ideology owing much to a failure to articulate a proper defence of its essentials. So this book is my contribution towards reviving that tradition, directly through the arguments it marshalls and indirectly through stimulating others to re-examine those essentials in a critical but sympathetic manner. I need hardly add that the stakes are very high.

Notes

1. With there being no comparable tradition of analysing the state in the UK as that in continental Europe (Dyson, 1980), many political scientists and most writers on public administration avoid the use of this concept in their analysis of the political and administrative system. Instead, they adopt a disaggregated approach, looking at the operation of public organizations and stressing their diversity. The main exception to this lack of interest in the idea of the state has been the work of Marxists who have been influenced by the continental European tradition. In a book like this, with its broad canvas transcending disciplinary boundaries and subsuming issues of philosophy and of policy, the concept is required, both for its substantive content and for its usefulness as shorthand. The word 'state' is used here more narrowly than in the work of Marxists such as Miliband (1969). Much later in the book, attention will turn to contrasting theoretical approaches to the analysis of the state, each leading to prescriptions as to its role (see Chapter 11).

2. The ratio of 60 per cent cited in Treasury (1976a) was calculated using volume figures for both public expenditure and GDP. This calculation cannot be replicated because Cmnd 6393 does not provide comparable volume figures for GDP. Therefore the Jenkins series measures both in cash. It cannot be extended beyond 1975/76 because the Table called 'Treasury Analysis of Public Expenditure' was discontinued after the 1976 Blue Book (Central Statistical Office, 1976a). Furthermore, the Jenkins series must rest on unrevised data, with the (then available) figures for GDP at factor cost being used from Central Statistical Office (1975, 1976b).

3. Before 1977, all the capital expenditure of nationalized industries was included in public expenditure. Subsequently, this was removed, to be replaced by the much smaller programme 5 (Government lending to nationalized industries). Similarly, all public sector debt interest was included before 1977 but the narrowed definition excluded that part which would be met from trading revenues. Not only are there continuing eccentricities in the way public enterprises impinge upon public

325

expenditure totals but the precise lines have continued to evolve from White Paper to White Paper (see Heald, 1982d).

4. The choice between volume and cash ratios can have a marked effect upon the declared trend of public expenditure. Crucially important are the sign of the relative price effect and the choice of base year for the volume series.

5. Public expenditure is calculated at market prices and thus includes certain taxes on expenditure. However, GDP at factor cost excludes taxes on expenditure but adds subsidies. In 1981, GDP at factor cost was only 84.9 per cent of GDP at market prices (Central Statistical Office, 1982b, p. 4). Using GDP at factor cost as the denominator in the public expenditure/GDP ratio will therefore produce a higher figure.

6. The reduction in public expenditure is £355 million, not £365 million, because of the way in which certain public service employees undertook to refrain from claiming national insurance benefits in consideration of their receiving unabated sick pay. As such payments were not treated as public expenditure (being regarded as transfers within central government), the savings in public expenditure are £10 million lower than the reductions in benefit expenditure (Department of Health and Social Security, 1982a).

7. A delightful example can be found in the oral evidence of George Younger, Secretary of State for Scotland, to the Committee on Scottish Affairs (1980, Q. 79): 'There is a complete difference in kind between allowing tax relief to people who provide their homes *at no expense to the State* and providing a grant to people to provide themselves with homes' (italics added).

8. A reconciliation is provided in each issue of *Financial Statistics* (for example, Central Statistical Office, 1983a, Table 2.4) between general government expenditure on the national accounts basis and public expenditure as defined in the latest White Paper. For example, the national accounts definition includes non-trading capital consumption but excludes certain public corporations' capital expenditure and nationalized industries' net overseas and market borrowing.

9. It has been argued by Beck (1976) that much of this growth has been illusory. The relative cost of providing public services is said to have increased sharply, with the volume of such services possibly contracting. A consideration of the issues raised by Beck's work is postponed until pages 177–86.

CHAPTER 3

1. This interpretation of Keynes (1936) was developed by Sir John Hicks and Alvin Hansen. The macroeconomy is analysed in terms of the goods

sector (equilibrium positions being defined by the IS curve) and the monetary sector (equilibrium positions being defined by the LM curve), with the level of real income being determined by the intersection of the IS and LM curves.

2. During the 1979 Conservative Government, the predictions of the Treasury model were increasingly discounted by Treasury ministers, suspicious of its Keynesian origins.

3. There is a close parallel between debates on public expenditure defini- tions in the 1970s and those of the early 1980s about the inclusion of all nationalized industry external finance, whether from the Exchequer or not, in the PSBR, a practice which is not followed in other countries (Treasury and Civil Service Committee, 1981c).

4. It should be noted that Ward and Neild used definitions of public expenditure receipts and the budget balance which differ from the official definitions. Their objective was to measure the change in purchasing power associated specifically with changes in budgetary policy which they defined to exclude any monetary consequences. Their measure of fiscal stance was therefore intended to indicate the effect of budgetary policy on aggregate demand, all other things remaining equal. The differences between the two series are due to a different base level of employment, the measurement of GNP at market prices rather than at factor cost and revisions to the national income accounts since the first series was calculated. They emphasized the importance not of the constant-employment budget balance in a particular year but of the change in fiscal stance over time.

5. The link between budget financing and money creation emerged as a central policy issue in all the industrialized economies during the 1970s. A recent OECD study (1982e) emphasized the importance of insti- tutional differences between economies in the financial and banking sectors and provided an interesting comparative survey of the financing of budget deficits.

CHAPTER 4

1. No significance should be read into the use throughout this book of the male pronoun which is merely adopted as a matter of convention. The available alternatives seem either awkward or forced.

2. Following Gray (1980), negative freedom and positive freedom will be described as two different conceptions of the concept of liberty, a practice differing from that of Berlin who did not consistently make this distinction. The terminological problems are illustrated by the fact that Berlin's two concepts of liberty are negative freedom and positive freedom! All page references to Berlin (1958) are to the 1969 version.

3. Although Taylor's (1979) imaginative example illustrates the point forcefully, it should be admitted that neither he nor anyone else has checked the empirical validity of the proposition about the relative incidence of traffic lights!
4. Although Gray (1980) has argued that MacCallum's triadic relationship may be non-neutral with respect to rival conceptions of liberty, the difficult cases which arise are not directly relevant to the concerns of this book.
5. On bureaucrats, Tullock (1979, p. 38) has written:

> The voting power of bureaucrats is, of course, very difficult to handle in a democracy. In a country like Britain, which does not have a written constitution, it would at least be theoretically possible for parliament simply to provide that bureaucrats and their families did not vote, but I would think a better scheme would be to set up a set of special constituencies in which bureaucrats and their families elected – probably by proportional representation, so that different bureaus would get adequate representation – their own representatives to parliament, and did not vote in the geographical constituencies. This method would give them weight in parliament roughly equivalent to their numbers but would also mean that they would face a very large number of MPs whose constituencies contained not a single bureaucrat.

On welfare beneficiaries, Richard Posner commented (on a paper containing some of the ideas of this chapter, delivered at Hertford College, Oxford in January 1980) that redistribution without the consent of the rich was 'legalized theft', implying that potential beneficiaries should not be allowed to vote on redistributional questions. This view stands as the polar opposite to Proudhon's (1840) famous denunciation of property as theft. Interestingly, Posner also provided a striking example of the ambivalence of free-market writers to the state. He vigorously dismissed suggestions that US farmers who were suffering financial losses from President Carter's grain embargo on the Soviet Union should be compensated, commenting that they fully understood the risks of 'trading with the enemy'.

CHAPTER 5

1. For a fuller explanation, see Bohm (1974), Layard and Walters (1978) or Laidler (1981).
2. The usual method of exposition is the Edgeworth box diagram, drawn in terms of a two-person, two-good economy. This restriction allows

the use of this neat geometric device: the results can easily be generalized using calculus. Indifference curves trace out an individual's preferences between two goods, each curve linking together combinations of these goods which generate equal levels of utility. The Edgeworth box diagram superimposes the indifference map of one person upon the other's, having first 'turned around' its origin by 180°.

3. When economists began to use the Pareto criterion as the basis for policy recommendations, it became obvious that the fact that no one could be made worse off was an exceptionally stringent requirement. Few practical policies would ever be sanctioned, thus preventing moves generating large efficiency gains but involving losers. This realization led to the development of a less stringent condition (a potential Pareto improvement rather than a Pareto improvement) which required only that everyone might be made better off after the policy change, via the mechanism of costless transfers. Compensation tests, such as the Kaldor–Hicks test (see Mishan, 1981), were designed to allow policy changes to be assessed on purely allocative grounds, with the distributional implications being incidental. They were not designed to enable allocation and distribution to be considered simultaneously, as were social welfare functions (see Appendix to Chapter 6). The criterion of a potential Pareto improvement formed the theoretical foundations for the later development of cost benefit analysis as a policy tool.

4. The most intractable issue confronting economists wishing to pronounce upon policy questions is the problem of 'second best'. If there are 'deviant' sectors in which the Pareto optimal conditions definitely cannot be met, it cannot be assumed that meeting hitherto unsatisfied efficiency conditions in other sectors will improve social welfare. In such cases, the efficiency conditions for these other sectors will be revised and will be much more complex than in the 'first-best' case. Mishan (1981) wryly noted that: 'The problem of Second Best has the distinction of being universally acknowledged while being, in effect, almost universally ignored or, rather coolly evaded' (p. 275). However, he continued: '. . . one should be able to contemplate the theorem without being wholly paralysed by it' (p. 296) and provided a thoughtful review of the extent to which first-best policy proposals must be amended. In a book such as the present one, it is inevitable that the problem of second best is given a wide berth. Although an issue of major theoretical importance and of practical significance for detailed policy, it is less relevant to the broad themes of this chapter, on the respective roles of the market and state.

5. For private goods, the necessary condition for overall Pareto efficiency is that the *common* marginal rate of substitution between any two goods should be equal to the marginal rate of transformation between those goods. For public goods, this condition is amended so that the

summed marginal rates of substitution should be equal to the marginal rate of transformation.

6. Strictly, the area under the demand curve is only an approximation of total utility. For a thorough exposition of alternative measures of consumer surplus, see Mishan (1981, pp. 145–97). For the purposes of the present analysis, an exposition in terms of the approximation makes it easier for the non-technical reader to grasp the essential points.

7. Those economists who defend the Pigovian tax/subsidy scheme counter that such a position totally underestimates the importance of bargaining costs in the large numbers case and the free rider problem (see Common, 1979).

8. There is an extensive literature considering the issues raised by Arrow's impossibility theorem, including much debate about the significance of his 'minimal' conditions. The issues are lucidly examined by Sen (1970) and Sugden (1981). What is important here is that the transition to collective choice generates formidable problems if such decisions are to be based on the values of individuals.

9. This mathematical term simply means that, at all budget levels, an increase in the bureau's budget will generate an increase in the bureaucrat's utility.

10. One of the most influential models of the political business cycle has been that of Frey and Schneider (for example, 1978) who claimed econometric support for their model. However, their work has been criticised by Alt and Chrystal (1981) who have made their own attempts to model government as an endogenous sector of the macroeconomy (Chrystal and Alt, 1979). They are critical of any attempt to attribute the growth of public expenditure to the political business cycle and prefer an explanation based on longer-term factors.

CHAPTER 6

1. The 'weighting' of gains according to the income group to which they accrue has been advocated by some of the foremost practitioners of cost benefit analysis (for example, Little and Mirrlees, 1974). However, the strength of the assumptions which have to be made about the shape of the utility function is sufficient to unnerve other economists, even many of those with no brief for the free market.

2. An indication of the size of additional cash transfers required to substitute for existing provision in kind is provided by the following examples relating to 1980/81. The average unit cost of a secondary school pupil in England was £964 (Boyson, 1982). For a family of two adults and two children aged between 11 and 15, cash to cover the cost of

the two pupils would amount to 63 per cent of the long-term supplementary benefit scale rate. Similarly, using average per capita expenditure for England, broken down by age group, replacement of the NHS by cash transfers would mean a supplement of 14 per cent (Finsberg, 1982b). Such a family makes heavy demands on educational facilities but relatively low demands on the NHS, thus emphasizing how use of welfare state services is related to the life cycle. For older age groups, replacement of the NHS by cash transfers would have parallel consequences.

3. As with studies of taxation, it is much easier to specify who immediately 'benefits' from particular items of public expenditure (that is the first round effects) than to trace through the induced changes in factor and product markets. For example, expenditure on education can, with suitable data, be allocated by sex, age and income group but the identity of the ultimate 'beneficiaries' depends, *inter alia,* on how the increased supply of educated manpower alters market wage rates.

CHAPTER 7

1. These nine types of accountability are those distinguished by Smith (1980) though he did not group them into political, managerial and legal accountability. For the sake of clarity, the term 'resource' accountability has been substituted for his 'economic' accountability as the latter term is potentially misleading.

CHAPTER 9

1. The implications of this definition of union density should be noted. Bain and Price (1980) included both employed and unemployed in the denominator because they were unable to distinguish in the numerator between union members gainfully employed and those who have continued to hold a union card during periods of unemployment, a widespread practice in certain industries. On such a definition, union densities will tend to fall during a recession if some proportion of union members losing their jobs also lapse their membership. However, it is possible that a union density restricted solely to those in employment might actually rise during a recession if the sectors with high densities, and the union members therein, fared better than the economy average.

CHAPTER 10

1. Marquand (1980) suggested that expenditure on regional policy enhanced the efficiency of the regional economies. However, this leaves

unsettled the net effect as it says nothing about the impact of the taxes which finance that expenditure. But Wilson's (1979) point remains unaffected by this qualification.

2. Short's (1976) category of 'regionally relevant' expenditure consists of public expenditure made 'in and for' a region. It therefore excludes expenditure incurred in a region, if the service is entirely national in character, such as defence, even though there are differential regional impacts on employment and income (see Heald, 1980c, pp. 20–7 for further discussion).

3. It is a measure of how little importance has been attached to such territorial mechanisms that there is no reference to the formula in Joel Barnett's account of his career at the Treasury (Barnett, 1982). However, in fairness, the name 'Barnett formula' was first used by Heald (1980d).

CHAPTER 11

1. One aspect of this change has been the growing significance and prestige of the 'think tanks' of the radical right: for example, the Institute of Economic Affairs, the Centre for Policy Studies and the Adam Smith Institute in the UK; and organizations such as the American Enterprise Institute in the USA. In contrast, the Fabian Society, enormously influential in an earlier period, has become peripheral and ineffective. Similarly, the National Institute for Economic and Social Research and the Brookings Institution, nominally uncommitted but in practice broadly sympathetic to the Keynesian social democratic state, have found their funding and prestige eroded. For an interesting discussion of the changed intellectual climate in the USA, see Miller (1981).

2. Patrick Minford is the most prominent academic exponent of the view that unemployment is voluntary, not involuntary, with his writings containing frequent reference to individuals choosing whether to work or to take leisure and benefits. Unemployment is caused by governments and unions, with the prescription being privatization, lower benefits and state action against unions. However, the tax/transfer system seems to take pride of place.

> The UK social security system gives indefinite and generous support in a way that sharply undercuts up to half of the economy's available jobs. . . . It is probably only habit, the desire to avoid upheaval, and the knowledge that the system must surely be changed in time, which prevent many more people from actually abandoning their existing jobs, rather than simply not making active efforts to find new ones (Minford and Peel, 1981, p. 6).

But it is not just the scope, coverage and generosity of the post-Beveridge tax/transfer system which is held to function in this damaging way: '. . . recent work on the UK has suggested that a large part of UK unemployment in the 1920s and 1930s was due to high social security benefit rates' (Minford, 1980, p. 9). It is beyond the scope of this book to attempt a detailed refutation of such views, but see Atkinson (1982). What needs to be stressed here is the way in which the changed ideological climate, in the economics profession and beyond, has made such views not just respectable but avidly welcomed by those looking for a convenient explanation for the return of mass unemployment.

3. The problems confronting any attempt to adopt a consistent use of terminology are illustrated by Crouch's (1979) use of 'reactionaries' for what in this book have been called the 'radical right' and 'radicals' for 'Marxists'.

4. Although the choice of the title of Hobbes's book (1651) was deliberate in that it powerfully conveyed the image of evil, Musgrave (1981) noted that it would be wrong to claim Hobbes's support for the stance of the Leviathan theorists. It should be noted that they use the term 'government' rather than 'state'.

5. A Standing Order of the House of Commons can hardly be interpreted as a written constitutional rule.

CHAPTER 12

1. Clark's (1945) 'safe limit' was 25 per cent of net national income. Clark (1977) drew attention to the changed convention which had involved a move from measuring net national income (involving a deduction for depreciation but expressed at market prices) to GNP at factor cost, recalculating his 1945 limit as 23 per cent.

CHAPTER 13

1. Table 13.1 provides a further analysis not considered in the text. Column 8 expresses asset sales as a percentage of gross capital expenditure and column 9 expresses the sum of charges and asset sales as a percentage of total gross expenditure. Asset sales have become a significant source of financing for capital expenditure, notably for housing. When interpreting the figures, it must be remembered that there are serious problems of comparability between the valuation bases for housing in column 5 (current capital costs, hence reflecting market values) and column 6 (receipts from disposal of public sector housing at large discounts on

market value). Furthermore, the 1979 Conservative Government's programme of special asset sales, intended to reduce the PSBR, is treated as an offset to the planning total but is not attributed to individual programmes.

2. The Department of Health and Social Security does not know the proportion of the population eligible for exemption. Although the proportion of the population exempt is not the same as the proportion of exempt prescriptions, the evidence on the latter indicates that it must be high.

Bibliography

Abramovitz, M. and Eliasberg, V. F. (1957) *The Growth of Public Employment in Great Britain*, Princeton, Princeton University Press for the National Bureau of Economic Research.

Acton, H. B. (1971) *The Morals of Markets*, London, Longman.

Acton, H. B. (ed.) (1972) *John Stuart Mill: Utilitarianism, On Liberty, and Considerations on Representative Government*, London, Dent.

Adam Smith Institute (1982) *Strategy Two: A Report on Public Services*, London, Adam Smith Institute.

Aldred, K. (1979) The Treasury Financial Information System, *Management Services in Government*, **34**, 90–102.

Alexander, J. and Toland, S. (1980) Measuring the public sector borrowing requirement, *Economic Trends*, No. 322, August 1980, pp. 82–98.

Allen, D. (1981) Raynerism: strengthening civil service management, *RIPA Report*, **2**, No. 4, pp. 10–11 and 15.

Alt, J. and Chrystal, A. (1981) Electoral cycles, budget controls and public expenditure, *Journal of Public Policy*, **1**, 37–60.

Armstrong, Lord William (1980) *Budgetary Reform in the United Kingdom*, Oxford, Oxford University Press for the Institute for Fiscal Studies.

Aronson, J. R. (1974) Financing public goods and the distribution of population in metropolitan areas: an analysis of fiscal migration in the United States and England, in *Economic Policies and Social Goals: Aspects of Public Choice* (ed. A. J. Culyer), London, Martin Robertson, pp. 313–41.

Arrow, K. J. (1951) *Social Choice and Individual Values* (1st edn), New York, Wiley. (2nd edn, 1963.)

Ashford, D. E. (ed.) (1980) *Financing Urban Government in the Welfare State*, London, Croom Helm.

Atkinson, A. B. (1982) Unemployment, wages and government policy, *Economic Journal*, **92**, 45–50.

Atkinson, A. B. and Stern, N. H. (1980) Taxation and incentives in the UK, *Lloyds Bank Review*, No. 136, April 1980, pp. 43–6.

336 Bibliography

Bacon, R. W. and Eltis, W. A. (1976) Britain's Economic Problem: Two Few Producers (1st edn), London, Macmillan. (2nd edn, 1978.)
Bailey, S. J. (1980) *The Restructuring of Local Authority Services under Conditions of Decline: A Case Study of the Education Service*, Centre for Urban and Regional Research Discussion Paper in Planning No. 16, University of Glasgow.
Bain, G. S. and Price, R. (1980) *Profiles of Union Growth: A Comparative Statistical Portrait of Eight Countries*, Oxford, Basil Blackwell.
Banham, J. M. M. (1977) *Realizing the Promise of a National Health Service*, London, McKinsey & Co.
Bank of England (1981a) Memorandum, in *Monetary Policy*, Treasury and Civil Service Committee, Third Report of Session 1980/81, II, HC 163–II, London, HMSO, pp. 41–59.
Bank of England (1981b) Is it the case that an increase in the PSBR has an effect on the economy only if it is unfunded?, in *Monetary Policy*, Treasury and Civil Service Committee, Third Report of Session 1980/81, II, HC 163–II, London, HMSO, Annex, p. 289.
Bank of England (1982) Inflation-adjusted saving and sectoral balances, *Bank of England Quarterly Bulletin*, 22, 239–42.
Barnett, J. (1982) *Inside the Treasury*, London, André Deutsch.
Baumol, W. J. (1967) The macroeconomics of unbalanced growth: the anatomy of urban crisis, *American Economic Review*, 57, 415–26.
Baumol, W. J. and Oates, W. E. (1972) The cost disease of the personal social services and the quality of life, *Skandinavska Enskilda Banken Quarterly Review*, 2, 44–54.
Baumol, W. J. and Oates, W. E. (1975) *The Theory of Environmental Policy*, Englewood Cliffs, New Jersey, Prentice-Hall.
Baumol, W. J. and Oates, W. E. (1979) *Economics, Environmental Policy and the Quality of Life*, Englewood Cliffs, New Jersey, Prentice-Hall.
Beaumont, P. B. (1978) The obligation of the British Government as an employer in the British Civil Service, *Public Administration*, 56, 13–24.
Beaumont, P. B. (1981a) *The Government as Employer in the Civil Service: A Best Practice Example?* London, Royal Institute of Public Administration.
Beaumont, P. B. (1981b) The right to strike in the public sector: the issues and evidence, *Public Administration Bulletin*, No. 35, April 1981, pp. 21–38.
Beaumont, P. B. and Heald, D. A. (1981) Public employment, in *Government Policy Initiatives 1979–80: Some Case Studies in Public Administration* (ed. P. M. Jackson), London, Royal Institute of Public Administration, pp. 16–41.
Beaumont, P. B. and Leopold, J. W. (1982) Public sector industrial relations in Britain: an overview, *Public Administration Bulletin*, No. 40, pp. 2–18.
Beck, M. (1976) The expanding public sector: some contrary evidence, *National Tax Journal*, 29, 15–21.

Beck, M. (1979) Public sector growth: a real perspective, *Public Finance*, **34**, 313–56.

Becker, L. C. (1977) *Property Rights: Philosophic Foundations*, London, Routledge and Kegan Paul.

Beenstock, M. (1979) Taxation and incentives in the UK, *Lloyds Bank Review*, No. 134, October 1979, pp. 1–15.

Beenstock, M. and Immanuel, H. (1979) The market approach to pay comparability, *National Westminster Bank Quarterly Review*, November 1979, pp. 26–41.

Beer, S. H. (1977) A political scientist's view of fiscal federalism, in *The Political Economy of Fiscal Federalism* (ed. W. E. Oates), Lexington, Mass., D. C. Heath, pp. 21–48.

Bennett, R. J. (1980) *The Geography of Public Finance*, London, Methuen.

Berlin, Sir Isaiah (1956) Equality, in *Proceedings of the Aristotelian Society, New Series*, LVI, London, Harrison, 301–26.

Berlin, Sir Isaiah (1958) Two concepts of liberty, in *Four Essays on Liberty* (I. Berlin), Oxford, Oxford University Press, 1969, pp. 118–72.

Bevan, G., Sisson, K. and Way, P. (1981) Cash limits and public sector pay, *Public Administration*, **59**, 379–98.

Black, Sir Douglas (Chairman) (1980) *Report of the Working Group on Inequalities in Health*, London, Department of Health and Social Security.

Blades, D. (1982) The hidden economy and the national accounts, *OECD Economic Outlook*, Occasional Studies June 1982, pp. 28–45.

Board of Inland Revenue (1980) Tax thresholds, *Inland Revenue Statistics 1980*, London, HMSO, pp. 71–4.

Board of Inland Revenue (1982) Tax thresholds 1949/50 to 1982/83, *Inland Revenue Statistics 1982*, London, HMSO, Appendix C, pp. 104–6.

Bohm, P. (1974) *Social Efficiency: A Concise Introduction to Welfare Economics*, London, Macmillan.

Borcherding, T. E. (ed.) (1977) *Budgets and Bureaucrats*, Durham, North Carolina, Duke University Press.

Boyle, L. A. (1966) *Equalisation and the Future of Local Government Finance*, Edinburgh, Oliver and Boyd.

Boyson, R. (1982) *Hansard*, 29 November 1982, col. 66.

Brandt, W. (1980) *North–South, a Programme for Survival: Report of the Independent Commission on International Development Issues*, London, Pan Books.

Brennan, G. and Buchanan, J. M. (1977) Towards a tax constitution for Leviathan, *Journal of Public Economics*, **8**, 255–73.

Brennan, G. and Buchanan, J. M. (1978) Tax instruments as constraints on the disposition of public revenues, *Journal of Public Economics*, **9**, 301–18.

Bridgeman, J. M. (1969) Planning programming budgeting systems, *O & M Bulletin*, **24**, 167–77.

Bridgeman, J. M. (1970) Planning programming budgeting systems II, O & M Bulletin, 25, 16–26.

Briscoe, S. (1981) Employment in the public and private sectors 1975 to 1981, Economic Trends, No. 338, December 1981, pp. 94–102.

British Medical Association (1977) Royal Commission on the National Health Service: Report of the Council to the special representative meeting, British Medical Journal, 29 January 1977, pp. 299–334.

Brittan, L. (1982a) Hansard, 30 March 1982, cols. 97–8.

Brittan, L. (1982b) The Government's economic strategy, in The 1982 Budget (ed. J. Kay), Oxford, Basil Blackwell for the Institute for Fiscal Studies, pp. 7–18.

Brittan, L. (1982c) Hansard, 28 July 1982, cols. 542–4.

Brittan, L. (1983) Hansard, 1 February 1983, cols. 84–96.

Brittan, S. (1976) An open letter to Professor Friedman, The Financial Times, 2 December 1976.

Brown, C. V. (1981) Taxation and the Incentive to Work, Oxford, Oxford University Press.

Bruce-Gardyne, J. (1982) Hansard, 30 March 1982, col. 102.

Brunner, K. and Meltzer, A. H. (eds) (1978) Public Policies in Open Economies, Amsterdam, North Holland Publishing.

Buchanan, J. M. (1961) Comment, in Public Finances: Needs, Sources and Utilization, National Bureau for Economic Research, Princeton, Princeton University Press, pp. 122–9.

Buchanan, J. M. (1962) Towards analysis of closed behavioral systems, in Theory of Public Choice (eds J. M. Buchanan and R. D. Tollison), Ann Arbor, University of Michigan Press, pp. 11–23.

Buchanan, J. M., Burton, J. and Wagner, R. E. (1978) The Consequences of Mr Keynes, Hobart Paper 78, London, Institute of Economic Affairs.

Buchanan, J. M. and Tullock, G. (1962) The Calculus of Consent, Ann Arbor, University of Michigan Press.

Buchanan, J. M. and Wagner, R. E. (1977) Democracy in Deficit: The Political Legacy of Lord Keynes, New York, Academic Press.

Burrows, P. (1977) Efficient pricing and government interference, in Public Expenditure: Allocation between Competing Ends (ed. M. V. Posner), Cambridge, Cambridge University Press, pp. 81–93.

Burrows, P. (1979) The government budget constraint and the monetarist-Keynesian debate, in Current Issues in Fiscal Policy (eds S. T. Cook and P. M. Jackson), Oxford, Martin Robertson, pp. 61–85.

Burton, J. (1978) Keynes's legacy to Great Britain: 'Folly in a Great Kingdom', in The Consequences of Mr Keynes (J. M. Buchanan, J. Burton and R. E. Wagner), Hobart Paper 78, London, Institute of Economic Affairs, pp. 29–75.

Burton, J. (1982) The varieties of monetarism and their policy implications, The Three Banks Review, No. 134, June 1982, pp. 14–31.

Butler, E. and Pirie, M. (eds) (1981) *Economy and Local Government,* London, Adam Smith Institute.

Butler, F. E. R. and Aldred, K. (1977) The Financial Information Systems project, *Management Services in Government,* 32, 77–87.

Byatt, I. C. R. (1973) Observation made during discussion of P. M. Jackson, The rising cost of local government services, in *Proceedings of a Conference on Local Government Finance,* London, Institute for Fiscal Studies, p. 95.

Cabinet Office (1981) *Efficiency in the Civil Service,* Cmnd 8293, London, HMSO.

Cabinet Office (1982a) *Administrative Forms in Government,* Cmnd 8504, London, HMSO.

Cabinet Office (1982b) *Efficiency and Effectiveness in the Civil Service,* Cmnd 8616, London, HMSO.

Carter, R. (1977) Justifying paternalism, *Canadian Journal of Philosophy,* VII, 133–45.

Central Statistical Office (1975) *Economic Trends Annual Supplement 1975,* No. 1, London, HMSO.

Central Statistical Office (1976a) *National Income and Expenditure 1965–75,* London, HMSO.

Central Statistical Office (1976b) *Economic Trends,* No. 270, April 1976, London, HMSO.

Central Statistical Office (1977) *National Income and Expenditure 1966–76,* London, HMSO.

Central Statistical Office (1981) The effects of taxes and benefits on household income, 1979, *Economic Trends,* No. 327, January 1981, London, HMSO, pp. 104–31.

Central Statistical Office (1982a) *National Income and Expenditure: 1982 Edition,* London, HMSO.

Central Statistical Office (1982b) *Economic Trends Annual Supplement: 1983 Edition,* No. 8, London, HMSO.

Central Statistical Office (1983a) *Financial Statistics,* No. 251, March 1983, London, HMSO.

Central Statistical Office (1983b) *Annual Abstract of Statistics: 1983 Edition,* No. 119, London, HMSO.

Cheung, S. N. S. (1978) *The Myth of Social Cost: A Critique of Welfare Economics and the Implications for Public Policy,* Hobart Paper 82, London, Institute of Economic Affairs.

Christie, C. (1982) The real Rayner targets, *RIPA Report,* 3, No. 1, pp. 7–9.

Chrystal, A. and Alt, J. (1979) Endogenous government behaviour: Wagner's Law or Götterdämmerung? in *Current Issues in Fiscal Policy* (eds S. T. Cook and P. M. Jackson), Oxford, Martin Robertson, pp. 123–37.

Civil Service Department (1980) Reductions in the size and cost of the Civil Service, in *Civil Service Manpower Reductions: Minutes of Evidence and*

Appendices, Treasury and Civil Service Committee, Session 1979/80, II, HC 712–II London, HMSO, Memorandum, pp. 1–3.

Clark, C. (1945) Public finance and changes in the value of money, *Economic Journal,* 45, 371–89.

Clark, C. (1954) *Welfare and Taxation,* Oxford, Catholic Social Guild.

Clark, C. (1964) *Taxmanship: Principles and Proposals for the Reform of Taxation* (1st edn), Hobart Paper 26, London, Institute of Economic Affairs. (2nd edn, 1970.)

Clark, C. (1977) The scope for, and limits of taxation, in *The State of Taxation* (A. R. Prest *et al.*), London, Institute of Economic Affairs, pp. 19–28.

Clarke, Sir Richard (1971) *New Trends in Government,* Civil Service College Studies 1, London, HMSO.

Clarke, Sir Richard (1978) (edited by Sir Alec Cairncross) *Public Expenditure Management and Control: The Development of the Public Expenditure Survey Committee (PESC),* London, Macmillan.

Clegg, H. A. (1979) *The Changing System of Industrial Relations in Great Britain,* Oxford, Basil Blackwell.

Clegg, H. A. (1982) Public sector pay and comparability: historical background and current issues, *Public Money,* 2, September 1982, pp. 39–43.

(Clegg) Standing Commission on Pay Comparability (1980a) (Chairman: Professor H. A. Clegg) *Report No. 9: General Report,* Cmnd 7995, London, HMSO.

(Clegg) Standing Commission on Pay Comparability (1980b) (Chairman: Professor H. A. Clegg) *Report No. 7: Teachers,* Cmnd 7880, London, HMSO.

Coase, R. (1960) The problem of social cost, *Journal of Law and Economics,* 3, 1–44.

Cobham, D. (1978) The politics of the economics of inflation, *Lloyds Bank Review,* No. 128, April 1978, pp. 19–32.

Cohen, G. A. (1979) Capitalism, freedom and the proletariat, in *The Idea of Freedom* (ed. A. Ryan), Oxford, Oxford University Press, pp. 9–26.

Collard, D. (1976) Review of C. K. Rowley and A. T. Peacock (1975) *Welfare Economics: A Liberal Restatement,* London, Martin Robertson, in *Economic Journal,* 86, 180.

Collard, D. (1978) *Altruism and Economy: A Study in Non-Selfish Economics,* London, Martin Robertson.

Committee on Scottish Affairs (1980) *Scottish Aspects of the 1980–84 Public Expenditure White Paper,* HC 689 of Session 1979/80, London, HMSO.

Committee on Scottish Affairs (1982) *Scottish Aspects of the 1982–85 Public Expenditure White Paper,* HC 413 of Session 1981/82, London, HMSO.

Common, M. S. (1979) External costs: myth or rationale for state intervention, *Omega,* 7, 385–98.

Confederation of British Industry (1981) *Report of the CBI Working Party on Government Expenditure,* London, CBI.
Conference of Socialist Economists' State Apparatus and Expenditure Group (1979) *Struggle over the State: Cuts and Restructuring in Contemporary Britain,* London, CSE Books.
Congdon, T. (1982) *Monetary Control in Britain,* London, Macmillan.
Convention of Scottish Local Authorities (1981) *Government Economic Strategy: The COSLA Critique,* Edinburgh, COSLA.
Convention of Scottish Local Authorities (1982) *Central/Local Government Relationships: A Time to Listen – A Time to Speak Out,* Edinburgh, COSLA.
Council of Civil Service Unions (1982) Evidence from the Council of Civil Service Unions, in *Efficiency and Effectiveness in the Civil Service,* Session 1981/82, Vol II. *Minutes of Evidence,* Treasury and Civil Service Committee, HC 236–II, London, HMSO, pp. 337–52 and 369–85.
Cranston, M. (1967) *Freedom: A New Analysis* (3rd edn), London, Longmans, Green and Co.
Crosland, C. A. R. (1956) *The Future of Socialism,* London, Jonathan Cape.
Crosland, C. A. R. (1974) *Socialism Now,* London, Jonathan Cape.
Crouch, C. (ed.) (1979) *State and Economy in Contemporary Capitalism,* London, Croom Helm.
Crouch, C. (1981) The place of public expenditure in socialist thought, in *The Socialist Agenda: Crosland's Legacy* (eds D. Lipsey and D. Leonard), London, Jonathan Cape, pp. 156–85.
Culyer, A. J. (1976) *Need and the National Health Service,* Oxford, Martin Robertson.
Culyer, A. J. (1980) *The Political Economy of Social Policy,* Oxford, Martin Robertson.
Culyer, A. J. (1982) The NHS and the market: images and realities, in *The Public/Private Mix for Health: The Relevance and Effects of Change* (eds G. McLachlan and A. K. Maynard), London, Nuffield Provincial Hospitals Trust, pp. 23–55.
Cyert, R. M. and March, J. G. (1963) *A Behavioral Theory of the Firm,* Englewood Cliffs, New Jersey, Prentice-Hall.
Dean, A. (1981) Public and private sector pay and the economy, in *Incomes Policies, Inflation and Relative Pay* (eds J. L. Fallick and R. F. Elliott), London, George Allen and Unwin.
Dearlove, J. (1980) Review of S. C. Littlechild *et al.* (1979) *The Taming of Government,* IEA Readings 21, London, Institute of Economic Affairs, in *Economic Journal,* 90, 454–5.
Department of Education and Science (1970) *Output Budgeting for the Department of Education and Science: Report of a Feasibility Study,* Education Planning Paper No. 1, London, HMSO.
Department of Employment (1977) Earnings of employees in the private and

Bibliography

public sectors: April 1970 to April 1977, *Employment Gazette*, 85, 1335–40.

Department of Employment (1978) The pattern of pay, April 1978: key results of the New Earnings Survey, *Employment Gazette*, 86, 1136–67.

Department of Employment (1979) The pattern of pay, April 1979: key results of the New Earnings Survey, *Employment Gazette*, 87, 965–1002.

Department of Employment (1980) Patterns of pay: early results of the New Earnings Survey, *Employment Gazette*, 88, 1089–97.

Department of Employment (1981) Patterns of pay: early results of the 1981 New Earnings Survey, *Employment Gazette*, 89, 443–9.

Department of Employment (1982) *New Earnings Survey 1982 – Part A: Streamlined Analyses and Key Analyses by Agreement*, London, HMSO.

Department of Health and Social Security (1982a) *Financial Effects of Statutory Sick Pay*, Mimeo.

Department of Health and Social Security (1982b) Question 11, in *1982 White Paper: Public Expenditure on the Social Services*, Social Services Committee, Session 1981/82, II, HC 306–II, London, HMSO, pp. 42–3.

Dilnot, A. and Morris, C. N. (1981) What do we know about the black economy?, *Fiscal Studies*, 2, 58–73.

Doern, G. B. (1981) Review of (Lambert) Royal Commission on Financial Management and Accountability (1979) *Final Report*, Ottawa, Government of Canada, in *Journal of Public Policy*, 1, 143–5.

(Donovan) Royal Commission on Trade Unions and Employers' Associations (1968) (Chairman: Lord Terence Donovan) *Report*, Cmnd 3623, London, HMSO.

Downs, A. (1957) *An Economic Theory of Democracy*, New York, Harper and Row.

Downs, A. (1960) Why the government budget is too small in a democracy, *World Politics*, 12, 541–63.

Drury, S. B. (1982) Locke and Nozick on property, *Political Studies*, XXX, 28–41.

Dunleavy, P. (1980) The political implications of sectoral cleavages and the growth of state employment – Part 1: The analysis of production cleavages (pp. 364–83), and Part 2: cleavage structures and political alignment (pp. 527–49), *Political Studies*, XXVIII.

Dupuit, J. (1844, reprinted 1969) On the measurement of the utility of public works, in *Readings in Welfare Economics* (eds K. J. Arrow and T. Scitovsky), London, Allen and Unwin.

Dworkin, G. (1972) Paternalism, *The Monist*, 56, 64–84.

Dyson, K. (1980) *The State Tradition in Western Europe*, Oxford, Martin Robertson.

The Economist (1982) Thatcher's think-tank takes aim at the welfare state, *The Economist*, 18 September 1982, pp. 25–26.

Education, Science and Arts Committee (1982) *The Future of the Theatre Museum,* Fifth Report of Session 1981/82, HC 472, London, HMSO.

Elliott, R. F. (1982) Comparative pay movements in the period since 1956, in *Inquiry into Civil Service Pay.* Vol. II. *Research Studies,* (Megaw) Committee, Cmnd 8590–I, London, HMSO, Research Study 4, pp. 129–69.

Elliott, R. F. and Fallick, J. L. (1981) *Pay in the Public Sector,* London, Macmillan.

Else, P. K. and Marshall, G. P. (1981) The unplanning of public expenditure: recent problems in expenditure planning and the consequences of cash limits, *Public Administration,* 59, 253–78.

Environment Committee (1981) *Council House Sales,* Second Report of Session 1980/81, HC 366–I–III, London, HMSO.

Estimates Committee (1958) *Treasury Control of Expenditure,* Sixth Report of Session 1957/58, I, HC 254–I, London, HMSO.

Expenditure Committee (1976) *Policy Making in the Department of Education and Science,* Tenth Report of Session 1975/76, HC 621, London, HMSO.

Expenditure Committee (1977) *The Civil Service,* Session 1976/77, HC 535–I–III, London, HMSO.

Feinberg, J. (1971) Legal paternalism, *Canadian Journal of Philosophy,* 1, 105–24.

Fiegehen, G. C. with Reddaway, W. B. (1981) *Companies, Incentives and Senior Managers,* Oxford, Oxford University Press for the Institute for Fiscal Studies.

Field, F. (1981) *Inequality in Britain,* London, Fontana.

Field, F., Meacher, M. and Pond, C. (1977) *To Him Who Hath: A Study of Poverty and Taxation,* Harmondsworth, Penguin.

Finsberg, G. (1982a) 'Prescription charges – level' *Hansard,* 29 March 1982, cols. 27–30.

Finsberg, G. (1982b) *Hansard,* 1 December 1982, cols. 223–4.

Forsyth, M. (1980) *Reservicing Britain,* London, Adam Smith Institute.

Forsyth, M. (1982) *Reservicing Health,* London, Adam Smith Institute.

Foster, C. D. (1971) *Politics, Finance and the Role of Economics,* London, Allen and Unwin.

Foster, C. D., Jackman, R. A. and Perlman, M. (1980) *Local Government Finance in a Unitary State,* London, Allen and Unwin.

Fowler, N. (1982) Speech to the 20th Anniversary Symposium of the Office of Health Economics in London on 23 September 1982, Department of Health and Social Security Press Release 82/292.

Frey, B. S. and Schneider, F. (1978) A politico-economic model of the United Kingdom, *Economic Journal,* 88, 243–53.

Friedman, D. (1980) Many, few, one: social harmony and the shrunken choice set, *American Economic Review,* 70, 225–32.

Friedman, M. (1953) The methodology of positive economics, in *Essays in Positive Economics* (M. Friedman), Chicago, University of Chicago Press.

Friedman, M. (1962) *Capitalism and Freedom,* Chicago, University of Chicago Press.

Friedman, M. (1976) The line we dare not cross: the fragility of freedom at '60%', *Encounter,* **47,** November 1976, pp. 8–14.

Friedman, M. (1980) Memorandum, in *Memoranda on Monetary Policy,* Treasury and Civil Service Committee, Session 1979/80, HC 720, London, HMSO, pp. 55–61.

Friedman, M. and Friedman, R. (1980) *Free to Choose,* London, Secker and Warburg.

Friedrich, C. J. (1955) The political ideas of neo-Liberalism, *American Political Science Review,* **49,** 509–25.

Fulton, Lord John (1968) *The Civil Service,* Report of Committee, Cmnd 3638, London, HMSO.

Galbraith, J. K. (1958) *The Affluent Society,* Harmondsworth, Penguin, 1962.

Galnoor, I. (1974) Reforms of public expenditure in Great Britain, *Canadian Journal of Public Administration,* **17,** 289–320.

Gamble, A. (1979) The free economy and the strong state: the rise of the social market economy, in *The Socialist Register 1979* (eds R. Miliband and J. Saville), London, The Merlin Press, pp. 1–25.

Garrett, J. (1978) Public Accountability, the Expenditure Committee and Public Accounts Committee, in *First Report of Session 1977/78,* Procedure Committee, Session 1977/78, III, HC 488–III, London, HMSO, Appendix 44, pp. 141–4.

Garrett, J. (1980) *Managing the Civil Service,* London, Heinemann.

Godley, W. A. H. (1976) Public expenditure 1970/71 to 1974/75, in *The Financing of Public Expenditure,* Expenditure Committee, First Report of Session 1975/76, II, HC 69–II, London, HMSO, p. 224.

Goldman, Sir Samuel (1973) *The Developing System of Public Expenditure Management and Control,* Civil Service College Studies 2, London, HMSO.

Goodin, R. E. (1982) Freedom and the welfare state: theoretical foundations, *Journal of Social Policy,* **11,** 149–76.

Gough, I. (1979) *The Political Economy of the Welfare State,* London, Macmillan.

Gray, A. and Jenkins, W. I. (1982) Policy analysis in British central government: the experience of PAR, *Public Administration,* **60,** 429–50.

Gray, C. (1982) Regional water authorities, in *Regional Government in England* (eds B. W. Hogwood and M. J. Keating), Oxford, Clarendon Press, pp. 143–67.

Gray, J. N. (1980) On negative and positive liberty, *Political Studies,* **XXVIII,** 507–26.

Green, D. G. (1982) Freedom or paternalistic collectivism?, *Journal of Social Policy*, 11, 239–44.

Gregory, M. B. and Thomson, A. W. J. (1981) The coverage mark up, bargaining structure and earnings in Britain – 1973 and 1978, *British Journal of Industrial Relations*, XIX, 26–37.

Gupta, S. P. and Hutton, J. P. (1968) *Economies of Scale in Local Government Services*, Research Studies 3, Royal Commission on Local Government in England, London, HMSO.

Gutmann, A. (1980) *Liberal Equality*, Cambridge, Cambridge University Press.

Hahn, F. H. (1980) Memorandum, in *Memoranda on Monetary Policy*, Treasury and Civil Service Committee, Session 1979/80, HC 720, London, HMSO, pp. 79–85.

Harris, R. and Seldon, A. (1976) *Pricing or Taxing?* Hobart Paper 71, London, Institute of Economic Affairs.

Hartley, N. and Bean, C. (1978) *The Standardised Budget Balance*, Government Economic Service Working Paper 1 (Treasury Working Paper 1), London, Treasury.

Hayek, F. A. von (1944) *The Road to Serfdom*, London, Routledge and Kegan Paul.

Hayek, F. A. von (1976) *Law, Legislation and Liberty*, Vol. 2: *The Mirage of Social Justice*, London, Routledge and Kegan Paul.

Heald, D. A. (1976a) The control of public expenditure, in *The Financing of Public Expenditure*, Expenditure Committee, First Report of Session 1975/76, II, HC 69–II, London, HMSO, pp. 199–203.

Heald, D. A. (1976b) *Making Devolution Work*, Young Fabian Pamphlet 43, London, Fabian Society.

Heald, D. A. (1979) Public expenditure and accountability, *Omega*, 7, 469–79.

Heald, D. A. (1980a) The rehabilitation of the market in social policy, in *Social Welfare: Why and How?* (ed. N. Timms), London, Routledge and Kegan Paul, pp. 55–92.

Heald, D. A. (1980b) The economic and financial control of U.K. nationalised industries, *Economic Journal*, 90, 243–65.

Heald, D. A. (1980c) *Financing Devolution within the United Kingdom: A Study of the Lessons from Failure*, Research Monograph 32, Centre for Research on Federal Financial Relations, Canberra, Australian National University Press.

Heald, D. A. (1980d) Territorial equity and public finances: concepts and confusion, Centre for the Study of Public Policy, University of Strathclyde.

Heald, D. A. (1980e) The Scottish Rate Support Grant: how different from the English and Welsh?, *Public Administration*, 58, 25–46.

Heald, D. A. (1981) UK energy policy: the economic and financial control of the nationalised energy industries, *Energy Policy*, 8, 99–112.

Heald, D. A. (1982a) Public expenditure in Scotland: memorandum by the specialist adviser, in *Scottish Aspects of the 1982–85 Public Expenditure White Paper,* Committee on Scottish Affairs, Session 1981/82, HC 413, London, HMSO, Appendix 1, pp. 75–92.

Heald, D. A. (1982b) Using Scottish instruments in pursuit of UK objectives, *Local Government Studies,* 8, 33–46.

Heald, D. A. (1982c) Local authorities, in *Government Spending in Scotland* (ed. M. Cuthbert), Edinburgh, Paul Harris Publishing, pp. 145–69.

Heald, D. A. (1982d) The financial relationship between government and public enterprises in the United Kingdom, Paper presented to the Franco–British Seminar on Public Enterprise at the University of Exeter, 9–11 July 1982.

Heald, D. A., Jones, C. A. and Lamont, D. W. (1981) Braking Mr. Younger's runaway train: the conflict between the Scottish Office and the local authorities over local government expenditure, in *The Scottish Government Yearbook 1982* (eds H. M. Drucker and N. L. Drucker), Edinburgh, Paul Harris Publishing, pp. 12–56.

Heald, D. A. and Steel, D. R. (1981a) Privatisation of UK public enterprises, *Annals of Public and Co-operative Economy,* 52, 351–67.

Heald, D. A. and Steel, D. R. (1981b) Nationalised industries: the search for control, *Public Money,* 1, June 1981, pp. 13–19.

Heald, D. A. and Steel, D. R. (1982) Privatising public enterprise: an analysis of the Government's case, *Political Quarterly,* 53, 333–49.

Heclo, H. and Wildavsky, A. (1974) *The Private Government of Public Money* (1st edn), London, Macmillan. (2nd edn, 1981.)

Hendry, D. (1981a) Econometric evidence in the appraisal of monetary policy, in *Monetary Policy,* Treasury and Civil Service Committee, Third Report of Session 1980/81, III, HC 163–III, London, HMSO, Appendix 1, pp. 1–21.

Hendry, D. (1981b) Comment on HM Treasury's memorandum 'Background to the Government's economic policy', in *Monetary Policy,* Treasury and Civil Service Committee, Third Report of Session 1980/81, III, HC 163–III, London, HMSO, Appendix 4, pp. 94–6.

Herrington, P. (1979) *Nor any Drop to Drink: The Economics of Water,* Occasional Paper, Sutton, Economics Association.

Heseltine, M. (1980) Ministers and management in Whitehall, *Management Services in Government,* 35, 61–8.

Higgins, T. (1978) Parliamentary control of public expenditure – a back bench revolt?, *National Westminster Bank Quarterly Review,* August 1978, pp. 26–35.

Hirsch, F. (1977) *The Social Limits to Growth,* London, Routledge and Kegan Paul.

Hobbes, T. (1651, reprinted 1968) *Leviathan* (ed. C. B. Macpherson), Pelican Classics, Harmondsworth, Penguin.

Hodson, J. D. (1977) The principle of paternalism, *American Philosophical Quarterly*, **14**, 61–9.

Hood, C. C. (1978) Keeping the centre small: explanations of agency type, *Political Studies*, **XXVI**, 30–46.

(Houghton) Committee of Inquiry (1975) (Chairman: Lord Douglas Houghton) *Pay of Non-University Teachers*, Cmnd 5848, London, HMSO.

Imber, V. (1980) *Public Expenditure 1978/79: Outturn Compared with Plan*, Government Economic Service Working Paper 31 (Treasury Working Paper 13), London, Treasury.

Jackman, R. A. (1981) The Block Grant in England, in *Public Expenditure and the Rate Support Grant*, Centre for Urban and Regional Research, Centre for Urban and Regional Research Discussion Paper 2, University of Glasgow.

Jackson, P. M. (1979) Financial control and responsibility, in *Scotland: The Framework for Change* (ed. D. I. MacKay), Edinburgh, Paul Harris Publishing.

Jackson, P. M. (1982) *The Political Economy of Bureaucracy*, Oxford, Philip Allan.

Jenkins, R. (1976) Speech at Coleg Pencraig, Llangefni, to the Anglesey Constituency Labour Party, 23 January 1976.

Jessop, B. (1977) Recent theories of the capitalist state, *Cambridge Journal of Economics*, **1**, 353–73.

Jessop, B. (1982) *The Capitalist State*, Oxford, Martin Robertson.

Johnson, N. (1974) Defining accountability, *Public Administration Bulletin*, No. 17, December 1974, pp. 3–13.

Jones, P. (1982) Freedom and the redistribution of resources, *Journal of Social Policy*, **11**, 217–38.

Joseph, Sir Keith (1979) Transcript of *The Charlton Interview*, 30 July 1979, London, BBC Television.

Kaldor, Lord Nicholas (1980) Memorandum, in *Memoranda on Monetary Policy*, Treasury and Civil Service Committee, Session 1979/80, HC 720, London, HMSO, pp. 86–131.

Kaldor, Lord Nicholas (1982) *The Scourge of Monetarism*, Oxford, Oxford University Press.

Kay, J. A. and Keen, M. J. (1982) *The Structure of Tobacco Taxes in the European Community*, IFS Report Series 1, London, Institute for Fiscal Studies.

Keating, M. J. and Rhodes, M. (1981) Politics or technocracy?: the regional water authorities, *Political Quarterly*, **52**, 487–90.

Keegan, V. (1982) The gap between industry's needs and those of Britain still seems to be yawning, *The Guardian*, 4 May 1982.

Kellner, P. and Crowther-Hunt, Lord Norman (1980) *The Civil Servants: An Inquiry into Britain's Ruling Class*, London, MacDonald Futura.

Kent County Council (1978) *Education Vouchers in Kent,* Maidstone, Kent County Council.

Keynes, J. M. (1936, reprinted 1973) *The Collected Writings of John Maynard Keynes,* Vol. VII: *The General Theory of Employment, Interest and Money,* London, Macmillan for the Royal Economic Society.

Kochan, T. A. (1977) A theory of multilateral collective bargaining in city governments, in *Public Sector Labor Relations: Analysis and Readings* (eds D. Lewin, P. Feuille and T. A. Kochan), Glen Ridge, New Jersey, Thomas Horton, pp. 142–59.

Kogan, M. *et al.* (1978) *The Working of the National Health Service,* Research Paper 1 for the (Merrison) Royal Commission on the National Health Service, London, HMSO.

Laffer, A. B. and Seymour, J. P. (eds) (1979) *The Economics of the Tax Revolt,* New York, Harcourt Brace Jovanovich.

Laidler, D. (1978) Mayer on monetarism: comments from a British point of view, in *The Structure of Monetarism* (ed. T. Mayer), New York. W. W. Norton, pp. 133–44.

Laidler, D. (1980) Notes on gradualism, in *Memoranda on Monetary Policy,* Treasury and Civil Service Committee, Session 1979/80, HC 720, London, HMSO, pp. 48–54.

Laidler, D. (1981) *Introduction to Microeconomics* (2nd edn), Oxford, Philip Allan.

(Lambert) Royal Commission on Financial Management and Accountability (1979) (Chairman: Allen Lambert) *Final Report,* Ottawa, Government of Canada.

Lange, O. (1938, reprinted 1964) On the economic theory of socialism, in *On the Economic Theory of Socialism* (ed. B. E. Lippincott), New York, McGraw-Hill.

Layard, R., Marin, A. and Zabalza, A. (1982) Trends in civil service pay relative to the private sector, in *Inquiry into Civil Service Pay.* Vol. II. *Research Studies,* (Megaw) Committee, Cmnd 8590–I, London, HMSO, Research Study 3, pp. 95–128.

Layard, R. and Walters, A. A. (1978) *Microeconomic Theory,* New York, McGraw-Hill.

(Layfield) Committee of Inquiry (1976) (Chairman: Frank Layfield) *Local Government Finance: Report of the Committee of Inquiry,* Cmnd 6453, London, HMSO.

Le Grand, J. (1978) The distribution of public expenditure: the case of health care, *Economica,* **45,** 125–42.

Le Grand, J. (1982a) *The Strategy of Equality: Redistribution and the Social Services,* London, Allen and Unwin.

Le Grand, J. (1982b) The distribution of public expenditure on education, *Economica,* **49,** 63–8.

Leibenstein, H. (1966) Allocative efficiency and X-efficiency, *American Economic Review*, 56, 392–415.

Leibenstein, H. (1973) Competition and X-efficiency: reply, *Journal of Political Economy*, 81, 765–77.

Leibenstein, H. (1975) Aspects of X-efficiency theory of the firm, *The Bell Journal of Economics*, 6, 580–606.

Leibenstein, H. (1976) *Beyond Economic Man: A New Foundation for Microeconomics*, Cambridge, Mass., Harvard University Press.

Lerner, A. P. (1944) *The Economics of Control*, London, Macmillan.

Likierman, A. (1981) *Cash Limits and External Financing Limits*, Civil Service College Handbook 22, London, HMSO.

Likierman, A. (1982a) Management information for ministers: the MINIS system in the Department of the Environment, *Public Administration*, 60, 127–42.

Likierman, A. (1982b) Efficiency in central government: Raynerism reviewed, *RIPA Report*, 3, No. 2, pp. 6–7.

Lindblom, C. E. (1977) *Politics and Markets*, New York, Basic Books.

Little, I. M. D. and Mirrlees, J. A. (1974) *Project Appraisal and Planning for Developing Countries*, London, Heinemann.

Littlechild, S. C. (1978) *The Fallacy of the Mixed Economy*, Hobart Paper 80, London, Institute of Economic Affairs.

Littlechild, S. C. (1979) What should Government do?, in *The Taming of Government* (S. C. Littlechild *et al.*), IEA Readings 21, London, Institute of Economic Affairs, pp. 1–15.

Littlechild, S. C. *et al.* (1979) *The Taming of Government*, IEA Readings 21, London, Institute of Economic Affairs.

Locke, J. (1690, reprinted 1967) *Two Treatises on Government* (ed. P. Laslett), London, Cambridge University Press.

Loevinsohn, E. (1977) Liberty and the redistribution of property, *Philosophy and Public Affairs*, 6, 226–39.

Lomas, E. (1980) Employment in the public and private sectors 1974–80, *Economic Trends*, No. 325, November 1980, pp. 101–9.

London Edinburgh Weekend Return Group (1980) *In and Against the State*, London, Pluto Press for the Conference of Socialist Economists.

MacCallum, G. C. (1967) Negative and positive freedom, *Philosophical Review*, 76, 312–34.

(MacDougall) Committee (1977) (Chairman: Sir Donald MacDougall) *Report of the Study Group on the Role of Public Finance in European Integration* Vol. I. *Report*; Vol. II. *Individual Contributions and Working Papers*, Economic and Financial Series B13, Brussels, Commission of the European Communities.

McLachlan, G. (1982) Introduction, in *The Public/Private Mix for Health: The Relevance and Effects of Change* (eds G. McLachlan and A. K. Maynard), London, Nuffield Provincial Hospitals Trust, pp. 1–18.

McLachlan, G. and Maynard, A. K. (1982) The public/private mix in health care: the emerging lessons, in *The Public/Private Mix for Health: The Relevance and Effects of Change* (eds G. McLachlan and A. K. Maynard), London, Nuffield Provincial Hospitals Trust, pp. 513–58.

McMillan, C. (1981) Fixing charges, *Public Money*, 1, June 1981, pp. 6–7.

Macmillan, H. (1938) *The Middle Way: A Study of the Problem of Economic and Social Progress in a Free and Democratic Society*, London, Macmillan.

Macpherson, C. B. (1973a) Berlin's division of liberty, in *Democratic Theory* (ed. C. B. MacPherson), Oxford, Clarendon Press, Essay V, pp. 95–119.

Macpherson, C. B. (1973b) Elegant tombstones: a note on Friedman's freedom, in *Democratic Theory* (C. B. Macpherson), Oxford, Clarendon Press, Essay VII, pp. 142–56.

Marquand, J. (1980) *Measuring the Effects and Costs of Regional Incentives*, Government Economic Service Working Paper 32, London, Department of Industry.

Marx, K. and Engels, F. (1848, reprinted 1968) *The Communist Manifesto* (eds L. Huberman and P. M. Sweezy), New York, Modern Reader Paperbacks.

Mayer, T. (ed.) (1978) *The Structure of Monetarism*, New York. W. W. Norton.

Maynard, A. K. (1975) *Experiment with Choice in Education*, Hobart Paper 64, London, Institute of Economic Affairs.

Maynard, A. K. (1979a) Pricing, insurance and the National Health Service, *Journal of Social Policy*, 8, 157–76.

Maynard, A. K. (1979b) Letter to *The Guardian*, 8 August 1979.

Maynard, A. K. (1982) The regulation of public and private health care markets, in *The Public/Private Mix for Health: The Relevance and Effects of Change* (eds G. McLachlan and A. K. Maynard), London, Nuffield Provincial Hospitals Trust, pp. 471–511.

Maynard, A. K. and Ludbrook, A. (1980a) What's wrong with the National Health Service?, *Lloyds Bank Review*, No. 138, October 1980, pp. 27–41.

Maynard, A. K. and Ludbrook, A. (1980b) Applying resource allocation formulae to constituent parts of the UK, *The Lancet*, 12 January 1980, pp. 85–7.

Meade Committee (1978) (Chairman: Professor J. E. Meade) *The Structure and Reform of Direct Taxation: Report of a Committee*, London, George Allen and Unwin for the Institute for Fiscal Studies.

Meerman, J. (1979) *Public Expenditure in Malaysia: Who Benefits and Why*, Oxford, Oxford University Press for the World Bank.

(Megaw) Committee (1982) (Chairman: Rt. Hon. Sir John Megaw) *Inquiry into Civil Service Pay* Vol. I. *The Inquiry's Findings*, Cmnd 8590; Vol. II. *Research Studies*, Cmnd 8590–I, London, HMSO.

Melville, Sir Ronald and Burney, Sir Anthony (1973) *The Use of Accountants in the Civil Service*, London, Civil Service Department.

(Merrison) Royal Commission on the National Health Service (1979) (Chairman: Sir Alec Merrison) *Report,* Cmnd 7615, London, HMSO.

Miliband, R. (1969) *The State in Capitalist Society,* London, Weidenfeld and Nicolson.

Mill, J. S. (1859) *On Liberty,* reprinted in H. B. Acton (ed.) (1972) *John Stuart Mill: Utilitarianism, On Liberty, and Considerations on Representative Government,* London, Dent, pp. 63–170.

Miller, D. (1976) *Social Justice,* Oxford, Clarendon Press.

Miller, D. (1983) Constraints on freedom, *Ethics,* (forthcoming).

Miller, S. (1981) Right on!, *The Times Higher Education Supplement,* 3 July 1981, pp. 11–13.

Millward, R. (1982) The comparative performance of public and private ownership, in *The Mixed Economy* (ed. Lord Roll), London, Macmillan, pp. 58–93.

Minford, A. P. (1980) The nature and purpose of UK macroeconomic models, *The Three Banks Review,* No. 125, March 1980, pp. 3–26.

Minford, A. P. (1981) Memorandum, in *Monetary Policy,* Treasury and Civil Service Committee, Third Report of Session 1980/81, II, HC 163–II, London, HMSO, pp. 8–21.

Minford, A. P. (1982) The development of monetary strategy, in *The 1982 Budget* (ed. J. Kay), Oxford, Basil Blackwell for the Institute for Fiscal Studies, pp. 75–85.

Minford, A. P. and Peel, D. (1981) Is the Government's economic strategy on course?, *Lloyds Bank Review,* No. 140, April 1981, pp. 1–19.

Minister for Reconstruction (1944) *Employment Policy,* Cmd 6527, London, HMSO.

Mirrlees, J. A. (1971) An exploration in the theory of optimum income taxation, *Review of Economic Studies,* 38, 175–208.

Mishan, E. J. (1981) *Introduction to Normative Economics,* Oxford, Oxford University Press.

Moore, B. and Rhodes, J. (1973) Evaluating the effect of British regional economic policy, *Economic Journal,* 83, 87–110.

Moore, B. and Rhodes, J. (1976) A quantitative analysis of the effects of the regional employment premium and other regional policy instruments, in *The Economics of Industrial Subsidies* (ed. A. Whiting), London, HMSO.

Morrison, H. (1983) Employment in the public and private sectors 1976 to 1982, *Economic Trends,* No. 352, February 1983, pp. 82–9.

Mueller, D. C. (1979) *Public Choice,* Cambridge, Cambridge University Press.

Musgrave, R. A. (1959) *The Theory of Public Finance,* New York, McGraw-Hill.

Musgrave, R. A. (1961a) Approaches to fiscal theory of political federalism, in *Public Finances: Needs, Sources and Utilization,* National Bureau of Economic Research, Princeton, Princeton University Press, pp. 97–122.

Musgrave, R. A. (1961b) Reply, in *Public Finances: Needs, Sources and Utilization,* National Bureau of Economic Research, Princeton, Princeton University Press, pp. 132–3.

Musgrave, R. A. (1981) Leviathan cometh – or does he?, in *Tax and Expenditure Limitations* (eds H. F. Ladd and T. N. Tideman), Committee on Urban Public Economics, Paper 5, Washington, D.C., The Urban Institute Press, pp. 77–120.

National Tax Limitation Committee (1980) A proposed constitutional amendment to limit federal spending, in *How to Limit Government Spending* (A. Wildavsky), Berkeley, University of California Press, Appendix A, pp. 127–33.

National Water Council (1980) *Charging Households for Water,* London, National Water Council.

Niskanen, W. A. (1971) *Bureaucracy and Representative Government,* Chicago, Aldine-Atherton.

Niskanen, W. A. (1973) *Bureaucracy: Servant or Master?* London, Institute of Economic Affairs.

Niskanen, W. A. (1980) The Short Amendment with comments and data by its author, William A. Niskanen, in *How to Limit Government Spending* (A. Wildavsky), Berkeley, University of California Press, Appendix B, pp. 135–42.

Norman, E. R. (1979) Denigration of capitalism: current education and the moral subversion of capitalist society, in *The Denigration of Capitalism: Six Points of View* (ed. M. Novak), Washington, American Enterprise Institute for Public Policy Research, pp. 7–23.

Normanton, E. L. (1978) Public Accountability, in *First Report of Session 1977/78,* Procedure Committee, Session 1977/78, III, HC 588–III, London, HMSO, Appendix 43, pp. 131–40.

Norton, P. (1980) *Dissension in the House of Commons, 1974–1979,* Oxford, Oxford University Press.

Nozick, R. (1974) *Anarchy, State and Utopia,* Oxford, Basil Blackwell.

Oates, W. E. (1972) *Fiscal Federalism,* New York, Harcourt Brace Jovanovitch.

Oates, W. E. (1977) An economist's perspective on fiscal federalism, in *The Political Economy of Fiscal Federalism* (ed. W. E. Oates), Lexington, Mass., D. C. Heath, pp. 3–20.

O'Connor, J. (1973) *The Fiscal Crisis of the State,* New York, St. Martin's Press.

OECD (1975) *Educational Development Strategy in England and Wales,* Paris, OECD.

OECD (1977) *Public Expenditure on Health,* OECD Studies in Resource Allocation, No. 4, Paris, OECD.

OECD (1978) *Public Expenditure Trends,* OECD Studies in Resource Allocation, No. 5, Paris, OECD.

OECD (1981a) *Revenue Statistics of OECD Member Countries 1965–80,* Paris, OECD.

OECD (1981b) *Long-term Trends in Tax Revenues of OECD Member Countries 1955–80,* OECD Studies in Taxation, Paris, OECD.

OECD (1982a) *National Accounts.* Vol. I. *Main Aggregates, 1951–1980;* Vol. II. *Detailed Tables 1963–1980,* Paris, OECD.

OECD (1982b) *Employment in the Public Sector,* Paris, OECD.

OECD (1982c) *OECD Economic Outlook,* No. 32, December 1982, Paris, OECD.

OECD (1982d) *Revenue Statistics of OECD Member Countries 1965–81,* Paris, OECD.

OECD (1982e) *Budget Financing and Monetary Control,* OECD Monetary Studies Series, Paris, OECD.

Orzechowski, W. (1977) Economic models of bureaucracy: survey, extensions, and evidence, in *Budgets and Bureaucrats* (ed. T. E. Borcherding), Durham, North Carolina, Duke University Press.

Page, C. S. (1969) Administrative costs of local authorities, in *Research Studies I,* (Wheatley) Royal Commission on Local Government in Scotland, Edinburgh, HMSO, pp. iv–11.

Page, E. and Midwinter, A. (1980) Remoteness, efficiency, cost and reorganization of Scottish local government, *Public Administration,* 58, 439–63.

Pareto, V. (1906) *Manual of Political Economy,* London, Macmillan, 1972.

Parry, R. (1980) *The Territorial Dimension in United Kingdom Public Employment,* Studies in Public Policy No. 65, Centre for the Study of Public Policy, University of Strathclyde.

Peacock, A. T. (1969) Welfare economics and public subsidies to the arts, *Manchester School of Economics and Social Studies,* 37, 323–35.

Peacock, A. T. (1978) Do we need to reform direct taxes?, *Lloyds Bank Review,* No. 129, July 1978, pp. 28–40.

Peacock, A. T. (1980) On the anatomy of collective failure, *Public Finance,* 35, 33–43.

Peacock, A. T. and Shaw, G. K. (1981) *The Public Sector Borrowing Requirement,* Occasional Papers in Economics No. 1, Buckingham, University College at Buckingham.

Peacock, A. T. and Wiseman, J. (1961) *The Growth of Public Expenditure in the United Kingdom,* Princeton, Princeton University Press for the National Bureau of Economic Research.

Peacock, A. T. and Wiseman, J. (1970) *Education for Democrats* (2nd edn), Hobart Paper 25, London, Institute of Economic Affairs. (1st edn, 1964.)

Pearce, D. W. (ed.) (1978) *The Valuation of Social Cost,* London, Allen and Unwin.

Perrin, J. R. (1978) *Management of Financial Resources in the National Health Service,* Research Paper 2 for the (Merrison) Royal Commission on the National Health Service, London, HMSO.

Pigou, A. C. (1920) *Economics of Welfare*, London, Macmillan.

Pliatzky, Sir Leo (1982a) *Getting and Spending: Public Expenditure, Employment and Inflation*, Oxford, Basil Blackwell.

Pliatzky, Sir Leo (1982b) Note, in *Budgetary Reform*, Treasury and Civil Service Committee, Session 1981/82, HC 137, London, HMSO, Appendix 18, pp. 163–4.

Plowden, Lord Edwin (Chairman) (1961) *Control of Public Expenditure*, Cmnd 1432, London, HMSO.

Poulantzas, N. (1969) The problem of the capitalist state, *New Left Review*, 58, 67–78.

Price, R. W. R. (1979) Public expenditure: policy and control, *National Institute Economic Review*, No. 90, November 1979, pp. 68–76.

Price, R. and Bain, G. S. (1983) Union growth in Britain: retrospect and prospect, *British Journal of Industrial Relations*, XXI, 46–68.

(Priestley) Royal Commission on the Civil Service (1955) (Chairman: Sir Raymond Priestley), *Report*, Cmnd 9613, London, HMSO.

Procedure Committee (1978) *First Report of Session 1977/78*, HC 588–I–III, London, HMSO.

Procedure (Finance) Committee (1982) *Minutes of Evidence*, Session 1981/82, HC 365–i–vii, London, HMSO.

Procedure (Supply) Committee (1981) *First Report of Session 1980/81*, HC 118–I–III, London, HMSO.

Proudhon, P-J. (1840) *What is Property?* reprinted in S. Edwards (ed.) (1969) *Selected Writings of Pierre-Joseph Proudhon*, London, Macmillan, p. 124.

Pryke, R. (1971) *Public Enterprise in Practice*, London, MacGibbon and Kee.

Pryke, R. (1980) Public enterprise in practice: the British experience of nationalisation during the past decade, in *Public and Private Enterprise in a Mixed Economy* (ed. W. J. Baumol), London, Macmillan for the International Economic Association, pp. 215–29.

Pryke, R. (1981) *The Nationalised Industries*, Oxford, Martin Robertson.

Pryke, R. (1982) The comparative performance of public and private enterprise, *Fiscal Studies*, 3, 68–81.

Public Accounts Committee (1978) *Department of the Environment*, Ninth Report of Session 1977/78, HC 299, London, HMSO.

Public Accounts Committee (1979) *Housing Associations and the Housing Corporation*, Fifth Report of Session 1978/79, HC 327, London, HMSO.

Public Accounts Committee (1980a) *Manpower Services Commission: Special Programmes*, Twenty-fourth Report of Session 1979/80, HC 763, London, HMSO.

Public Accounts Committee (1980b) *Department of the Environment: Housing Corporation*, Twenty-third Report of Session 1979/80, HC 741, London, HMSO.

Public Accounts Committee (1981a) *The Role of the Comptroller and Auditor General*, First Special Report of Session 1980/81, HC 115–I–III, London, HMSO.

Public Accounts Committee (1981b) *Department of the Environment: Housing Corporation*, Eleventh Report of Session 1980/81, HC 328, London, HMSO.

Public Money (1981a) Information: a public good? (unsigned article), *Public Money*, 1, September 1981, p. 3.

Public Money (1981b) Efficiency in the Civil Service (unsigned article), *Public Money*, 1, December 1981, pp. 8–15.

Rae, D. (1981) *Equalities*, Cambridge, Mass., Harvard University Press.

Rawls, J. (1972) *A Theory of Justice*, Oxford, Clarendon Press.

Rayner, Sir Derek (1982) Note on progress with Rayner exercises, in *Efficiency and Effectiveness in the Civil Service*, Treasury and Civil Service Committee, Session 1981/82, HC 236–II, London, HMSO, Memorandum, pp. 85–9.

(Redcliffe-Maud) Royal Commission on Local Government in England 1966–69 (1969) (Chairman: Lord John Redcliffe-Maud) *Report*, Cmnd 4040, London, HMSO.

Rees, J. C. (1960) A re-reading of Mill on liberty, *Political Studies*, VIII, 113–29.

Regan, D. E. and Stewart, J. (1982) An essay in the government of health: the case for local authority control, *Social Policy and Administration*, 16, 19–43.

Reid, D. J. (1977) Public sector debt, *Economic Trends*, No. 283, May 1977, pp. 100–9.

Reisman, D. (1982) *State and Welfare: Tawney, Galbraith and Adam Smith*, London, Macmillan.

Ridley, N. (1982) *Hansard*, 1 December 1982, cols. 179–80.

Robbins, L. (1938) Interpersonal comparisons of utility, *Economic Journal*, 48, 634–41.

Robinson, A. (1978) *Parliament and Public Spending*, London, Heinemann.

Robinson, D. (1982) Public sector pay: the case for an incomes policy, *Public Money*, 2, June 1982, pp. 25–31.

Rose, R. (1981) What if anything is wrong with Big Government?, *Journal of Public Policy*, 1, 5–36.

Rose, R. (1982) *Understanding the United Kingdom: The Territorial Dimension in Government*, London, Longmans.

Ross, W. (1977) Approaching the archangelic?: the Secretary of State for Scotland, in *The Scottish Government Yearbook 1978* (eds H. M. Drucker and M. G. Clarke), Edinburgh, Paul Harris Publishing, pp. 1–20.

Rothenburg, J. (1970) Local decentralization and the theory of optimal government, in *The Analysis of Public Output* (ed. J. Margolis), New York, National Bureau of Economic Research, pp. 31–64.

Rowley, C. K. (1978a) The 'problem' of social cost. Prologue to S. N. S. Cheung, *The Myth of Social Cost: A Critique of Welfare Economics and the Implications for Public Policy*, Hobart Paper 82, London, Institute of Economic Affairs, pp. 11–18.

Rowley, C. K. (1978b) Liberalism and collective choice: a return to reality?, *Manchester School of Economics and Social Studies*, **46**, 224–51.

Rowley, C. K. (1979a) Buying out the obstructors?, in *The Taming of Government* (S. C. Littlechild *et al.*), IEA Readings 21, London, Institute of Economic Affairs, pp. 107–18.

Rowley, C. K. (1979b) Liberalism and collective choice, *National Westminster Bank Quarterly Review*, May 1979, pp. 11–22.

Rowley, C. K. and Peacock, A. T. (1975) *Welfare Economics: A Liberal Restatement*, London, Martin Robertson.

Royal College of Physicians of London (1971) *Smoking and Health Now: A New Report and Summary on Smoking and its Effects on Health*, London, Pitman Medical.

Royal College of Physicians of London (1977) *Smoking or Health: The Third Report from the Royal College of Physicians of London*, Tunbridge Wells, Pitman Medical.

St John-Stevas, N. (1983) *Parliamentary Control of Expenditure (Reform) Bill*, Bill No. 19, Session 1982/83, London, HMSO.

Samuelson, P. A. (1954) The pure theory of public expenditure, *Review of Economics and Statistics*, **36**, 387–9.

Samuelson, P. A. (1955) Diagrammatic exposition of a theory of public expenditure, *Review of Economics and Statistics*, **37**, 350–6.

Savas, E. S. (1980) Comparative costs of public and private enterprise in a municipal service, in *Public and Private Enterprise in a Mixed Economy* (ed. W. J. Baumol), London, Macmillan for the International Economic Association, pp. 253–64.

Savas, E. S. (1982) *Privatizing the Public Sector: How to Shrink Government*, Chatham, New Jersey, Chatham House Publishers.

Schumpeter, J. (1943) *Capitalism, Socialism and Democracy*, London, George Allen and Unwin.

(Scott) Committee (1981) (Chairman: Sir Bernard Scott) *Inquiry into the Value of Pensions*, Cmnd 8147, London, HMSO.

Scottish Office (1982) *The Rate Support Grant (Scotland) Order 1982*, Session 1981/82, HC 143, London, HMSO.

Seldon, A. (1977) *Charge*, London, Temple Smith.

Seldon, A. (ed.) (1979) *Tax Avoision*, IEA Readings 22, London, Institute of Economic Affairs.

Seldon, A. (1982a) The necessity of unemployment, *Journal of Economic Affairs*, **2**, 194–6.

Seldon, A. (1982b) Is the public sector organised in the interests of the public?, *Public Finance and Accountancy*, November 1982, pp. 40–1.

Selowsky, M. (1979) *Who Benefits from Government Expenditure: A Case Study of Colombia*, Oxford, Oxford University Press for the World Bank.

Semple, M. (1979) Employment in the public and private sectors 1961–78, *Economic Trends*, No. 313, November 1979, pp. 90–108.

Sen, A. K. (1970) *Collective Choice and Social Welfare*, Edinburgh, Oliver and Boyd.

Short, J. (1976) *Public Expenditure in the Northern Region and other British Regions*, Technical Report No. 12, Newcastle-upon-Tyne, Northern Region Strategy Team.

Short, J. (1981) *Public Expenditure and Taxation in the UK Regions*, Farnborough, Gower Publishing.

Short, J. (1982) Public expenditure in the English regions, in *Regional Government in England* (eds B. W. Hogwood and M. J. Keating), Oxford, Clarendon Press, pp. 191–216.

Simons, H. (1948) *Economic Policy for a Free Society*, Chicago, University of Chicago Press.

Smith, A. (1759, reprinted 1982) *The Theory of Moral Sentiments* (eds D. D. Raphael and A. L. Macfie), Oxford, Clarendon Press, 1982.

Smith, A. (1776, reprinted 1982) *The Wealth of Nations*, Harmondsworth, Penguin.

Smith, B. (1980) Control in British Government: a problem of accountability, *Policy Studies Journal*, 9, 1163–74.

Smith, C. T. B., Clifton, R., Makeham, P., Creigh, S. W. and Burn, R. V. (1978) *Strikes in Britain*, Department of Employment Manpower Paper No. 15, London, HMSO.

Spann, R. M. (1977) Public versus private provision of governmental services, in *Budgets and Bureaucrats: The Sources of Government Growth* (ed. T. E. Borcherding), Durham, North Carolina, Duke University Press, pp. 71–89.

Stanyer, J. (1974) Divided responsibilities: accountability in decentralised government, *Public Administration Bulletin*, No. 17, December 1974, pp. 14–30.

Stapleton, R. G. (1981) Why recession benefits Britain, *Journal of Economic Affairs*, 2, 7–11.

Stein, H. (1980) The big issues: defense and inflation – how to pay for survival, Statement to the Committee on the Budget, US Senate, March 4, 1980, reprinted in *AEI Economist*, March 1980, pp. 1–6.

Stein, J. L. (1982) *Monetarist, Keynesian and New Classical Economics*, Oxford, Basil Blackwell.

Stigler, G. J. (1970) Director's law of public income redistribution, *Journal of Law and Economics*, XIII, 1–10.

Sugden, R. (1981) *The Political Economy of Public Choice: An Introduction to Welfare Economics*, Oxford, Martin Robertson.

Sugden, R. (1982) Hard luck stories: the problem of the uninsured in a laissez-faire society, *Journal of Social Policy*, 11, 201–16.

Supplementary Benefits Commission (1977) *Annual Report for 1976*, Cmnd 6910, London, HMSO.

Tait, A. A. and Heller, P. S. (1982) *International Comparisons of Government Expenditure,* Occasional Paper 10, Washington, D.C., International Monetary Fund.

Tawney, R. H. (1913, reprinted 1979) Poverty as an industrial problem, in *The American Labour Movement and Other Essays* (ed. J. M. Winter), Brighton, The Harvester Press, pp. 111–28.

Tawney, R. H. (1931, reprinted 1964) *Equality,* London, Unwin Books.

Taylor, C. (1979) What's wrong with negative liberty?, in *The Idea of Freedom* (ed. A. Ryan), Oxford, Oxford University Press, pp. 175–93.

Taylor, C. T. and Threadgold, A. R. (1979) *Real National Saving and its Sectoral Composition,* Bank of England Discussion Paper No. 6, London, Bank of England.

Thatcher, M. (1980) The first Airey Neave Memorial Lecture, London, 3 March 1980.

Thatcher, M. (1982) Speech at the Lord Mayor's Banquet, Guildhall, London, 15 November 1982.

Thomson, A. W. J. (1979) Trade unions and corporate state in Britain, *Industrial and Labor Relations Review,* 33, 36–54.

Thomson, A. W. J. and Beaumont, P. B. (1978) *Public Sector Bargaining,* Farnborough, Saxon House.

Thomson, A. W. J. and Heald, D. A. (1979) Collective bargaining in the public corporations, *Personnel Management,* 11, No. 9, pp. 22–7 and 42.

Tiebout, C. M. (1956) A pure theory of local expenditures, *Journal of Political Economy,* 64, 416–24.

Tiebout, C. M. (1961) An economic theory of fiscal decentralization, in *Public Finances: Needs, Sources and Utilization,* National Bureau of Economic Research, Princeton, Princeton University Press, pp. 79–96.

Tobacco Advisory Council (1982) Memorandum, in *Budgetary Reform,* Treasury and Civil Service Committee, Session 1981/82, HC 137, London, HMSO, Appendix 16, pp. 158–61.

Tobin, J. (1970) On limiting the domain of inequality, *Journal of Law and Economics,* 13, 263–78.

Tobin, J. (1981) The monetarist counter-revolution today – an appraisal, *Economic Journal,* 91, 29–42.

Treasury (1963) *Public Expenditure in 1963/64 and 1967/68,* Cmnd 2235, London, HMSO.

Treasury (1969) *Public Expenditure 1968/69 to 1973/74,* Cmnd 4234, London, HMSO.

Treasury (1972) *Public Expenditure White Papers: Handbook on Methodology,* London, HMSO.

Treasury (1975) *Public Expenditure to 1978/79,* Cmnd 5879, London, HMSO.

Treasury (1976a) *Public Expenditure to 1979/80,* Cmnd 6393, London, HMSO.

Treasury (1976b) Control and presentation of public expenditure, *Economic Progress Report*, No. 80, November 1976, pp. 1–3.

Treasury (1977) *The Government's Expenditure Plans*, Cmnd 6721–I and II, London, HMSO.

Treasury (1978) Public expenditure – gross or net presentation, in *Memoranda on the Control of Public Expenditure*, Expenditure Committee (General Sub-committee), Session 1977/78, HC 196, London, HMSO, pp. 11–13.

Treasury (1979a) *The Government's Expenditure Plans: 1979/80 to 1982/ 83*, Cmnd 7439, London, HMSO.

Treasury (1979b) *Needs Assessment Study-Report*, The report of an interdepartmental study co-ordinated by HM Treasury on the relative public expenditure needs in England, Scotland, Wales and Northern Ireland, London, HMSO.

Treasury (1979c) *The Government's Expenditure Plans 1980/81*, Cmnd 7746, London, HMSO.

Treasury (1979d) Budget procedures, *Economic Progress Report*, No. 109, May 1979, pp. 1–3.

Treasury (1980a) *Financial Statement and Budget Report 1980/81*, Session 1979/80, HC 500, London, HMSO.

Treasury (1980b) *The Government's Expenditure Plans 1980/81 to 1983/ 84*, Cmnd 7841, London, HMSO.

Treasury (1980c) *Monetary Control*, Cmnd 7858, London, HMSO.

Treasury (1980d) Monetary policy and the economy, *Economic Progress Report*, No. 123, July 1980, pp. 1–4.

Treasury (1981a) Simulations on HM Treasury, London Business School and National Institute models, in *Financing of the Nationalised Industries*, Treasury and Civil Service Committee, Eighth Report of Session 1980/81, III, HC 348–III, London, HMSO, Appendix 17, pp. 69–70.

Treasury (1981b) Costing unemployment, *Economic Progress Report*, No. 130, February 1981, pp. 4–7.

Treasury (1981c) The impact of recession on the PSBR, *Economic Progress Report*, No. 130, February 1981, pp. 1–4.

Treasury (1981d) *The Government's Expenditure Plans 1981/82 to 1983/ 84*, Cmnd 8175, London, HMSO.

Treasury (1981e) Background to the Government's economic policy, in *Monetary Policy*, Treasury and Civil Service Committee, Third Report of Session 1980/81, III, HC 163–III, London, HMSO, Appendix 3, pp. 68–93.

Treasury (1981f) *The Role of the Comptroller and Auditor General*, Cmnd 8323, London, HMSO.

Treasury (1982a) *The Government's Expenditure Plans: 1982/83 to 1984/ 85*, Cmnd 8494–I and II, London, HMSO.

Treasury (1982b) The budget balance: measurement and policy, *Economic Progress Report*, No. 144, April 1982, pp. 1–4.

360   Bibliography

Treasury (1982c) Trends in civil service pay compared with other indices, in *Inquiry into Civil Service Pay*. Vol. II. *Research Studies*, (Megaw) Committee, Cmnd 8590–I, London, HMSO, Research Study 2, pp. 70–94.

Treasury (1982d) The public sector for the public, *Economic Progress Report*, No. 145, May 1982, pp. 1–4.

Treasury (1982e) The contingency reserve and the contingencies fund, *Economic Progress Report*, No. 150, October 1982, pp. 1–3.

Treasury (1982f) The operation of cash limits, in *Budgetary Reform*, Treasury and Civil Service Committee, Session 1981/82, HC 137, London, HMSO, Memorandum, Appendix 2, pp. 126–7.

Treasury (1982g) *Autumn Statement 1982*, Session 1982/83, HC 10, London, HMSO.

Treasury (1983a) Making a Budget – 2: the Finance Bill procedure, *Economic Progress Report*, No. 153, January 1983, pp. 4–5.

Treasury (1983b) *The Government's Expenditure Plans 1983/84 to 1985/86*, Cmnd 8789, London, HMSO.

Treasury and Central Statistical Office (1979) *Guide to Public Sector Financial Information: No. 1, 1979*, London, HMSO.

Treasury and Civil Service Committee (1980a) *Monetary Control*, Third Report of Session 1979/80, I and II, HC 713–I–II, London, HMSO.

Treasury and Civil Service Committee (1980b) *Memoranda on Monetary Policy*, Session 1979/80, HC 720, London, HMSO.

Treasury and Civil Service Committee (1981a) *Monetary Policy*, Third Report of Session 1980/81, HC 163–I–III, London, HMSO.

Treasury and Civil Service Committee (1981b) Adjusting the PSBR for inflation – the real and nominal PSBR, in *Monetary Policy*, Treasury and Civil Service Committee, Third Report of Session 1980/81, I, HC 163–I, London, HMSO, Annex to Chapter 6, pp. xcix–c.

Treasury and Civil Service Committee (1981c) *Financing of the Nationalised Industries*, Eighth Report of Session 1980/81, HC 348–I–III, London, HMSO.

Treasury and Civil Service Committee (1982a) *Efficiency and Effectiveness in the Civil Service*, Vol. I: *Report*, Session 1981/82, HC 236–I, London, HMSO.

Treasury and Civil Service Committee (1982b) *Budgetary Reform*, Session 1981/82, HC 137, London, HMSO.

Tullock, G. (1979) Bureaucracy and the growth of government, in *The Taming of Government* (S. C. Littlechild *et al.*), IEA Readings 21, London, Institute of Economic Affairs, pp. 21–38.

Van Lennep, E. (1981) Opening address, in *The Welfare State in Crisis*, Paris, OECD, pp. 9–12.

Vane, H. R. and Thompson, J. L. (1979) *Monetarism: Theory, Evidence and Policy*, Oxford, Martin Robertson.

Waddington, D. (1982) *Hansard*, 25 November 1982, cols. 571–2.

Wagner, A. (1883) The nature of the fiscal economy, extract from *Finanzwissenschaft* Part I, Third edition, Leipzig, in *Classics in the Theory of Public Finance* (eds R. A. Musgrave and A. T. Peacock), London, Macmillan, 1958, pp. 1–8.

Wagner, R. (1975) The anti-social activities of the public sector, *The Banker*, 125, 1503–11.

Walters, A. A. (1969) *Economics of Road User Charges*, World Bank Staff Occasional Papers, Baltimore, Johns Hopkins University Press.

Wanniski, J. (1979) Taxes, revenues, and the 'Laffer Curve', in *The Economics of the Tax Revolt* (eds A. B. Laffer and J. P. Seymour), New York, Harcourt Brace Jovanovich, pp. 7–12.

Ward, T. S. (1982) Privately supplied update of figures in T. S. Ward and R. R. Neild (1978) *The Measurement and Reform of Budgetary Policy*, London, Heinemann for the Institute for Fiscal Studies.

Ward, T. S. and Neild, R. R. (1978) *The Measurement and Reform of Budgetary Policy*, London, Heinemann for the Institute for Fiscal Studies.

Wasserman, G. J. (1970) Planning programming budgeting in the police service in England and Wales, *O & M Bulletin*, November 1970, pp. 197–210.

Weale, A. (1978) Paternalism and social policy, *Journal of Social Policy*, VIII, 157–72.

Webb, M. G. (1980) Energy pricing in the UK, *Energy Economics*, 2, 194–8.

(Wheatley) Royal Commission on Local Government in Scotland 1966–69 (1969) (Chairman: Lord John Wheatley) *Report*, Cmnd 4150, Edinburgh, HMSO.

Whynes, D. K. and Bowles, R. A. (1981) *The Economic Theory of the State*, Oxford, Martin Robertson.

Wildavsky, A. (1980) *How to Limit Government Spending*, Berkeley, University of California Press.

Wilkinson, G. and Jackson, P. M. (1981) *Public Sector Employment in the U.K.*, Public Sector Economics Research Centre, University of Leicester.

Williams, A. (1966) The optimal provision of public goods in a system of local government, *Journal of Political Economy*, 74, 18–33.

Williams, A. (1967) *Output Budgeting and the Contribution of Microeconomics to Efficiency in Government*, CAS Occasional Paper 4, Civil Service Department, London, HMSO.

Williams, A. and Anderson, R. (1975) *Efficiency in the Social Services*, Oxford, Basil Blackwell.

Williams, B. (1962) The idea of equality, in *Philosophy, Politics and Society* (eds P. Laslett and W. G. Runciman), Second Series, Oxford, Basil Blackwell.

Williamson, O. E. (1975) *Markets and Hierarchies*, New York, Free Press.

Willis, J. R. M. and Hardwick, P. J. W. (1978) *Tax Expenditures in the United Kingdom*, London, Heinemann for the Institute for Fiscal Studies.

Wilson, T. (1979) Regional policy and the national interest, in *Regional Policy: Past Experience and New Directions* (eds D. Maclennan and J. B. Parr), Glasgow Social and Economic Research Studies 6, Oxford, Martin Robertson.

Wolf, C. (1979) A theory of nonmarket failure: framework for implementation analysis, *Journal of Law and Economics*, 22, 107–39.

Wollheim, R. (1956) Equality, in *Proceedings of the Aristotelian Society, New Series*, LVI, London, Harrison, 281–300.

Wright, M. (1977) Public expenditure in Britain: the crisis of control, *Public Administration*, 55, 143–69.

AUTHOR INDEX

Index

SUBJECT INDEX

accountability in the public sector 151 – 73
Adam Smith Institute 306, 317, 332
alcohol
    legal restrictions on consumption 105,
    132
    taxation of 79, 291, 294
allocative efficiency
    conditions for 85 – 9, 98, 329 – 30
    effect of charges on 91 – 2, 99 – 102,
    138 – 9, 301 – 6
    implications of externalities for 97
    property rights secure 102 – 3
Armstrong Report 196 – 7, 203
asset sales 333 – 4

balanced budget rule 271 – 4
Bank of England 46, 272
Barnett formula 247, 332
Basnett, David 229
Baumol's disease 114 – 15, 177
behavioural theories of the firm 89, 116
benefits in cash
    disincentive effects of 139 – 40, 145
    education spending replaced by 143,
    330 – 1
    freedom reduced by eligibility criteria for
    79 – 80
    hostility to 7, 38, 55
    IEA's views on 90
    NHS replaced by 330 – 1
    paternalism of 134
    restriction of voting rights of beneficiaries
    76, 328
    significance of transfer payments 11,
    130 – 1
    territorial uniformity of 248 – 9
    versus benefits in kind 137 – 41, 144 – 5,
    242, 330 – 1

benefits in kind 134, 137 – 41, 144 – 5,
    242, 330 – 1
    see also benefits in cash
Berlin, Isaiah
    views on equality 125
    views on freedom 59 – 64, 74, 77, 327
Beveridge, William 5 – 6
black economy 293, 308
Boulding, Kenneth 109
Boyson, Rhodes 314
British Medical Association 159 – 60, 303
Brittan, Leon 15, 245, 301, 306, 320
Brittan, Samuel 37
Brookings Institution 332
Buchanan, James 90, 109, 268
Budget, the 169 – 70, 197 – 8
budget deficits 273, 327
    see also balanced budget rule and Public
    Sector Borrowing Requirement
bureaucracy
    absence of incentives for efficiency
    116 – 18
    budget-maximizing theories of 110 – 14
    of the welfare state 79 – 80
    privatization to check 117 – 18, 306 – 16
bureaucrats see public officials
Burns, Arthur 268
Burton, John 109
Butler, 'Rab' 5

capitalism
    as the source of freedom 68 – 77
    implications of Keynesian theory for 3 – 4
    implications of Paretian theory for 86, 94
    Marxist views on 260 – 3, 267
capitalist state
    Marxist theories of the 261 – 70, 275 – 6
Carey, Peter 168

Index